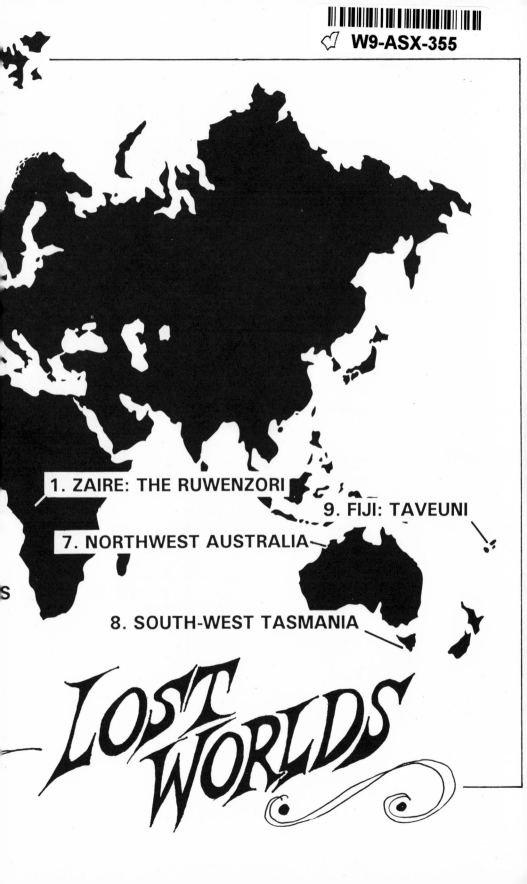

LOST WORLDS

Also by David Yeadon

Adventure Travel

THE BACK OF BEYOND
SECLUDED ISLANDS OF THE ATLANTIC COAST
NEW YORK'S NOOKS AND CRANNIES
BACKROAD JOURNEYS OF SOUTHERN EUROPE
HIDDEN CORNERS OF BRITAIN
BACKROAD JOURNEYS OF THE WEST COAST STATES
HIDDEN CORNERS OF NEW ENGLAND
HIDDEN CORNERS OF THE MID-ATLANTIC STATES
EXPLORING SMALL TOWNS IN CALIFORNIA (2 Vols.)

Travel Guides

NEW YORK: THE BEST PLACES
FREE NEW YORK
NEW YORK BOOK OF BARS, PUBS AND TAVERNS
WINE TASTING IN CALIFORNIA
HIDDEN RESTAURANTS OF CALIFORNIA (2 Vols.)

Others

SUMPTUOUS INDULGENCE ON A SHOESTRING—
    A Cookbook
WHEN THE EARTH WAS YOUNG—
    Native American Songs and Chants

THE
BUNGLE-
BUNGLE
— Northwest
Australia

LOST WORLDS

Exploring the Earth's Remote Places

written and illustrated by
DAVID YEADON

HarperCollins*Publishers*

HarperCollins books may be purchased for educational, business, or sales promotional use. For information, please write: Special Markets Department, HarperCollins Publishers, Inc., 10 East 53rd Street, New York, NY 10022.

FIRST EDITION

Designed by David Yeadon

Library of Congress Cataloging-in-Publication Data
Yeadon, David.
  Lost worlds : exploring the earth's remote places / David Yeadon.
  p. cm
  ISBN 0-06-016656-8
  1. Yeadon, David.   2. Voyages and travels—1981–   I. Title.
G465.Y425   1993
910.4—dc20   92-54755

93 94 95 96 97 HC 10 9 8 7 6 5 4 3 2 1

For **Peter Hillier**

pilot, philosopher and friend;
the man who gave me yet
one more life
and widened my smile.

The saving of the self:

The point of life is to know, love and serve the soul.
*Thomas Moore (**Care of the Soul**)*

Life is either a daring adventure or nothing.
Helen Keller

I was not born to be forced. I will breathe after my own fashion.
Henry David Thoreau

The saving of the earth:

We have done, and continue to do, terrible things to the Earth in the name of "progress."

I believe it is still very much in the balance, whether we can succeed in rescuing ourselves and the Earth from the consequences of our arrogance and folly. There's no room for the unbelievable complacency of those who claim that we have already done enough, and that our economic prospects will be undermined if we make too much of a song-and-dance about the environment. The truth is that there will be no singing and no dancing if we don't take far more drastic measures than we have to date.

The wounds we have inflicted can be healed; the Earth can be "saved" from further destruction. But if it is to be done, it must be done now. Otherwise, it may never be done at all.
*Jonathon Porritt—**Save The Earth**—Turner Publishing, 1991.*

CONTENTS

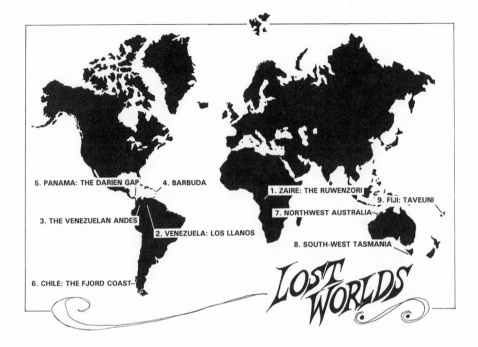

5. PANAMA: THE DARIEN GAP   4. BARBUDA

1. ZAIRE: THE RUWENZORI   9. FIJI: TAVEUNI

3. THE VENEZUELAN ANDES

7. NORTHWEST AUSTRALIA

2. VENEZUELA: LOS LLANOS

8. SOUTH-WEST TASMANIA

6. CHILE: THE FJORD COAST

Lost Worlds

WORDS OF THANKS

So many individuals gave encouragement and support during my travels. Without their kindness I might never have completed my journeys—or this book. In particular I would like to thank:

Richard Agar, for his hospitality at Exmouth in Western Australia.

Parker Antin, for his book *Himalayan Odyssey* and his enthusiasm for my adventures.

The legendary **Doña Barbara**, who gave meaning (tinged with menace) to Venezuela's Los Llanos.

Jan Beck, for his help in reaching Zaire's Mountains of the Moon.

Tim Cahill, for his kind words on my previous book, *The Back of Beyond*, which gave me heart for these journeys.

The late **Bruce Chatwin**, for his beautiful book *The Songlines* from which I learned so much about the Australian outback.

Sir Arthur Conan Doyle, for the pleasures of his book *The Lost World* and for the dreams he made me dream.

Phil Cooper, pilot and companion, for his calm and composure over the notorious Western Arthurs range in South-West Tasmania.

Tom Cronin, for his ongoing interest in my adventures (and his desire to join me as a video-recordist for WHBG, Boston).

The Cuna Indians, for their hospitality in Panama's Darien Gap and their explanation of "The Golden Time."

Lynne Cupper, my sister, and husband **Burford**, who offered sanctuary and fine sustenance during my homebound stopovers in England.

Jose Diego, llanero and lover of the wild places, for his tales and insights during my Los Llanos odyssey.

Monica and Herman Ehret, for their constant support and love.

The **Estrada family**, for their kindness and hospitality in Venezuela's Los Llanos.

Ormond Eyre of Taveuni's Maravu Plantation Resort, for an evening of kava and fine conversation.

Bill Foley of **Westchester Book Composition**, for transforming a spotty manuscript into perfect galleys.

"Frigatebird Sam," for his company and revelations on the island of Barbuda.

Bob Geeves, a wilderness-man par excellence, for his stories and bush-wisdom (but not his snoring!) at Melaleuca in South-West Tasmania.

Stephanie Gunning of HarperCollins, for always making the process of book-creation seem so easy.

Linda Halsey and the staff of *The Washington Post Travel Section*, who faithfully encouraged me in my wanderings and published numerous extracts from these journeys.

Don Hammerquist, a true "King in a Grass Castle" rancher at Western Australia's Mount Augustus, for his tales of the "jackaroo" life.

Peter Hillier, to whom this book is dedicated, who saved my life (and this book) in Australia.

Michael and Marianne Hume, my white-water–enthusiast friends, whose experience on the cutting edge of life makes some of my adventures pale in comparison.

The late **Deny King**, for the comfort of his hikers' hut and the inspiration of his "writing-shack."

Eric Leed, for the insights of his book *The Mind of the Traveler* and the pleasure of our conversations.

Anne Morrow Lindbergh, for the inspirations from her little book *A Gift from the Sea* on the island of Barbuda.

Graeme Macarthur and Murray, my hosts and companions in the Bungle Bungle of Western Australia.

Maika, Mitieli, the four fishermen, and the villagers of Navakawau on Taveuni (Fiji), without whom my visit would have been far less rewarding.

Thomas Moore, for his wonderful book, *Care of the Soul*, which helped my spirit through so many rough patches.

Jan Morris, whose books are among my favorite traveling companions.

Paco, my guide into the Venezuelan Andes, whose energy and endurance were inspirational (if occasionally irritating!).

Nancy and Sam Paskin, who are always the first to ask about my journeys.

Dan Peebles, for his help in extracting me from a mud hole in the Australian outback.

Bob Poole of *National Geographic*, for constant encouragement to this world wanderer.

Wilf and Joan Proctor, for living life to the full and always being there.

Lela Prym of Taveuni's Garden Island Resort, for her kindness and Julia Roberts smile.

The Pygmies of Zaire's Ituri Forest, for one night of magic following that strange "bangi" afternoon.

Lanny Riley, for his tales—and truth—about Tasmania's "hidden history" (and an excellent breakfast!).

Juan Felix Sanchez and his wife, **Epifania**, from whom I learned so much in the El Tisure valley of the Venezuelan Andes.

Christine Schillig of HarperCollins, for her support with this book and her subsequent decision to wander the earth in search of her own lost worlds.

Peter Swales, my Australian skipper and companion on the almost-disastrous sail down the fjord coast of Chile (and special thanks to *Christine*, his boat, for her amazing endurance).

Scott Swanson of **Lost World Adventures**, for his company and conviviality in Venezuela.

Joan Tapper and the staff of *Islands Magazine*, for inviting me to share some of my "lost world" discoveries with readers.

Paul Valcoze, for his company and quiet insights on that long boat journey into the heart of Zaire's darkness.

Mike Ventura, a fine photographer, with whom I plan to enjoy more odysseys.

"Walrus" Wade, Australian outback pilot and raconteur, for getting me safely across the great "Never-Nevers."

Kurt Wassen and his team of fellow-mountaineers for helping me down from Zaire's Mountains of the Moon.

Aubrey and Rosemary Webson and their two children, **Amber** and **Kamali**, for their kindness on Antigua and enduring friendship.

Barbara and Peter Willson, tin miners at Melaleuca in South-West Tasmania, for their company and English humor.

Bill Winkley, a fellow writer, for his hospitality and advice in Fiji and the endurance of his friendship.

Claude Yeadon, my late father, whose spirit wafts through these pages, and my late mother, **Margaret**, whose love of open-ended travel taught me so much.

Lynn Yorke of the *National Geographic Traveler*, who shares my love of places unexplored.

And special thanks, once again, to:

Hugh Van Dusen, my HarperCollins editor and friend, who creates the best welcome-home dinners.

And finally—my wife **Anne**—for all her help in preparing the manuscript, her prayers during my long absences, and her love.

INTRODUCTION

I have a confession to make. If confessions embarrass you, please feel free to ignore what follows and leap right into the chapters. Book introductions are usually pretty dull anyway. I rarely read them—particularly those with a confessional element. I assume that if the writer—particularly a travel writer—lugs a backpack of guilts and hang-ups and phobias around, the burden will quickly become apparent, sometimes nauseatingly so, in the flow and flux of the writing.

Come to think of it, I have a number of confessions.

First: I am happily—very happily—married to Anne, and have been for twenty-five years (plus a little prematrimonial get-acquainted time). So—in my travels I'm not escaping from a broken love affair or a pending divorce; I'm not looking for a replacement wife or any other relationship "thing" that might otherwise permeate these pages with purple-prosed angst or feel-sorry-for-me diatribes. I'm just your average happy wanderer who misses his wife (and best friend) far too much during his adventuring, who finds solace from homesickness and occasional depression either in silence or overactive sociability, and who is one of the most reluctant postcard and letter writers I've ever known. Fortunately, my mate puts up with my long lapses in communication, prays for me regularly, and comforts me wholeheartedly when I return—wan, weary, and, more often than not, whacked out.

Second confession: I love traveling. And thus I dislike travel books written by authors whose catalogs of miseries, morose complaints, and know-it-all arrogances seem to demean the very concept of open-eyed, open-minded and open-ended travel.

To repeat: I love travel. I have loved its sear and serendipity since I first wandered away from home in Yorkshire, England, through the open gate of my grandparents' garden and into the wild and unknown streets outside—at the age of three. Thanks for the timely intervention of a "bobby" I was restored to domestic disharmony (my father was temporarily in disgrace for leaving the gate unlatched), but not before I'd been pursued for blocks by a belligerent Scottish terrier, almost fallen down an open manhole, enjoyed the remnants of an ice-cream cone someone had kindly left stuck in a privet hedge, and attempted a little well-acted bribery at a corner shop by bawling my head off until I was given a free bag of licorice candies.

It was a relatively short journey by grown-up standards but in toddler terms I had entered a universe of delights and spine-tingling terrors. And I learned a few lessons that lasted. I learned that fear generates fear and aggressiveness (the more alarmed I was at the growling of the terrier, the more ferocious he became, until I banged him on the nose with a branch); I learned that danger can lurk in the most benign places (the open manhole in a very respectable suburban street of hedgebound homes); I learned that living off the land was both feasible and delightful (the discarded ice cream was the best I'd ever tasted); and I learned that drawing too much attention to myself could jeopardize my adventuring escapades (the shop owner who had donated the bag of candies also immediately called the police).

But I digress (another typical problem with introductions).

The lure and love of travel has been a prime component of my nature for as long as I can remember, despite all my efforts to live the straight and proper life (fifteen years as a city planner), to marry (much to the surprise of my family—and also my wife, I think), to become an avid consumer (far too many clapped-out cars) and even a social acolyte (a miserable boat trip with London's toffee-nosed, stinking rich jet set at the Henley Regatta put an end to that brief experiment).

Then things changed. One near-death and other soul-jarring experiences made me, in common with many others, face the fact of my mortality and adopt more of an "only-one-life" policy. Without regurgitating all the round-robin arguments and rationalizations that plagued me for a while, I will simply say I eventually recognized the power and impetus of the child within, the child who had never lost his lust for things wild and undiscovered, for places and people that most of us only read about (in books like this, perhaps), for experiences that stretch the envelope of existence to the breaking point.

And so, hand in hand and heart in heart, Anne and I discarded much of the baggage of our overdirected and driven lives and learned to enjoy a simpler, less cluttered existence. We became explorers—starting small in a VW camper (just a plain green bus—no LSD-inspired graphics on this one), writing a little, sketching, and exploring America's great wildernesses. Books began to emerge almost by accident. We were in our James Campbell stage, finding our own "bliss" and letting our souls lead us wherever they would. We had little money, no "security," few possessions of any importance, no plans, and no unwanted ties—and we were ridiculously happy. We were—in the best sense of that overworked word—free. Free of the parts we had thought to be ourselves, only to realize that our true selves had been railroaded and ramrodded for years by forces and influences that were not of our choosing. For a while we became children again, children of the earth, delighting in its power and mystery and, in turn, the power and mystery of our own lives. We roamed; we rested on mountaintops and by quiet streams and lakes far from the churning confusions and clamor we had once accepted as life's ransom; we talked and read and thought and sang (funny

the things you find yourself doing when you "let go"), we wrote
... and somehow more books emerged.

Now, that was all a long time ago. Since those early days
Anne has experienced numerous challenges working with blind
and visually impaired populations around the world and I, with
a few interesting diversions along the way, have just completed
this, my sixteenth illustrated travel book. Sometimes we travel
together, sometimes we don't. We've shared many strange and
wonderful experiences; we've gained a considerable amount of
knowledge and maybe even a little wisdom. Exploration—both
inner and external—is still the driving force behind our lives.
Travel has become an active metaphor of life itself—the celebration
of uncertainty, curiosity, unpredictability, "luck," fear, hope, and
wonder—the wonder of places untouched and untrammeled, the
double wonder of self-discovery and the discovery of the earth's
secret places and lost worlds, the wonder of being alone in lonely
remote regions in an increasingly homogenized world that sometimes seems far too overdiscovered, the wonder of sharing experiences and insights with others. . . .

Which leads to confession number three.

My own enthusiasm for travel and the inner exploration that
comes from making oneself vulnerable and reliant upon one's
own resources continually increases my empathy for fellow travelers with similar attitudes. "World wanderers," "Earth Gypsies"—call them what you will—seem to have the knack of
tapping into their own rich seams of self-dependence, courage,
and clear-mindedness. I listen, entranced as a child, to their tales;
I share their fears and tribulations; I celebrate their endurance and
their fascination in life as they hone down the cutting edges of
their own perceptions and walk the razor's edge of their own
mortality.

Recently I talked with two friends, Michael and Marianne,
both white-water enthusiasts, as they attempted to distill the essence of their experiences on some of the wildest rivers in the
world. First understand that these two people are pure main-
stream America. They pay all their worldly dues, they work long
hours at regular jobs, they have a home with an irritatingly large
mortgage, they mow their own lawn, they do their own home

repairs, they pay their full share of taxes, life insurance, credit card and utility bills . . . they're "normal."

They just have this one little quirk. They enjoy playing on the edge of mortality; they have this thing about white-water adventuring . . .

MICHAEL: "And so off we go, and the waves are crashing—you hit the waves, the waves hit the boat, you get thrown all over the place . . . you're holding on to your paddle and you're hanging over the side of the boat, water churning off rocks, huge waves everywhere, and you're bouncing around like crazy . . . and then it's over for a while and you say, 'That was nothing.' And you want to go on because you don't know what's going to happen next . . . but deep down inside you're thinking: I hope we flip—I really hope we flip!

"It's one of the greatest feelings to take on nature—to take on these rivers. The river gives you everything it's got and you get through it—at the end of the day you get through it. I'm not suicidal—I'm not going to do a river where I know I'm going to die if I don't know what I'm doing. . . . I'm not going to take on a challenge like that if I don't feel I'm up to it. . . . I respect there are forces out there that are greater and better than I am and I have to learn to face them . . . I want to be a part of it. . . . I like the feeling of nature beating on me—giving me its best—facing it—looking at it right in the eye and coming through.

"The magic is you get to go to places that very few people have gone—you get to see the real country—you're actually there, in this canyon, this gorge . . . you get to keep all the memories— the dangers, the feeling of being on the edge of things, being in these beautiful places with nature at its best, its wildest . . . and you're part of it all.

"It leaves its mark. You're stronger, you feel more confident . . . you feel you can face things better than before . . . it's something you can always draw on . . . nothing has got anywhere close to what I had to face on those rivers . . . you feel so . . . *alive!*"

MARIANNE: "I'm a perfectionist. I want things done right, I want results, I want things perfect . . . but when you're on the river, it's not perfect, you have to let go, stop controlling. . . . I suppose you learn to have faith that somehow you'll be okay.

"I remember one time on the Moose. We were there for the snow runoff—real rough—beautiful—and I fell in on the worst rapids, boat flipped . . . what scared me most was that it was so cold that I couldn't catch my breath. Then I got pinned under the boat—my head was banging on the keel. . . . I was trying to breathe in the air pocket. . . . I was panicking.

"Then it was slow-motion. Everything changed. After that first panic I just gave in to it . . . you've just got to go with it, don't fight it. . . . Sometimes it seems like an eternity, so much longer when you're pinned underneath . . . but somehow there's that peace . . . you feel really free, just letting go like that. . . . The shock only hits you when you're out of the rapids and you remember how cold you are. It doesn't take long before you hit the shore, but it can seem like forever on that last stretch.

"But you survived—that's the big thing. You give it your best shot and then you learn to have faith. . . . That sense of letting go is the best feeling you'll ever have . . . you know you're part of something so much greater than yourself and that you'll be okay no matter what happens. . . . And you carry that feeling with you. . . . You become a true optimist."

Which is a key fourth confession: I too am an incorrigible optimist, not just in terms of my own personal well-being, but also in the belief that our fragile planet will survive intact despite the enormous threats of overpopulation, disease, pollution, the destruction of the wild environment, and the mindless eradication of natural resources.

Optimists are not very fashionable species today in the aftermath of the 1992 Rio conference and the gory, pessimistic gloating of "Greens" in all their myriad forms and frenetic guises. Of course I've seen the destruction—driven by roaring greed and the lure of quick wealth. I've walked through the burned-out rain forests of Panama; I've seen the eroded slopes of southern Tasmania's mountains after the clear-cutting of ancient forests; I've seen pollution in all its varied forms in India, Latin America, Africa, the South Pacific islands, the Mediterranean, and the United States. I know those threats are real and must be remedied.

Regrettably the remedies are rarely simple. The issuing of eloquent eulogies, strict dictates, and hand-wringing homilies will do little to stem the tidal waves of human hopes, material expectations, and Western-inspired concepts of "progress." My years as a city planner taught me the dangers of fast, slick solutions based on a naive obliviousness to the enormously complex and entangled forces that create, shape, and define the destiny of cities. Invariably, too little time is given to understanding the cause-and-effect whiplash effects of ill-shaped "solutions" to urban ills. In the United States in particular we seem to have a habit of pouring great caldrons of cash into the sinkholes of problems without ever seriously examining the endlessly porous nature of the bedrock. And there we stand on the edge—peering into the maw—asking ourselves, "Where did it all go? What happened to all our solutions?"

I remember my time in Panama, on the edges of the almost impenetrable Darien Gap jungle (see Chapter 5). I was talking with members of a campesino (peasant) family. In the distance the ancient rain forest was in flames. From another direction huge trucks were emerging from the deep darkness of the jungle laden with freshly felled trees.

"I thought the government had banned tree-felling in these forests," I said.

"They have," replied the wife.

"So why are these trucks here?"

Shrugs all around.

"And the burning," I said. "I thought the government had banned the burning of the forest."

"They did," said the wife again.

"So why the burning?"

"To make a farm."

"For whom?"

"For us—for our families. We have to make a living."

"But in other parts of Panama, this hasn't worked. The soil is no good for farming. After four or five years there's no farm left."

"Yes," said the woman's son, "but in four years we will have a video machine. . . . "

A few days later, after an arduous journey through the Darien

7

jungle by canoe and on foot through some of the hardest—and hottest—hiking territory on earth, I entered a small Cuna Indian community high in the mountains. I was far from the burning and logging frenzy to the north and sat talking with the chief's son in the shade of huge forest trees. The Cuna are one of the last tribal groups in Latin America to withstand the scourge of conquistadors, colonialists, and modern-day capitalists in a relatively unscathed state. They have been labeled by anthropologists as the last original democracy on earth and still conduct their affairs in the heat of community debates. They resist progress in the Western sense and regard their rain forests as sacrosanct:

"We believe the forest is part of the Golden Time," the chief's son told me, "a time of balance. The forest is our home, our pantry, a place for our medicines. Yet every year it is threatened. There have been so many plans to take our trees, make our islands into places for tourists, build roads through our forest, and bring cattle into the lowland along the coast."

He went on to explain that after laborious petitioning of the government and with the help of U.S.-based institutions, the Cuna have so far managed to safeguard their sacred forests and maintain their traditional way of life. Western scientists now work with the tribespeople to study the ecological cycles of the Darien rain forest and the medicinal properties of plants unique to this region.

"You see," the chief's son told me, "there are many things in our forest which may help other people. We do not have to destroy it. We can live here. The balance can be kept."

Hence my optimism. I believe we are beginning to learn to appreciate and maintain fragile balances. Also, in questioning many of our own modern-day mores, in realizing the complexity of the problems we have created for ourselves, and in looking again at the knowledge, cohesion, and balance of so-called primitive societies, we are becoming far less myopic in our thinking and possibly more modest about our once-bombastic sense of endless change and progress.

And a final reason for my optimism. The journeys undertaken for this book and its precursor (*The Back of Beyond: Travels to the Wild Places of the Earth*, HarperCollins, 1991) have made me realize just how wild and unexplored much of our planet remains. My

8

wanderings through "lost worlds"—places seemingly untouched by the horrors of mindless decimation and the hyperbole of the "end-of-the-earth" doomsayers—reinforced my faith that we, and these places, will survive. Just to know that such "lost worlds" exist at all—untouched, unspoiled—is succor for the spirit of wonder in each one of us. It is my hope—my optimistic hope—that these journeys will help a little to rekindle that spirit and reinforce our efforts to maintain and protect the great wildernesses of our earth.

We are learning to tread softly in these secret places and to safeguard a world we barely comprehend. We are learning to accept its gifts gratefully, to take only what we need (and continually reexamine the need for these "needs") and to hold its bounty in trust for the future. It is our world—our only home. We are the earth—and the earth is us.

And—last confession—I love it.

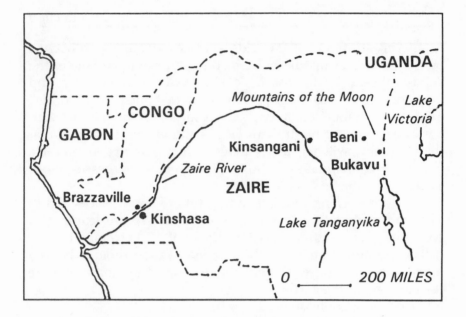

1. ZAIRE'S RUWENZORI
To the Mountains of the Moon

"It was like traveling back to the earliest beginning of the world, when vegetation rioted on the earth and big trees were kings. An empty stream, a great silence, an impenetrable forest. The air was warm, thick, heavy, sluggish. . . . The stillness of life did not in the least resemble a peace. It was the stillness of an implacable force brooding over an inscrutable intention. It looked at you with a vengeful aspect."
—Joseph Conrad, *Heart of Darkness*

Just think about it. Soaring ice and glacier-wrapped peaks rising almost seventeen thousand feet out of the scrub, forests, swamps, and grasslands of lowland Zaire and Uganda. The third highest mountains in Africa. Vast, majestic, sky-scratching, cloud-smothered pinnacles in the middle of millions of square miles of unexplored, unmapped wilderness.

Henry Morton Stanley, the man who sought out the elusive Dr. Livingstone in 1871 and became the first European explorer to see this mystical mountain massif, called it just that—Ruwenzori. A simple Bantu expression meaning "hill of rain" or "rainmaker." He recorded his sighting as:

> A sky-piercing whiteness ... which assumed the proportion and appearance of a vast mountain covered with snow.

Those two irascible wanderers Richard Burton and John Speke were convinced the Nile was born here. Burton referred to the massif as the "Lunatic Mountains" because of the old legends of men being driven to madness trying to seek them out in a region covered by clouds for most of every year. But the two men never proved their hypotheses to the satisfaction of the walrus-mustached, sideburned doyens of exploratory knowledge sipping their ports and brandies in the mahogany- and portrait-walled confines of Britain's Royal Geographical Society.

The wonderfully foolish, courageous, desperate (and very erotic) expeditions of these two men merely added confusion and cartographical conflict to the neat-minded "Empire" protagonists in their sagging leather wing chairs.

"Nonsense!" they said.

"Wrong measurements," they said.

"Let's have another drink and toast the Queen," they said.

And so two more "life must be more than this" exponents were dumped into the ash cans of dubious notoriety. Lives of soaring adventure ending in squalid squabbles, mutual backstabbing—and ignominious deaths.

The "Mountains of the Moon"! What an enticing prospect. A red rag to this wandering bull. Hidden in their almost perpetual cloud cover, they definitely exist. We know that from later, better-organized expeditions. But even Ptolemy guessed the presence of the "Lunae Montes" somewhere in the center of the continent.

Aristotle referred to "a silver mountain" in the heart of Africa, and Aeschylus wrote of "the Gods' great garden [the Nile Delta] fed by distant snows."

The region is still a mysterious lost world today. People have vanished here, dying in blizzards, being swallowed up by moss bogs, or tumbling off the edge of ice-sheened precipices. French mountaineer Bernard Pierre described it "a place not of this planet."

But it *is* on this planet and I had to see these peaks. Touch them. Trample over their glaciers and ice fields. Explore the strange foothills where familiar flowers and plants back home—heather, lobelia, groundsels, and ferns—grow into tree-sized specimens, where three-foot-long earthworms ease through mossy bogs, and where one of the oddest creatures on earth, the rock or tree hyrax (a rabbitlike member of the elephant family with hooves and a humanlike shriek) frolics in the always-wet gloom of fantasy forests seen nowhere else on earth. I had to come here and experience these hidden wonders in deepest central Africa for myself.

My destination was the town of Beni in eastern Zaire, couched on the lower flanks of these great Ruwenzori Mountains. However, I began my journey a long way from Beni, over eleven hundred miles to the west, in the capital city of Kinshasa (Leopoldville) on the great Zaire (Congo) River—the Amazon of Africa. Getting to the mountains presented experiences and challenges that, by themselves, could have filled a good half of this book.

Part I—Kinshasa to Kisangani by Riverboat

Chaos. Absolutely bloody, sweaty pandemonium.

I though I'd get there early. "Board at dawn," an official of the riverboat told me. "Afterwards—all crazy!" Well—it was barely dawn. The sun was still below the horizon. And it was already crazy. Passengers—hundreds of them—tumbling across the docks, down metal plates that pretended to be a gangplank—goats, pigs, bundled chickens, caged monkeys, buckets full of vegetables and meat, baskets bulging and covered with sacks, women in bright flowery frocks carrying babies papoose-style, little children dragging even smaller children, an Indian merchant balancing twelve bound rolls of printed fabric on his head, three Bantu tribesmen manhandling an enormous trunk with brass padlocks and a Christmasy ornamentation of stickers and transit labels. And soldiers too—big fellows with angry faces and automatic rifles and a penchant for pushing and bawling at the churning, shouting, screaming mass.

I hardly had a chance to see the boat from the quay. *The General* something or other—a lopsided, low-in-the-water, rusty white five-deck creature pierced with tiny windows—mother to a flotilla of five even rustier barges strapped with frayed cables to its superstructure and to one another. Together they were easily the size of a football field. My ticket indicated I had a "to-share" cabin in the main vessel. Most of the crowd was surging farther forward into the shadows of the single- and double-deck barges. Over three thousand people were in there, I was told later, for our seven-hundred-mile, eight-day ride from Kinshasa to Kisangani (Stanleyville). I don't know how many were in the main boat, but it felt like a floating palace compared to the stifling claustrophobia of the prisonlike rooms and passageways on those barges.

I found my room. Two bunk beds and a porthole encrusted with explosions of rust and black cobwebs. Couldn't open it. Wouldn't make any damned difference anyhow. Never been in a tiny space so hot before. Sweat pouring. Wanted to dump my pack but nobody around, no key, so dragged it back up on deck and sat in a small patch of shade, wondering what the hell I was going to do with myself for the next eight days.

Time passed very slowly in the sweltering heat. They'd said the boat would leave at ten A.M. It was now one P.M. and still no sign of departure. More shouting, desperate passengers—more goats and chickens. Finally a great blast of steam, whistles, gongs, and soldiers giving vent to their pent-up anger by dragging away two raggedly dressed men who tried to leap for the side of the boat as it creaked and sagged into the main channel of the river. Howls and yells from friends or family on board. Didn't make a bit of difference. The soldiers had something to punch and pound at last. God—sometimes I hate Africa.

UP THE ZAIRE RIVER
— Zaire

And then again, sometimes I don't. Ten or more miles upstream, things settled down. People came out on the long veranda with stools and folding chairs; there was the chink of beer bottles, even the aroma of food being cooked somewhere deep in the growling bowels of this ungainly boat-barge conglomeration. A breeze too. And shade. Now we were getting civilized. Kinshasa was gone. Farewell, festering, unworkable city of four million. The locals call it Boubelleville—Trash Can City! A remarkably accurate description in spite of a patina of modernity in the form of broad boulevards and modest high rises. All for show, though. The truth lies beyond the gleaming towers.

The jungle was edging in. Miles and miles of it in all directions tumbling to a ragged halt along torn, timber-strewn shores. Might not be such a bad journey after all. The cabin was a hellhole, but what the heck, I would stay on the deck.

I was wondering if the sun was melting my brain. Couldn't seem to focus on anything serious. All that noise and crush and panic had unloosed some idiot in my skull. I needed some relief. A beer first and then maybe someone to talk to.

"Hello."

I looked up and saw a man about forty or so with graying hair, a lean face closely shaved, wearing a blue T-shirt and a crisply pressed pair of white safari shorts. (And carrying a generous supply of bottled beer.)

"I think you would enjoy a drink?"

I thanked him, maybe too profusely.

"May I sit with you?" he asked, and smiled.

"Please. I could do with some company."

Paul was a French citizen who had lived in Zaire most of his adult life ("since I discovered African women"). After the normal introductory chitchat I asked him to tell me a little about this strange and mysterious country. Vaguely, from shards of schoolboy history, I remembered tales of atrocities and unbelievable cruelties inflicted on the Congo nation by Belgium's King Leopold II. But Paul gave these tales flesh and blood. Too much blood.

"It was possibly the worst example of colonial rape ever inflicted on an indigenous people," he said. "Even today I have friends in Belgium who will not talk—they refuse to discuss this period of their history. It is still hard for them to imagine such

16

things as were done. I think they would prefer to forget. You see, Leopold was—ah, wait a minute—I am going too fast. Let's begin with the Portuguese. One Portuguese man. A navigator, Diogo Cao, who discovered the Congo River in 1482. He thought it was just another bay and then found a river of such a size that it pushed out fresh water thirty, forty miles into the Atlantic. He could not understand a river of that enormity. We now know it is the fifth largest river in the world—almost five thousand kilometers long. Do you remember the others?"

I hadn't expected the question and dredged my mind for the answers: "Er—the Amazon. Yes, certainly the Amazon. The Nile ... the Mississippi, and ..."

"The Yangtze, my friend. Never forget the Yangtze."

"Right."

"So—Signor Cao met the people—the Bakongo tribe—and sailed upriver as far as the Caldron of Hell—a very difficult part of those rapids that fill the last four hundred kilometers of the river below Kinshasa—the old Leopoldville. The things he offered them—gifts, education, the world's most powerful religion, and personal friendship with King John of Portugal—seemed to please the Bakongo King, Nzinga, and what happened in the early fifteen hundreds was possibly one of the best relationships between an African and a European nation. We French—the British, the Spanish—we all had our dreams of riches and power, but Portugal for a while—well, they seemed happy just to convert, educate, and help the development of the Congo without destroying it."

"That didn't last too long, though. Not from what I understand."

"Well—you are so right. Portugal became greedy—they saw how rich all the other colonial powers were becoming—and they joined the slave trade. And other things too. Then the Arabs moved in from the Middle East. Other countries got involved. Many of the native kingdoms were destroyed. Pirates, profiteers, planters—everyone tried to grab a bit of the Congo. Your Dr. Livingstone came too—he talked about 'taming, educating, and Christianizing these savages of darkest Africa.' And the tribes themselves. They also began to destroy one another." He sighed. To him, Zaire's history was still something very alive and tangible.

"So how did King Leopold get into all this?"

17

"Leopold? Ah—well. That was another Englishman, your Mr. Stanley, who came here looking for Livingstone, you remember, and then he seeked—searched for—someone—someone very rich—to invest in developing this place—this 'Amazonia of Africa.' In the 1880s Europe was carving up Africa—deciding who would have which bits. King Leopold had made a lot of money with his shares in the Suez Canal and was angry that Belgium didn't seem to be getting much in the way of colonies in Africa. Somehow—I don't know how—Stanley persuaded the European governments to let Leopold start a private company to collect ivory and rubber—and anything else that made a profit. So the king now had his own private colony—the whole Congo, eighty times the size of little Belgium—all his, to do with what he wanted."

"And what did he do?"

"He made a lot more money. That's what he did. He killed or starved eight million Africans; he cut off the hands of workers who gathered the rubber if they did not collect enough. His soldiers made fortunes too. The more hands they brought to him— they smoked the hands to preserve them and put them in big straw baskets—they more they got paid. I think that is what inspired the writer Conrad—another one of your Englishmen—to write that famous story 'Heart of Darkness.'"

"Yes—I know the story well."

"Then you know what I'm talking about. It was unbelievable what happened. Unbelievable! A whole country of this size, at the mercy of this tyrant—this idiot—in Belgium."

"Didn't Britain put a stop to it all?"

"And France. France too protested. Oh—and Mark Twain too. He wrote a vicious satire about Leopold. In 1908 the country was taken over by the Belgian government. Leopold was discredited. It became the Belgian Congo and for a while things got better. New cities were built. Many mines were dug for copper, diamonds—later uranium. Many got rich. The Belgians—even some of the natives."

"Did the tribes have any political power?"

"None. And that, of course, was the problem. The Belgians kept promising them power but did nothing."

"So—what happened?"

"Patrice Lumumba. That's what happened. He created riots

18

and demanded freedom. That was in 1958. And"—Paul laughed loudly—"he got it. In a year or so the Belgians were gone. They took everything. Just walked—or maybe they ran—away."

"And left a hell of a mess behind."

"And left a mess. Yes. And a hell. That's exactly what they did. Maybe they thought that if things got really bad they'd be invited back. Who knows? But they certainly left a mess. A few days after independence in 1960 the place went crazy. The whites who had stayed were murdered or driven out, the country started dividing itself up, back into the old tribal regions. Roads, machinery, towns—all were destroyed. The Belgians sent troops back in—there were more massacres. Then the United Nations took over for a while and tried to bring the tribes together—then the tribes started using mercenaries and within a year you had a bloody—very bloody—civil war. Lumumba was murdered—some say by people paid by American CIA. Mobutu tried to establish himself as leader but was forced to resign. Dag Hammarskjöld tried to stop the fighting between the UN troops and the mercenaries, but he was killed—very mysteriously—in a plane crash. It was terrible. The country was destroying itself. Then the Simba terrorists came along—believing they were immune to bullets. Doing terrible things. So more mercenaries came—'Mad Mike' Hoare and others as mad as he was. They were as cruel as the Simbas—killing everyone, anything. The massacre of the whites—the 'mateka' of Stanleyville [Kisangani] was one of the worst things the Simbas did. I can't even tell you how horrible it was—it would make you ill. Eventually the mercenaries destroyed most of them—but it was a bad, bad time."

Paul paused to take a long pull on his Primus beer and gave me a second one. Our shade had shifted, so we moved farther down the deck back into the still-sweltering shadows. Across the broad Zaire River large islandlike mats of water hyacinths slipped by, speckled with blue flowers. The water was possibly a good two miles wide now; I could see the straggly jungle, misted by heat haze, easing slowly—very slowly—by. Behind that riparian riot of vegetation lay what? The map showed nothing except puce-green swaths of blank paper with no roads, no villages, no mountains. Just endless jungle covering almost three million square miles, laced by spidery tributaries. Empty, unused, unexplored. The old Africa—the Africa of V. S. Naipaul's *A Bend in the River*:

Africa is big. The bush muffles the sound of murder, and the muddy river washes the blood away.

And other Naipaul lines that touch the mystery of this silent place:

The bush is full of spirits; in the bush hover all the protecting presences of man's ancestors . . . the river and the forest are like presences, and much more powerful than you. . . . You feel unprotected, an intruder. . . . You feel the land taking you back to something that is familiar, something you had known at some time but had forgotten or ignored, but which was always there.

Conrad captured a similar spirit in "Heart of Darkness":

Going up that river was like traveling back to the earliest beginnings of the world . . . an empty stream, a great silence, an impenetrable forest. . . . You thought yourself bewitched and cut off forever from everything you had known once— somewhere—far away—in another existence.

The vast Congo basin has drawn writers like moths to its tantalizing flames: Graham Greene creeping through the alleys of Leopoldville seeking, savoring the atmosphere and tension and stupefying sense of humid doom for his *A Burnt-out Case*, Gide and his *Journey to the Congo*, and Céline's *Journey to the End of the Night*, Helen Winternitz's more recent *East Along the Equator*, and Peter Matthiessen's *African Silences*. So many more too. Explorers, world wanderers, diarists, sociologists, UN missions, church missionaries, get-rich-quick Trumpies, seekers of the sensual and the strange—all coming here looking for insights, understanding, wealth, cheap sex, adventure. Who knows, maybe even early death. The death wish that seems to urge Greene-like characters to slither into this wilderness and disappear. While others—like me, I suppose—come merely to wander, and to wonder.

Paul nudged my arm. "Hello, David. Where are you?"

I didn't know where I was. Limbo-landed again. Off in the infinities of this incredible place. With a mind at first reaching out, trying to touch the edges, discovering the edgelessness of things and being content for the moment at least to pause—and to dream.

"Sorry, Paul. I was just thinking." Thinking what, though? I tried to explain. "It always amazes me. Particularly in Africa. The horrible histories—the cruelties, the inhuman violations, the genocides, the greed... and yet it all looks so peaceful, so untouched. The jungle grows back again—that patient jungle—so patient—covering the scars, breaking the buildings into dust, grinding and squeezing it all down into its roots... as if none of the terrors and tortures had ever happened; as if there was no break between what was, what is, and what will be."

Paul smiled, sipped his beer, and wiped the corners of his mouth delicately with long, sinewy fingers.

"You talk like a writer."

It was my turn to smile. "But what I can write is so pathetic against... all this. The power of it. The horror of it. It's... too big!"

"Now you sound like a white African."

"Like you?"

"Yes—like me. You are saying—feeling—what I have felt for ... what? All of my time here, I think. And it has been a long time. Thirty years."

"And you're still here."

"Oh, yes, of course. You can never really leave, you know. Even if you leave."

"Yes. I can sense that. I'm beginning, but only beginning, to understand why."

"Oh—I think by the time you leave, you will understand maybe a little better. In Africa—and in Zaire particularly, David, always remember it—that French saying: 'Plus ça change, plus c'est la même chose.' The same thing. Different disguises but always the same thing."

We drank our beers in silence, watching the river ease by like thick syrup, flattened by the appalling heat, undisturbed by breezes, reluctantly rippled only by the boat.

"And Mobutu. How are things now under President Mobutu?"

Paul's expression changed. The smile withdrew and his

21

mouth became a thin gash. He looked over his shoulder as if nervous about eavesdroppers and his voice became a sad whisper.

"Oh, David. I could tell you so . . . so many things. He has been president now for over twenty-five years. Twenty-five years of crazy schemes and useless industrial projects and useless dams and airports and useless wars. He has told people what to wear, what to think, what to believe. Zaire has now, I think, one of the largest debts in the world, it is one of the poorest and one of the hungriest places on earth in spite of all its wonderful earth, minerals, gold . . . thirty-five million people with an average income, if you can call it that, of less than one hundred and fifty dollars a year! Yet Mobutu is one of the richest men alive today. Do you know what his full name is—Mobutu Sese Seko Kuku Ngbendu wa za Banga—it means 'the great warrior who conquers everything.' Maybe it's true—he has conquered everything—for himself. And all thanks to our support of him—French money, Belgian money, British money, U.S. money—and, of course, your CIA. He has hidden it all away—billions of dollars—and his people get"—outstretched arms again "this! Yet we all keep this man alive, we let him do whatever he wants to do. We are still the power behind his throne."

"Twentieth-century colonialism?"

Paul lowered his voice even further.

"David. This is dangerous. Please be careful what you say and what you do here. Things may look so very beautiful and peaceful as we go up this river, but Zaire . . . it is a very strange country. You—all of us—have to be careful what we say and who we say it to. This man keeps power in the old-fashioned way— terror, fear, informants—sometimes very friendly people who get very rich by saying bad things about you to the police. And money. Lots and lots of money . . . our money!"

"It's incredible."

"It's Africa," said Paul quietly.

"So why do you stay?"

"Ah. That question again. That old question. Why do I stay? Sometimes I just don't know. . . . " He took a long pull from his beer. "A writer once wrote—I forget who it was, but it doesn't matter—he wrote, 'I could always move on—though where, I didn't know. And then I found I couldn't move. I had to stay.' "

"Sounds a bit like Naipaul."

"Possibly. I don't remember."

"So. You have to stay?"

He gave one of those wonderfully French shrugs, with out-stretched arms and raised eyebrows.

"I have to stay . . . that's all. I have to stay, David."

The sun was setting now and music roared up from the barges. Paul seemed talked out and went off to his cabin for a nap. I stayed on deck for a while, enjoying the evening breezes. But the music got louder and louder. Too loud to ignore. What was going on down there in those barges? Time to explore.

And what an exploration!

This was not a boat, it was a community. A floating mini-city complete with bars, discos, banks, snack stands, merchants in little cramped compartments, gamblers, vendors of smoked monkeys that looked like wizened charcoal-shrouded fetuses, and smoked bats, smoked crocodile, and smoked fish (I think it was fish), butchers (watching a goat struggle in its bloody death throes is not conducive to a hearty appetite), bakers—who knows maybe even candlestick makers, old whores, young whores, fat, thin, angelic, vampish, and just plain ugly whores. And smells—marijuana, roasting goat, roasting monkey, laundry, toilets that don't work, sweat, incense, cheap perfumes, beans—vast caldrons of beans—tea, boiling maize, boiling fish stew (the most popular dish, served with hot pepper sauce), fresh-cut pineapples, stale beer. And sounds—the music, of course, scores of different cheap cassettes playing on equally cheap boomboxes—screams, the cries of children, shrieks of chickens about to be lopped, topped, tailed, trussed, and turned over blazing fires, the flapping of wet washing in river breezes strung out in gay lines of color resembling the slum streets of Naples. . . .

The alleys (sometimes with names!) between the metal-box cabins were like Oriental bazaars, lit by flaring, spitting oil lamps. You could buy just about anything here: illicit herbs, antibiotics, condoms, baskets, blankets, fabrics, fruit, fish, all those smoked oddities, cheap glittery jewelry, cheap glittery women, second-hand dresses and pants, platters of fat squirming grubs (ready for deep frying into a popular snack), live baby crocodiles, an amazing assortment of ballpoint pens adorned with familiar Fortune 500 logos, pirated cassettes in cracked plastic boxes, notions, potions, and lotions of all descriptions, plastic shoes and sandals from Hong Kong, cigarettes (sold individually), cheap watches—and beer. Crate upon crate of Primus and Congo beer. Half the boat's cargo seemed to be beer.

"Hey, *bonjour*, white—buy me a beer." The call came from a bunch of men who seemed bored with their gambling on the upper deck of one of the barges and were looking for distraction.

I smiled, waved, and shrugged.

"Okay, man—we buy you beer!"

I joined them.

"So where you going, *citoyen*?" The use of the French vernacular created a rumble of laughter.

"I'm not a *citoyen*—I'm from the USA."

Raised eyebrows, a few ooh-la-las, and more laughter. Someone pushed a warm beer into my hand. Someone else patted my back. (Where was my wallet? Oh, right, in my ankle strap, under the sock. If they tried a pickpocket technique they'd find nothing. Why am I always so suspicious at first? Because you've been ripped off in so many places that it's second nature, comes the reply.)

"So—you like our country?" The questioner was an older man with a thick mat of curly gray hair and a long scar from hairline to chin on the left side of his face. He had finely drawn features—not unlike the notorious explorer of eastern Zaire, Richard Burton.

"So far, I like it," I said, and slurped my beer with the others.

"And what about our beloved president?" the older man asked with a lopsided grin. He looked a little drunk. He was leading me on. Trying to get me to commit verbal indiscretions. I remembered Paul's warning.

"I don't know. We haven't been introduced yet." Not much of a response, but it made them all laugh and another bottle of beer arrived in my spare hand.

"And you would like to meet him—yes?"

Time to shift the conversation away from Mobutu. I'd read far too much about his "personality cult" and his dreaded henchmen to offer an unbiased reply. Certainly he'd brought a measure of centralized control and calm to this chaotic land—but at what cost to his poor *citoyens* and *citoyennes*, and at what cost to us, the ill-informed, gullible, boondoggled, and bamboozled taxpayers back home?

"Is it always as hot as this?"

"*Tout le temps*, man. All the time."

I shifted position to get a little more of the night breeze. The engine vibrations from the main boat ran through the metal deck and made my backside tingle. At least there were no mosquitoes up here. The breeze kept them away.

A row broke out farther down the deck. One of the merchants from the dark alleys below stormed up the steep iron steps and across the warm metal plates pocked with rivets, scattering gamblers, knocking over one of those interminable boomboxes (and killing it, I think—or at least the Bob Marley reggae racket ceased abruptly), and stomping right up to a small wizened man wrapped in a grubby cotton cloak. He had been huddled with his wife, two children, and three baby goats, sipping a beer. The tirade was in that strange lingua-franca which seems to be the only way, other than the "lingala" river language, that the two-hundred-plus tribes of Zaire have found to communicate with each other.

The merchant's brawlings and cursings momentarily silenced the carnival-mood passengers. Dancers stopped, more boomboxes were turned down, and swigging ceased. Distractions of any kind were always welcome up here. Eight days of ceaseless travel is a long time and a good fight or shouting match was just the thing to break the beer-boozed, marijuana-mellowed monotony.

Although I have a reasonable grasp of French as spoken in France, I have a hard time with its ethnic derivatives, Creole-inspired or otherwise. I couldn't understand a word of the merchant's roar, but it seemed to have little impact on the old man. He merely lowered his head and disappeared deeper into his grubby cloak. There were sniggers and giggles. The merchant was obviously losing this particular battle—and losing face too. In desperation he seized one of the man's baby goats, raised it high above his head like a scimitar, paused to shout one more string

25

of invectives at the old man, and threw the squealing creature overboard.

The giggles ceased. The closest thing to utter silence reigned on the deck. No one moved for a few seconds and then there was a sudden rush to the side to see what had happened to the poor kid. I stood too and could see it in the boat lights, struggling gamely against the waves made by the prow, making for the now-invisible shore at least a mile away. Surely it would never arrive. The creature seemed barely weaned. What a lousy thing to do.

I was tempted to grapple with the merchant (Oh, when will I learn to mind my own business?) but he vanished in the surge of bodies, doubtless returning to the sweaty sanctuary of his metal-box "store" below. The old man still sat immobile, head down in his cloak. His wife looked miserable but seemed to accept the incident as some kind of just punishment for sins I couldn't fathom. Only the children cried—both of them—tears pouring down their faces as they held the remaining two baby goats close to their thin bodies.

I remembered a line from Naipaul again: "It was unnerving, the depth of that African rage, the wish to destroy, regardless of the consequences."

Two minutes later the whole incident was forgotten. Music blared again, bottles chinked, card games recommenced, and my compatriots returned to their interrogation.

"Where in America you are from?" asked one of them.

"Didn't you see that?" I was outraged at all the nonchalance. "Didn't you see what that guy just did?"

Tolerant smiles and shrugs from my group. "Wait until the murders come," murmured the man who had originally invited me over.

"Murders—what murders?"

"Aha, *mon ami bon*—these boats are very strange. Many things happen. It is a long way to Kisangani, over twelve hundred kilometers."

More giggles and shrugs. "Have another beer."

"No, no, thanks. I have to get back to my cabin. I'll see you later. Maybe."

David in retreat. Not a happy sight. Not a happy man. Sensing a secret world here. Who knows what vendettas and feuds

and drug-crazed attacks—even murders—might plague this floating Dante's Inferno of three thousand hot, hungry, harassed—
and drunk—*citoyens*.

I needed rest!

Only I didn't get much. My stuffy, smelly cabin was now
occupied by three other gentlemen, all large, all snoring and fart-
ing like flatulent hippos. I lay on my bunk, watched the largest
cockroaches I've ever seen anywhere skitter across the floor in
search of nighttime snacks. I stuck cotton wool in my ears and
prayed for sleep. In the end I gave up and went outside onto the
open passageway, lay down on the warm metal, and dozed fit-
fully, wafted by cool breezes which, once again, kept the mosquitoes away.

Dreams came. Strange dreams of snakes. Huge liquid snakes
with hundreds of glinting silver eyes. Possibly sparked by those
lines from Conrad about his Congo (now Zaire) River:

> [It is] an immense snake uncoiled, with its head in the sea,
> its body at rest curving afar over a vast country, and its tail
> lost in the depths of the land.

The name of the river and the country stems from a phonetic
Portuguese mangling of the ancient Bantu language word *rizadi*,
meaning "the great river that devours all rivers."

How appropriate. In my dreams I felt I was being devoured
in the snakelike river itself. Things tumbled by in the churn, wash,
and drag of the current—bodies horribly mutilated, bits of bodies,
baroque curlicues of blood and gore, cows, decapitated crocodiles,
creatures all encrusted in black burned skin like those "smoked"
monkeys, bats, and tree squirrels, enormous fish heads with open
mouths and teeth that flashed like scimitars, and, of course, poor
struggling baby goats, bleating, shrieking in the surge of that
endless river of my dreams. . . .

It was not a pleasant night.

Morning came, not in the quiet purplings and pinks and slow
tangerines one might expect, but in another jarring riot of churning bodies and screams and shouts.

Scores of lithe, virtually naked men and youths were teeming up vine ropes and over the side of the barges like some kind of Hollywood-staged pirate invasion. What the hell was happening now?

The other passengers were less surprised. Many had pulled out their folding seats and were enjoying a grandstand view of our slow passage by a small riverside town. High above on the bluffs I could see a church tower (vague echoes of hymns wafting through the thick air), faded pastel buildings, and three once-ornate but now-overgrown European-style mansions. Lower down a straggle of thatch and bamboo shacks stretched along the ocher-earth bank in both directions, before fading into the jungly scrub.

The locals were out in their tree-trunk–adzed pirogues—dozens of them—all vying for positions close to the barges to allow their occupants to clamber on board with their trading bundles of trussed cocks and geese, turtles, huge manganza and catfish, crocodile tails, sacks of writhing live grubs, baskets of flailing eels, huge branches of bananas, bags of manioc and maize.

Chaos once again: bodies tumbling into the water, pirogues overturning in the wash of our floating monolithic boat, their occupants cursing, laughing, yelling, and still managing to scramble onto the barges with their bundles.

So this was how it worked. The merchants on the boat not only sold and traded with its passengers, but also with the occupants of river towns and villages as we moved slowly upriver. Smoked meats and fish and fruit exchanged for incense, baskets, blankets, beer, cassettes, and all the other junk heaped down below in the barges. A movable market. Rampant capitalism released in this vast nothingness. A Milton Freidman frenzy of barter and banter. Goods and money changing hands at a Hong Kong pace as the *piroguistes* tried to complete their transactions before the boat moved higher up the river into unfamiliar water, by which time they stood a good chance of losing their pirogues in the turbulent wake or having them (and themselves) crushed against the barges or ground into one of those insidious sandbanks that plague this ever-changing river.

I struggled through the confusion of bodies to get closer to the action.

The merchants were pure money machines now, fever-faced

and slit-eyed—bargaining with Levantine dexterity, spraying handfuls of filthy bank notes like confetti, making the villagers fight and grovel for attention, scything the *piroguistes'* expectations of fair deals to panic-selling levels. Others were trading directly from their boats, hoisting up dripping gutted fish and clutching at the fluttering money tossed overboard, money which in a month or two would be almost worthless in inflation-wracked Zaire.

On shore stood their wives and children, waving, cheering them on like spectators at a ball game, screaming encouragement—faster, faster! More, more! Shouts, curses, violent but brief arguments, spittings, fist waving, people tumbling on the slippery decks slick with fish scales.

I watched one small boy—an apprentice *piroguiste*—trying to maneuver his thin and very wobbly craft between the others and shouting at the merchants to attract their attention. In his left hand he held three curled and crisp-smoked monkeys threaded on a rope. No one had noticed him and our boat was moving away from him, huge diesels churning the muddy water behind us, whistles blasting. Ever more frantically he waved his meager offering. I shouted at one of the merchants nearby and pointed to the little boy. He had just completed what looked like a highly lucrative deal and, a minor miracle, I saw him smile and gesture to the boy, who paddled his pirogue furiously to catch up with us and then hurled his blackened bundle at the outstretched hands of the merchant.

It missed.

It hit the side of the barge below the rail with a sad little bump and fell down into the churning water below.

The look of despair on the boy's face sliced right through my gut. His only trading item lost—and possibly on his first venture out into this wrenching, slit-throat man's world where nimble hands and nimble brains were vital to success.

The merchant laughed, shrugged, and began to turn away. But then—surprise—that hard-bitten, money-driven man stuck a grubby hand deep into a trouser pocket, pulled out a few notes, rolled them into a ball, and threw them like a major-league pitcher right into the boy's hands. Then he smiled, waved, and vanished into the madness.

The boy did the nearest thing to a jig that you can do in a pirogue, waved at me and the already-vanished merchant, and paddled frantically back to shore. Two little girls, maybe his sisters, came rushing down to greet him and ogle at the fistful of cash he carried with him proudly up the red sand beach.

We were passing an island and the captain was steering a little too close to shore. A few of the pirogues became caught on roots and snags. Panic set in. Bodies leaping off the barges, splashing in the water between the pirogues. More swampings, more cursings and laughter. A few hardy men tried to keep up with us and make last-second deals, flailing frantically with their long paddle-poles, but soon they too dropped behind as our boat creaked and groaned out into the main channel again, back into the breezes, back into the limbo land of this vast and mysterious river.

The hours slid by. The river widened, eight or nine miles now from bank to bank.

I passed the time reading and sketching and even trying one of the meals in the restaurant for first-class passengers—an odd and tasteless concoction of manioc, beans, and old unsalted meatballs made of unidentifiable meat. I decided to stick to the snacks so lavishly displayed and cooked on the little stands down in the bazaars and decks of the barges. As a result I am now a still-living connoisseur of crisp-roasted caterpillars, sliced crocodile tail, monkey casserole, catfish stew, conchlike snails served with liquid fire, aka pepper sauce, and curried beetle grubs (not to mention tidbits of half a dozen or more smoked jungle creatures).

In the scourge of afternoon heat people slept under tarpaulin canopies and anywhere else they could find shade. The river was misty, sheened in a humid haze, through which the sun was a silver shimmering blur leaching the color from the scene.

I rarely went to my cabin. It was far too hot during the day and full of unwashed, rumbling bodies at night. I preferred the gangway, where I could follow the shadows, doze a little, smell the burning wood from the always-active barbecues, capture a breeze or two, and even imagine I heard drums—distant and echoing—from the line of jungled shore on the far horizon.

Occasionally I'd spot a crocodile or a floating log—it was hard to tell the difference. At one point, as we followed a channel marked by more floating mats of water hyacinths (usually evidence of adequate river depth and lack of sneaky sandbars) I saw four large mounded creatures wallowing in the shallows by a river island. I had misplaced my binoculars and in the zoom lens of my camera it was hard to distinguish their shapes. I think they were hippos.

Even in the sudden downpours that came out of nowhere in the middle of the afternoons I managed to stay outdoors under the broad canopies of the boat's superstructure. The rain thrashed and pounded the river into submissive flatness and carried in it the smell of fires and wet earth and rotting jungle.

As evening closed in, the earthy aromas were more intense and the breezes fresher. Then came the night (that all too quick transition from dusk to darkness one always experiences on the equator), with yet another surge of disco music and fights and dancing and boozing and all the other more illicit activities deep down in the subterranean dankness of the barge bottoms, where people sat and gambled and fought and loved and slept on tiny rectangles of straw matting. Our huge spotlights attracted brilliant flashing streams of moths and flying insects like endless fireworks displays.

Thunder rumbled in the distance and surges of sheet lightning flashed across the silent jungle shores, reflected in the dark waters.

And then the dawns. Those slow cool dawns, as we eased up the still river, bathed in winey morning air, watching the striations of color push away the stars and the Africa-black night and bathe the boat and its sleepy-eyed occupants in liquid essences of gold and amber and lemon before the first smack of heat and the beginning of another long day. Edging ever deeper into the heart of darkness. . . .

Life on the boat, at least on our section of the main boat, settled into a series of lazy reveries. Occasionally Paul and I would meet and chat and introduce ourselves to other passengers. But for long periods I just sat and watched the slow brown-silver river, sometimes broad and vast as a desert, sometimes broken in a filigree of channels between mud-shore islands. Except for the occasional fisherman and his family living in straw huts shaded by palms, bamboo, and papyrus fronds, the islands were devoid of visible life. Torrents of sounds came from their jungled depths, particularly in the evening, but I rarely saw any of the sound makers. Like so much in this vast country, they were invisible—their presence indicated more by suggestion than perception.

The journey eased on, days slipping into nights and slowly into days again. The heat was still merciless, but I'd found ways to alleviate its impact—sleeping, moving around to find choice, shady places fanned by river breezes, dousing myself regularly in water and letting it evaporate slowly, or, when really necessary, uplifting my mood with a glass of almost lethal "Whiskey-Zairois," whose moonshine contents I can only guess at. Sex had been offered me in a multitude of variations but not accepted. How could any sane individual consider hearty couplings in this torpor? A slow, gentle Thai-style massage maybe, after a cold shower—but no one thought to offer that.

I should have known all this calm and languor was too good to be true.

The unpleasantness began innocently enough one afternoon as we passed a series of small fishing villages beyond Mbandaka. We were cruising calmly up the western side of the river quite close to the bank. Drums echoed occasionally in the forest—an ancient system for indicating the progress of the boat *to piroguistes* farther upstream. I was doodling rather ineffective sketches on a pad stained with beer and sweat.

A thin, weasely-faced man, perhaps in his mid-forties, with a skin the color of cold cappuccino, edged up the long, open veranda near my cabin. There was something officious about him, tinged with an undoubted penchant for forelock pulling in the presence of appointed superiors. His dress was innocuous enough. He wore a rather grubby white shirt, pink tie, creased gray trousers stained at the cuffs, and plastic, imitation-leather shoes. His smile, when I looked up and nodded a good afternoon, was exactly what I thought it would be—tight and false. In fact, downright unpleasant. The very epitome of Uriah Heepishness.

"*Parlez-vous Français, monsieur?*"

"A little, yes—but I prefer English."

"Ah—I am not so good by my English."

"Ah."

I was hoping that might be the end of our little chat. Rarely do I take such an instant dislike to newly met individuals, but this particular one exuded mistrust and guile.

"*J'pense que*—I am sorry—I will try the English. . . . I see that you are artist."

"I'm sketching—yes."

"Ah—yes, artisting."

I smiled. His new word had an amusing ring to it. Unfortunately, he took my smile for encouragement and crept closer (I mean really crept, as if he sensed that at any second I might take a swing at him with my pencil).

Then he was peering over my shoulder.

"Ah, *les villages*—the villages. Yes."

He began a flurry of noddings. Either that or he had a very bad attack of the tics.

"You are very good, *monsieur*. Your artisting—*c'est trés bonne!*"

"Thank you."

"You have many like this?"

"Quite a few, yes." Looking back, I should have shut the sketchbook and shut myself up too. But instead I flicked through a few of my other quick doodles, including a few I'd done when we were invaded at that little town with all the pirogues.

"Ah, yes. You have many. Very good."

He stood—or rather stooped—for a while and was silent. When he started up again I could have sworn he almost reached up to pull his forelock.

"I am sorry to interrupt you."

"No, no—that's fine."

"Excuse me, *monsieur*, but do you have a beer?"

"No, sorry—I've just finished the last one."

"Ah, yes."

More silence. I was getting a little irritated now. I don't like sketching when people are watching and he gave no indication of moving on.

"Ah—I see you smoke cigars."

"Yes. Yes, I enjoy the occasional cigar."

"Excuse me, *monsieur*—but do you have one cigar for me?"

"I'm sorry. I'm out. My cigars are all back in the cabin." I wished I'd had one. He may have left me alone.

"Of course."

The throb of the boat's engine ran through my body like a vibrator bed. A pleasant sensation, made even more relaxing by the river breezes which Uriah Heep was now effectively blocking.

"I wonder, *monsieur*. I am needing of buying something. Is it possible that you have a little—excuse me—a few zaires for me—*un petit cadeau*."

Okay, I'd had it. My patience had gone now and I wanted my breeze back—and my solitude.

I turned and gave him my stern look.

"I am sorry, I don't have a beer, I don't have a cigar, and I don't have any zaires on me at the moment. Now, if you don't mind . . ."

And he did it! He actually reached up and touched his forelock. Didn't exactly pull it, but near enough to confirm all my expectations.

"Ah. Eh, *bien*. I will leave you now. *Adieu, monsieur*."

Five minutes later I'd forgotten about him. But the following morning as we docked in Lisala it was obvious he had not forgotten me.

We slid slowly through more floating mats of hyacinths and made a dainty landing at the old, battered docks below a steep bluff. I was told we had a three-hour stopover so I decided to disembark and go exploring.

The long stairway up to the top of the bluff was shaded by trees. On the top, breezes blew away my almost constantly pumping sweat. From glimpses of the other small river towns with their decaying, vine-shrouded European mansions and crumbling civic buildings, I didn't expect too much of Lisala—but surprise, I discovered cool gardens, a large mission and church, and a broad plaza full of music and beer-chugging locals. I was looking forward to joining them, but suddenly found myself in the company of two soldiers carrying automatic rifles. And some way behind them, who should be there but that hunched little weasel, Uriah Heep. The glint in his shaded eyes was sheer maliciousness; his smile was as tight and false as yesterday, but there was some other expression in his face—vengeance! Not a pleasant sight.

He kept his distance, shuffling his feet in the soft sandy surface of the avenue, while the soldiers informed me that I was obliged to accompany them to the immigration and customs offices.

My initial alarm gave way to increasing confidence. All my papers were in order. I had my medical and vaccination forms, and my British passport was safely in my bag with its splendid "requirement" written in copperplate type on the inside cover. The ring and rhythm of its language always impressed me and I reproduce it here for all those who've never really studied the intricacies of one of Her Majesty's passports:

> Her Britannic Majesty's
> Secretary of State
> Requests and requires
> In the Name of Her Majesty
> All those whom it may concern
> To allow the bearer to pass freely
> Without let or hindrance,
> And to afford the bearer
> Such assistance and protection
> As may be necessary.

Splendid—almost pure colonial rhetoric! "Without let or hindrance." I love that line.

I started to hum quietly and nonchalantly, but the soldiers seemed unamused. Their fingers tightened on their guns. One of them even grasped my elbow. I shook him free and he didn't try again, but his look reminded me to exercise caution. Show respect David, I thought. This is Zaire and the Queen of England is a hell of a long way away.

Behind the pleasant river bluff facades of Lisala, the town

became increasingly unkept and overgrown: sidewalks buckling and sprouting weeds, broken lampposts, old colonial buildings boarded up, with cracked, mold-flecked walls, decaying shutters, and collapsing roofs.

We entered a particularly decrepit specimen up a flight of lopsided concrete steps.

A few people in ragged clothes lay sprawled on the porch surrounded by children with reddening hair (a sure sign of malnutrition), goats, and the remnants of a meal of manioc and little else.

The soldiers paused at the top of the steps and Uriah Heep darted past, through the torn fly-screened door, his eyes and face hidden behind hunched shoulders. The door slammed shut and we waited. It was hot. Very hot. No breezes here. I cursed my penchant for perspiration. My mother once told me it was a genetic characteristic of her side of the family, but here it might be taken for nervousness or downright panic.

However, I didn't feel any panic. This would, I thought, be one of those amusing little misunderstandings ideal for dinner table dialogue after a fine meal, during the Stilton and port phase. How would I tell it? "Well, anyway, there I was wandering about this pleasant little plaza in the middle of the Belgian Congo. . . . "

A voice boomed inside the building and the soldiers broke my reveries by rushing me through the door past what was once a magnificent double-curve staircase and into a dark, dirty back room where the servants' quarters must once have been in the "soirée and dansantes" days of Belgian hegemony.

A man in a wrinkled uniform sat with his back to a spider-web–laced window at a small desk. His face was silhouetted against the sunlight that struggled in between the dust and decayed webs. Uriah Heep was nowhere to be seen. The soldiers pushed me into a rickety cane chair and stepped back to the doorway.

It was very quiet and very hot. Oh, yes—and here comes the perspiration, I thought, rolling out of my pores, now the size of meteor craters.

"Papers." The officer extended his long fingers and I gave him my passport and all the other bureaucratic claptrap neatly packaged in a leather case. It all looked very impressive, until he started pulling out its contents with disdain and scattering them over his dusty desk like wastepaper.

The passport seemed to fascinate him. I have an extra large one to accommodate all the visas and stamps of my travels and he started at the beginning and laboriously perused each smudgy symbol and signature, some going back over eight years.

I began to hum to myself again—just a tiny, almost inaudible hum, you understand—but it seemed to annoy him. He looked up, stared at me until I stopped, and then resumed his exacting perusal.

I watched a fly in the window, moving slowly down the screen in the heat. It was making straight for a web in the bottom corner where dried bits of bodies and wings of its compatriots lay in a dusty pile. Surely it could see that they were the remnants of flies like itself; surely it could see the web through its complex multilensed eyes; some of the strands were bright gold in the sunshine. Apparently not. The dumb thing walked straight into the web, struggled pathetically to release itself as the spider emerged from the pile of fly detritus, and watched. After a minute or so of writhing about, the fly had effectively wrapped itself into a neat compact bundle ready for spider lunch. And the spider obliged, casually approaching and tapping the bundle to ensure there was no more fight left in the fly and the settling down to a long, leisurely repast.

A frisson of fear jingled down my neck and spine. Maybe there was a touch of fly in me and my spider was sitting directly across the desk. . . .

He'd dismissed the passport and was now flicking through the other papers.

"Medical—where is?"

"Ah, you speak English. I wonder, sir, if you could please tell—"

"Medical—where is?" he repeated louder.

I pointed to a neatly folded series of vaccination cards, all with U.S. medical stamps and signatures.

In the gloom of the room I could feel, rather than see, his smile. It didn't feel to be a nice smile. Far too spidery for this increasingly uncomfortable fly.

"No good."

"Why no good, sir?" I asked as gently as I could.

"No Zaire medical."

"No. These are from the United States of America." I said the words slowly and majestically, as if describing some celebratory doctorate of honor.

"No good. No Zaire medical."

Bullshit! No one had told me I had to have my up-to-date vaccination forms validated in Zaire.

"Zaire doctor. He must sign."

"I was not aware of that. Your people let me into this country. They saw these documents."

"New regulation." I could feel the spider now. Lunch was almost ready.

And Mobutu too. I suddenly noticed a dusty photograph of the president on the wall to the left of the officer, replete in his leopard-skin hat, the "Great-Warrior-Who-Conquers-Everything" staring right at me, eyes wide open and lips smiling, just a little. Under the photograph was a plaque in French: LISALA. BIRTH-PLACE OF OUR PRESIDENT.

"Do you have a doctor here? Can he sign these papers?"

"No doctor. Away."

"You have no doctor anywhere in this town?"

"No doctor."

"So—what do you want me to do?"

That smile again. And Mobutu's too. I was trapped in their little game. Somewhere nearby, maybe peeping through a keyhole with his mean little eyes, was Uriah Heep. I could sense him. And he'd be smiling that weasel smile. He'd got even with me for my brusqueness of yesterday.

"You must stay. Until doctor comes."

"Stay here. In Lisala?"

He nodded.

"When will the doctor come?"

Smug smile and elegant French shrug (outstretched hands and all).

"But I am on the boat, going to Kisangani. I have a ticket and a cabin."

He played his ace. "Also you have drawings."

"Drawings? What drawings?"

"Of ports on the river."

Now it all became hideously clear. No wonder Heep had been so happy to see my sketch pad.

"Those are drawings of the villages and the people. That's all."

"They are of ports."

"Not ports. Just the villages. And no one told me I couldn't sketch on the boat." But to be honest I had heard unpleasant travelers' tales of tourists whose cameras and film had been confiscated for photographing "forbidden subjects." But surely a few innocent sketches didn't count.

"They are for my book. A book on my travel here."

"Ah—you are writing book. On Zaire?"

"Yes. That's why I am here."

"But you come as tourist. Not journalist."

"I'm not really a journalist. I'm an author—I write travel books and I use my sketches in my books. I have one of my books back in the boat. I can show you." I was really nervous now. There wasn't much time before the boat left, and things were getting a bit too complicated.

The officer knew that too and decided to provide a succinct summary of my position.

"So." He leaned back in his creaking chair and held his hands in prayer position. "You have no medical stamps. You are journalist, not tourist, and you are drawing our ports."

This fly was well and truly webbed. The spider could feast on me at his leisure. I could sense that arguing the finer points of his accusations would only make things much worse and I'd miss the boat and be stuck in this place for God knows how long.

The solution, of course, was predetermined. I emerged from that horrible little room ten minutes later, $20 lighter (a small fortune in the Zaire black market), and carrying my medical papers on which he'd scrawled illegible signatures. As I hurried away back to the boat I'm sure I heard laughter—lots of laughter—rattling the tin roof and broken shutters of that once-regal mansion. I never saw Uriah Heep again, but his ghost followed me throughout the rest of my journey across this strange and dangerous country.

The last night on the boat, after another long chat with Paul (who praised the way I'd handled the "unpleasantness" at Lisala), I gave myself up to the romp and reggae of the barge bars, drinking far too much beer and "whiskey" and home-brewed palm wine, dancing with some pirogue fishermen who popped in for a bit of a shindig after successfully selling their thrashing river fish, dancing (but only dancing) with the whores, even dancing with myself at one point, I think, while the room roared and hands clapped and I flung my anger and frustration away in the heat and the haze and the happy-go-lucky headiness of that crazy music on that crazy boat. . . .

Part II—Kisangani to Beni—Overland Through the Pygmy Forest

At last I was in Kisangani, the first leg of the long journey over. Only I didn't want to be in Kisangani. In fact, I had no more desire for towns or sodden heat or soldiers or corrupt officials or even (strange for me) a change of diet in the town's restaurants. I wanted to be on the road, driving through the bush. I wanted to get to the Ruwenzori Mountains and feel their cool breezes and touch the ice on their summits.

I found Kisangani—the old Stanleyville—far prettier than Kinshasa but still a rather depressing place, as one might expect from the town that inspired Conrad's "Heart of Darkness" and was the home of V. S. Naipaul's sad and cruelly treated store owner in *A Bend in the River*. A battered sign by a ramshackle hotel told me I was now at the geographic heart of Africa, but even that didn't do much to cheer me up. King Leopold's headquarters had once been located here; Conrad's notorious Kurtz had his base here; the Simbas committed some of their worst atrocities here in the mid-sixties, followed by Tshombe's white mercenaries, who did equally atrocious things to the Simbas. Not a very encouraging history in this discouraging place.

I'd seen the same sights in other river towns—broad, weed-clogged avenues lined with crumbling buildings; overgrown gardens given over to grunting, rooting, bellowing, and pissing goats, pigs, chickens, and geese; African families living like outcasts among the tumbling porticoes of more of those once-pristine European mansions—the whole decrepit disassembling of an empire that meant nothing to most of Zaire's indigenous inhabitants. Nothing, that is, except forced labor, forced religion, irrelevant education, cruel punishment, and perpetual poverty.

You could sense it all here. All the horrors. That great cultural maw between the conquerors and the conquered. And you could sense Conrad's "vengeful aspect," the "implacable force brooding over an inscrutable intention." The jungle returning, absorbing the crud of dead dreams; the people attempting to re-create the old traditions of village life in the abandoned shells of aborted colonialism.

It was too much for me—the sparse, meager offerings at the outdoor market, beggars with wizened legs and arms, buildings still pockmarked by bullet holes, more slinking Uriah Heep types (no sketching or photography for me here), and the endless mud, tin, and cardboard slums surrounding a few last pockets of carefully nurtured Belgian bourgeoisdom. I had to get out. Fast.

It was surprise time again. I managed to arrange a lift with a burly Belgian truck driver. Jan spoke a French dialect I couldn't understand and only limited English, but he seemed the silent type anyway, content to play heavy metal tapes, smoke terrible cigarettes, and drink freely from his cargo of beer. His destination was the same as mine—Beni—four hundred miles or so to the east in the Ruwenzori foothills along what I'd been assured were undoubtedly the worst roads anywhere in the world. "But," an informant in Kisangani had told me, "you'll be passing through one of the most wonderful primeval forests on earth—the Ituri. No one has any idea of the things to be found in there—trees, birds, animals, insects—thousands of species never seen or recorded." This was a bonus I hadn't expected. How wonderful? I wondered. Will I be tempted to dally awhile? Will I ever reach Ruwenzori?

At first the road had a semblance of surface on it. The red mud and dust had congealed into a passable if corrugated track and we passed by areas of low scrub and tiny gardens of manioc, fruit trees, and maize. A few ambitious locals had strung up unappetizing selections of dead forest animals for sale on long strands of vines: bush rats, monkeys, hyraxes, bats, and fat porcupines, their once-upright quills now hanging down in black and gold cascades, covering their heads.

"They good meat," Jan said as we barreled along. "You want?"

Normally I might have accepted the offer, but in that early, sticky morning the invitation lacked appeal.

"No. Thanks, Jan, I'm fine for now."

He handed me the first of countless beers. "This best for breakfast!"

After a few miles we left traces of Kisangani far behind and entered the tall, dark forest. It crowded in on us at the side of the track and formed a high cathedral-like ceiling above us. Intricate weaver bird nests hung like huge suspended raindrops from the trees. Large yellow and turquoise butterflies tumbled among the wildflowers at the edge of the gloom, a few dying ignominious deaths on our windshield. I picked one off. Its wingspan was over five inches and patterned in an intricate filigree of curled black lines like a Dubuffet artwork. And the lines themselves were patterned in microscopic white dots, some of which had even tinier black centers. Why so much detail? Why such richness and complexity of design? Was it for mutual identification, or camouflage? Surely the tiny white dots—some hardly larger than a pinprick—would be indistinguishable while the butterfly was in flight. Was it merely accident—a genetic exercise in Pollock-randoming? I looked more closely. No, it couldn't be that. The dots had distinct micropatterns, a kind of evenly spaced zigzag along the black bands, which themselves were less than a sixteenth of an inch wide. And I knew that if I put this wing under a microscope I'd see even more intricately designed subpatterns and, under an electron microscope, a whole new level of aesthetic delights—all as exactingly articulated.

Was it all for the pure delight of a cosmic mind? The Creator rejoicing in the details of his own creation? "God in the details?"

I've used that Mies van der Rohe phrase so often, particularly in my one-time career as urban planner and architect-collaborator. We knew all too well what it meant in those days. We knew how the grand design of a hotel lobby or an office tower boardroom could be compromised by inappropriate door handles or even something as apparently insignificant as the precise shade and texture of the grouting on a vast tile floor.

But the phrase has developed other meanings in my travels. As I see and touch unfamiliar leaves, animals, tree barks, insects—yes, and butterflies—I am amazed not only by the rampant variations of such creations (more than twenty thousand different species of beetles, for example, on earth today!) but how each one is a complete and whole design solution in itself, right down to the juxtaposition of cells and ultimately, I suppose, molecules. Each infinitely small hair on the leg of a pepper-grain-sized flea has more construction specifications than the most sophisticated of automobile engines.

"You like them?" Jan asked as I stroked the soft-textured brilliant blue wing of the dead butterfly.

"Yes—they're beautiful. I was just thinking—"

"Too many. Make mess!" he snapped and turned on the windshield wipers to scrape off the residue of their broken bodies.

It would be too difficult to explain what I was thinking. So I drank my breakfast beer and celebrated silently, amazed once again by the incredible wholeness and wonder of each smidgen of life around us.

We passed through small ragtag roadside villages consisting mainly of mud and thatch huts. Descendants of the Bantu tribe, dressed in an odd assortment of logo T-shirts and bright kanga cloth wraps, sat in the shade of mango trees, pounding and cooking manioc, the staple diet of rural areas. They were friendly and so were we. Lots of mutual waving as we bounced by.

After about fifty miles the track began to show signs of severe wear. Sections of it had collapsed and slid off into valleys that appeared between the forest scrub. We passed occasional remnants of overturned trucks that had tumbled off the road and into the trees below.

"In rains. Very bad. Sometimes two, three weeks to Beni," Jan said, puffing on a never-ending chain of cigarettes.

"Three weeks to cover four hundred miles!"

"Sometimes never arrive!" He laughed and pointed to yet another scavenged truck in the half-light of our tunnel-like track.

"Holes in road big . . ." he tried to think of a suitable simile in English, "like elephant. Big like elephant! Truck go in. Splash. No truck. Go right under. Bye-bye."

Once again I thanked my instincts for leading me here in December, supposedly one of Zaire's dry seasons (although fierce rainstorms on the river had left me suspicious of such predictions).

"You think now is a good time for travel?"

He shrugged a big French shrug and opened another bottle of beer with his teeth.

I was getting used to French-style shrugs in Zaire. It was almost a national expression—silent but oh so full of meaning. In a country where few things work as they should, where petty anarchy seems to have replaced centralized bureaucracy, where nothing is what or where you expect it to be, a shrug is often the only answer to important questions and the only solution to most problems.

"When Belgium here, many good roads. One hundred and fifty thousand kilometers. All good." Jan imitated the sound of a racing car and waved his hand to suggest the speed and evenness of the colonial highway system. "Now—" he jumped up and down in his seat to simulate the impact of the bumps and gashes in the roads (he didn't need to. We were jumping up and down quite enough as it was. Involuntarily), "terrible!'

Another long silence, interrupted by the squeaks and bangs of the bouncing truck. I wondered how long it would be before our cargo of beer became a frothy chaos of broken bottles shooting their contents into the air like a grand fireworks extravaganza.

Jan eventually leaned over and whispered "Mobutu take all!" He'd obviously been waiting to tell me his secrets about this strange country, but why the whisper? Surely he didn't think the truck was bugged! Nothing much else works here. Bugs certainly wouldn't. But then again, almost everyone else I'd met who had something critical to say about the country or its much-feared leader tended to transform into a whispering, look-over-the-shoulder informant.

"He take everything. 1974. Belgian farms, shops, houses, cars—everything. Take and give to his family and friends. He say "This is for my people!" but people not get rich. Mobutu get rich.

Big! All copper—all diamonds. All for Mobutu. He is very powerful. He say, 'All people change names to native names. No more French or Belgian names.' He say Zairois all part of 'popular revolution movement.' 'We must all sacrifice things,' he says, and then he takes all money and builds big palaces for him—for himself! Rich friends ride around in big cars—very fat and fancy—but no roads, nowhere to go! That's Zaire—nowhere to go!"

I vaguely remembered testimony given to a congressional committee in the United States some time back in the early eighties by an exiled prime minister of Zaire. His tales of corruption made the antics of such masters of the art as Idi Amin, Noriega, and Marcos seem amateurish and unambitious by comparison. Hundreds of millions—some say as much as ten billion—of U.S. aid dollars, plus hefty slices of off-the-top loot from nationalized mining and import-export companies poured into Mobutu's secret bank accounts and made him—unofficially, of course (that is, not to be found in the Fortune list)—one of the richest men on earth, outflanked only by the Sultan of Brunei and maybe America's Sam Walton (late owner of Wal-Mart stores).

"Yes, Jan, I've heard some pretty frightening stuff about Mobutu. Sometimes it's hard to know if it's all true."

Jan laughed loudly and the truck swung alarmingly as he took both hands off the wheel and pushed the hair out of his eyes. "It's all true! I live here since thirty years. From Independence. I will tell you many things."

And he did. In his slow, hesitating English I was given a bookload of boondoggling schemes, tales of murders and political purges, tales of sexual goings-on in the Mobutu clan that even the Marquis de Sade might have found unpublishable. Worst of all were the stories of the poor Zairois themselves living in this huge, fertile, mineral-rich basin of 1.5 million square miles, who seem to have been given the mere scraps of unsatiated greed and left to glean their meager *cadeaux* gifts and pitiful incomes based on mutual bribery as best they may.

It was a long diatribe of half whispers and violent curses. Jan seemed to really care for the people of this battered, dysfunctional country. It was the "clan" members and the hangers-on of the Mobutu court and the politicians he couldn't abide.

He left his biggest broadside until last.

"And you are American?"

"No, not exactly. I'm British, but I live most of the time in America. In New York."

"Well—who is to blame?"

"I don't know, Jan."

"The Americans! The CIA! The politicians. Your President Reagan, your Bush. They meet—met—with Mobutu. Twice they met with Mobutu. In the American big house. . . ."

"The White House."

"Yes, the White House. And they did nothing. They said nothing. They gave him more money!"

I nodded. I remembered tales of Mobutu taking over two floors of the Waldorf-Astoria in Manhattan for his state visit retinue of wives, mistresses, and hangers-on. But most American voters didn't know Zaire from Zanzibar and hardly noticed the irony of all that U.S. generosity and genuflecting. One wonders if even Reagan himself was aware of the idiosyncrasies.

But I was tired of all the tirades.

"Jan, you may be right. I have met many people here in Zaire who think like you do. From what I've seen, this is a country that needs a lot of help. What do you think can be done? You've lived here a long time. What ideas do you have?"

(Please, Jan—don't say "Give it back to Belgium" or I'll start blasting at you about what Leopold and the Belgians did to this place when they had a chance to make it work.)

He shrugged and went back to puffing his cigarettes and drinking his beer. Another long silence.

"Have you seen pygmies?"

"Where. Here in Zaire?"

"Yes. We have many small people who live in this forest. You will see them. They do not have cars and refrigerators and televisions and money. They hunt animals to eat. They know how to live. Simple. Not greedy. All the others—pouf!"

Was that his solution? A back-to-basics regimen for the populace? It seemed that many Zairois were doing that anyway. Going back to the old life—the small gardens, the ancient communities of rural villages deep in the vast hinterlands of the Zaire basin. Leaving the worn-out colonial towns behind and reinventing themselves in the deep shadows of the forests and the broad grasslands. Zaire is still a work in progress, even though concepts of both "work" and "progress" seem very different here.

We drove a long way that day and on into the night over the chronically bad road. Jan seemed to have an innate knack for avoiding potholes and mud holes long before I even saw them. Finally he suggested it was time for some sleep after a casual dinner of fruit, salami, and bread we'd brought from Kisangani, and we curled up on our cab seats.

His snoring was not conducive to my rest.

The next day we hit a muddy stretch about two hundred miles into the forest. We skidded a little on a steep drop into a valley, banged over the last remnants of a rusty Belgian pontoon bridge across a ferocious earth-colored river, and set off at a rattling pace up the other side. Around a bend we came almost bumper to bumper with another truck splayed across the gooey road, effectively blocking it.

We skidded to a halt on the steep slope. Jan looked unconcerned.

"Is nothing," he said, and stepped out of the cab to greet two blacks who were sitting on the running board of their truck looking equally unconcerned. It was a long conversation and by the look of their hand gestures and belly laughs it had more to do with sexual exploits and conquests than moving a stuck truck.

I was about to join them when Jan returned to the cab.

"Is okay. We push them."

As he rolled back to line up our vehicle with theirs, two figures suddenly emerged from the deep forest at the roadside. They were tiny men, far less than five feet tall, and dressed in nothing except loincloths held by vine ropes around their waists. The deep coffee-colored skin of their arms and faces was covered in painted black markings, lines, crescents, and circles, similar in some ways to the markings I'd seen on the Choco tribespeople in Panama's Darien region. They carried three-foot-long bows and a few metal-tipped arrows stuck in their vine belts.

"Jan. Pygmies. Are those pygmies?"

"Ah." He smiled. "Efe people. The old people of Africa. Pygmies."

"Where did they come from? Is there a village around here?"

"No, no. No village. They come from forest."

I didn't have much time to stare. Jan was revving hard on the engine and pushing the rear bumper of the splayed truck. Wheels spun, globs of mud flew everywhere. The spray from the other truck's rear wheels smothered our windshield. Jan flicked the wipers on and we peered out through a miasma of smeared ocher earth.

Slowly, very slowly, the truck ahead began to move and straighten out on the track. One of the blacks standing on the running board by the open passenger door of the truck was yelling and gyrating like a cheerleader. More gratings of gears, groans from transmissions, mud flying everywhere. But we were all moving slowly uphill in a slithery zigzag pattern. The yells and cheers got louder as we finally reached a level patch, where Jan paused to make sure the truck could pull itself, and then roared past it with great blasts on his horn. I looked for the pygmies, but they'd vanished, back into the forest.

A half mile or so farther on, Jan stopped briefly to clean off the windshield; he stared down the track until the other truck finally came into view, and then roared off again.

"Great stuff, Jan! You were kind to do that."

He gave me a surprised look. "Why? It is what we do. If we do not, nobody moves. All get stuck!"

Well—okay—that's true. There's no emergency tow-truck system on this or any other rural highway in Zaire. It was obviously in everybody's interest to help everybody. The thought left a pleasant, confident feeling in my gut—we'd get through. No matter what condition the roads, we'd get through because everyone else had to get through.

"Do you know much about the pygmies, Jan?" I asked later.

"Oh—a little." He puffed happily on his cigarette for a while and then began a long, disjointed monologue about the people he called "Efe."

"In this place—in the Ituri Forest here—are old Bantu people. Different names now—BaBira, BaLese, other names. They live in villages near roads. They don't like the forest. Too dark. But they like forest meats—monkeys, porcupine, hyrax—you see them. And duikers too—they like duikers—little deer, like small dogs. Very nice. Also small buffalo—red buffalo—smaller than pygmies. Very angry. You must hunt buffalo with much caring. And pygmy elephant—people say they live in high grasses, but I have never seen. So, pygmy—BaMbuti people—like forest. They wander about...."

"They're nomadic?"

He seemed annoyed by the question.

"I don't know your word."

"Never mind."

"Okay. So pygmies wander about. Make huts like round hats with mangungu leaves and grass. Very quick. Two hours to make. And they get meat with arrows. Very good shots. And they find bee honey. Big pieces. Then they bring to BaLese villages and sell for other food—manioc, maize, other things which BaLese grow in gardens. So—everybody happy."

He paused to pry off another beer-bottle cap with his teeth.

"Many pygmies live here in Ituri—maybe twenty thousand. No one can count. They always moving. But much—most—around Mount Hoyo near Beni. Very happy people. Always singing, dancing. Lots of smoke. Lots of eat. Food. Lots of food. Big mushrooms. Sometimes kill okapi—giraffe of the forest—but him is very difficult to shoot with arrows. Has big ears and walks very quiet. And now if they shoot they have trouble with government. Special animal now, the okapi."

He paused and seemed to be listening to the engine. Then he began again, "I like pygmy people very much. Like I say before—no televisions, no big houses, no . . . ."

He was listening again and this time he looked worried. We drove in silence for a few more rutted miles. He kept changing gears and testing his acceleration until finally the engine gave a horrendous gasp, followed by a low whine and then a gurgle. And stopped.

Now, breakdowns are different from stuck-in-the-mud antics. Breakdowns mean nuts and bolts and grease and wrenches and pinched fingers and long hours of cursing and not much in the way of extraneous activity. Except constant beer swilling and cigarette smoking. And a breakdown is what we had, along a particularly dark stretch of forest, miles from anywhere, according to my map.

Jan didn't have a spare whatever it was he needed and apparently neither did the only other truck that passed us in our two-hour wait at the side of the track.

"Shall I walk to the next village and see if I can find what you need?'

"No. Mambasa is only place," he said, followed by a long string of invectives, only a few of which I recognized as Anglo-Saxon.

"But Mambasa's a long way east from here."

He finally gave up cursing and shrugged.

"Okay. Listen, please. You stay. I go to the next village and send man to stay with truck—and the beer. After he come, you get ride with someone and I see you in Beni. Okay? If no ride come, you wait too."

Seemed to make sense—so with another shrug and a wave he set off down the track, turning once.

"Beer in back. Enjoy!" he shouted, then laughed and vanished around a bend almost as quickly as the pygmies.

It was suddenly very quiet. The first time in two days I'd been aware of silence. Even as we'd slept in the cab the previous night the air had been filled with screeches, clicks, rasps, and crackles (and Jan's snoring). A mosquito coil had kept out the biters, but the noises were so intense and so close that I hadn't enjoyed much in the way of rest.

But now it was all silence. Unnerving at first, then strangely calming. Everything felt to be at peace in the heat of the day. I opened another beer and sat in the shade, thinking about nothing in particular.

I must have dozed off. When I opened my eyes three little men were sitting beside me. They were all coffee-skinned and thin-boned with wide noses, big eyes, bulging cheekbones, and broad smiles. They were smoking strange cigarettes wrapped in what looked like very old yellow parchment. More pygmies. Where the hell do they come from?

I smiled and offered them each a beer. They accepted and drank daintily from their bottles, giggling softly.

One of the men passed me his cigarette. It seemed impolite to refuse it, so I took it and pretended to puff on it. They all giggled again and the man indicated that I should inhale the tobacco or whatever it was. I examined the cigarette more carefully. The paper was actually a leaf—a very thin and delicate leaf, not unlike paper. I took a longer drag, carefully. Untreated tobacco can be strong stuff. This wasn't. Not at all. It went down smoothly—no burning, no irritation, no gagging.

"Very nice," I said, and handed it back. But he wouldn't accept it. In fact, he'd already lit another using some smoldering ashes wrapped tightly in a wad of green leaves. A unique form of portable lighter. He indicated that I should continue smoking. So I did and we sat in silence for a while watching butterflies in the light shafts.

It really was a very pleasant tobacco, earthily aromatic with a rich blue smoke that wafted up into the trees in lovely curlicues, changing into golden patterns when it passed through patches of sunlight. Like coiling serpents. The curves began to fascinate me. Some were pure rococo—rich, fat, and pompous. Shapes full of the sureness and certainty of themselves. Others became longer and more tenuous with a finely tensed art nouveau line. Almost erotic. As they slowly broke apart they resembled Klee patterns of happy bouncing curves and circles, and then eventually hung suspended in the soft light, a series of perfectly balanced Miró mobiles.

After what must have been quite a long period of watching the cigarette smoke patterns, I decided to stand up and stroll around. Then I sat down again. Quickly. Well, actually I sort of slithered back down. My legs didn't seem to want to stand at all. Nothing of me felt like moving. My head was dizzy in a rather peculiar way. It wasn't nausea or anything. It was just that my body seemed to be sinking gently into the ground while my head was off by itself, floating, spiraling upward, watching butterflies, watching the smoke again, enjoying the edges of the dark leaves gilded in golden sunlight, tracing the snakelike outlines of vines and strangler figs as they coiled up the trunks of trees high above before disappearing into the cathedral-roofed canopy over the track.

A head trip!

I heard the words aloud in my brain—"Your head's taking a head trip and leaving your body behind"—and burst out laughing. More like giggles—childish giggles. The three pygmies were giggling too and puffing away on their cigarettes.

I couldn't stop the giggles. My whole body was tickled by them—my feet, my hands, even my stomach—all tickling with these ridiculous giggles. . . . Time rolled on and the giggles still kept coming. My world was a harmonic whole of laughter and smoke curlicues. . . ."

"Bangi!"

Someone was speaking. A long way away. I looked up and there was a face. A tall man with Rastalike hair standing over me holding something at his side. A strange metal thing with shiny horns sticking out the front. A bicycle! Of course. Well here's a happy how d'you do—a stranger with a bicycle who keeps saying things at me in a loud voice.

"You smoke bangi!"

There were more giggles at the side of me. I turned and my three pygmies were still sitting contentedly by the track, sipping their beers and nodding—"Bangi—*oui*—bangi." What the hell is bangi? I thought. I must have actually said it too because the tall man with the bicycle started up again.

"Bangi is Zaire marijuana. They give you marijuana. You gone!"

Really? But I'd only taken a few casual puffs of their cigarette, spurred by politeness rather than intent. It must have been a powerful concoction indeed. One I could do without in the future.

"I make coffee. You be better."

The man was being very considerate. Who was he?

"Where Jan put coffee?"

Oh, Jan's friend. That's right. The man from the village coming to look after the truck.

My head had rejoined my body and my mind seemed to be focusing better on the situation at hand.

"Behind his seat. In the canvas bag. I think."

Soon I smelled the coffee bubbling in a battered pan on Jan's tiny kerosene stove.

The man's name was Amit or something that sounded like Amit. He brought my coffee in a chipped enamel mug. It was black, thick, and very strong.

"So—you like Zaire bangi?"

"Er—no, not exactly. I thought it was some kind of jungle cigarette."

He laughed, exposing a huge mouth of bright white teeth. "Well—you right. Bangi is Efe tobacco. They smoke all the time. They say it makes them good hunters—I think it just makes them happy. All the time."

"Well, they certainly seem happy."

I turned and smiled at my three conspirator-companions. They smiled, giggled, and nodded. Then one of them spoke to Amit. Amit listened and translated.

"They would like to take you to their houses. In the forest. Would you like to go? Do you feel okay?"

"Another cup of this coffee and I could walk to Beni."

He poured another cup out of the battered pan.

"So—would you like to go with them?"

"How will I get back to the road?"

"They will bring you back."

"Where?"

"Here."

"Right here?"

"Yes."

"Is it a long journey?"

"Not so far. Maybe a few kilometers. Not far."

"It'll be dark in a few hours."

"So—you can stay with them tonight. Come back in morning."

"You'll be here?"

"Of course. Jan has go to Mambasa and then come all way back. He will be long time. I will be here all night."

"Are these good men? I don't want any more of their bangi."

"They good men. They are Efe. Efe are good people. They are forest people."

I couldn't think of any more questions to ask. I stood up, this

PYGMIES
in the Ituri Forest — Zaire

time without falling down. The coffee had given me new energy—
and sanity. I groped in my backpack for some chocolate I'd bought
in Kisangani, offered it around, and gobbled the remnants myself.

"Okay, Amit. I'll go."

The pygmies seemed delighted and did a little bouncy jig by
the side of the track, stirring up the red dust.

"Ah," said Amit, "if you can see them when they dance . . ."

"Yes, Jan told me they love dancing."

"It very big thing for them. Very important. Most Zaire people, we have forgotten the dances. But Efe live in deep places.
They remember."

I said good-bye to Amit and promised to be back early in the
morning. I had no idea where I was, where I was going, or what
would happen, but somehow I trusted the three little men who
hopped around me and then led me off through the high grass
and stands of whispering bamboo at the roadside and into the
forest. Their forest.

It is difficult to explain what happened during the next few hours.
Maybe it was the aftereffects of the bangi, maybe I was confused
by the zip-zap sequencing of events, or maybe there's real magic
in the forest that doesn't take kindly to crude revelations in written
words.

There are stories that metaphorize the Ituri Forest as Eden,
the first paradise on earth. Of course every nationality values,
even reveres, its own country. The Balinese, the Nepalese, the
Mongols, the Navajo, the Tuaregs of the Sahara, the Sri Lankans—
each believe their land to be the most beautiful of places, the place
where the earth, as we know it, began. And—being of a flexible
and a generous nature—I usually agree with all of them. Beauty
understood through the eyes of its beholder, and shared with that
beholder, is beauty indeed. I have seen many places where the
earth began and fell in love with each one of them.

But the Ituri Forest was something I'd never experienced
before. There was something utterly overwhelming about its silence, its space, and its majesty. Enormous trees, with roots that
eased out of the earth like the smooth backs of dolphins, rose
scores of branchless feet into twilit canopies, where they exploded

in soft profusions of sun-dappled leaves and vine flowers of purple, yellow, and scarlet. Hundreds of air plants (epiphytes) drooped over the topmost branches like shaggy-haired kittens. Vines hung down like hairy ropes, inviting me to climb into the uppermost reaches and explore the busy territories of the white-nose and blue monkeys, the hornbills, and dozens of other species who rarely if ever visit the open forest floor.

I hadn't expected such openness. In other rain forests I'd explored, particularly in South America, the layering of the plant species was far more intense and frenzied. Here I walked through the equivalent of an English beech forest, bouncing on the moist, mulchy earth, admiring its rich range of bronzes, ochers, and golds. There was no need for panga knives to cut through the brush. There was hardly any brush. No stinging plants, no vicious thorns, no sticky fly-catchers, no razor-edged leaves. Only a few smaller trees and occasional flurries of fat-leaved bushes, but mostly space and cool air that seemed to fill my body with sweetness and wonderful calming silences in the green half-light.

How different this was from the tangle of Panama's Darien jungle and the impenetrable tumult of Tasmania's rain forests. I walked as if floating—effortlessly, easily through the quietude—following my three guides, who strolled barefoot across the soft surface, barely making a sound.

Two lines from Baudelaire that Paul had shown me on the boat seemed to capture both the magic and the mystery of the forest:

Nature is a temple in which living columns sometimes emit
    confused words.
Man approaches it through a forest of symbols which
    observe him with familiar glances.

(I particularly like the "familiar glances." Sometimes I sense that.)

It was evening when we arrived in a slight hollow on the forest floor. The cicadas were off again, making their ritual, ear-scratching racket. Fires were burning in the soft half-light and I could see five domed huts in an arc around a larger fire. Shadows flickered across the hollow and on the bushes and tree trunks. Figures moved about—children, young girls with faces painted in red and black lines, and older women, all naked except for loincloths made from a thin bark.

My three companions were greeted with broad smiles and laughter. Some of the women began singing quiet simple songs, more like mantras, as they pounded manioc with heavy wooden pestles.

We all sat down by the large fire and a boy, thin and coyly shy, carried a three-foot-long tube of bamboo and placed it in the hands of one of the men. It was a communal pipe with a small bowl already filled with compressed bangi leaves. The man reached out to the fire, scooped up a few glowing embers, placed them on top of the bangi, and inhaled deeply. Blue smoke rose again in those now-familiar curlicues. I decided not to stare at the ever-changing shapes in fear of starting up the whole hallucinatory process again. And, as politely as I could, I declined to participate as the pipe was passed around the circle. I needed no stimulants that night. It was enough just to be here, deep in the forest with its night cries and curious sighing sounds. (Breezes in the canopy? Or the soft breathing of the forest gods that the pygmies revered and their Bantu cousins feared?) I was happy to listen to the sleepy chirps and coos of invisible flycatchers, warblers, sunbirds, and pigeons high in the canopy; I was content just to be here with these friendly people, the last authentic hunter-gatherers on earth, who seemed to accept me so openly, without undue curiosity or the banter of bad-English questions that had bombarded me elsewhere in Zaire.

Other men joined us by the big fire. The women, still humming softly, sat with their pots by the fires preparing food or weaving intricate nets of liana rope, which, I learned later, the pygmies used for hunting duikers and other species of miniature antelope.

The pipe was refilled and continued its way, mouth to mouth, around the main fire. One of the men began a low, guttural chant, his chest reverberating like a taught drumskin. Others joined in, imitating the sounds of forest birds. They swayed together to the slow rhythm in a haze of bangi smoke.

Someone—another young boy—began a delicate dance in the flickering shadows beyond the fire, stirring up little clouds of dust. He seemed to be playing two roles, first as a hunter in the forest, carefully stalking on tiptoe; then he became the prey, possibly a small antelope, low to the ground, moving, then pausing, sniffing the air, then moving on again. The men turned to watch, emitting the long sad cries of an antelope. The boy hesitated, depicting the confusion of the animal. The cries continued. The boy imitated the long, leaping run of the antelope, darting in and out of the shadows. The men began to clap quietly—the antelope became more alarmed, leaping harder and faster, whirling through the dust clouds. The clapping increased—the antelope ran—the clapping got louder—the boy suddenly did a somersault and thrashed his legs and arms about, depicting the animal's entanglement presumably in one of the hunting nets the women were weaving by the huts. The men suddenly leapt up from the fire, surrounded the boy captured in the imaginary net, and began a rapid circular dance around his writhing form. Six, seven, eight times they danced around him, clapping and laughing. Then they stopped as suddenly as they'd begun. One man knelt down and with an imaginary panga knife slit the throat of the boy-antelope. The boy gave a rather too realistic shudder and lay still among the settling dust.

There was a brief silence followed by soft laughter from the women and wild leaps from the men. The boy rose up, smiled, and vanished into the shadows. The men continued their leaping and laughing and then, one by one, returned to sit by the fire and resume their bangi smoking.

The whole event lasted only a few minutes. It had been so impromptu, so casually introduced and ended, that for a while I wondered if I'd imagined it all, swept away again in a hallucinatory haze from all that bangi smoke. But then the boy joined us by the fire and the men slapped his back and thighs, congratulating him on a fine performance. A small intense ritual deep in the forest, not for me, but for themselves. A reaffirmation of their own lives and their links with the life of the forest itself. A part of their daily rhythm, as natural as sleeping or eating.

And eating is what we did next. The women carried chunks of hot meat and wild yams from their cooking pots on large green leaves and handed each of us a hefty portion. I suddenly realized how hungry I was. I hadn't eaten anything except half a bar of melted chocolate since my breakfast of coffee and cheese with Jan.

The meat was delicious—sweet, tender, and full of juice. The men seemed to be speaking the lingala language, of which I understood almost nothing. But they knew I was curious about the animal origins of our dinner and pointed, with gales of laughter, to the boy, the dancer, who was eating with us. I understood and laughed with them. I was eating antelope or duiker, the creature imitated in the boy's dance. I praised the meal so profusely that the women brought me two more enormous helpings and stood grinning behind the men, watching me eat every mouthful, washed down with a communal bowl of what I think was home-brewed palm wine. It was a sweet, seemingly innocuous concoction, but after four long gulps I felt wonderfully light-headed and sleepy.

Maybe I even dozed off. Perhaps I was more tired than I realized. Later on I was vaguely aware of hands lifting me and helping me across the clearing toward one of the huts. I think I tried to protest. I felt like staying where I was, lying under the high canopy of dark forest trees, but a hut seemed to have been requisitioned for my use and the last I remember was slipping down onto hard-packed earth and fading off into sleep with the soft cooing of voices all around me. . . .

Dawn sounds and smells awoke me. The screech of Columbus monkeys, birds declaring territorial boundaries in the treetops, the aroma of rekindled fires, the hum of women's voices, the click and patter of falling leaves and pods from the buo trees. I peeped out of my small domed hut through which light trickled in thin shafts between the dried leaves of the thatch. On the fringe of the clearing I saw profusions of flowers—tiny pink blossoms like impatiens, gloriosa lilies, streams of mauve hibiscus blossoms, and what looked like a substantial patch of six-foot-high marijuana plants.

Two little girls saw my bearded white face emerge and ran away screaming in a combination of terror and delight.

One of my friends of yesterday came over and smilingly indicated that it was time to return through the forest to the truck.

I nodded and smiled back. How could I explain that I really didn't want to leave? That I'd like to stay a few more days and see more of the dancing and learn more about their lives, their hunting, their customs. But I knew that it wouldn't be fair to Jan. Even though he was a self-contained man and used to long periods alone on the road, we had established an amicable bond and I knew that if I didn't return he'd more than likely come looking for me.

So—I had to leave. But not before I'd been invited to share a bounteous pygmy breakfast of honeycomb chunks dripping with sweet nectar gathered the previous day from a nearby bee colony. The sugar surged through me like a drug, filling me with energy and eradicating all the sloth and weariness of last night.

I thanked the women for their kindnesses, the young man for his dance, and the children for their morning smiles. Then I was off again with my three friends, back through the green-blue light of the cool forest, back to the road, back to my Beni-bound schedule.

Although I could discern no actual trail through the forest, we arrived a couple of hours later at exactly the same spot where I'd been introduced to bangi the day before. There was the truck and there was Jan finishing off the repairs.

He greeted me as if nothing peculiar had happened. As if my stroll into the hidden forest world of the Ituri pygmies was the most obvious way for me to spend my time while he was gone.

I found a few gifts in my backpack for my friends—a metal comb, a pack of cigars, and a Swiss army–style knife. They offered me a wad of bangi wrapped in green leaves. Jan nodded that I should accept, so I did and later, much to his delight, gave it to him. We said brief farewells. I turned to see if I could find some more chocolate for them, but they vanished. Zap. They were gone. I peered into the dark forest and listened for the sound of departing feet. Nothing. They disappeared as quickly and quietly as they had come.

Much as I loved the forest and its deep silences, I was ready for open spaces again. And colder air; how I longed to breathe long,

61

heady lungfuls of cold air. It seemed weeks since I had actually enjoyed the pleasures and the brain-calming effect of long inhalations and exhalations. On the river particularly, the air had often seemed old, used, stagnant. The slight breezes of morning and evening were always so short-lived. In the torpid heat of the day and night I always seemed to be out of breath. The air had felt far too thick to reach deep into the tissues of my lungs and tickle my capillaries. My brain had felt oxygen-starved and sluggish. My body had felt sluggish and old.

But we were definitely climbing now and the road was better. Still terrible, of course—cracked, potholed, and corrugated, but free of those huge mud holes which, in the rainy season, can hold up convoys of trucks for weeks and even, as Jan had told me, swallow up smaller vehicles into their pernicious bogs.

The forest thinned out. The carefully layered profiles of vegetation became more anarchic—a rampant battle for air and light. The ordered hierarchy of plants and trees I had seen in the Ituri now became ragtag tangles of greenery, broken by small BaLese tribal farms and cleared sections and sinewy swaths of savanna. The air was cooling too as we climbed laboriously toward a high plateau.

Suddenly, after negotiating a steep incline up through the last fringes of forest, we emerged on a broad grassy plain, and there they were! The magnificent Ruwenzoris—looking so close and so tactile I felt I could almost leap out of the truck, bound across the bouncy grass, and start my ascent immediately. Knifing through their almost perpetual cloud cover, a series of purpled peaks patterned with flashing snowfields and glaciers rose up into a perfect blue sky.

I'd been waiting for this moment for so long. Even Jan, who'd seen these same vistas many times before on his interminable drives along this hell highway, stopped his incessant cigarette puffing, rolled his truck to a standstill, and sat staring at them, smiling. We climbed out of the cab and strolled a short distance up the track. After the incessant growl and churn of the diesel engine and the endless racket of his heavy-metal tapes, there was nothing now but silence. A pure silvered silence and cool winey air, which I sucked down in great breaths. A few scarlet-winged butterflies fluttered and flashed over the dusty scrub at the roadside. Other than that there were no movements, no sounds any-where. The plain rose slowly ahead of us to a jumble of grassy and forest-free foothills, and then came enormous surges of gray-blue granite cliffs, arêtes, and ridges rising through clouds to those sharp sparkling peaks.

It had been worth all the agonies and angst of the journey so far just to see this.

But I knew there was to be more—much more. The adventure had hardly begun. In the shadowy clefts and high valleys of those mountains were some of the strangest places on our planet. Life-forms and gigantic hybrid plants to be found nowhere else on earth. One of our most mysterious lost worlds. A place I had waited twenty years to explore and touch. A place that was show-ing itself to me in a splendor I had hoped for but never expected. I was high and happy. I grasped Jan's hand and shook it. He laughed and slapped my shoulder.

"So—you like?" he shouted.

"Absolutely bloody marvelous!" I replied, and we broke out more beer to celebrate the occasion and toast those oh-so-splendid mountains.

While Beni was yet one more faded, jaded Zairois town, at least it had a transitory cosmopolitan air due to the large numbers of truckers and merchants from Uganda, Kenya, and Rwanda who used this place as a transit and trading center. The large market plaza was a redolent hum of smells, noise, and activity, but it was too hot to dally there.

Jan decided to make his delivery and head back to Kisangani the same day, not even pausing to enjoy a night on the town among the ramshackle beer joints and the painted ladies. I thanked him with a few gifts from my backpack and went off for a night of luxury at a hotel with running (cold) water and a res-taurant of sorts. An air-conditioner stuck in the cracked window of my room overlooking the main street looked as if it had never cooled anything in years. I banged it, kicked it, and finally took the cover off to find it had no working parts inside. Just a rusty metal box. A symbolic relic of fine ambition leached of life—not unlike Zaire itself. It was hot, so I showered again and let the water evaporate by itself with the window open until the flies and noise and smell of roaring trucks on the streets set my teeth on edge. With the windows closed and the remnant of a torn curtain pulled across, I finally faded into sleep, bathed in sweat.

I'd planned on spending a couple of days resting up for the trek into the mountains, but after that one night in Beni I realized I'd probably regenerate my energy far better in the mountains away from this nonentity of a town.

Part III—Into The Mountains of the Moon

Early in the morning, after a hasty breakfast of eggs and stale bread, I bought some provisions for the hike ahead and walked to the truck terminal to find a lift to the starting point of the Ruwenzori trail. The clouds were much lower than yesterday and the mountains were hidden. Fickle creatures, I thought, although I'd been warned that for more than three hundred days a year they were cloud-covered, rain-lashed and snowbound, and even though I'd chosen the time of my arrival here carefully to coincide with the "dry season," there were no guarantees of basking in the kind of vistas I'd enjoyed with Jan the day before.

"Don't weaken," I told myself as the fifth effort to cadge a lift failed. "You've made it this far. You can only keep going."

Finally I paid a small fee in U.S. dollars to the driver of a small van ("Dis tin' you askin' is not law. Much trouble with police. Give me *cadeau*—gift—five dollars. American." We settled on three.) And off we bounced, leaving Beni behind in a trail of pink dust.

We climbed steadily toward a rock-strewn pass and one of those African vistas that makes your mind go all gooey and your heart skip an alarming number of beats. This continent always amazes me by its size, just as it has amazed every other explorer and writer. You can never really grasp its scale. The view before me was of sinewy rivers, shards of hazy forest, lakes, small farms and villages, great slashes of red earth looking like fresh tiger scratches on exposed flesh, and roll after roll of Ireland-green foothills brightened by recent rains and soft valleys, some resembling the dales of Yorkshire (without the drystone walls), others more reminiscent of Appalachian "hollers." The scene seemed vast, endless. Yet as I defined its dimensions on my now-tattered map I saw it was a mere pinhead of printed paper against the enormity of the African landmass. An insignificant, irrelevant semi-quaver of space lost in the grand symphony of mountains, deserts, forests, swamps, airy plateaus, river basins, and more than sixteen thousand miles of coastline from the "Skeleton Coast" of Namibia to the bleached beaches of Morocco and Tunisia, to the empty desolation of Somalia's Benadir and the rugged mountain-bound bays of South Africa.

That's another reason why the Ruwenzori had drawn me for so long. It was the wonder expressed in the writings of early explorers that made me think of this region as the epitome of all things African—huge, inaccessible, and full of secrets. You can sense this spirit in Henry Stanley's words when, at his camp at Lake Albert in Uganda in 1888, the clouds pulled back for a brief period and revealed a vision never before recorded by a white man:

> A peculiarly-shaped cloud of a most beautiful silver color, which assumed the proportions and appearance of a vast mountain covered with snow, drew all eyes and every face seemed awed . . . for the first time I was conscious that what I gazed upon was not the image or semblance of a mountain but the solid substance of a real one.

He had found Ptolemy's "Mountains of the Moon," and although he never climbed them (Lougi Amadeo di Savoia, Duke of Abruzzi, was the first white to ascend and map the Ruwenzori in 1906), Stanley carried that magnificent vision with him to his death in 1904. "It was perhaps the most wondrous moment in all of my African journeys," he wrote to a close friend.

I expected nothing less for myself.

But this time the clouds failed to lift as they had done the previous day. As I unloaded my backpack at a small straggle of huts by the roadside and set off along the narrow trail to base camp in the foothills, I prayed that the weather would improve and that I'd be given that chance I'd waited for so long, to touch the summit of Mount Margherita (the 16,763-foot peak on Mount Stanley), the third highest peak in Africa—and by far the most

65

splendidly profiled. There are eight separate peaks here altogether in an area of seventy by thirty miles, including Mount Speke and Mount Baker, all around 16,000 feet, but Margherita was the one I wanted to conquer.

Unlike the volcanic cones of Mount Kilimanjaro and Mount Kenya, the Ruwenzori are relatively recent granite peaks thrown high above the African plains by tectonic plate movements less than two million years ago along the vast Great Rift Valley to the east, which stretches four thousand miles from the Jordan Valley deep into Zimbabwe. The intrusion of these enormous upended Archean massifs into the atmosphere creates a sudden updraft of western air flows laden with moisture from the soggy Congo basin, resulting in an annual precipitation on their slopes of almost seven feet, much in the form of blizzards and ice storms across the summits. Swamps and bogs on the lower slopes, glaciers and icefields higher up (striated with crevasses), and treacherous walking and climbing conditions are characteristics of this region. I had pitons for my boots and some warm clothing, but this was another of my solo ventures and I was not equipped for long grapplings with a bare and frozen mountain.

I stayed that first night in a pleasant little guest house surrounded by scrub jungle and was told by the elderly black man who brought my dinner of manioc and pork that a party of four Germans had passed through earlier in the day and would be well on their way to the second camp at Kalongi hut.

That's okay, I thought, I prefer to have the mountain to myself. But then the next morning the interminable Zairois tangle began. A young man in a shabby uniform approached and announced that a string of "new regulations" had just been decreed by the government. I'd had my fill of "new regulations" back at Lisala and this time I was ready.

"You must take guide and porter," he said, staring at me with that mix of Zaire humor and anger which only made him look confused.

"I don't want a guide or a porter."

"To Mount Stanley, very difficult. Five, six days up-down. You must have."

Then he told me the going rates. I could have hired ten Nepalese porters for the price and was loath to part with more

U.S. dollars for *cadeaux*—gifts. Especially for something I didn't need. So I lied.

"I'm with the German party—the four Germans, y'know, who left yesterday. I have to walk quickly to reach them."

He looked even more confused.

"Also I am a writer." I showed him a rather ragged copy of one of my earlier books and pointed to my photograph on the dust jacket. He studied it carefully. Then I played the final card. "Look, I must hurry. I need good photographs. This is for very important American magazine."

He was totally perplexed.

Time to go. I heaved on my backpack and walked away as quickly as I could, squelching and splashing through the muddy earth, soaked by early morning drizzle.

He called out, but I could tell his heart wasn't really in it. I'd got what I wanted. I was off—alone—into these mysterious mountains.

A couple of hours later I was less certain of my decision. The terrain was difficult now; the neat little patchwork fields of manioc, bananas, and maize were far behind and I climbed upward through eight-foot-high *pennisetum* "elephant" grass and spray-topped papyrus. Then the forest closed in, leaving me a narrow muddy trail and a tunnel through the tangle of lianas, aerial roots, strangled vines, and groping branches. Familiar-looking ferns reached eight feet into the thick humid gloom, and beard moss, similar to the Spanish moss found on the swamp cedars and live oaks of Deep South United States, hung over the trail in long tentacled strands. I felt as if I were a child in a *Honey, I Shrunk the Kids* kind of world. A world of recognizable plants that had suddenly become giant-sized. Familiar, yet threatening.

And then came the great tree ferns. I was suddenly back in a picture-book scenario of precoal-age earth when dinosaurs roamed and pterodactyls flew and these enormous thirty-foot-high specimens with dark trunks and winglike leaves filled the wet forests and swamps. I welcomed the hummingbirds and the gold and amber butterflies that bounced through the rare shafts of sun—at least they were of recognizable size. Even the occasional tiny lizards and little mold-green snakes that crossed my trail were reassuring signs that some things were still as they should be in this peculiar place. I looked for the Ruwenzori's unique three-horned chameleon and those yard-long earthworms but saw nothing except vast armies of soldier ants on the move through the half-light. I wondered if I might come across one of Zaire's famous gorilla families, but I knew their Djomba sanctuary was way to the south. Two large white and black monkeys gave a fine display of very ungorilla acrobatics and then vanished screaming into the forest.

I was in a region of deep gorges and gullies. Occasionally views would open up between the hagenias, giant orchids, and gloriosa lilies which sinewed themselves around the ferns, and I'd peer out across mist-shrouded clefts hundreds of feet deep. The higher parts of the mountains were, as I'd expected, lost in the clouds. In fact, I hadn't seen anything of Mount Stanley since that sudden revelation before Beni. My role was just to keep walking and climbing and trust to luck that I'd finally reach a cloud-free summit.

When I arrived at Kalongi base hut I was around seven thousand feet up on the slopes and the air was cool and refreshing. In spite of the mud and the tangle of the forest, I felt far less exhausted than I'd expected. Time to celebrate, I thought, but the hut itself was hardly appropriate for a hedonistic interlude. One broken bed, not a single window intact, missing floorboards, cobwebs of Ruwenzori scale, and abundant evidence of animal rather than human occupation. But there was a black sooted-encrusted stove which I crammed with scraps of branches and twigs and in five minutes had a blazing fire, hot enough to warm me and heat water for a dehydrated food supper. Hardly gourmet fare, but, as I hadn't had a really decent meal in more than two weeks, my palate and stomach gleefully accepted curried shrimp and long-grain saffron rice despite its cardboard-and-paste taste.

Night came quickly. I rolled out my foam rubber mat and waterproof sleeping bag, took a couple of swigs from my flask of whiskey-Zairois, and fell into a seamless sleep.

It had obviously rained heavily during the early hours. I lay next to a pool of water at dawn and wondered why, if someone had gone to the trouble of constructing this hut, someone else couldn't come along occasionally and patch up the roof and floorboards and windows. But then I remembered: This is Zaire and one learns not to expect Swiss Alps efficiency in these wild climes. At least I was dry. My faithful waterproof sleeping bag had resisted all onslaughts except a small reconnaissance team of ants that, sometime deep in the night, had bivouacked and feasted on my arms.

Breakfast consisted of my always-effective Kendal Mint Cake and lukewarm tea loaded with sugar. Lots of energy stimulants but not really an ideal repast for what was to come on that second day of the climb.

It began innocently enough. More of the same branch- and root-tangled forest—no, let me say it—jungle. Jungle seems to be a nonword in today's environmentally correct dialogue, but *forest* is far too euphemistic here. This place was a ragged riot of vegetation, little resembling the finely tiered layers of a true rain forest. A free-for-all razzmatazz of trees, vines, creepers, ferns, roots, and flowering bushes. And a new addition. Heather trees. A species I'd only seen once before in the wild and cloud-bathed heights of Gomera, one of the least known of the Canary islands.

Back home in Yorkshire, England, I was used to the benign, ankle-high surges of heather filling the moors of Brontë country and blossoming into a fall haze of tiny lavender flowers. But here in the Ruwenzori, everything was written large and heather grew into twenty-foot-high trees with distorted, writhing limbs, foot-snagging roots, and dense leaf canopies that turned day into dusk. Exciting, enticing, a fantasy of entrancing forms—but lousy hiking territory.

I prayed I wouldn't snap a leg. The idea of being helpless in this unearthly place set up a jangle in my head. How would I get down? Who—if anyone—would find me before the soldier ants had their way with me and left a pile of moldy bones and a backpack full of aluminum-packed dehydrated curiosities to be mulled over by morose Zairois officials?

My mind was playing its tricks again. C'mon, I told myself. The brain saps energy quicker than anything. Seal it off. Compose a letter to Anne. Write a poem. Anything to suppress the silly yammer. . . . Invent a song and keep singing it! So I did (to a robust marching tune):

(Chorus)   Well—here I am
                just a lonely man
                lugging my way through the trees.
                Now I know I am
                just a happy man
                Singing this song to the breeze. . . .

(Verse)   Oh—it's a new day again
                and I'm squelching through the rain
                ignoring the pain
                becoming insane
                whistling like a train
                feeling kinda' vain
                'cause I've nothing to gain
                from weepin' like a drain
                or acting like a zane-y
                crazy man. . . .

(Chorus)   So here I am. . . .

And it worked! God love us, it worked. I was fresh and frisky again as I fought with roots and branches, conquering the ridges and the mud holes and catching glimpses of mist-wisped canyons through infrequent gaps in the fervent foliage.

Sometime around midafternoon I emerged from the forest onto a barren plateau of broken rock to find the sun shining spasmodically through gashes in the high cloud cover. I needed a break and sat down abruptly on a boulder to feast on more energy-giving mint cake.

All was silence. The mists eased by in tattered strands, catching briefly in the tops of the trees. There were no sounds at all— no birds, no monkeys, no perpetual squelch of mud-caked boots, not even the sound of my own pumping heart and panting lungs. And once again came the mood that makes this kind of exploration so rewarding—the sense that I had the whole place all to myself and everything was just fine, in spite of my momentary weariness.

The silence, alas, did not endure for long. In the middle of my mellowness came one of the most terrifying screams I have ever heard—a gut-wrenching cacophony of agony, fear, and anger all rolled into one violent pitch. It was both human and animal and echoed down the rocky clefts and up the fogbound granite cliffs of the mountains.

"What the hell. . . ."

I waited for a second scream. My mind whirled with possibilities, from the more modest—a frightened hiker behind me, challenged by a snake—to the plain outlandish—the return of Zaire's notorious Simba terrorists, whose habit it had been to emit shrill shrieks before committing violent murders—or even the sound of one of their victims, horribly mutilated and dismembered before death!

There was no second scream. And then I remembered that the tree hyrax, the tiny member of the elephant family with hooves for feet, was said to emit a pretty intense signature call when disturbed or alarmed.

Was that what it was—that odd little anomaly of the animal kingdom? Or had it been human, as I'd first thought?

Should I go back into the forest to find out, or . . . I chose the "or" alternative, grabbed my backpack, and set off up the trail at a pace that made me realize my weariness was a sham and I had amazing reserves of energy previously untapped.

Fear does that.

After twenty minutes of half running, half scrambling up slippery mud slopes I began to wonder if I'd made a serious mistake by not bringing a guide-porter with me. I'd still seen no sign of the German hikers far ahead of me and my backpack seemed much heavier at the height of nine thousand feet than it had at the starting point, around four thousand feet.

To add insult to indecision, I had now left the forest behind and was entering a strange world of high bamboo groves, neck-tall nettles (a far more vicious sting than the relatively benign species back home), and vast open heaths of thick spongy moss bog. If I kept to the narrow trail I was safe, but the moss lured me with false paths ending abruptly in lichen-surfaced bogs that look firm-surfaced until I trod on them and watched them collapse like lumpy porridge. At one juncture I'd taken the wrong route and ended up thigh deep in a rotting morass of this peaty mud and dead vegetation. To make matters worse, the mists were becoming thicker, approaching pea-soup intensity in places.

I was not a happy hiker. I tried a few bars of my marching song, but my heart wasn't in it. I was mud-caked, cold, and a little frightened. This leg of my long journey to the Ruwenzori was not quite what I'd expected. In fact the whole thing was rapidly becoming a right royal screwup.

Now I knew I should have hired a guide.

Things went from bad to terrible. More dark, dank swaths of heather forest with snagging roots and eerie tentacles of beard moss dangling from the branches and brushing my face (memories of the old "Ghost Train" horrors of seaside fairs back home when invisible spider-webby threads would envelop my head in the blackness). There were infrequent delights too in the form of beautiful forest orchids and scarlet fuchsias hanging from the trees like fat bunches of grapes—but such sights seemed only to intensify the malevolent evil and danger of the place.

One particularly nasty tangle of moss-shrouded roots grabbed my ankles and sent me sprawling into the slime of the trail. At first everything seemed fine: My backpack straps had held and nothing in my body seemed broken. But as I stood, a sear of pain shot up my right leg and my ankle felt to be on fire. Oh, boy—not that! Not a broken, or even a twisted ankle. Not in this place.

I knew that if any damage was done, sitting down to rest would only increase the swelling. So I moved on slowly, hobbling, as the ankle throbbed and gave me fiery branding-iron shocks if I put too much pressure on it.

I was exhausted and close to tears. I knew that even at the next base hut, Mahangu, I'd only be around eleven thousand feet—still six thousand feet below the peak of Mount Margherita. What to do? The ankle was obviously not broken, but I'd messed it up badly in the fall. If I turned back I could possibly reach the Kalongi hut by nightfall. If I kept on going I might be lucky enough to find the Germans at the Mahangu hut.

I decided to cut myself a long bamboo walking staff and keep climbing.

The remaining four hours of the day's hike are better not remembered in detail. Even now, as I write, I find my mind merely giving me flashes of recollection—more ethereal bamboo groves bent by the winds, each delicate pointed leaf edged with silvered moisture; more grab-and-scratch heather trees; more moss bogs sprinkled with tiny white flowers. And everything sheened in a drizzly gray mist that soaked through my layered clothing, leaving me shivering and utterly miserable. When was I going to see those mystical mountains I'd come so far to explore and touch? If the mist persisted even during this so-called dry season, then what was the point of going on? Even reaching the summit would be a rather pathetic experience if I couldn't at least enjoy vistas across central Africa. But on the other hand, I'd come too far to give up. The weather might improve . . .

Only it didn't.

I staggered into the Mahangu hut at dusk to find it empty and as miserable as Kalongi. The only compensation was a generous pile of branches and twigs near the stove left behind presumably by the elusive Germans. I soon had a fire going, and in spite of the rapidly increasing cold I felt safe and warm, cocooned in my sleeping bag trying to eat another cardboard concoction of dehydrated fantasy food. The ankle had gotten through the rest of the day without further trauma; it was discolored and puffy, but the pain was muted.

I fell asleep before finishing dinner.

Things looked more promising on the morning of the third day. The mists had lifted—not far enough to expose the summits, but I could look back the way I'd come and be amazed by the power and majesty of the scene. Huge serrated granite ridges, deep clefts and gorges, broken cliffs and screes, and those deep tangled forests and emerald green moss bogs—a splendid riot of scenery. Even if I stayed here and went no farther I'd enjoy a semblance of satisfaction.

No, you wouldn't, my adventurer voice informed me. You'd know you failed.

So I kept on going.

The ankle complained a little, especially when I squeezed its swollen components into my damp boot. But it responded well to a tentative stroll around the hut. I'd been lucky. It could have been a lot worse. I was going to make it to the top after all!

The trail began the same way it had ended the previous evening. More snarled roots and mud slides and boggy patches. I discarded my bamboo walking staff, now badly cracked, and cut a fresh one.

The sun began to appear in patches and the mists lifted even higher as I entered one of the strangest regions of the Ruwenzori. I'd heard about it from a couple of world wanderers I'd met on the riverboat but never expected to find such an other-planet environment.

There were no trees now, just great upward sweeps of moss and high-elevation grasses. But rising out of this relatively benign surface was a Hollywood film set for a days-of-the-dinosaurs fantasy movie. Enormous twenty-foot-high versions of the familiar ankle-high lobelia surged like fiery spears into the clearing sky; equally tall groups of triffidlike groundsels and senecios, crowned with thick cabbagelike rosettes of leaves, rose on ancient thigh-thick trunks encased in the dead and rotting layers of previous "crowns." The chill breezes made these creatures sway as if alive; their brittle appendages rattled like skeleton bones.

Scattered between these enormous freaks of nature were large golden-tinged mounds of moss that had surged unchecked over long-dead and fallen groundsels. Other, less familiar plants filled in the spaces—bushes with fat spongy leaves and thin candlelike flowers, tall shrubs that felt like latex foam, great swaths of ferns and bracken bathed in mist-moisture, and, in the clefts of distant cliffs, what looked like giant gorse bushes sprinkled with bright lemon flowers.

An alien, magical place.

I sat on a lichen-covered rock and gazed around in open-mouthed awe. The expression "lost world" took on new, fresh meanings here. I gave thanks that my ankle had held up and that I hadn't been forced to turn back the previous day. To have missed this experience would have been one of the greatest disappointments of all my lost world odysseys.

There are sound scientific reasons for the profusion of such unique species in this very high environment—a lack of competitive forest, which allows plants to grow to previously unrecorded heights, supported by vast amounts of year-round rain, rich mineral soils, and unusually high levels of ultraviolet radiation. But such explanations in no way diminished the impact of just being here, touching these strange growths and experiencing the deep mysteries of this place.

I arrived late in the afternoon at the third hut, Kiondo, and, once again, found the place empty. My energy seemed boundless. The day's walk up through the "pterodactyl territory" had been relatively easy, with no mishaps. The mist had vanished, the sun was shining, and the high clouds were lifting off the peaks. Maybe at last I'd see what I'd been hoping to see for days—the summits of the Ruwenzori.

A path meandered away from the hut to the ridge of Musswa-Messo, a mere five hundred feet or so higher up. I was already at fourteen thousand feet and it looked like an easy stroll. According to my map I'd be able to get a much better view of the mountains from that vantage point, so I left my backpack in the hut by the stove and set off up the springy moss-flecked ground singing my walking song.

And I had it all.

As I scrambled up the last few feet to the grassy summit, the remaining shards of cloud slid off the peaks and there they were: Mount Stanley, Mount Margherita, and the other peaks; the enormous Stanley glacier, cracked and broken and blinding white; the appropriately named Lac Vert and Lac Noire nestled in their mountain bowls; and, far below, the great swaths of giant lobelia, seneca, and groundsel I'd hiked through earlier in the day. The vista was incredible—ice-etched ridges, the broken frost-shattered pyramids and pylons of granite pinnacles, snowfields as smooth as cake icing—all backdropped by a searing cobalt-blue sky.

In places where the Stanley glacier had cracked to reveal the interior of its two-hundred-foot-thick ice pack, I could make out the precise layerings of the seasonal ice accumulations, some divided by dark bands of soot and windblown charcoal carried to those heights during gigantic bush fires on the western plains of Zaire and the Congo.

It was getting colder as the sun eased down into the hazy plateau thousands of feet below, but I was reluctant to leave my aerie. This was exactly what I'd come to see—the splendor of Africa's most mysterious mountains. The discomforts of the cold hut were meager enticements. I remained where I was, silent and happy.

THE MOUNTAINS OF THE MOON
— Zaire

And tomorrow I'd try for the summit of Margherita. Up the long rock walls, across the ice fields, to touch the 16,763-foot peak. It looked so close. So accessible. It was all waiting for me. Worth every one of the terrors and tribulations of the long journey from Kinshasa.

But fate works in odd and often unkind ways. Coming down from Musswa-Messo I was so entranced by the evening clarity of the scene and the soaring perfection of the peaks, I forgot that I was still on dangerous ground, slick with mud and littered with loose rocks.

The fall came so suddenly I hardly noticed it. One moment I was gazing at the glacier, the next I was flat on my back in the mud and scree with my ankle—my right ankle again—badly twisted and sending those now-familiar spears of pain up my leg and thigh.

Goddamn it! I'd done it again. Further damaging the already weak joint. And this time I knew it was more than a mere bruising. Something felt very wrong. If it wasn't broken I'd certainly torn tendons and Lord knows what else. My left elbow had also taken a hell of a knock on a piece of jagged granite and my lower arm and fingers felt numb.

Much later, after hopping down the few hundred feet to Kiondo hut, I lit a fire, removed my boots, wrapped the now-blue and swollen ankle in tight elastic bandages, and cooked another tasteless dehydrated dinner. I then swallowed a cluster of aspirins and tried to sleep.

But fate hadn't finished with me yet.

During the night a rainstorm began and a furious howling of cold winds blew the pouring water right through the smashed windows. Sleep was impossible and, although my waterproof sleeping bag gallantly kept me dry, my mood descended to pitlike depths. The ankle throbbed and gave me those branding-iron burns every time I tried to move it to a more comfortable position. Swigs of whiskey-Zairois had no impact on the pain or my increasing depression.

The early morning light merged with the miasma of the scene. Except there was no scene, really. It was just fog. Wafting masses of the stuff. Blowing through the windows in wraithlike curlicues and billowing about outside the hut.

The lukewarm coffee tasted like mud. I ate the last of my chocolate and mint cake in the hope of releasing some latent energy. My mood only worsened. I'd been shown all that was before me—so close, so tangible—only to have it whisked away like a dream. To climb farther was obviously impossible; even to descend was highly questionable with an ankle as fragile as a feather.

I hit the bottom of the spiritual barrel and began to wallow in surges of self-pity and self-recrimination.

Then—voices. Faint at first, then louder. Shouts, laughs, cheers. A lot of people, by the sound of it.

And a lot of people it was—four red-cheeked, dripping wet bronzed faces peering at me through the open doorway, and behind them a bunch of black faces with foreheads covered by the burlap straps of loads on their shoulders and backs.

"Ah—*guten morgen!*" A giant of a man beamed at me in my sprawled state by the smoldering fire. Everyone else smiled too. The elusive German climbers had finally turned up and I began to feel better immediately.

And better still, because they replenished the fire, made fresh coffee, and handed me slabs of salami and bread and strong cheese, and told me tales in broken English of the terrors they'd experienced on the higher slopes when they'd attempted to make the climb that morning from the final hut. Blizzards like they'd never known before, even in the Austrian Alps; two of the party almost lost over an ice fall; winds that blew them off their feet even when they weren't moving.

They had decided to abandon the climb and get down to the lower huts as soon as possible. Their guides had told them it would get much worse and by the look of the fog outside I agreed with them.

One of the climbers inspected my ankle with long physician's fingers and declared it badly sprained but possibly adequate for the hike down if I avoided any more falls. He bound it up again tightly in fresh bandages and helped me squeeze it into my boot.

Half an hour later we were on our way down, moving through the mists that made the giant lobelias and groundsels look even more ominous and otherworldish. I was dreading the tangles of the heather forests, but the climbers had appointed one of the porters as my personal guardian and physical support on the rougher slopes.

For much of the way the pain and discomfort of the ankle focused my mind on the trail. I was hardly aware of anything except the nature of the ground directly in front of me. Every root and rut was noted and avoided. On the more difficult stretches I leaned on my porter with my arm around his shoulder. He seemed amused by the familiarity. Maybe even pleased that he'd been able to relinquish his heavy pack for the relative ease of supporting this weary, pain-wracked wanderer. I taught him some of the lines to my marching song and we sang it together in terrible disharmony as the downhill trail went on and on and on. . . .

The next day, back in Beni, I treated the four Germans to the closest thing to a slap-up dinner my modest hotel could provide. Not a memorable feast but certainly a memorable celebration of their concern and kindness.

They were as disappointed as I that we'd not made the summit of Margherita, but, after downing more than our sensible share of Primus beers and glasses of whiskey-Zarois, we peered out of the grubby windows in the evening light and laughed ourselves daft at the view.

Zaire had won. For a few brief tantalizing moments Mount Stanley and all the other peaks sparkled brilliant gold and orange in the setting sun, ice fields flashing, ridges outlined in silver . . . then they slowly vanished again back into their cloud cocoon. A final ironic reminder of our mutual failure. Only our laughter outlasted the brief sighting as we all realized we were content just to have been here and to have shared the visions of this strange and magnificent—if occasionally malevolent—place.

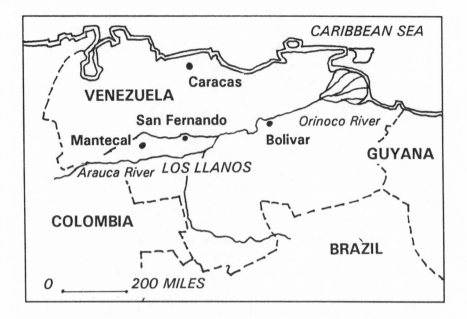

CARIBBEAN SEA

VENEZUELA

Caracas

San Fernando

Mantecal

Orinoco River

Bolivar

GUYANA

Arauca River LOS LLANOS

COLOMBIA

BRAZIL

0 _____ 200 MILES

2. VENEZUELA'S LOS LLANOS

Exploring Infinities

It was all the fault of a novelist who couldn't make up his mind what to write next.

In 1927, around about Easter, Rómulo Gallegos was wandering South America in search of inspiration for his next book. He was a restless, impetuous man constantly starting projects and then abandoning them in favor of new ideas. But he found abundant grist in Venezuela, where citizens are full of tales and the country itself is an incendiary catalyst of inspiration. The scenery is remarkably diverse—from the uncrowded white sand beaches of the Caribbean coast and islands and the great sprawling delta of the Orinoco to the frost-shattered peaks of the high Andes and the mysterious "lost worlds" of the Gran Sabana, where hundreds

81

of vertical-sided mountains (*tepuis*) rise like unearthly totems out of the trackless Amazonian jungle.

Gallegos was boggled by options. His publisher was restless. Two manuscripts lay stranded in midinspiration. He was not a happy man.

Until he met the *llanero*—a cowboy of the plains.

Now, *llaneros* love to talk. Any subject will suffice, but one close to their hearts is their homeland, Los Llanos, a vast six-hundred-mile-long by two-hundred-mile-wide plain in the heart of Venezuela occupying almost a third of the nation. The southern part, drained by the slow-flowing Apure and Arauca rivers, is the wildest part of the Llanos. The land has many of the features—or rather, nonfeatures—of the sprawling grasslands of Brazil's Pantanal and the Argentina pampas. To call the region flat is like calling a Lamborghini a car. It is one of the flattest places on earth. Beyond a few scraggly hummocks (*matas*) of mapora palms and araguaneys (Venezuela's national tree), the eye scours the horizons for any sign of variations in the unremitting horizontality. A little less rain and the place would be a desert stretching out to hazy infinities in every direction. But it does rain. Incessantly, between May and November, turning the plain into an enormous shallow lake. Birds flock here by the millions. Some leave at the onset of the dry season, but most remain, making Los Llanos one of the earth's most important breeding reserves and a hot spot on ornithologists' maps. Well over 250 species make their homes here, not to mention the alligators, capybaras (almost hunted to extinction when the Catholic church announced that, as the creature could swim, it could be eaten on "fish Fridays"), foxes, peccaries, agoutis, anteaters, tapirs, howler monkeys, ocelots, coati, wild boars, anacondas, and even the elusive jaguar.

The famous explorer/navigator Alexander von Humboldt wandered this wild region in 1800 and wrote in his *Travels in the Equinox Regions of the New Continent*:

> The first view of the Llanos fills the soul with a feeling of infinity and through this feeling destroys any sensibilities of space, moving the intellect into higher realms. In the same instance there is the impression of clear surface—dead and rigid—like a desolate planet. Equal in size to the central por-

tion of the Sahara it appears at times like the sea of sand in Libya and another time like the green pastures of the Central Asian steppes.... One becomes weary below the endless open sky... the contemplation of the horizon that continually appears to retreat from us; one loses hope of ever reaching anywhere.

Little has been done to tame and cultivate the Llanos. Cattle ranches—some the size of the Florida Everglades—offer the only real source of livelihood for the *llaneros*. But these cattle are not the docile, udderbound creatures of home; they are wild and ferocious, making the life of the *llanero* cowboy an arduous and adventure-filled existence. Real Wild West stuff (before the West was Hollywood-hyped and Roy Rogered into a Saturday afternoon popcorn pastime).

So Gallegos met this true grit-and-guile *llanero* somewhere on the edge of the strange wilderness. And he listened to his tales— tales of midnight roundups (the cattle are too clever to be caught during the day); legends of the "black gods," "Evil Eye" indians, and the *brujos* (sorcerers); epics of family blood feuds among the regal ranch owners. Murder, mayhem, magic, mosquitoes, mystery, and misery. All the great themes of a great novel. Life on an outback that most people never knew existed. A place where property was the pillar of power and law was whatever the *llanero* barons said it was.

But there was something missing. And Gallegos kept listening.

Then came the story of Doña Barbara.

Now, here was the key ingredient to a truly enduring novel of Venezuelan history. A woman—a woman landowner in a time of total patriarchal domination. A woman who could corral cattle and break in horses better than any man. A woman without scruples who could eradicate anyone who stood in the way of her aggressive ambitions to own all of the Llanos and everything in it—the great rivers teeming with anacondas, alligators, stingrays, electric eels, and deadly piranhas; the endless grasslands and jungle *matas*, where the birds nested and the cattle hid; the vast marshes and quicksand bogs, where antagonists could easily be dispatched to early graves.

Doña Barbara. A nineteenth-century queen of the Llanos. A maven of magic and the black arts. A woman. A witch.

Gallegos worked like a madman. Discarding previous manuscripts, he threw himself into research and romantic speculations. He gleaned every nuance, cajoled ranchers into revealing their fears and fantasies (Doña Barbara was a striking woman and not averse to using beauty and bed to accomplish her schemes), and struggled to separate myth from mundanity.

Writing day and night, he had his manuscript ready in twenty-eight days. Publishers tumbled over themselves to meet his price. It was printed in 1929 in Spain, gained immediate fame and awards, and was eventually translated into twenty languages. Gallegos rode the crest of international celebrity for the rest of his life. Doña Barbara was raised to the level of legend and the Llanos with her. The *llaneros*—previously dismissed as uneducated, untamed wild men—became the stuff of South American machismo and manliness. A nation found its new heroes of the free life— an anarchistic celebration of the unchecked human spirit, male and female.

After reading Gallegos's *Doña Barbara*, I had to come to the Llanos. Still a "lost world" even today, the place drew me in like a mosquito to hot flesh. My other journeys in Venezuela—my search for the hermit of the Andean Tisure Valley, my struggles in the tepuis of the Gran Sabana—were all wonderful adventures, but I knew that one day I'd enter the Llanos and lose myself in its hazy horizons. And if luck stuck with me, I'd return with something special, something unique. Like Gallegos, I was lured by its legends and—like others before me—I was fascinated by the cruel, sensual, enduring spirit of Doña Barbara.

The truck pitched and bucked like a wild stallion on the rutted earth track. I was in the back with my bags, smothered in dust and screening my eyes from a blazing—and still hot—sunset. It was February, the heart of the dry season. There had been no rains since November. The truck left a trail of spuming dust for a mile back down the track. The driver—an old *centaur* cowboy— was crazy. At least that's how it seemed. He thought he was back on his horse. He tried to avoid every pothole by riding his vehicle like a bronco. Most times he failed and the poor vehicle cracked and snapped—metal on metal—as the shocks surrendered to the beating and rocks spewed out from under the tires like machine-gun bullets.

There were birds everywhere. Thousands of them. Spoonbills, jaribu storks, white and scarlet ibis, egrets, herons, vultures, and hawks. But asking him to stop so I could photograph them was like trying to slow an avalanche with a bucket. I thumped on the truck roof, but he just leered at me through the grimy rear window and let out some *llanero* howl like a rodeo holler. I gave up. The birds would have to wait. I padded myself in with my bags to keep the blood flowing in my legs and backside. I'd asked to sit in the open back so I could enjoy the sun and the scenery. Only I wasn't enjoying them much at all.

Somewhere way out there in the burnt-green wilderness was a ranch, Hato la Trinidad de Arauca, of almost one hundred thousand acres. Modest by Llanos standards, but still pretty big. I'd made arrangements to stay here for a while with the Estrada family who had recently opened a lodge as a place of refuge for weary explorers. The Estradas have been *llaneros* for five generations and are hoping to raise capital to keep their cattle land in a natural state, uncultivated and undeveloped. Other ranchers are constantly planning elaborate schemes for farming the rich earth and domesticating their herds of wild cattle, but Hugo Estrada and his family believe the Llanos is far too important as a breeding ground and safe haven for endangered wildlife to be changed.

But there is more to Hugo Estrada's ambitions than environmental philanthropy. There is the memory—the presence—of Francisca Vazquez de Carrillo, the notorious Doña Barbara. Her ranch, Mata de Totumo, adjoined the Estrada ranch, and her reputation as a sorcerer kept most *llaneros* well away from its dark jungly hummocks and deadly quicksands. They called it El Miedo, The Fear. Legends abounded about the place: ghosts of Doña Barbara's outcast lovers who haunted the creeks and sloughs, seeking to fill "the eternal holes in their souls"; a wizardly "partner" she called "Socio," who helped her maintain her mastery of the black arts; fierce cutthroat compatriots whose duty it was to seize land, cattle, and property without regard to such incidentals as deeds and laws; strange rituals and sacrifices undertaken in her "conjuring room" to preserve her powers—and always the growing size and wealth of her ranch as she amassed land and cattle using every device in her devious, and deadly, arsenal.

So this is where I was heading, to the *campamento* of Doña Barbara, to meet the modern-day Estradas. And I hoped it was going to be worth all this banging about and dust chewing in the back of a beaten-up truck.

On the way down I had paused in the sweltering little cow town of Mantecal on the edge of the southern Llanos. It happened to be carnival time, a pre-Lent bacchanal of parades and costumed children. (Dressing up like a Llanos jaguar seemed to be very popular.) Everyone was out in the streets, dancing, cheering, and whooping it up near the iron-railed enclosure where the *llaneros* held their regular *toros coleados* rodeos. These were supposedly crazy affairs—cowboys competed to throw angry bulls by their tails. I would have loved to photograph one of these unique events but instead had my cameras and recording equipment almost ruined by a sudden dousing from buckets of cold water thrown by laughing revelers. No one had warned me that one of the highlights of *carnivale* was to go around soaking unsuspecting victims. I was obviously an ideal candidate and left the merry little town dripping and cursing and trying to dry out all the sensitive electronics of my equipment.

The sun had gone now. We were far from the madness of Mantecal. The air had a chill to it, like a desert after dusk. The horizons were muted and vague in the purpling sky. Mystery crept in. I remembered a passage from the Gallegos book:

> The Llanos is at once lovely and fearful. It holds, side by side, beautiful life and hideous death. The Plain frightens, but the fear which the plain inspires is not the terror which chills the heart; it is hot, like the wind sweeping over the immeasurable solitude, like the fever lying in the marshes. The plain crazes; and the madness of a man living in the wide lawless land

leads him to remain a Plainsman forever. There is madness in the languid desolation—the unbroken horizon enclosing nothing but emptiness—a sprawling wilderness land of struggle and peril, with as many horizons as hopes.

But one man had apparently been unmoved by all the maudlin tales of mystery. Don José Natalio Utreva, head of the Estrada family in the late 1800s, admired the courage and fortitude of Doña Barbara. He knew the power of legend and myth over the lawless *llaneros*. He understood that the only way that Doña Barbara could hope to survive in that harsh wilderness was by determination. She was proud, and clever—but not the evil witch others claimed her to be.

They were close—how close is not recorded. They called each other *pariente* (relative) and they became compatriots in the endless plots and ploys of the ranchers. When Doña Barbara disappeared in 1922—or died (after Gallegos's book it was hard to separate fact from fiction)—the Estradas purchased much of her land, and her memory—her presence—has been protected down through the generations. Today, on the Estrada ranch, there is a memorial to her, shaded by a great divi-divi tree; her adobe and thatch house has been rebuilt by members of the family and furnished simply in traditional nineteenth-century *llaneros* fashion.

We arrived well after dark after more hours of bumping and banging in the back of the truck. There were stars everywhere, new unfamiliar patterns. As the driver switched off the engine the silence hummed, broken only by the ear-itching saw of the cicadas. Fifty yards away was the Doña Barbara Lodge, built originally by the Estradas for their Llanos ranch hands. Lights shone outside the small rooms. After hours of crashing through the wilderness, seeing nothing but brown-green horizons, the place looked like a palace. I rose up from the truck bed like a dust-coated apparition, then promptly fell down again. My legs were numb. They had forgotten how to stand.

Someone was coming toward me. A tall thin man silhouetted by the lights. I managed to haul myself out and leaned against the rear fender, clinging on to the truck for support.

"A good drive, yes?"

I tried to say something witty, but my mouth was dry and caked with grit. What came out was somewhere between a croak and a grunt.

"I am Francisco. Welcome to the *hato*. Hugo Estrada is my father and he will meet with you later."

I smiled and nodded.

"Have a wash. Then dinner. Leave your bags. Someone will bring them."

Sounded fine with me.

There were twenty rooms at the lodge, all previously used to house ranch hands. Mine overlooked a tree whose upper trunk was encased in a bulbous five-foot-high termite nest meticulously shaped out of mud and straw. The lights from the lodge also illuminated the wings of a small plane in an adjacent field, a very convenient form of transportation in this wilderness. The moon was out now, large and low on the horizon, bathing nearby trees and the endless plain beyond in silver light.

In the shower the layered dust on my head and body coagulated into rivulets of mud. A reflection in the cracked mirror made me look like a swamp thing newly emerged from the bog. Not a pretty sight.

Dinner was a splendid affair. The Estradas—the father, Hugo, and his wife, Beatrice, his son, Francisco, two daughters, Carmen and Ixora, and their children—greeted me like a lost relative, offered me a choice of cold beer or fresh fruit juices, and led me to the buffet table set under the stars in the outdoor dining area. Due to bad planning on my part I hadn't eaten since the morning and was ravenous. And here I was, faced by a feast of soups and entrées of fried fish, steak, chicken in hot sauce, pastas, rice, fruit, and salad, all served with home-baked breads and little *arepa* loaves. Hugo, the stocky don in his early seventies, with a broad white mustache, twinkling eyes, and a ready smile, followed me along the buffet table. "Take more," "Try the bread," "Don't miss this," "That's not enough," "This is fresh papaya juice—is very good after long journeys."

I tried to eat slowly, responding to questions and asking a few of my own, but the delicious dishes occupied most of my attention. Then came dessert—some decadent concoction of grated coconut, pureed mangoes, and caramelized sugar. I attempted to limit my intake, but Beatrice would have none of my gustatory modesty. As soon as I'd finished she gently removed my plate with a smile and returned with an even larger second helping, plus a glass of sweet *chichi* blended from rice and milk, and a slab of cheese made every day at the Estradas' small dairy from "tame-cow" milk.

"You like?" asked Hugo, eyes twinkling again.

"I like very much. I'm glad I came."

The family nodded approval.

"Tomorrow, if you wish, you can take a horse early in the morning. The birds are beautiful then," said Hugo.

"Sounds like a great idea."

"Good. Five-thirty is a good time. One of the men will bring your horse."

We talked about the wildlife and Hugo Estrada's plans to keep most of his ranch in a natural state.

"The other ranchers—we are not always agreeing on matters. Some want to begin cultivation and keep all the cattle tame for cheese and meat. They use chemicals for spraying. They burn their land. They say it makes better grass for the cattle. But when they burn they destroy the places for the birds. Many animals die. It is not good for the Llanos. This is a special place in Venezuela. In the world."

Beatrice brought me a book the family keeps in which guests at the lodge had described their feelings about Hato La Trinidad. I read:

I love this land—the land of the Llanero who needs only a knife, a horse, a hammock and a fishing line. . . .

Strong yet gentle—the land and the people.

I toast to the Estradas—a family working hard to keep a balance between man, his enterprises, and nature! The preservation of God's creation.

One comment referred to Doña Barbara:

Do you represent the dark side of the Llanos—the jaguar, the piranha, the stingray, the electric eel? . . . perhaps you practiced both good and evil witchcraft for you have surely left us a strange and enchanted land.

Much later I thankfully tumbled into bed to rest before an early start to my "enchanted land" explorations.

By six I was out on the plains—just me and my sleepy horse. The sun rose slowly over the gallery forests by the river, flecking the araguaney trees, jasmines, and acacias with silver-gold light. From the lower trunk of one of the araguaneys grew two exotic rosa de la montana flowers—fiery balls of bright red—glowing like miniature suns. Over in the ranch house palms I heard the resident colony of buff-necked ibis beginning their morning litany of shrieks and scratchy caws. Nearby at the stables the *llaneros*—the "midnight cowboys" of the ranch—were unsaddling their horses after a long night of rounding up the cattle. Way off in the distance I heard the eerie calls of howler monkeys.

At the edge of the *mata* I disturbed a cluster of parrots. They scattered like litter in a hurricane, a hyped-up half-flight of flailing green wings and frantic screeches. Whatever hope I had of quietly photographing the storks and herons by the watering holes was gone. Two five-foot-high jaribu storks rose up in slow laborious flaps from their sentry positions overlooking the half-dry ponds, followed by dainty lines of snowy egrets, white ibis, three whistling herons, and a single scarlet ibis like a flash of red flame. Only the spoonbills remained, trailing the shallows with their strange scooping beaks. Oh, and a macaw too. He sat with his enormous bill, way up in a palm, knowing he was safe and wondering what all the fuss was about anyway.

Something brown and big moved through the sawgrass on the far side of the water hole—maybe a capybara, over three feet high, the largest rodent in the world. A shadowy undulating mass of black closer in turned out to be a bunch of vultures feasting on the remains of fish left behind by the storks and herons. Obviously food was more important to them than fear of an unexpected intruder.

I moved on as slowly and silently as I could across the lightening plain. My horse seemed pleased not to be called upon to gallop. Galloping is not a forte of mine. A lazy saunter suits me much better and it seemed an appropriate pace for such a lovely early morning.

The plain stretched out to misty horizons in all directions. I tried to imagine what it must look like in the rainy season—a vast, seemingly endless lake, sparkling under a hot sun or black as pitch as storms lash its surface. So big. So splendidly remote and untamed.

I could ride for days across this land and see nothing but the plain. No village, no houses, no signs of man's existence here. Just the breezes, the occasional flurry of birds by a waterhole or over a *mata*; possibly the fleeting shadow of a jaguar . . . nothing more. Boundless space under a vast blue sky. . . .

I envied the *llaneros* their freedom. They live their own lives as they have done for generations, hunting the wild steers under the midnight stars, singing their songs of love and lust for this vast tempting plain. Simple, uneducated men, but wise in the ways of this "strange and enchanted" land. Their land.

Which for a while felt to be my land too. I knew so little of its secrets and its dangers, yet I could sense its power in these huge empty horizons. A power that seeemed to pour into me as I rode into the morning light, making me proud to be here and, for a while, proud just to be me, needing nothing.

Much later on, after lunch, I was introduced to José, one of the supervisors of the *hato*'s workers and cowboy-*llaneros*. I wanted to know more—much more—about the life of the *llaneros* and to understand the Doña Barbara legend.

José was middle-aged, with a sinewy body and a sun-burnished face, wrinkled like worn leather. He spoke good English and seemed to enjoy nothing more than sitting in the shade of a palm near the lodge, telling me tales of his heritage and his homeland.

"What was that phrase again?"

" 'Horse first and woman later.' The old *llaneros* used to say it always. They said many true things. Like the hares of the dawn. Do you know what they are?"

"No."

LOS LLANOS
Venezuela

He smiled. "They are those little round clouds on the horizon. Pink and then gold in the sunrise. You see them most days."

"Tell me some more."

"You maybe think *llaneros* are just ignorant cowboys." He didn't wait for my rebuff. "Well—it's true. Education, schools, big-city things are not very important here. They used to call this 'the kingdom of the *cimarrones*'—the wild ones. When the Spaniards were here in the 1700s they sometimes would give convicts a choice of imprisonment in the dungeons or deportation to the Llanos. Escaped slaves—they were brought from the Caribbean islands—came here too. So you can imagine what a wild place this was. *Llaneros primitovos* they called us. No one trusted us and we trusted no one. Life was simple. Cabins of adobe and thatch. Hammocks for sleeping. A palisade fence to keep out the wild cattle and the jaguars. Storerooms for cassavas, beans, and corn; a smokehouse where salted meat dried; stables, pigsties, a place for the rope cutter, and a big calabash shade tree by the poultry yard. Sometimes a dairy near the corral for the tame cows and a room for making cheeses from the milk. That was all. Simple."

"In some ways it doesn't seem too different today," I said. "I know there are trucks and bikes—there's Hugo's plane—but things are still pretty basic. The *llaneros* seem to live—"

"The *llaneros*!" He grinned. "We'll never change. We're still the same as before. We do not make friends easily. We are suspicious of people—even people we know. That is our history. We still don't trust laws and lawyers. We trust only the knife and the gun and the 'red glory of death.' We learned that from Pancha Vazquez—or maybe she learned it from us!"

"Who's Pancha Vazquez?"

"The one you call Doña Barbara. We called her other names."

"So I've heard."

"Ah—don't laugh. Maybe some of the stories were a little—how you say—'blown up,' but Pancha had powers. Real powers."

"Such as?"

"Well—they say she 'pocketed' men. She knew the secrets of Camajay-Minare, the black god of the Orinoco. She learned from the Indian women how to make special things from herbs and roots. She gave the men love potions and then did what she liked with them. When she was finished, she—or maybe the wizard, the 'partner'—got rid of them. That woman had her own cemetery! She had all the secrets from the Indians—the Evil-Eyed, the Breathers, the Prayers. She became very rich. She buried pots—big clay jars—full of twenty-dollar gold pieces. People think they're still here. They dig for them. They even dug in her grave. They found nothing. No gold. No bones. Nothing."

"Maybe she was bluffing. Life must have been hard for her here."

"Hard! Sure it was hard. It was hard for everyone. But she was tough. She could lasso a bull out in the open as well as any peon. She could fight the Cunaviche rustlers and win. She could beat the best lawyers in Caracas—they called Llanos law the law of Doña Barbara. She knew where—which *matas*—the bulls and their herds would hide in when she took the men out at night to tame the cattle and bring them back to the dairy. Many horses were torn to pieces under her by those bulls, but she got away, mounted a spare, and brought them back to the *hato*."

He looked at me warily to see if I still believed him and nodded when I nodded.

"Smuggling too. That's when you take unbranded cattle that wander onto your *hato*. She believed in the 'right of the noose.' It was—it still is—a great roundup game out here. And she was good at it. Maybe the best."

"Tell me about those roundups."

He paused, remembering his younger days, perhaps, when a horse—usually without a saddle and ridden barefoot—meant freedom and the open plain for days on end.

"They are bloody days. You can lose horses—plenty of them. Those steers are wild. We didn't use them for meat or milk much in the old days—only the tames ones. It was the hides that counted. Most of them are still out there, still unbranded. There aren't many fences. What is on your property is yours. But they don't want to belong to anybody. They like things the way they were—free and open."

"So how do you round them up?"

He laughed and lifted his head. I could see his bright eyes flash under his straw hat.

"The trick is to get the bulls away from the herds. If they keep with the cows they lead them all into the *matas* and we lose them. So we have to get them—one by one—get him to charge you, lasso him—maybe even castrate him if there is time and then get the boys circling the herd to calm them all down. Sometimes we get some tame ones coming in from the next ranch—something about a stampede that just draws them in. So we end up with a few with other brands on them. We can fix that. We all do it."

"Is it dangerous?"

He laughed again. "You don't have time to worry about that with the noise. The steers are scared—and mad. They want to be back on the prairie—the bulls are mad because they've lost control; the cows are mad because they've lost their calves; there are horns and ribs crashing and horses getting bloodied up. And the men yelling—and you never know if the herd will break out again— someone not where he should be—a few seconds and they're out of the circle and all across the plain. Then I get mad too!"

"Bet it makes you wish the rains would come."

He paused, letting the memories subside and chuckling to himself. Finally he began again.

"The rains." He was still chuckling. "Well—there's no round-ups deep in the rains, but at the beginning there's the big one. All the ranchers get together and pick their best cowboys—their *centaurs*—and work each ranch rounding up for branding in the corrals. We have the *desmontrencaje* to separate the cows from the yearlings, brand them, notch their ears with the mark of the *hato*, and keep a tally on strips of leather cut with the point of a knife. Just like the old Spanish settlers. Nothing much has changed since their days. After that it's quiet for a while. The Barinas wind brings the big storms and the lakes start to form. Then we get all the old songs—guitars, *cuatros* [ukuleles], harps, calabash rattles, the corridos—we make up verses to tunes we know, dance the *joropo* to criollo music, we roast the veal over the fire, sprinkle on the *aji de leche*, cook the bananas and yuccas—and blow cigar smoke at the mosquitoes. We called this the time of 'guid, cup and ham-mock.' Lazy days. You can't go anywhere. Most of the tracks are gone under the lakes. Sometimes we organize a *toros coleados*—a crazy rodeo where the *llaneros* compete to throw bulls by their tails. Very crazy! But most of the time we just do nothing."

"Don't you get restless?"

"Restless? Maybe. But it is the way it is. It's all we know.

Things are set that way. Everything works with the seasons. After the first rains the herons and egrets return—all the *matas* and waters are covered with white birds. Way back—years ago—we called it the 'time of the feathers' when the molting began. Like snow. The lakes and the *matas* were covered in feathers. We'd go out in the canoes—all of us—singing like madmen—and collect them, bundle them up, and sell them to the fancy merchants in San Fernando way down the river. They called that city 'the feather capital of the world'—people there got rich using our feathers—they even built a palace by the river, like something from Venice. And here we were fighting the alligators, the piranhas—and the malaria. That was the bad part. Malaria. You began to shiver, then you'd turn white, then green. Soon the crosses appeared on the higher ground. We lost many men that way. There was no cure in those days. Lots of praying, plenty of magic potions from the *brujos*, dancing the *joropo* to drive out the fever—but no cure."

"The plainsmen—the *llaneros*—they were tough men?"

"Yes, tough—and they still are tough. And suspicious, superstitious, rough with women, rough even with friends. There is a saying: 'A plainsman will be a plainsman for five generations.' It's true. It gets in the blood—the spirit of this plain."

"It still seems a hard life."

"Of course it's hard. But the *llanero* knows nothing else. To him it is just the way life is. The seasons as the pendulum—a great pendulum—backwards and forwards across the plain, life-death, life-death, from flood to the fires of the drought, from fires to flood." He stretched out his arms and shrugged. "It's all they know. For a long time it was all I knew."

The next day, Hugo's son, Francisco, suggested some piranha fishing on the Arauca River, a few miles from the lodge.

He was a tall man in his early thirties with the face of a boy and a quick humor. Educated at Cornell and the University of Texas, he spoke clear English.

"Can you eat piranhas?" I asked.

"Of course, if they don't eat you first," said Francisco. "They call them *caribes*—flesh-eaters. Another name for them is 'donkey castrators'! Donkeys keep away from the rivers. Not much meat on piranhas, though—they're lean so they can swim fast—but what you get is good. Want to try?"

I'm a worse fisherman than I am a hunter. I don't get much pleasure out of hooking and shooting things. I'd rather take photographs, or just watch. The last time I'd fished for food was years back, way up on the California coast near Big Sur. Someone had told me that around sunset I'd catch all the sunfish I could eat in the sloppy surf. Bait wasn't necessary, they said. Just a good polished hook. Sure, I thought. Another fisherman's tale. But I tried it—just a bit of nylon line and a bright hook—and voila! Sunfish after sunfish came flapping in eagerly trying to devour the metal. After catching eight in as many minutes I gave up. It was too easy. Didn't seem fair somehow. I cooked them and ate as many as I could to justify the slaughter. But my heart—and my stomach—weren't convinced. It was not a memorable meal.

So—somewhat reluctantly—I went to fish for piranha.

At the place we launched the canoe the Arauca River was about a quarter mile wide. Thick and silty, it eddied like melted coffee ice cream around fallen trees in the shallows. The banks were mud ramparts, hard and cracked, pierced by the roots of jungle scrub. It was very quiet. And very hot. The breeze from the motor-powered canoe did little to reduce the sear of the sun on my skin.

We didn't talk much. It was too hot to think. Lines of cormorants and egrets, standing on the mud flats like expectant spectators, watched us pass.

The snout of an alligator nudged through the water, followed by a couple of bulbous eyes. Iguanas, sunbathing on the bank, scurried for cover as we eased by. Colonies of rare hoatzins (fat partridge-shaped birds with disheveled arrays of head feathers) went into paroxysms of raucous cawing if we came too close to their tree perches, and climbed higher into the branches using tiny claws on their wings. Vultures, hawks, and falcons skimmed the sky in slow art nouveau curls of flight; herons and storks stood rigid as reeds on the river's edge, pretending to be invisible.

The river had a timeless feel to it, untouched, unmolested, flowing somnolently eastward to join the Apure and eventually the great Orinoco two hundred miles farther downstream.

I felt mesmerized by the heat and the drone of the engine as we moved on against the current. In gaps between the riotous flurry of trees and thick scrub along the top of the bank I caught glimpses of the plains again, shimmering empty infinities, beguiling, beckoning with promises of . . . what? Freedom? Release? I never quite pinned it down. Why this fascination with nothingness? Gallegos's "immeasurable solitude," and "the madness of languid desolation." But at least I wasn't alone in my madness. The *llaneros* knew it too and gave their lives to it, generation after generation.

"We're here," said Francisco.

He pointed to a scrub-shaded creek on the far side of the river.

"In the floods that creek leads right to the lodge. Good fishing all the way."

We eased out of the swirl of the main stream into this fetid backwater. Francisco cut the engine and the heat doubled in intensity. "Now, piranhas!"

He became a flurry of activity, chopping bait, fixing the hooks to our lines, and scattering nuggets of advice like bird seed.

"They're fast. When you feel the bite, jerk hard. Watch their teeth; they'll take chunks out of your fingers. Hit them hard with this"—he showed me a thick wooden club—"very hard. And they still may not be dead. Sometimes they'll bite even when they are dead. Be careful. Don't let them flap around the boat. Put them in the bucket. They can leap high. Take your ear off. . . ."

I wish I'd stayed back at the ranch.

But it was too late now. Francisco was showing me how to cast. First try and my hook stuck in the side of the canoe. He was patient. I sweated and learned. After three limp casts I began to get the feel of it.

At first nothing much happened.

"It can take time," Francisco whispered. "But when they know there's food they'll be all around us."

Still nothing.

And then, suddenly, the first bite. More of a violent grab, actually. I jerked my line and the hook shot out of the water like a bullet, almost hitting Francisco in the face. The bait was gone.

A big chunk of chicken neck gobbled right off the hook, leaving nothing but a tiny remnant of wet skin.

He laughed softly. "You have to jerk much faster. They're clever—and always hungry."

Then it was his turn for a bite. I saw his line go taut. He pulled back instantly and the surface of the water broke. Something silver and orange flew across the surface of the creek, flailing and writhing, scattering spray. Then it vanished. Then it was back, this time closer to the canoe. A very angry little creature indeed, trying to bite itself off the line with two white rows of half-inch-long dagger-shaped teeth. Francisco carefully lowered the flailing creature onto the floor of the boat, where it continued to flap in paroxysms of rage. A quick club to its head and there was silence. He removed the hook cautiously, never taking his eyes off those teeth, and dropped the supposedly dead creature into the bucket. Only it wasn't dead. With a massive show of determination it leapt clean out and tried to attack my sneakers.

"Watch out," shouted Francisco, as he pounded its head fiercely again with the club. After that it didn't move. But I didn't trust it and eased farther down the boat away from the bucket.

Francisco laughed. "Wise move."

Two minutes later it was my turn. A big one this time, eight inches from teeth to tail, angrier than the first and beautifully marked with highlights of sunset red on its sparkling silver-gold body. I wasn't up to the clubbing, so I passed the flailing fish to Francisco, who quickly silenced it and added it to the bucket.

They were hungry, these piranha. Our catch accumulated quickly, but the bait supply dwindled rapidly as the lucky ones grabbed lunch and escaped before either of us was fast enough to jerk the line. Peering over the side of the boat I occasionally saw them streaking like skinny torpedoes through the shallows. Francisco watched them too.

"Last month a woman was lost in the river. It does not happen often. She must have cut herself, maybe grazed her foot on a sharp branch. They say she slipped and the piranhas attacked. Like sharks they go crazy when there's blood in the water. Her husband was there on the bank. He heard her shout and before he could get to the river she was gone."

"What happened?"

100

He shrugged. "They never found her."

I felt nervous. "I wish you hadn't told me that."

"It's best you know. This river is very dangerous. Many of the alligators have been killed by poachers—Indians—but there are a few left, the big, mean ones. And stingrays, electric eels—even anacondas. The old ones can grow to fifty feet."

I looked long and hard at the river. It eased on past the creek, its smooth surface benignly placid in the hot silence. I remembered that Gallegos line—"The Llanos is at once lovely and fearful." A fickle place, a place of violent and sudden death in the midst of sweeping beauty. Even under that blazing sun, cold shivers scampered up and down my spine.

I looked again at the river. There was movement now, out there in the middle, far beyond the swirls and eddies of the shallows. Something black, cutting the surface and then disappearing. More than one. Things with fins.

"Dolphins," said Francisco. "Freshwater dolphins."

"Dolphins too?"

"Oh, yes. And manatees. They play here. There are many. Sometimes you see the dolphins leap. Sometimes you just see a fin. They're lazy today."

A strange and wonderful place, this Llanos.

Francisco declared fifteen piranha and one rather weary catfish to be enough for dinner and suggested we make our way back. That was fine. Fishing still didn't hold much fascination for me.

There was no need to start the engine. The current carried us downstream and the breeze was refreshing after the wet heat of the creek. The dolphins followed us for a ways playfully and then vanished.

"Indians. Fishermen." Francisco pointed to the far bank after we'd floated a couple of miles. I saw them. A huddle of brown figures on a small shaded beach gutting a pile of enormous fish—a few peacock bass (*pavon*), long gray catfish, a fang-toothed aymara, and some bright red beauties I couldn't name.

"Where'd they catch fish like that?"

"In the main river. With nets."

"Makes our catch look a bit pathetic."

Francisco laughed. "Ah—you haven't tasted ours yet. Much better."

We eased over to the group, who watched us briefly and then continued their gory task, throwing the innards into a cracked wooden calabash. Two twenty-foot-long canoes were pulled up on the sand, each carved from a solid tree trunk.

A man dressed in a pair of ragged jeans walked out into the shallows to greet Francisco. He carried one of the larger fish and gave it to him. They obviously knew one another and a rumble of conversation began as if they were continuing a previous discussion. Apparently that's exactly what it was.

"He's trying to sell me one of his canoes." He pointed to the larger one, a fine dark brown specimen, smooth on the outside and patterned with ax marks inside. "We talk about this every time we meet."

"How much is he asking?"

"Fifteen hundred bolivars—about thirty dollars."

"That's all!"

Francisco shrugged and smiled. "Every time it gets a little less. One day I'll buy it."

"It's beautiful."

"Yes, I know."

The conversation ended with smiles. No deal today, but they both knew that the transaction would take place. One day. Soon.

We left the Indians still cleaning their fish and drifted off again downstream. Half an hour later we were back at the launching place and pulled the boat out of the water and high up the bank.

"Dinner soon. Your first piranha dinner."

In the evening, after that memorable piranha dinner (Francisco was right—not much flesh but good eating), I spent some time with Hugo Estrada, the don of La Trinidad. We sat together in the easy chairs by a large mural painted on the outer wall of the lodge. It depicted the now increasingly familiar themes and sights of the region—the vast green horizons, the cowboys on their wiry little horses, the capybaras, the birds, the deadly jaguar.

Hugo gestured at the painting. "You know all this now, eh?"

"I'm learning," I said. "But I'm still curious about you. Francisco has told me about your career as an agricultural adviser to the government, your honorary doctorates, your policies to limit imports and help Venezuela develop its own industries. I've seen that hallway in your ranch with all your awards and citations. Photographs of you shaking hands with presidents—"

Hugo smiled (twinkling eyes again) as he interrupted me.

"Ah—but did you see the room at the end?"

"Yes, I did. The one with that huge poster of the New York skyline."

"Well—that picture is very important to me. You must understand that it is very easy here to get used to everything and you don't want to leave. You become a king—here is all your domain. And it's good weather, good things to see every day, beautiful birds and animals—so why leave? you think. Why leave? But that is not good. Not good for me. You need to remember other places. Big, big places. Then you don't become a king. You understand?"

I nodded.

"Kings can be dangerous." He chuckled. "I know. I've worked with many men—ministers, presidents, very rich men. When they start to think like kings . . . very dangerous. For them, for everyone. And so—I remember other places. Like New York!"

He paused to refill our drinks and we sipped them quietly for a while under yet another night sky pinpricked with a billion stars.

"The Indians also do the same for me."

"You mean the Indians around today—the ones I saw on the river with Francisco?"

"No, no," he said with a laugh. "We have problems with them from time to time. Especially the Cuivas who live over in Colombia. They fool around here at times. We go after them, but they just run back to Colombia. The Yaruro are good people, though. Good fishermen and good workers. But—no—I am talking about the ancient tribes—the ones who were here maybe ten thousand years ago. Between the Orichuna and Arauca rivers we have found many signs of their culture—thousands and thousands of pieces of pottery with beautiful designs and different colors. It's not our clay—from some other place. And stones. We

103

find lots of stones—and we don't have any stones here at all. We think they were here for a very long time. We need to have proper studies of their culture."

"No one's doing any research?"

"No—not seriously. But I have much to tell them when they do. Tomorrow I will show you one of their burial urns—five feet high, a beautiful round shape, and made without a wheel." We stopped talking for a while and looked at the star-filled sky.

"It's good to be here," I said.

Hugo chuckled. "Others ask me why I spend so much time on the *hato*. And I tell them—just look around you."

He spread his arms wide and laughed.

The next day I was with Francisco again. He took me first to the old family ranch house full of portraits, shelves of books, and sideboards filled with crystal glasses and old family dinnerware. Outside, shaded by coconut palms, he maintained a series of breeding areas for some of the endangered species of the Llanos—anteaters, land tortoises, and alligators.

"Most of the alligators have been killed by poachers," he told me. "We have to try and do something to fight back."

After his U.S. education, Francisco had decided to reject lucrative offers of employment in the States and return to his father's *hato* to continue the work of improving the ranch—trying to maintain, as he put it, "a benevolent control of balance."

After long miles of rough riding on his Jeep across the endless plains, we arrived at the dairy, where a small herd of tamed cows were being milked by a ranch hand.

"Time for breakfast," he said. Once again we had left very early at dawn, and it was only eight-thirty.

He led me into one of the cool, adobe-walled rooms of the dairy and pointed to two white wheels of cheese bathed in the limpid morning sun.

"Pick one," he told me.

I selected the smallest, an eight-pound beauty with a curdy aroma, and we sat at a table outside drinking small cups of strong black coffee and eating slices of succulent cheese on slabs of *arepa* cornbread baked for us by his sister Carmen the night before.

"Do you ever age the cheese?"

"Not usually—we eat it too fast! But sometimes we wrap a special cheese in a skin of coffee beans and cloth and bury it underground for a year or so. It's really hard when it comes out, but the flesh is much whiter than this—and so good!"

An hour later we were strolling on a broad beach of fine white sand by the slow-moving Arauca. Francisco pointed out small black nuggets of a hard rocklike substance embedded in the sand.

"*Azabache*. Petrified resin from the trees. You'll always find it here. The *llaneros* carve it into tiny figurines and animals. You can buy them in the fancy stores in Caracas. It's quite valuable!"

More rough and dusty driving in the Jeep across the ranch trails brought us to a large circular cattle pond. It was hot now. The sun had given up its early morning coquettishness and now pounded down like a hammer on our heads. The water was just too tempting. Not bothering to undress, I just jumped in, sneakers, jeans, and shirt, and bathed in the wonderful cold wetness of the pool.

Within minutes the sun had burned off all the moisture and I was dry and dusty again as Francisco led me to one of the ranch's most unusual sights—a magnificent Italian statue of Christ carved from white Carrara stone standing high on a plinth, its arms outstretched toward the infinities of the Llanos. An inscription below the statue read in Spanish, LORD, BLESS OUR PLAINS.

"We call him Cristo de la Mata—this is the center of the *hato* and my family decided that we needed something special here in this wild place to remind us of the important things."

Around the Christ figure were four smaller carved angels representing the races of the Llanos—Indian, black, white, and mestizo.

"Your family has a great love for this place," I said.

"Of course," he replied. "It has been our life for five generations."

He handed me a folded piece of paper from his pocket with a poem written on it.

"My father composed this."

I reproduce the verses in full because they seem to capture the spirit of the Estrada family's work and caring for this wild land:

Our Father Who Is in the Land

Our father who is in the land
mixed with the flowers, the rain and the wind
present in birth, life and the urn,
immersed in souls, laughter and the kisses.

Bring forgiveness into proud minds
and in the same manner forget those many sins
that man in his life, commits every day,
not knowing what he is doing or why he has done it.

Bless the skies ruptured by man,
keep the land free of blood and steel,
take care of the children without breast or bread,
keep him that dies without ever living.

Our father who is in the land
bless your world, my country and my home,
and protect us always, in every moment
even if we sometimes forget, everything you are.

Much later on in the day, as we bounced back toward the lodge along more rough tracks, Francisco announced, "And now for Doña Barbara."

"I was wondering when I'd see her grave."

"Well, you seem so curious about her, I've been saving it for last."

Not far from the old ranch we followed a winding footpath through the scrub to her memorial set behind an iron railing and shaded by an old divi-divi tree. It was a special moment for me; after all the reading I'd done and all the tales I'd heard, I was finally in a place Doña Barbara herself had loved and spent her tempestuous life protecting.

Nearby was the replica of her simple adobe and thatch home. In its cool shady rooms you could feel her presence. A hammock tied between two wooden veranda posts seemed to be waiting for her.

"How do you feel about all the tales of witchcraft and sorcery—all those Gallegos stories?"

Francisco smiled. "Oh, I don't take them too seriously. She was a tough woman—a real fighter. She possibly created most of the myths herself to scare people. If people believe you can cast spells, they cooperate—they respect you. I think that was all it was. Maybe."

"But you're not totally sure?"

"Well—there are one or two things that happened . . . it makes you wonder. But how will we ever know? The important thing was that she survived. She faced the challenges and won. She was a woman for her times. A real woman."

The hammock beckoned. Behind the house a flight of egrets flashed in the sun. In the flowers by the veranda hummingbirds sucked nectar and a jaribu stork, erect as a palace guard, watched us from a nearby lagoon. In the heat of the day the hammock offered languid leisure for Doña Barbara and all the people of the Llanos. A place to pause and remember Hugo Estrada's phrase—"Just look around you."

I spent many more happy days on the ranch discovering its secret places, and the memories still return: the swift dawns with breezes smelling of wild mint and cattle, as a million birds begin their morning clamor; flights of red ibis like long ruby rosaries; the white cranes high in the silver-gold light, serene and silent; corrals holding unbroken horses crying for the freedom of the plain; sand devils thrown up from the sun-dried land by sudden flurries of wind and sent swirling across the wilderness like writhing apparitions; the dainty paraguaton flowers that sweeten the air of the musty *matas*; the sense of being slightly drunk with the sunlight, the sweeping wind, and the open plain stretching away in every direction. And then those nights with the prairie, asleep, black, and silent below vast traceries of stars. . . .

I remember my last night after a long and delicious dinner. The sun had finally set, but twilight still glimmered across the western plain; a girdle of dark clouds was cut by the sharp circular horizon of the savanna and, beyond that invisible stretch of silent land, a full moon rose, silhouetting scattered *matas* with their scrawny palm tops. The silence of the night eased across the flatness. A silence that, for centuries, huddled groups of *llaneros* have broken with songs, laughter, and tales of prairie hobgoblins, "nights of white shadows," mysterious horsemen, and "the weeping woman" who leads men to drown in river pools and quicksands. But their laughter would pause at any mention of the Familiars. These were the most feared of all prairie apparitions. They often brought omens of disease and death, loss of wealth and property, terrible adversities, and were the ghostly outcomes of one of the strangest customs of the Llanos.

In line with ancient superstitions, whenever a new ranch was established a live animal would be buried beneath the first corral to be erected so that his spirit—the Familiar—imprisoned in the earth of the property, might protect and defend its owners in perpetuity.

Nowadays there are other, less elusive spirits protecting the Llanos—the spirits of infrequent visitors to this strange land who share the visions of Doña Barbara, the Estradas, and other enlightened ranchers, and hope for its preservation.

I add my hopes to theirs.

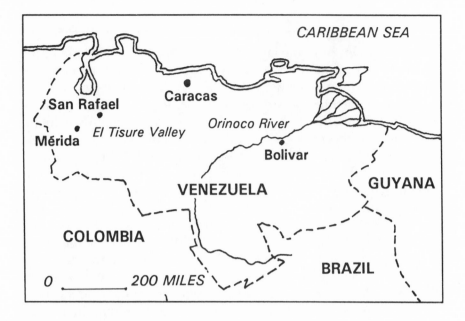

3. THE VENEZUELAN ANDES
Seeking the Hermit

The story had a certain appeal.

There was once a wise young man who was a judge and a highly respected citizen of a small town in the Andean region of Venezuela. One day in 1943 without warning he decides to dump all the honors and material benefits of a secure and prosperous life and, along with his wife, goes off over the mountain passes to a remote valley cut off from the world. There he builds a primitive house out of rocks, grows his own food, rears his own livestock, and lives a simple, silent existence.

For a long time nothing is heard of the man until tales begin to trickle down from the jagged peaks of the Sierra Nevada range to the towns of the Mérida Valley. Tales of a church he has built by himself, stone by stone, with a tall tower and bells, of wooden carvings depicting Calvary and the saints of Christendom, of beautiful rugs and cloth woven by the man on his own loom. Tales too of the man's wisdom and his kindness to occasional strangers who wander into his lonely outpost in the valley of El Tisure. Eventually his reputation as the guru of the mountains encourages arduous pilgrimages by hardy souls in need of advice and spiritual nurture. . . .

As I said, the story had a certain appeal.

I'd come to Mérida, the charming little "City of Gentlemen," a few days before in search of Venezuela's Andean grandeur and had found it in abundance. High above the narrow Spanish-flavored streets and churches of this regional capital rose the soaring Sierra peaks and ranges, snowcapped and shining in a warm spring sun. Glaciers sparkled among the arêtes of Pico Bolívar (16,427 feet), the tallest mountain in Venezuela.

I had taken the cable car (*teleferico*), the longest and highest in the world, up the slopes of Pico Espejo (15,634 feet), and gasped for elusive oxygen while photographing the mountain ranges and the statue of the Virgin of the Snows overlooking the Colombian border. I had explored the city's markets, marveled at the opulence of a wedding at the cathedral, watched Ecuadorean folksingers in the Plaza Bolívar play their strange flutes and odd-shaped guitars, heard the wild cheers of the crowd at the municipal cockfight, enjoyed the hearty—and typically inexpensive—steaks and fresh trout dinners in the city's traditional restaurants, and danced till I dropped to the sambas and tangos of Mérida's pre-Lent carnival.

But—as always—I was restless for adventure. Something different, something challenging. Something more than trinkets and travelers' souvenirs to take back home. Something with meaning and endurance.

A journey to find the hermit of El Tisure! What a fine climax to my stay in this beautiful and wild region. I needed a bit of quiet wisdom and insightfulness anyway to balance the hedonistic pace of Mérida.

So that's how I came to be sitting on this mule, under a

brilliant blue sky, heading slowly away from the Mérida Valley and climbing ever higher toward a fourteen-thousand-foot pass over the mountains and into the secret wilds beyond—the "lost world" of El Tisure.

My young bright-eyed guide Paco, always smiling (and occasionally laughing at my antics to mount and control my headstrong mule), let me saunter ahead on the stony track while he murmured softly to his own well-behaved horse and cajoled an irritable donkey carrying our supplies and equipment.

We passed the tiny stone farmhouses on the lower slopes occupied by the *minifundista*, the small landowners of the Andes. Some of the fields on the steep hillsides had been leveled in terrace fashion based on the ancient *poyos* originally constructed by the Timoto-Cuica Indians. But most were merely cleared of stones, which now formed miles of serpentine stone walls and were plowed horizontally with the contours by teams of enormous oxen. I tried to photograph them, but my mule refused to stop.

It was so good to be away from the city and among the broken treeless hills of the *paramo* uplands, swaying through sweeping pastures of yellow *frailejon* flowers, whose pale green stems and leaves were coated in white velvety fur. Venezuelans have a soft spot for the wild *paramo* and its characteristic hardy plant. They write songs and poems about it, claim dramatic medical properties, blend the pith into a kind of jam, and wrap home-churned butter and little goat cheeses in its fuzzy leaves to give them "perfume." When nothing much else grows in the high Andean ranges but spiky grasses, heather, and mosses, you have to admire its tenacity, and beauty. A hillside of golden *frailejon* flowers is a soul-warming sight.

We paused for a lunch of fruit and coarse *arepa* cornbread. I had watched Paco's mother bake the small rounds in her rock-walled kitchen in San Rafael. The tiny room had no chimney and blue smoke, cut by shafts of sunlight through a tiny window overlooking the pig pound, wraithed around our heads before slowly easing through chinks in the pantile roof. She was a small plump woman with one of those strong Indian faces that seemed to be hacked out of Andean gneiss. But when she smiled through the smoke her features immediately softened into girlish femininity. I liked her, even though I couldn't understand a word of her soft chatter. And I think she liked me too because she picked our lunch loaves very carefully, smelling each one, tapping the hard, almost black crust with her fingers before wrapping them in cheesecloth and sending us off into the hills with a blessing and a final smile.

We let the horse, the mule, and the donkey graze by a stream which tumbled over large boulders into a deep pool, clear as uncracked crystal. It was hot in the sheltered spot we'd selected for lunch, out of the valley breezes. The water was tempting, so I stripped off and plunged in.

And almost plunged right out again. The pool was virtually ice and the hot sun made it seem even colder.

Paco laughed through his mouthful of *arepa*, spraying crumbs. In his broken Spanish-English I heard him explain that the water in the stream had come from melting snow and ice fields in the mountains high up above the pass.

I tried to fake nonchalance as I splashed about, aware that my body was rapidly losing all feeling.

"It's fine, Paco. Once you get used to it, it's fine. Come on in!"

Paco shook his head and continued spraying *arepa* crumbs. But, to be honest, it *was* fine after a while. My torso emerged tingling and invigorated and I lay back in the grass to let the sun dry me, enjoying the tickling sensations as veins began to run again.

After lunch the narrow path began to rise more steeply toward a vast wall of rock that seemed to grow higher and more ominous as we guided our animals between the broken boulders. Where was the pass? I looked for an inviting cleft between the jagged mountains, but all I could see was that rock face. Surely we weren't going to clamber over that thing?

Apparently we were.

The path zigzagged across more screes of sharp rocks, descended into clefts, crossed tumbling streams, and then climbed ever higher, heading straight for what looked like the insurmountable barrier. Maybe you'd make it with ropes and pitons, but with animals and a donkey laden with packs of food and sleeping bags and cooking equipment? Crazy idea! No wonder the wise old man who'd cast off all society's trappings was known as "the hermit." He'd discovered a place well and truly shut off from the world. Well, he'd better live up to all the tales told about him. This was going to be a far harder journey than I'd first thought.

Back in Mérida, when I announced my plans to a few friends I'd made in the city, there'd been raised eyebrows, low whistles, and decidedly cynical grunts. But no one warned me I'd be climbing vertical rock faces and maybe using up yet one more of my catlike lives. They were envious. I could feel it. Maybe a little resentful that I could travel where I wished, allowing all the time needed, while they stayed home in the city living responsible, hardworking lives.

Well. It was my fault for maybe being a little too dismissive of the challenges and not doing enough background research on what I was letting myself in for. And now I could hardly change my mind. I was in it for the duration. I couldn't go back and explain that it was a more difficult journey than I'd bargained for. After all, we world wanderers (even this rather overweight one) have a certain reputation to keep. And they'd given me a wonderful farewell dinner, plied me with excellent wines, and toasted to my success. I had to succeed, for them—and for me.

So—onward and upward.

And upward and upward.

The rock wall now loomed like the Hoover Dam over us. I could see clouds across the high crags being slit to ribbons by the frost-shattered ridges.

Then the real climbing began. Surprisingly there was a path of sorts between piles of smashed rocks, but it was too steep for mule riding. We dismounted and began to drag our reluctant mounts higher and higher up the cliff face.

At eight thousand feet in San Rafael, where I'd arranged for my guide and transport, the air had been invigorating, full of the scent of flowers. Now we were around eleven thousand feet and I was aware of diminishing oxygen. My breaths were shorter and my body complained of thin air. I stopped leading the mule and let him make his own way up the narrow path. I had enough problems dragging my own weight up the steep face.

I tried not to look up. It was just too depressing to see the wall looming above me. Step—inhale—step—exhale. A slow

113

steady rhythm was best. One step after the next, allowing the hypnotic pace to reduce thought to the now and nothing more.

Paco seemed unfazed by our change of pace. He'd made this journey before and didn't mind telling me.

"This is the easy bit," he called out, grinning like an idiot.

Thank you, Paco. Just what I needed to hear.

And of course he was right. Compared to what came later, this was a country ramble.

It became colder too. The mists were beginning to creep down the rock face. The top of the pass was blocked from sight by swirling wraiths of ribboning cloud. Soon we disappeared entirely into the cloying dampness. At times I lost the path and had to clamber back over mossy boulders to find my way again.

After two hours of this I was drained of all energy. Only the mental rhythm—step, inhale, step, exhale—kept me moving ever upward. Pilgrims seeking out the lonely hermit must really be burdened with problems to make this journey. I wondered what comforts they brought back with them. Apparently Juan Felix Sanchez, for that was his name, was known to speak in elliptical wisdoms, zenlike in their simplicity—or complexity, depending on your attitude. I'd heard similar tales in Nepal of mountain-bound gurus to whom the frantic faithful flocked in search of insights and gleamings of timeless knowledge. They say you value what you struggle for. In which case this was going to be a most enlightening journey.

The rock wall was almost vertical now. Somehow the animals climbed surefooted up the serpentine path, which was only a couple of feet wide. I was puffing and wheezing like a leaky steam engine. It was only that pungent quote from Shakespeare's *Macbeth* that kept me going:

> . . . stept in so far that
> Returning were as tedious as go o'er

Paco was at the rear, still smiling and cajoling the donkey who, every few minutes, would bray out his anguish at having to carry our hefty load of food and equipment up such a ridiculously steep path.

Upward and upward; thirteen thousand feet and still climbing.

We were now totally smothered in the mist. Nothing existed outside the pounding of my heart, the rasp of my oxygen-starved lungs, and the scratch of boots on hard rock.

Upward and upward.

Surely we must be near the top of the pass by now. It was getting darker. My watch told me it was six-thirty P.M., too late to make it down the other side in safety. That meant a night on the mountain. Not a welcome thought. We'd obviously set out on the journey too late in the day. Paco had warned me about this, but I'd ignored him in my enthusiasm for getting started. An enthusiasm that had now diminished to surly resentment at the fickleness of these mountains.

Then suddenly all my mumbling and grumbling ceased as a blast of frigid wind tore at my wet parka and almost sent me tumbling backward down the rock wall. My eyes were reduced to narrow slits and I could see nothing in front of me except slabs of ice-coated rock. But at least they were horizontal slabs, not vertical. Like a graveyard of fallen headstones. The top of the pass!

There was little time or enthusiasm for rejoicing. We both pulled our hoods tightly around our faces and tried to take shelter behind a boulder as the wind and clouds tore past us.

Paco had to shout to make himself heard in the maelstrom.

"Welcome to La Ventana—"the place of the winds"! We go down a little way. Find somewhere out of the wind. Make camp." Then he added ominously. "This is not good. We leave too late."

Yes, Paco, I know. And it was my fault.

The animals sensed our moroseness. They too knew things had gone wrong and made odd whinnying noises, beginning the descent warily, placing their feet delicately on the loose icy rocks of the path.

Fortunately, as we moved lower, the wind dropped. By nine-thirty P.M. we had found a sheltered spot in a rough circle of tumbled boulders and agreed to stop and spend the night. There were patches of brittle grass and *frailejon*, so at least the animals would have something to eat. We untied the packs and pulled the rolled sleeping bags off the shivering little donkey.

"You want some soup?" asked Paco.

"Great idea," I think I said as we both scrambled into our waterproof sleeping bags, but I don't remember anything else. Maybe Paco cooked and drank some soup, but I was already asleep, cocooned in duck down and dreaming of those long, leisurely dinners I'd enjoyed with my friends back in the cozy candlelit restaurants of Mérida that now seemed so far away. . . .

Sometime in the middle of the night I awoke briefly. It was still very cold, but there was no wind and no cloud. The black sky was a vast scattering of stars. The moon shone between the peaks of the mountains, silvering their summits. The silence buzzed in my ears. Only the soft breathing of Paco huddled in his sleeping bag reminded me of where I was and what I was doing.

Dawn came as a fanfare: sudden surges of peach and amber across the layered ranges. Far below, the tangled valleys were filled with lavender mists.

Paco was already up, hunched over the butane stove trying to boil water for coffee (almost an impossibility at fourteen thousand feet). The animals looked fine, heads down, munching on the ice-flecked grasses. The sun rose rapidly; dun-colored hills turned bronze and the whole mountain panorama beckoned us to move on, deeper into this lost world of the Venezuelan Andes.

The descent was slow and difficult. Ice still coated the narrow path and we moved cautiously on the slippery rocks. But our spirits were different now. The worse had been overcome and we knew that somewhere down there, deep in one of the valleys, was a house, shelter, a place to cook a decent meal—and Juan Felix Sanchez.

Finally we saw the house, a rambling structure of black rock topped by sections of tin roof set against a hillside of wild bushes. There were no other buildings, no other sign of human habitation anywhere in that vast sweep of valleys and mountains. But curls of blue smoke, easing out from under the roof (no chimneys once again), made the place seem friendly, beckoning.

116

As we approached we noticed small rock shrines, one in the shape of a cross, one a tiny chapel the size of a doll's house set by a swirling stream. We crossed the stream lower down and dismounted on a pasture of close-cropped grass at the side of the house. A cock crowed. A dog barked. Other than that there was no noise at all.

"They will be inside," said Paco.

We crossed a second stream by way of a bridge of broad stone slabs and entered a dusty corral. Ahead of us a doorway led through to an enclosed courtyard. A couple of oddly shaped benches stood by the one outer wall of the house, pieced together from wood planks supported by sections of twisted branches. On a low plank table lay two clay bas-reliefs. The clay was still moist and someone had left them to dry in the sun. The figures were crudely shaped, but it was obvious that they depicted two scenes from the stations of the cross.

We entered a dark room built of black rock. Thin strands of sunlight filtered through chinks between the unmortared joints. Still nobody.

Paco pointed to a thick wooden door to our left. It was slightly ajar and smoke trickled out. We pushed it open and entered a smoky room entirely without sunlight and lit only by a smoldering fire. At first I could see nothing. My eyes hadn't adjusted from the sear of sunlight outside. Paco eased past me and moved toward the fire. There were grunts of recognition and then he was speaking quietly—almost reverently—and stooping to greet someone beyond the flames. A figure rose up, small and hunched. Another figure remained seated in the shadows. I eased forward across the earth floor. A hand—warm and rough-skinned—reached out. I saw a dark smiling face and a magnificent silver mustache. Eyes sparkled in the glow of the fire.

"I am Juan Felix Sanchez. You are welcome." He spoke Spanish in a slow gravelly voice. His hand gently squeezed mine and led me to a bench by the fire.

"Sit down. You will have some tea."

At the mention of tea, the second figure arose.

"This is Epifania. She will make tea for you."

I think Epifania smiled, but it was hard to tell with her face half hidden behind the shawl. She shuffled across the floor to

117

bring two cups and then filled them from an enormous black kettle on the fire.

Whatever was in that odd-tasting brew worked its magic. Within minutes I felt relaxed and refreshed. All the aches in my bones after that cold night on the mountain eased away. It was time to get to know my hosts.

The conversation was slow, punctuated by periods of friendly silence as we all sipped together. Juan had obviously greeted many curious visitors to his remote retreat over the years and I was doubtless asking the same tedious questions as everyone else. But he answered quietly and politely as I tried to piece together the history of his unusual life.

As I'd been told in Mérida, he had left behind his important title as president of the community council and all the trappings of a prosperous legal career back in the San Rafael Valley. Along with his dogs, bed supplies, seeds, a container of fingerling trout to stock his own trout pond, some livestock, and a devoted wife, he had moved into the El Tisure Valley in 1943 and, except for a few rare occasions, had never ventured away from his simple home in almost fifty years.

"There was no reason to go anywhere," he murmured softly. "Everything was here."

The house had grown amoebalike over the years from a tiny shepherd's shelter to this warrenlike complex of rooms and court-yards. On an upper level reached by a crude ladder made from tree branches he had built his own loom and wove his own rugs and thick cloth. Occasionally outsiders would come and stay to help him in the slow extension of his home, but usually it was just Juan and Epifania building the place together, rock by rock, over the years.

At one point as he talked he quoted something I couldn't quite understand. I asked him to repeat it and Paco translated:

> The dead are not those who
> rest in a cold tomb:
> The dead ones are those who
> have dead souls
> and continue to live.

"Did you write that?" I asked.

Juan suddenly started chuckling and spilled his tea over his stained trousers.

"No, no. That is on the gate of a cemetery in Mérida. I remember reading it when I was a boy. But it is very true—yes?"

We laughed and nodded.

"Were there many dead souls in San Rafael? Is that why you left?"

Juan smiled and shrugged. As I later realized, he rarely answered questions directly.

"A soul is all you have," he said. "Everything else is . . . " he shrugged again and left the sentence unfinished.

By late afternoon I was sitting with Juan on an old wooden bench set against the corral wall outside his home. We were both drinking an herb tea of some kind prepared by Epifania. She was a shy woman whose face was always partially hidden by the shawl draped over her head and held in place by a broad-brimmed straw hat.

The sun was still bright and hot, burning my face as we laid our heads back against the wall and watched the chickens peck in the dust of the corral. On the hillside in front of us our horse, mule, and donkey nibbled happily on fresh green pasture. Behind them a waterfall tumbled off rock ledges into a series of cool dark pools before becoming a stream again, chittering away behind us.

I turned to look at Juan. His eyes were closed now. A bushy walruslike mustache hung down on either side of his mouth, which curved up slightly in a smile that never seemed to vanish. His dark brown skin was lined and leathery, his chin fuzzy with a silver stubble of unshaved hair. For a man in his eighties he had the face of a mischievous boy—part cherub, part imp. His two pet parrots, bright green with red markings, cackled at one another while nibbling on a pile of sunflower seeds left by Epifania. There was a peace about the place and I was glad to be here.

* * *

When Juan awoke I began to ask him about his church built on a hillside a short walk from the house, but he seemed to grow impatient.

"Have you been there?" he asked.

"No, not yet. We've only just arrived."

"Well, go first. Then we talk."

Paco leaned over and whispered, "Sometimes what he does not say is more important than what he says."

Oh, boy. The zen was beginning.

It came again when I asked if I could see some of his weaving.

"You can see my weaving if you can see my weaving," he replied. Then he laughed, spilling tea again, and reached across to touch my knee. "You are a good man, Señor David. A good man."

Paco looked pleased at the remark, which seemed to have no epigrammatic whiplash. I held his hand. "I like you too, Juan."

More laughs and choking. Then his face turned serious and he said quietly, "I will tell you a story."

Paco leaned forward. Epifania was nearby but, as seemed to be her custom, said nothing.

Juan coughed and spat, then began.

"There was a man, a good man of the mountains—a hermit—who had an angel for a friend. Every day, at the hour of prayer, the angel would come to greet him and they would walk together. If the man needed advice the angel would give it to him, and before he left he would always remind the man to go out to do an act of charity every day. The man obeyed and was known and loved by everyone he met for his kindness.

"One day, when the man was walking on a path in the mountains, he saw two soldiers with a third man tied up like a prisoner. 'Why is this man tied up?' asked the kind man.

" 'He has done wrong. The law has sentenced him to be hanged.'

"The man of the mountains asked if the prisoner could be released, but the soldiers refused. The man then said, 'He who does it pays for it.'

"The soldiers placed a strong stick between the branches of two trees and hanged the prisoner.

"That night at the hour of prayer the angel did not appear

to the man of the mountains and he was very sad. The same the next day, and the next.

"Then on the next day after that the angel came to him and the man asked him why he had not appeared on the three days before. 'What you did was a bad thing. You said to the soldiers who were going to hang the prisoner, "He who does it pays for it." You did not give advice to the men. Instead you said "He who does it pays for it" and for that God will chastise you.'

"The poor man of the mountains was very sad. 'Does that mean that I will not be saved?'

"The angel replied: 'You must go now and remove the man who has been hanged. Bury him. Take the stick they hanged him on, place it on your shoulder, and everywhere you go you must take it with you. Whenever you sleep place the stick by your head and when the stick becomes alive with flowers, you will be saved.'

"The little man—the hermit—was very sad but obeyed the angel. He took down the body. He buried the man and carried the stick with him every day—everywhere he walked—on his shoulder. At night, every night, he put the stick at his head, hoping that it would come alive in the morning with flowers."

Juan paused in the middle of the narrative. Epifania filled his cup with more tea and he drank slowly. There was something in the way he told the tale that made it seem personal. I was tempted to ask but was learning to cut the questions and just listen.

Soon he began again.

"After becoming very old the hermit still carried the stick with him and slept with it next to his head every night. Then one stormy night, when he was very far from his home in a wild part of the mountains, he saw a small house. He was in need of shelter and in the house was an old woman. The man said, 'Señora—please do me a favor and let me stay here for the night in your house.'

"Many times the woman refused, but the man begged, 'I am old and very tired. I will sleep anywhere.'

"Still the woman refused and said, 'I have two sons who are thieves. If they see you here they will kill you.'

"But the man was too weary to go farther and told the woman the story of his punishment and the stick he must carry. 'Let me stay,' he said again. 'Whatever happens will happen.' Finally the woman did not say no anymore and he found a place in the stable and put his stick in the corner against the wall.

"When the sons came back to the house they sensed the man was there and were going to kill him. But the woman said they must not, and she told them the tale. She said that there was something strange about the man and his punishment.

" 'God is watching him,' she warned them, and the sons were alarmed.

" 'Only for that small wrong God is punishing him for so long? What punishment will we have to endure, then? We have killed many people!'

"That night the sons repented of their terrible crimes and the following morning went to see the hermit. But the hermit was dead and his stick, leaning against the wall of the stable, was alive and full of flowers. The sons were saved that day because they repented. And that is my story."

There was a long silence.

Paco had been quietly translating the long slow tale in case I missed some of its subtleties. (I've tried to write it down as it was told, but even now I'm not sure I understand all its meanings.) I watched Juan's face, hoping he'd explain more about the story and why he'd chosen to tell it to us. Was it somehow about him—about his life? Maybe about his one-time position as a judge? Was he the hermit? Had he lost his angel somewhere along his life? Or had he found something else? Had his stick flowered? . . .

The questions kept bouncing around my head, but I now realized that Juan was unlikely to answer them. In the true spirit of zen, you find your own answers.

As it grew darker we thanked Juan and Epifania for their hospitality and left to prepare our meal in the courtyard. They both smiled and Juan murmured something quietly to Paco.

"He says we can sleep in the room off the courtyard. There are bamboo beds. And we can stay as long as we wish. He wants you to go and see his church tomorrow.

After dinner (a remarkably unmemorable mush of a meal) I went to check out the beds in the dark room off the courtyard. Like much of the house the walls were monolithic creations of unmortared stone through which the cold night air whistled. The bed was constructed of sections of tree trunk and the raised sleeping platform consisted of thin strips of bamboo placed close together and covered with a few goat and cow hides. Paco seemed quite happy with the accommodation, but I found the utter blackness of the room oppressive and decided to spend another night out in the open.

I found a small hollow covered in soft pasture turf close to the waterfall behind the house. It was cold, but the sky once again was a vast panoply of brilliant stars. Slipping on an extra pair of trousers and second shirt under my parka, I snuggled down in the waterproof sleeping bag and lay back, listening to the night breezes in the bushes.

My mind dabbled with the intricacies of infinity. Stars do that to me. Those constant patternings of sparkle-matter—the same patterns that have intrigued astronomers down the ages—suggest permanence, stability, and balance. As two-dimensional designs they fascinate—but as three- and four-dimensional actualities they tear at the edges of a finite mind, invoking a kind of momentary madness. No wonder the ancients preferred the concept of a flat earth and used ridiculous logical contortions to prove that the earth, sun, and moon were the focus of the universe. How they must have resented the conflicting mathematical evidence of other realities—larger, mind-bending actualities.

And now, today, when we know that we're nothing but specks of matter in an inconceivably vast infinity of random chaos, how do we place ourselves? How do we find meaning within our little finite minds, so easily boondoggled by an act as simple as looking at stars? How do we relate big bangs, expanding and contracting universes, antimatter, parallel realities, and all the implications of $E = MC^2$, to our day-to-day lives full of petty concerns, hopes, frustrations, all ending inevitably in death? How do we keep a faith in any ultimate meaning and purpose when all around us, every day, are these overwhelming reminders of our apparent insignificance? Does Juan have answers for these kinds of questions?

Casting off all the tempting diversions of life as he had done—prosperity, power, status, community, sensual pleasures—is certainly one way to clear the mind and the spirit for deeper perceptions and insights. But does it lead merely to a more sophisticated definition of unanswerables? Or is there really a mind behind matter, order within chaos, a nonmaterial spiritual reality of which we are all part?

A short film I saw years ago dabbled with the actuality of infinity—both inner and outer. Beginning with the hand of a bather on a beach somewhere, the film simulated first an outer journey of 10 to the power of 10, leading the viewer from a place ten inches above the bather's hand (10 to the power of 1), to 100 inches (10 to the power of 2), and so on until at 10 to the power of 10 we vanished into a virtual infinity of endless space. Then the same journey was undertaken inward, into the hand itself, down through the pores, into the spaces between cells, then into whirling molecules, then between the particles of molecules, and on and on until at 10 to the power of 10 we disappeared into the infinities of inner space—equally deep, equally as intangible as the outer universe itself.

The film lasted ten minutes or so—it was a short documentary for schoolchildren, I believe—but the images and its impact have remained with me for years. The idea of everything we perceive possessing the same fathomless infinities—everything interconnected in endlessness—was both alarming and comforting at the same time. The film didn't try to suggest any spiritual significance to its revelations. We each have to figure that out for ourselves, I suppose. But for me, it gave stargazing a whole new dimension and here I was once again under those same stars, cocooned in my cozy sleeping bag, letting the possibilities pulsate through my sleepy brain.

Which suddenly wasn't so sleepy anymore.

Something was out there moving about in the grass. A dark thing, keeping low to the ground among the faint moon shadows. And it was coming my way, toward my comfortable hollow by the waterfall. I never thought to ask Juan or Paco about night creatures in this lonely silent valley. Wolves? Coyotes? Do they exist in Venezuela? I knew there were jaguars way down in the plains of Los Llanos, but what about up here in the wilds of the Andes?

The thing kept coming. Larger and darker than before. I reached out to find a stone or something to scare it away, but all I had were my boots. Well—better than nothing. I eased up slowly to a sitting position and prepared to aim . . . and then was greeted by a gentle *woof*, a wagging tail, and a wet nose nuzzling my beard. It was one of Juan's dogs, curious about this stranger who preferred to sleep out in the cold rather than on a perfectly comfortable bamboo bed.

I stroked its head and it gave a little whining noise. Maybe it was hungry. I groped around in my bag and found a bar of chocolate. It vanished in two bites. I lay back again and the dog decided to join me, stretching full length against my side. It was a lovely sensation. I forgot about the infinities and all those unanswerable imponderables. A friendly dog was just what I needed. So what if it was, just like me, a walking universe of endless space. It was a tactile, warm, and furry universe—and a fine sleeping companion.

Juan, wearing a traditional wool ruana cloak, joined Paco and me for coffee in the courtyard as the sun rose over the mountains, burning off stray strands of morning mist. We had just finished washing ourselves in the stream and were still tingling and flush-faced from the icy water.

"Paco tells me that you are an artist," Juan said.

"Well—I do a lot of sketching."

"Can you do faces? People faces?" he asked.

"Yes. I enjoy sketching faces."

There was silence. We sipped the strong coffee and I knew he'd left a dangling question.

"Juan—I would like to sketch you and give it to you as a gift."

I'd obviously said the right thing. His leathery face buckled into a hundred creases and furrows and he chuckled.

"That would be very good. I will fetch my hat."

He returned wearing a stained, weather-bashed straw hat decorated with a broad band of woven cloth in once-bright reds and indigos.

"Did you weave that band yourself?" I asked.

He smiled and nodded. "And the hat. I made the hat. Many years ago."

He chose to remain silent and serious as I sketched. Doves cooed, chickens scratched in the dust of the corral. Our donkey bellowed out a greeting to the morning from the hillside above us and Paco watched entranced as the lines coalesced into a face on the sketch pad.

I decided to draw him just the way he was, with his ragged mustache, unshaven chin, and big watery eyes. I wanted to capture his kindness, his wisdom, his sureness of purpose, and his amazing endurance for almost five decades in this remote hideaway. I think I managed some of the above and gave the drawing to him.

He looked at it thoughtfully for a long time. Maybe I'd been a little too honest with the sketch. Maybe he was hoping for something different, less face lines maybe, less of the scrubby beard.

He lifted himself up from the bench without a word and went inside the house. Paco looked perplexed. Had I offended the man in some way? That can be a problem when you sketch people's portraits. You never really know how they see themselves and I'd never learned the street artists' clever techniques for graphic flattery.

He returned shortly, without the sketch and without his hat, and sat down on the bench. He asked to use my sketch pad and my pen. I gave them to him.

Slowly—very slowly—in a shaking hand—he began to write something on paper. I think he had arthritis in his fingers. Each letter seemed to be a struggle. But then he came to the final signing of his name and let go with a grand flourish of filigree lines that resembled some of the more elaborate signatures on the Declaration of Independence. He handed the pad and pen back to me and I could barely make out the words in Spanish. Paco seemed to have less problems and translated a very flattering—and very moving—statement. I think I blushed. Juan obviously liked his sketch and according to his message our friendship would be "eternal as heaven."

Then he dipped into a pocket of his torn jacket and brought out a shard of dark rock. He asked for my hand and placed it gently in my palm.

"This is a piece from the first stone of my church. Keep this to remember me."

I nodded and thanked him.

"And now," he said, smiling again, "I would like you to go and see my church and come back and talk with me again."

Which was exactly what I had planned to do.

Paco decided to stay behind and help Juan with some rock-lifting project (yet one more extension to the house?) so I walked over the pasture and across the stream alone. On the far side of the narrow valley a path climbed the hillside between more bright patches of *frailejon* flowers. The air off the mountains was crisp and fresh. I carried Juan's little piece of stone in my pocket and felt as frisky as a fawn in that blue and gold morning.

I was repressing all thoughts of the return journey over the dreadful La Ventana and enjoying the easy uphill walk. As I moved higher the vistas opened up like a huge diorama—range after range of mountains purpling with distance, more sinewy valleys disappearing into morning mists. What a wonderful land Juan had found for his life! A little lost world untouched by anything except the elements and his own enduring spirit. In the rush, rigor, and hype of modern-day life we need all the Juans we can find to remind us of other possibilities, other perspectives.

The church came suddenly, around a bend in the track, perched on the edge of an alarming drop into the next valley. It sat, squat and compact, in bold stone simplicity on a sloping site, shaded by wind-shaped conifers. A twenty-foot-high stone tower with a belfry rose up beside the main door. In front was a tall cross decorated, Gaudi-like, in fragments of pebbles, pottery, and glass. Small shrines and memorials to individuals known and admired by Juan filled the space between the church and the high stone retaining wall by the path.

I entered through a narrow gate and climbed the steps to the church. The blue-painted iron door squeaked open. At first it seemed very dark, but as my eyes adapted to the glimmer of filtered sunlight, I found myself in a long, narrow space about thirty feet long bound by more bare stone walls and with a sloping flagstone floor leading to an altar. A few chairs and benches made from more of those twisted branches and stumps so loved by Juan lined the walls. An enormous font, hollowed from a boulder, stood on a stone plinth decorated by chips of colored rock.

The power of the little church lay in its simplicity. It seemed to have grown directly out of the earth itself. For year after year,

127

from 1952 to 1970, Juan and Epifania had built this place and its tower rock by rock and dedicated it to the Virgin of Coromoto. It's hard to imagine the energy, the sweat, the back-snapping toil that went into such an effort. And yet the church exuded a spirit of calm, peace, and effortlessness. In the same way that the great pyramids seem to deny the agony and the superhuman labor that went into their construction by their overwhelming purity of form, so here the clarity of Juan's vision suppressed all thoughts of the personal struggle during its creation.

Light filtered through a section of transparent roofing material and bathed the altar in gold. In contrast to the starkness of the nave, here was a compact riot of symbolic objects and colorful ornaments. An old car headlight set in the wall above peered down like an eye of God. A tracery of rosaries and religious pendants dangled over the three-stepped levels of the altar. Fresh flowers in clay pots (who had placed them there?) filled most of the first level, followed by tiny religious statues and postcards on the second, and candles, miniatures of Christ, the Madonna, and the saints, and more flowers on the third. Every level was filled with objects; there was no room for anything else.

I sat on the cold flagstones at the base of the altar for a long time. I'm not a religious person in any formal sense, but Juan's little church touched something inside me. Maybe it was the sureness—the certainty—of his own faith. Surrounded by all this evidence of his labor and his love, I felt a certain diffuseness, an uncenteredness, in my own ramblings and meanderings. While opposed to dogma and "only one answer" diatribes in all their multifaceted forms, I maybe am drawn a little too much into the gentle anarchy of my own life, avoiding spiritual commitment, sacrificing focus for the exploration of open-ended possibilities and alternatives. Most times I am content to play with the options, but once in a while, when faced with something as strong and moving as this place, well, I begin to wonder. . . .

And there was more wonder to come.

I opened the door of the church and stepped out into—nothing! The earth had vanished. Everything was pure white light. No mountains, no valleys, no trees—nothing but light. I blinked. It was cloud. Bright white cloud filling the valley and blocking out everything. Apparently a regular occurrence in this strange place, but I didn't know that then.

I wandered up the hill behind the church, carefully following the narrow path. The cloud whirled around me blown by a strong wind. Then figures began to emerge, dwarf-sized and hunched among the *frailejon*—wooden figures, carved with boldness out of the limbs and trunks of pine trees. Juan's "Calvary"!

I continued to climb up the path. The figures had an eerie quality but there was grace and life in their crudely shaped features. Juan had a knack of giving tactile existence to lifeless chunks of wood. And nowhere was that more evident than on the three huge crosses that suddenly reared out of the mist at the top of the hill. This was his Golgotha—his shrine to the suffering of Christ, impaled by nails on a cross. His head, bound by the crown of thorns, hung loosely on his breast, looking down at his mother kneeling by the base. On either side, on smaller crosses, were the two criminals who died with Christ, their outstretched arms lashed by ropes to the horizontal beams.

It was an overwhelmingly powerful creation. Even in the rough-hewn figures you could sense the agony of death and the grief of the mourners on the rock-strewn ground below the crosses. Behind the figures, Juan and Epifania had formed a pile of broken boulders to emphasize the remoteness and isolation of Golgotha.

I shivered in the swirling mists. The place had far more impact than all those realistic blood- and gore-stained Christ figures I'd seen in Venezuelan Catholic churches. I could sense the agony and the horror of the artist himself expressed in these primitive figures. Juan must have felt those nails through his own hands.

Then something very odd began to happen. As I stared at the tortured faces and the hands of Christ outstretched in agony, the mists began to clear and sunlight touched the crosses and piled boulders. Within a couple of minutes the hill was bathed in a brilliant afternoon light; the carved wooden bodies turned from a dead gray to a rich resin bronze. The place no longer seemed threatening and full of misery. There was a sense of new life now, new vigor in the figures—a resurrection in sunlight!

The cynical, agnostic part of my brain rebelled at such thoughts. I could sense it chuckling at the naïveté of this often

FÉLIX SANCHEZ
g His SHRINE
the Merida Andes
VENEZUELA

confused individual, moved almost to tears by a trick of fickle microclimate—the sudden presence of warmth and light in the midst of a chilly cloudbound afternoon. All the tangled thoughts of my night under the stars came rolling back, trying to reduce the impact of the moment to the insignificance of over-emotiveness and a passing hysteria.

But as I left the hill and the little stone church, something remained with me . . .

The days eased by in El Tisure and I spent time with Juan sitting quietly in his sunlit corral, sometimes talking, sometimes silent.

I remember one strange and moving incident. During one of our long silences in the shade of the corral wall, I fell asleep and dreamed. The dream ended as abruptly as it had begun. I found I was crying. Big, hot tears were squeezing between my closed eyes and rolling down my cheeks.

I opened my eyes and saw Juan looking at me and smiling. "I'm sorry. I had a dream."

"Yes. It was a very good dream," Juan said.

He didn't ask me. He told me.

"Yes it was. It reminded me of something—somebody—I keep forgetting."

"Yes."

"My father," I said. Those damned tears kept on rolling.

"Yes."

"He was a good man. Like you. He cared about so many things . . ."

Juan nodded as if he knew more than I wanted to tell him.

I tried to laugh. "Wow—that was something. I haven't thought about him for a long time—far too long."

Juan smiled and, once again, he reminded me so much of the father I loved—the kind, vulnerable, wise man behind the stern-father mask.

"He was a good man," Juan said.

"Yes he was—how do you know?"

He laughed quietly as if the answer was so obvious it hardly needed saying: "Because you are his son."

132

Then he leaned over, squeezed my hand and repeated the phrase—"because you are his son."

Looking back I wish I could have learned more from the man but as he said in one of his indirect responses to yet another of my questions—"You can only learn what you already know. When you know all that you have always known, the learning is done."

I often think of his soft laughter and of that hidden valley way back in the Venezuelan Andes. Maybe one day, when all our travelings are done, Anne and I will find our own El Tisure, our own timeless place of focus and freedom. If we do, we'll take something of Juan Felix Sanchez with us—his smile, and that shard of stone from his little shrine in those remote mountains.

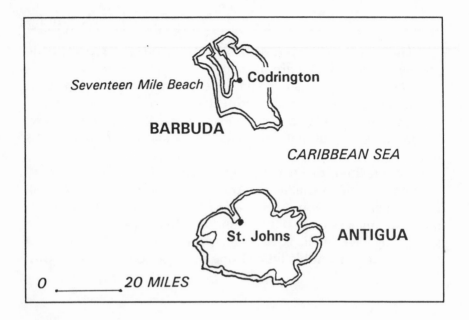

4. BARBUDA
All Alone in Paradise

I had decided to take a couple of weeks off from world wandering and adventuring and fly down to Antigua for a little laid-back lollygagging. But Antigua was beginning to pall.

Now, don't get me wrong. I've got nothing against Antigua. In fact, I have dear friends who live there and who took great pains to show me the delights of their Caribbean island, including visits to more lovely beaches than I really wanted to see. "One for every day of the year," they boasted. After a fourth day of beach-hopping I believed them.

Of course it wasn't all beaches. We strolled the old waterfront streets of the capital Saint Johns, visited the teeming Sunday market, ate delicious island concoctions at palm-shaded restaurants, and admired the island's exclusive and ultra-expensive resort enclaves. We also spent a frenzied Sunday afternoon of reggae and dancing on the windy hilltop of Shirley Heights overlooking the historic Nelson's Dockyard and the blue-hazed outlines of St. Kitts-Nevis and Montserrat out in the turquoise ocean. I watched a cricket match featuring Antigua's most beloved citizen, Viv Richards, played the ancient African game of warri with the locals, became embroiled in furious rum-laced debates with the editor of a radical island newspaper, and visited with a "family" of agrarian Rastas living a marijuana-laced life in a secluded valley, well away from the tourist beaches.

But after a week or so of all this activity I was ready for something different, something slower-paced, something that needed a backpack and little else.

Then someone whispered to me about tiny Barbuda.

I hadn't realized that Antigua had a sister-island about twenty-five miles to the north. (More of a stepsister, actually, almost ignored by her large and well-endowed sibling.) A place with hardly more than a thousand residents—untouched, unspoiled, unincorporated into the maelstrom of modern-day enigmas that impact Antigua. A Robinson Crusoe paradise where I might discover what the Caribbean looked like and felt like before the twentieth century came carousing in, cluttering quiet coves with condos, releasing plagues of package-tour promoters and Fantasy Island resort developers. A little lost world, here in the heart of the Caribbean. Something I'd not expected.

It was so good to be on the ocean in a small boat bouncing across the choppy waves under a cloudless blue sky. I was the only passenger and Sam "Frigatebird" Jackson, the skipper, gave me snippets of Barbuda history during our three-hour journey.

"You won't think it once y'see it—it's only a tiny place, 'bout twenty miles tip to toe—but it's got a history long as a frigate bird's wings."

"I meant to ask you, Sam—why do they call you Frigatebird?"

"Ah—you jus' wait 'n' see. I'm not going to be tellin' you everythin' before we gets there. This ain't no ordinary place an' you got to take it in gradual—like drinkin' strong punch."

I liked the man already. He must have been in his sixties, with his crinkled face a dark rich mahogany color and a substantial belly that overhung his bleached jeans and strained every stitch of his pale blue T-shirt.

"So—'bout this place's history. They all tried to tame it like all the other islands—the British and the French. Tried to plant their plantations 'n 'all that in the 1600s. But it wouldn't take. Couldn't get it goin' right 'cause of them Carib tribes. They were real mighty men, those Caribs. Didn't like people comin' in and claiming their land—even though tha's what they done to the people that lived here before they came. Got rid of them pretty fast—the Caribs just came in and took what they wanted. Sometimes they stayed. Sometimes they moved on. But the Europeans, they always came back and 'round 'bout 1680—after King Charles II leased the island to this family called Codrington for 'one fatted sheep a year'—they attacked with six war canoes and chopped up most of Codrington's men and messed up all the plantations."

"So that's why the island is so untouched today?"

"Hey—wait a minute. We not started yet. There's plenty more. Those British settlers don't give up so easy. Few years later they were back again and the Codringtons built themselves a castle, this time on a hill—th' only hill Barbuda's got—and started breedin' slaves for their Antigua sugar fields. You heard of them slave stock farms before, ain't you?"

I suppose I had, but it's not a part of British colonial history that I like to dwell on, so I mumbled something incoherent and Sam continued.

"Well—then the French decided it was their turn and came in 'round 1710 and blew up the castle and took all the slaves. I tell you, these were wild days 'round this part of the Caribbean. All the stuff people get upset about now—y'know, all that government shenanigans stuff and all the fuss about too much development?—tha's tame compared to what went on here two hundred, three hundred years ago. Even after the French got kicked out there were plagues of smallpox, then some Englishman tried to set up his own little kingdom here, then there were slave riots and problems with the Codringtons' lease, and then came the War of Independence in the USA and the Americans stopped trading with the British West Indies and everybody was going bankrupt. I tell you, this place might look like paradise, but it was a hellhole for a hundred years or so. Then the British tried to give it away and when nobody would take it they said Antigua had to look after it and that's the way it still is—Antigua and Barbuda—one country but two different places. Real different."

And how right he was. This little lost world in the middle of one of the earth's most intensively developed tourist regions is the epitome of peace and apartness. Long, low vistas of unbroken, unpeopled beaches greeted us as we sailed north through Gravenor Bay, past the ruins of an old stone martello defense tower built as a rather ineffective bastion against the French, and then up alongside the long sandbar separating Codrington Lagoon from the ocean. Over a hundred wrecks are recorded in the shoals and reefs around the island. It is a treasure hunters' paradise (Mel Fischer has been here numerous times with his treasure-hunting expeditions) and ideal for scuba diving, except most scuba divers don't even know the place exists.

Entering the lagoon at its northern tip near Goat Point was a tricky business and Sam was unusually silent as he nudged his small boat through the ever-changing curlicues of sand banks and channels and patches of sharp coral heads.

Mangroves rioted along the low shorelines and behind them lay a ragtag mass of palms and thick jungly undergrowth that rose to a hazy series of limestone hills known as the Highlands.

The ocean breezes had stilled and it was hot as we edged southward down the widening channel into Codrington Lagoon. There was no sign anywhere of activity. It was almost as though we'd entered our own uncharted island and had the place all to ourselves—surely an impossibility in the Caribbean. And when Sam suggested we "stop off an' get some beer in town" my worst fears were awakened.

"Town! What town?"

"Codrington. Just a couple of miles down."

I shouldn't have worried. "Town" consisted of a post office, a police station, and a few pastel-shaded tin-roofed shacks hidden in the low scrub.

"That's the town?"

"Yeah," said Sam, "that's all there is. But there'll be some beer around somewhere."

"There's no other place on the island. Just this?"

"That's it. There's people living and gardening back in a

ways, but there's less than a thousand folks on Barbuda and you likely won't see a one of them."

Codrington seemed deserted, but Sam managed to find some beer at a friend's house and we sat in the shade of palms over-looking the lagoon. Behind us was a riot of flowering bushes—bougainvillea, red ginger, hibiscus, frangipani.

After a while Sam said, "Y'asked me about my name—Frigatebird. You want to see why they call me that?"

"Sure."

Half an hour later we were easing across the main lagoon toward the mangrove swamp northwest of "town." Sam was grinning. "These birds are real beautiful."

"What birds?"

"Jus' hold on," he said, "till we get 'round into the small lagoon."

We left the open water behind us and entered a strange, silent world of thick mangroves and narrow channels bounded by reeds. It was hot now; the tradewind breezes were blocked by the dense vegetation and our T-shirts were quickly drenched once again in sweat. Sam was pointing and whispering, "You see 'em now?"

What I'd taken to be puffy white flowers among the mangrove bushes slowly became faces—lovely down-covered faces with sil-ver-gray beaks and calm, curious eyes. Scores of them, watching us as we edged closer to the marshy shore.

"You can tell the male birds. Look for the red balloons."

"The what?"

"The red balloons—they puff up those red pouches over their necks. Like balloons. Gets the lady birds crazy when they're mat-ing."

I saw them now, among the deep green of the mangrove leaves, lots of bright red "balloons" all blown up for our benefit.

As we floated closer to the nests I expected commotion, panic, and a great flurry of wings. But nothing happened. The birds just sat there, bobbing their heads as if in greeting, and watching us with those lovely quiet eyes.

"Ain't they something," said Sam.

"I've never seen birds so tame," I whispered.

"They got no reason to be feared. Don't see many folks out

138

here. And they don't taste so good—so no one shoots 'em. They just let 'em be."

We paused within six feet of a nesting group. I snapped away with my camera and they continued to nod appreciatively.

"Now watch this," said Sam as he eased himself slowly out of the boat and into the shallow water. The birds turned to observe him but made no other movements as he crept slowly toward a nest, now only a yard or so away. He was making a low clicking sound that seemed to intrigue the birds. They stretched out their long necks as if to greet him.

It was magic to watch as he slowly extended an arm and began to stroke the soft white feathers of a male frigate bird's head. Gradually his hands slid down the neck and rested on the top of the coffee-brown and black wing feathers. I watched the bird's eyes. They were still calm—almost sleepy—as Sam stroked downward toward the tips of the wings. Then, very gently, he began to stretch out the wings themselves. They seemed to unfurl like umbrellas until, fully outstretched, they were a good six feet from tip to tip. The other birds stared, curious but unconcerned, as Sam began to lift the creature by its wings out of the down-covered nest. Its dainty white webbed feet hung unprotestingly against the broad vee of its dark tail feathers.

I was so amazed I almost forgot to photograph the process. Sam was still making those soft clicking noises and I felt an urge to giggle. I had never seen such a trusting relationship between a man and wild creature before. We get so used to the fear and timidity shown by animals and birds that we accept it as a normal state. But we're wrong. Surely this is the true state—a state of trust and mutual confidence in a place where fear has not yet been introduced.

Sam lowered the bird gently back into the nest, slid back to the boat, and smiled.

"Now—ain't that something," he whispered.

"I don't believe you did that."

He laughed softly. "If the chicks had been around like in early spring, it mighta been harder. They get a bit edgy when the youngsters come. But they fine now."

He was silent for a while, still touched by a place he knew so well. Then he added: "An' you should see 'em fly. They go up soaring—up to two thousand feet and more. . . . Lord, they so beautiful."

And, as if in agreement, five males blew their red balloons simultaneously while the females nodded their downy white heads.

We floated deeper and deeper into the mangroves and saw hundreds more frigate birds, all equally tame and unconcerned by our presence.

"Sam, this is a wonderful place."

Sam smiled and nodded.

"Sam, I'm going to stay."

"You goin' to stay where?"

"Here. On the island. Maybe find a beach and just stay here awhile."

He looked serious.

"There's a place you can stay in Codrington. I can—"

"No. I just want a beach and a bit of shade. I've got enough food for a few days. And water. I've got water."

He looked at me and grinned.

"We got a real live Mr. Robinson Crusoe here!"

"Yes—that's it. A few days of Robinson Crusoe living. There aren't many places left like this—especially in the Caribbean. I'd like to give it a try."

He shook his head and chuckled. "You crazy."

"Yes, I know."

He thought for a while. "Listen—if you go on the east side over by the caves there's a whole lot of beaches. No one goes there."

"What about on this side?"

"Well—there's a beach—a real long one—Seventeen Mile Beach, they call it—goes all the way down the other side of the lagoon. Pink sand, palm trees. . . . "

"And no people?"

"Yeah—no people. No one. You got miles and miles of beach and no one. Couple of ponds with good water. Tha's 'bout it."

"Can you show me how to get there?"

He burst out laughing. "You jus' like what they say about the Barbudans. People in Antigua think they crazy. Always doin' things different. Don't want development, don't want tourists.

Wan' to just be left alone. They kept asking them British to let 'em go independent of Antigua. They still write to the queen asking! They wan' to keep their land communal like it's always been. They claim they got 'rights' since way back when they were slaves. They don't want to be in the 'Bird Cage'!''

"What Bird Cage?''

"Y'know—the Birds—Vere Bird, Lester Bird, Vere Bird, Jr.— all them Bird family that runs Antigua.''

I laughed. It was the first time I'd heard the expression, and from all I'd learned on "the big island" it seemed most appropriate.

"There's this guy, Arthur Nibbs, young lawyer born on Barbuda. Chairman of the Barbuda Council. He really tells 'em: 'Barbudans'll do a mass suicide on the beaches if they don't get independence from Antigua.' He said that and most of 'em here, they agree with him. They just wan' to be left alone. To be like they've always been. They like bein' free—they like bein' Robinson Crusoes!''

"I think I know how they feel," I said.

"Yeah, well. You still crazy.''

I suppose I was, but I did it anyway. Sam had to go back to Antigua but said that either he or one of his friends would be back in Codrington in four days.

"I'll see you in town if you ready to go back then," he said.

"I'll buy you a beer.''

"No—you get a beer from me if you make it!''

Sam let me off the boat a mile or so south of the mangrove lagoon. A narrow path wriggled away from the reedy shore and disappeared into a mass of thorn bushes and cactus.

"You walk on through, less'n a mile, till you get to the beach on the other side. Shame you don't have a gun. There's wild pigs in there and deer. You sure you got enough food?''

"Yes, I'm fine." It was more of that dehydrated package stuff, but all I needed was a fire and some water. I'd also gotten some nylon line and a couple of hooks in one of those Boy Scout fishing kits.

He still looked uncertain. I think he was really convinced I was crazy.

"Sam—stop worrying. We're only talking a few days!''

"Yeah, I know."

"So—see you Thursday."

"Yeah."

"Good-bye, Sam." He was beginning to make me feel nervous.

"Yeah. Okay." He chuckled. "Best of luck, Crazy Crusoe! Tha's what you are. Dam' Crazy Crusoe!"

His boat was soon a tiny speck in the broad blue lagoon.

It is suddenly very quiet. The evening chirps and clicks and cricket-scratchings have yet to begin. Everything is still and limp in the late afternoon heat. I'm on my own again and it feels wonderful.

The thorn bushes are worse than I'd expected and I keep losing the almost invisible path and ending up in impenetrable thickets with four-inch thorns that reach out and snag every bit of clothing and flesh they touch.

According to a sweat-stained map that Sam had given me as a parting gift, it is only half a mile or so across the narrow peninsula to the beach. But the path doesn't seem to want to go straight. It twists and loops like lacework, keeping to the higher ground above swampy patches covered in enticing low grasses.

And then, it's there. An ocean of sloppy, slow-moving wavelets, shimmering in a heat mist; a fringe of low, bent palms offering welcome shade and a beach of the most beautiful pink sand I've ever seen anywhere in the world.

Actually to call it merely a beach is an insult. It is a magnificent, slowly curving strand of talcum-soft silica stretching into hazy infinities in both directions. Untouched, unbroken, unspoiled by any sign of human intrusion. No buildings, no boats, no people, no nothing. Just me and this perfect place—this little lost world set in a turquoise ocean under a dome of blue sky. All mine!

Here I am, I thought, singing again in my solitary madness.

Poor old Sam. He'd felt my "madness" and seemed worried. I sense it too now but feel elated—and I remember some words from Anne Morrow Lindbergh's beautiful book, *A Gift from the Sea*:

The sea does not reward those who are too anxious, too greedy, or too impatient. To dig for treasures shows not only impatience and greed, but lack of faith. Patience, patience, patience, is what the sea teaches. Patience and faith. One should lie empty, open, choiceless as a beach—waiting for a gift from the sea.

I have nowhere special to go, nothing to do. I don't even have to think, if I can persuade my restless mind to switch off for a while and become part of this beautiful place.

Be patient, I tell myself.

And slowly, slowly as a rising tide, the calm comes.

At one point, meandering across the endless sands, letting the grains tickle my toes, I look down on my mind as if floating over a familiar turbulent landscape. And what clutter I see there— what a jumbled topography of fears and feelings and disjointed, shadowy memories. Like an attic into which I throw things haphazardly, promising myself the pleasures of sorting it all out one day into neat piles and boxes. I've noticed I do that with my studio back home—letting it become a chaotic mess of papers and drawings and slide boxes and half-finished writings and notes to myself and broken pencils and unread magazines. And then— suddenly—in a whirl of organizing glee I file, fold, pack, stack, and rack all the clutter into neatly labeled packages, sweep the floors, clean the windows, wash fingerprints and coffee stains and cigar ash from my desk. And it's new again. A model studio, almost fit to be photographed for the glossy "house" magazines. . . . Ah. If only minds could be tidied up so neatly and so quickly.

But there again. Unlike my studio, which is the only working space I have, my head has other spaces I can enter, spaces beyond the finite mind, that are far less cluttered. A little cobwebby, perhaps, from underuse, but lean and roomy and fresh. Spaces to dream in; spaces in which to experience new sensations and see new patterns of understanding; spaces to explore, as seemingly infinite as this beach and the ocean that skitters and dances and plays across its pinkness.

I realize once again that the magic of "lost world" exploration is not to be found merely in the external adventures and discoveries—wonderful and terrifying though they are—but in the lost

143

worlds that such experiences lead us to find within ourselves. Those "other spaces" in the spirit that beckon and tantalize us all but in which we spend far too little time.

The sun is sinking now, easing down through the darkening blues into brilliant layers of scarlet, crimson, and old gold. The haze lifts as the heat diminishes and I can see, way on the edge of the horizon, the purpling peaks of Nevis, Saint Eustatius and—very faintly—the volcanic pyramid of strange little Saba. The far western outposts of the Leeward Islands. Dramatic and mysterious in profile, but all gentle, peaceful places, still unspoiled by the rampant tourist extravaganzas that have raped and pillaged the more popular Caribbean islands.

And here I am. On the quietest, most peaceful place of all. Alone. Enjoying my Robinson Crusoe fantasies and writing snippets of thoughts to myself as the sunset gilds the trunks of the leaning palm trees and sends shimmers of gold threading across the frothy tops of lazy waves. Lying quietly here, with no thoughts except this one.

When I allow my eyes to really see, freed from the filters of the mind, I'm amazed at how much I don't see most days. In the mystery and silence of this evening I'm tingling. I feel renewed in some way, excited by the smallest details—a flash of light on the crystalline surfaces of sand grains; the purposeful, determined movements of a tiny crab, hardly bigger than a dime, scurrying along the edges of the sloppy surf; the slow circle patterns traced in the sky hundreds of feet above me by five frigate birds, wings outstretched but unmoving, merely floating on the spirals.

I'm here, emptied, waiting to be filled again.

I strip off everything and stroll into the ocean, letting the water lick around my ankles. I hear the suck of surf, the gentle grasp of the tide, the rumble of pebbles moving in the deeper places, and sense the slow rounding down of everything.

I walk in until the sea reaches my navel and then turn to lie on my back, letting the warm water hold me, moving me slowly into the shore, then easing me out again. Solitude seems so natural now. Life welcomes the void and fills me—with little secrets.

Much later I find a bowl of soft sand between two palms. I

spread out my groundsheet, spray myself against an expected onslaught of mosquitoes that never comes, and light a small fire of dead palm fronds and broken branches dragged from the scrub behind the beach. I plan a dinner from a handful of dehydrated food packages and then realize I'm not hungry. How about a fish? About time you tried out that little Boy Scout box with the nylon line and the brightly colored float. But somehow the idea of actually killing something and eating it doesn't appeal. A handful of dried fruits and raisins is fine.

And then something very odd. A sudden change of mood. I feel very alone. Even vulnerable.

A shiver of fear starts in my neck and jiggers all the way to my toes. Fear of what? I can't pin it down. I just have this need for company. For some familiar sound or voice. Even a radio. . . . That's it. My trusty little shortwave radio. My dependable friend that keeps me in touch with the world in the remotest of places. I reach out for my backpack and feel around in the dim light for its familiar form. Out it comes, earphone and all. Switch it on. It's already switched on. And there's no little red light to tell me I'm tuned in to the BBC World Service, or Radio Moscow, or Voice of America—or even Radio Cuba. Nothing at all. Just a useless black plastic box with two burned-out batteries and no replacements. Well—I didn't know I was going to go wandering off like this. I'd planned to be back in Antigua with Sam tonight. If I'd have known I was going to do this dumb Robinson Crusoe thing I'd have brought all kinds of stuff—my tiny tape player, more food, a flashlight, books.

I scribble depressing thoughts in my notebook: A loneliness creeps in with the dusk, lowering the ceiling of thoughts, closing off feelings, edging out the adventure.

A voice inside niggles: So now you're really on your own, mate! My mind whirls around like a caged monkey, trying to find a way to subdue this surge of loneliness and these odd fears. It's crazy. There I was, an hour or so ago, blissfully floating in the ocean, writing little mellow thoughts to myself, absorbed in the silence and stillness of this place. And now here I am, struggling like a straightjacketed madman, desperately seeking noise and distraction, unable to return to those calm, tranquil spaces in my head.

It's all so ridiculous. This earth wanderer, explorer of wild places and lost worlds, panicked because his stupid shortwave radio won't work and scared by the sounds and rustling movements in the scrub behind me.

There's something in there! that damnable little voice shrieks inside my skull.

But what? Sam said there were no snakes here—at least none that are dangerous. Maybe a few wild pigs, but most of those were supposed to be way off on the other side of the island around the caves and clefts of the limestone Highlands. So what the hell is moving back there?

I turn to stare into the thick scrub. In the light of the dying fire I can see nothing except dark shadows.

Forget it, I tell myself. Enjoy the last of the light, faintly pink behind the black silhouettes of the far islands. Get your head back to where it was before. Have a drink of rum. Write another one of those scribbles to yourself. Stop thinking! Just enjoy being here.

But I am right.

There *is* something behind me. I can hear it moving closer now, coming through the scrub toward me. The faint crack of a twig; a rattling of dry leaves. Something is there. . . .

I sit absolutely motionless. Whatever it is may not have seen me. And I can escape easily. A fast trot into the sea—even a quick scamper up one of the palm trees. I'm safe.

And the deer thinks so too.

It steps daintily out of the bushes a few yards to my left, lifting small feet in a tiptoe motion, easing across the spiky grasses.

It seems a very small deer, hardly more than hip height. Maybe a young fawn. And barely distinguishable from the shadows in the last glimmers of dusk. Except for the eyes. Bright, full, and unblinking. Staring straight at me.

We both remain absolutely still. Its tail and ears are erect. I don't sense any fear in the creature. Perhaps a little caution, but mostly curiosity.

It takes a couple of steps toward me, shaking each of its front legs as it walks, and then pauses and lowers its head, maybe as a way of seeing me better. Maybe even a gesture of acknowledgment. I've never been so close to a deer before except in a zoo and I breathe as quietly as I can. I know little about these animals, although I've always loved the gracefulness of their movements.

The deer raises its head again and allows its tail to drop. Its eyes are still fixed on mine. Such calm eyes. Beguiling.

I suddenly have a flash of the monkey I'd once watched long ago in the rain forest of Costa Rica's Tortuguero National Park. An old whiteface, sitting in a banyan tree, staring at me with dark, stern eyes set in a wrinkled and strangely human face. I remember the sensation I'd had—that the creature somehow knew exactly what I was thinking and feeling. He seemed very old and wise and even a little sad at what he saw below him. He just sat there, never shifting his gaze. My guide had whispered to me, "I seen him before. I know him." The jungle was utterly still; nothing moved. And then he was gone. A few waving leaves, a quick shadow in the gloom, and then nothing.

"Bet he could teach you a few things," my guide had said.

And that's the feeling I have once again. Somehow in the stillness and calm of that small deer I sense an enormous know-ingness. It is almost talking to me with those eyes. I stare back and for a while nothing happens. Everything is very quiet and still. Even the surf is silent. And then I feel a great warmth well up inside, a surge of something milky, spreading out to my arms and fingers and up into my head, easing out all the yammer and fear and loneliness and replacing it, once again, with the sheer joy of just being here in this lovely place.

I can't stop a grin from spreading across my face. I feel cleansed of all the garbage of the previous hour. The more I smile, the better I feel.

The ravings of a crazy man? Sam would have thought so, but then he'd said something on our trip over I hadn't really absorbed at the time but which was similar to my feelings now. We'd been watching the birds and then the antics of a couple of turtles as we entered the narrow channel through the coral heads at the top end of the lagoon.

"They can live to be a coupla hundred years old, those turtles. Been goin' long before us humans came along. They got the wisdom of a few million years behind 'em."

In the deer's soft, calm eyes I sense the essence of those wisdoms. Not the noisy "I got it!" revelations of human perceptions—things to be debated and dissected and discarded at will—but something much deeper, much more ancient, much more enduring.

And then, like my Costa Rican whiteface monkey, it is gone. A shake of the head, a flick of the tail, and gentle dainty retreat into the dark scrub behind the palms.

I sit for a long time in silence, letting the joy-waves ride up and down my body. I don't need the radio now. I don't need company, or distractions. All those elusive fears, the loneliness, are gone.

For tonight, at least, I just need me.

Time doesn't really exist anymore. My watch is stowed deep in the backpack and my body begins to respond to its own rhythms. Rhythms of which I'm too often unaware. I sleep when I'm sleepy or when it's too hot to walk out on the open beach. I boil a packet of beef stroganoff for breakfast because I suddenly feel like eating beef stroganoff. Halfheartedly I try fishing in the shallows with the line and float and a bit of leftover beef as bait. But I think even the fish can sense I'm not really trying. And it's too hot anyway. They're doubtless off in deeper, cooler places doing whatever fish do down there in the heat of the day.

I scribble more thoughts to myself as I stroll through the surf in the early evening. And the beach just goes on and on—endlessly arcing away in both directions, mile after mile of soft pink sand unmarked by footprints or anything else that suggests the island has ever seen a human here before.

It's all mine.

That one thought keeps dancing through my head like a woodland sprite. Rarely if ever have I felt so free and unencumbered by plans or projects or fears or uncertainties. I have no guides to worry about—or, as is more usually the case, to worry about me. I have no one to meet, nothing to do, nothing to say, nothing even to think, if I don't feel like thinking.

And that's what I'm enjoying most. The lack of thinking. For much of the time my mind is content to see without looking, to feel without analyzing. Just to be. To walk softly in the glimmering light . . . and disappear!

I am learning to expect nothing—to expect no expectations. So what comes? Lovely surprises, of course, all the time. The perfection of a shell in all its whirling wonder; the shapes in a piece of driftwood—two horses, a hand, a mountain landscape in miniature, a breast pertly nippled; the incredible life in a dead vine still clutching, strangling, a withered tree trunk. So many moments in a single moment!

Letting go, flowing with the flow of things, and, for a single second, being infinite.

I find myself walking on tiptoe even in the soft sand, so as not to bruise that special silence before dusk, before the noises in the bushes and the cool evening breezes that make the palm fronds go *clacker-clacker-clacker*.

And after all this today, more surprises tomorrow.

I've hardly begun.

Because I've slept during the day I feel like walking at night under a creamy half-moon and a canopy festooned with star patterns. The beach is a silver strip, edged by a sparkling sea that hardly moves at all: In the quietness of this night I meet myself again and rediscover so many things I'd forgotten.

Finally sleep eases in, so I spread out the groundsheet, bunch up the backpack as a pillow, and drift off with a final thought for the day: I hope all this never ends; I hope I never arrive.

On the third day—I think it's the third day anyway—there's a storm, a real humdinger. Out in the west, among the silhouetted islands, the sky is clear and bright. But in the other direction it's as black as a mine shaft. I don't think I've ever seen a sky as black anywhere. The wind, a few minutes ago nothing more than a pleasant trade breeze, bashes into the palms like a prizefighter going for a knockout in the first round. The surf itself turns black, showing its true colors, discarding the simpering turquoises and royal blues, throwing off its limpid lappings on the shore, and gathering muscle by the minute. The gentle chitter of pebbles in the undertow is replaced by an ominous grinding and pounding as coral boulders, deeper down, begin to move against one an-

A HOMAGE
—To a beach,
a shell
and Frigate bird Sam
— BARBUDA

other. The sea seethes up the pink beach, now turning blood red as the first egg-sized splatters of rain hit, sending up sprays of fine silica. It races far higher up the sand than before, pauses as if in frustration that it has failed to reach the tree line, and then tears back down the slope of the beach to consolidate itself in even higher, blacker waves that rise up like ancient battered walls to surge forward once again.

This is the ocean I love and admire. This is when you feel its strength and majesty—when you know it can destroy boats, men, houses, even whole communities, in the power of its latent spirit. You become too beguiled and entranced by its apparent docility in the Caribbean; you forget how oceans can shape and meld whole continents; you ignore its primeval force and nature.

But not now!

I find a hollow away from the gesticulating palms and flying fronds, up close to the sturdy thick scrub. And I watch as the rain thrashes the grasses, breaking them and pounding them into the soft earth. I don't think I'd like to be a palm tree in this storm. They've learned the benefits of flexibility—they sway and bend and throw their fronds high like the outstretched gesticulating arms of Arab women at a wake—but each storm saps their strength, weakens their roots, stretches their fibrous trunks to the breaking point, and leaves them more vulnerable to the next on-slaught. I've seen dozens of them on my walk, dead and discarded like driftwood, half buried in sand, their broken roots still scream-ing at the air—eternal reminders of battles fought and lost in the seething, scathing tumult of hurricanes.

I am lost in the power of the storm. Soaked, shivering (the wind is actually cold), and shocked by the suddenness of it all, I give myself up to its roar and its rage.

On and on, blacker and blacker, louder and louder. Maybe this really is a hurricane. With my radio out of action I've heard no warnings. My one hope is that Sam is comfortable and safe at home and not out on the ocean in this maelstrom. The growling and grinding from the surf is almost animal-like now. A fierce, teeth-tingling sound. Waves hit the shore like mortar shells, ex-ploding in fury and froth, scattering rocks and shells and detritus up the beach and sucking the sand back into the depths with snakelike hisses.

I'm safe—or at least I think I am. I'm not a palm waiting for the final root-snapping blast. I have the luxury of sheltering in my sandy hollow and watching the spectacle like a young thumb-sucking boy at a circus. And I love it. I almost feel to be part of the storm's spirit; I'm in the roll and heave of the black waves; I'm in the shrieking wind and the exploding rain-eggs. I'm out of myself and wrapped in the magic and mystery of it all. . . .

What seems like hours later, the calm comes almost as suddenly as the storm. The wind dies. Waves toss in confusion like a restless army without generals and then subside, losing their dour color and adopting, chameleonlike, streaks of their previous blue and turquoise hues.

The beach is a mess. A battlefield of broken things marking the line of fiercest attack. Way up the sand a couple of palms have fallen. I can see the threadlike runners off the main roots waving like flags of surrender in the dying wind. The scrub behind the palms is still intact, a few discarded leaves and twigs, but otherwise undefeated.

There are coconuts everywhere, blown from the palm tops by the storm. I pick up a couple, smash their shells with a rock, and drink down the sweet liquid inside.

I'm drying out fast. The sun is hot again and the stickiness of air increases as the rain evaporates. The sand is harder now, compacted by the storm, and I begin my walk again on a firm surface. The beach seems to slope more steeply than before, its softer top surface stolen by the surf, revealing a coarser grain. Still pink, though.

There are shells and bits of shells everywhere, but they're all empty. Are they merely the discarded garbage of the seabed or have the terrified occupants—conchs, hermit crabs, sea snails—fled to the deeps, abandoning their perfectly formed castles to the fickleness of the surf hordes?

Ridiculous thoughts. The occupants and their castles are complete entities. One can't exist without the other. I've become a hurricane-harassed brain. Can't think straight. But the thought persists. Why are they empty? And so many of them. Wonderful whorls of calcium, so finely etched and colored. Architects and engineers would benefit from studying their microstructure—Corbusian elegances of form-following-function; Miesian essays of detail and exactness of fit; Robert Graves's blendings of colors and subtle wit, and a Gaudi-like robustness and flair for sheer arrogance and idiosyncracy of design. A universe of forms at my feet. A mathematician's total knowledge all in one curled snail shell. Perfect three-dimensional geometry. All here.

I thank the storm for its gifts. And then I thank this little island. So compact, so rich, so whole. I am learning something here.

Back at home, Anne has a lovely poster on the wall in her studio. A photograph by Elliot Porter of lonely surf-pounded rocks on some island in Maine. But the words on the poster irritated me:

> I am not lonely
> I am merely alone

We have a marriage that has endured and strengthened over twenty-five years and at first I couldn't understand the idea of her feeling alone. Alone from me, our cats, our lakeside home, and all the myriad details of our lives. But shimmers of comprehension were shining through, polished by the storm.

I think back to my sudden surge of loneliness a couple of days ago, that great gloom that fell over me for a few hours. And then I realize that I'd come through it with the help of that deer with the calm eyes. We couldn't talk, we couldn't communicate in the traditional sense, but the deer had restored the wonder— the knowledge—that I have always known somewhere deep down.

I come back to Anne Morrow Lindbergh's book *A Gift from the Sea* once again:

How wonderful are islands! The past and the future are cut off; only the present remains. Existence in the present gives island living an extra vividness and purity. One lives like a child or a saint in the immediacy of the here and now. Every day, every act, is an island, washed by time and space, and has an island's completion. People too become like islands in such an atmosphere, self-contained, whole and serene; respecting other people's solitude, not intruding on their shores, standing back in reverence before the miracle of each other individual.

We have to be alone to touch our inner selves. For if we cannot touch ourselves, how can we ever truly touch anyone else?

I pick up the shell again and stroke it. A thing so whole, so complete. A product of its own world, its own complex net of dependencies and threats and terrors and truths. And yet, by its very nature—alone. In my hand. And something to take home with me.

John Donne got it right and wrong. "No man is an island" makes sense in a hundred measurable ways. But ultimately we are all islands and if we don't face up to that truth and rejoice in the possibilities of solitude, we miss out on one of the gifts of life.

This island has revived *my* island. This little lost world has given new life to my own personal world. Fears, loneliness, hurricanes, noises in the night—I can accept them all now. And love too. Love is larger now; deeper in—deeper out.

In another day or so, after many more miles of sand and scrub, I'll be meeting Sam again. I'm looking forward to that. I remember the knowing way in which he caressed and held the frigate bird and stretched its wings to show me their size and their beauty. Sam, I'm sure, knows and loves this island, but he also knows and loves *his* own island, within. There is something complete about the man. A completeness I'm learning to find within myself, thanks to a deer, a storm, and a shell.

Funny, isn't it? Perhaps all the answers are all around us. We merely have to pause, see, and understand.

It is evening again; the sun scatters strands of golden tinsel across the bay. And wisps of silver cloud, pluming—just for me.

Thank you, little lost world of Barbuda.

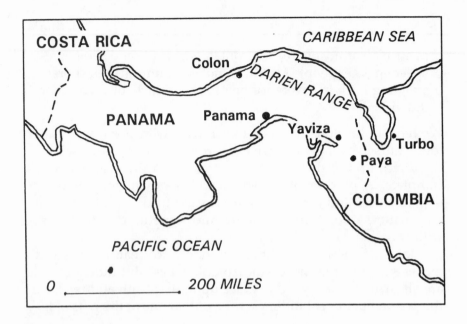

5. PANAMA—
THE DARIEN
Lost in the Golden Time

"Then I felt like some watcher of the skies
When a new planet swims into his ken;
Or like stout Cortez when with eagle eyes
He stared at the Pacific—and all his men
Look'd at each other with a wild surmise—
Silent, upon a peak in Darien."

Keats

The idea of the Pan American Highway has always intrigued
me. Tim Cahill's record-breaking auto road odyssey with Gary
Sowerby from its southern endpoint in Argentina's Tierra del

156

Fuego to the last few feet of bumpy track by the Beaufort Sea in northern Alaska (*Road Fever—A High Speed Travelogue*, Random House, 1990) only increased my fascination at this route, over fifteen thousand miles long, passing through such a kaleidoscopic wealth of scenic and cultural variations from latitude 50° S to latitude 70° N.

Conceived by the Pan American Highway Congress in 1925 and boasting a spectacular array of engineering and logistical feats, this amazing road has one glitch, a place where it surrenders its magnificent continuity and admits defeat against enormous topographical obstacles. That place is the Darien Gap in Panama, where Central and South America meet in a narrow and pernicious jungle, mountain, and swamp-clogged peninsula less than 100 miles wide and 150 miles long.

One traveler described it back in the sixties as "packed with incredibly dense vegetation, threaded with rivers and streams, and thought to harbor head-hunting Indians as well as poisonous snakes ... the Darien Gap has long frustrated every attempt to travel the full length of the Pan American Highway."

On most world maps you can barely make out the region at all. You wonder what all the fuss is about. But its impact on the highway is unmistakable. After crossing the tortured wilds of Patagonia, the notorious Atacama Desert of Chile, the western fringes of the Amazonian Basin, and a dozen other places once thought to be impassable, the road gives up at the port of Turbo in Colombia and travelers are obliged to spend tedious days arranging transit on a ship to Colón at the northern end of the Panama Canal. And all to avoid the terrors of this 150-mile-long "gap"!

Lurid reports have trickled back from world wanderers about this place. "A hellhole," "the worst jungle in the world," and even (to borrow Winston Churchill's description of the Soviet Union) "a riddle wrapped in a mystery inside an enigma."

In spite of its notorious reputation, little has been written about the Darien, and the place remains a tantalizing lost world—an ideal candidate for my explorations.

And so—off I went to Panama, hiking boots polished, backpack brimming, and expectations exhilarated by recent press tales of defeated expeditions and the strange habits of native tribes somewhere deep in the gloom and swampy morasses of this truly enigmatic region.

Panama City, following the graft and kleptocratic regime of Noriega, was not a place to dally in. Beyond the high-rise patina of urban sophistication on the edge of the shantytowns and around the vulture-encrusted rubble heaps, there was a mood of anarchy and creeping chaos—too many booze- or drug-crazy youths in clapped-out cars roaring around the city looking for something to distract them from the stupor of the streets. Many of the stores, looted and decimated by the locals during the U.S. "invasion," were still boarded up. Banks, the lifeblood of Panama City, were open but seemed to sport more security guards than customers. Highways were littered strips, the haunt of packs of wild dogs by night and their human equivalents during the day.

I found little reason to linger and, after making my travel plans known to the disinterested authorities, I was relieved to be busbound heading east to the end of the road at the village of Yaviza. Finally I was off to the Darien to satisfy a decade of personal curiosity.

The first eighty or so miles were tolerable enough as I bounced along with a dozen Indian-featured passengers in a gaily painted minibus of a species known to older Panamanians as *chivas* or "nanny goats." Salsa music blasted from a cracked speaker above the driver's head. He only had the one tape, which he played over and over again, although it wouldn't have made much difference if he'd had a whole library of salsa cassettes—that stuff all sounds the same to me. An endless frantic bongo-and-brass racket whose frenetic energy drove passengers into a deep stupor. Sweaty too. The music seems to exude heat and, even with all the windows open, I sat in moist misery wondering why so many of my "lost world" adventures seem to take place in such torrid climes. Next time, I vowed, I was going to stick to the cold places— maybe the Falkland Islands or Greenland or even Antarctica itself. This Yorkshire body, with genes generated in the cool Irish bog country of County Cork, does not adapt well to perpetual sauna-bath sorties. Maybe there's a subconscious masochistic intent to my wanderings. Maybe there are deep-seated guilts in my psyche that need to be expunged by the torment and torpor of travel in such uncomfortable places. A hair-shirt harangue for an overly hedonistic life? Maybe even. . . .

The road ended abruptly. Without any warning we bumped off the edge of the tar and onto a corrugated mud track, formed into peaks and troughs and ditches by trucks and getting worse by the minute. At first the driver didn't appear to even acknowledge the sudden change and careened along even faster. He was an aggressive, arrogant fellow who called himself Zolo! (yes—he pronounced his name with the exclamation mark), blasting through mud sluices and skimming over the ruts in what looked like a frantic effort to lift the minibus off the ground and establish a kind of gravity-defeating hovercraft ride that would bring us to our destination in a state of suspended animation.

I had to give the man credit. A few times he almost made it, as we seemed to float weightlessly above the craters before crashing to earth with a jarring crunch and ominous creaking of springs and chassis. But at least we were on level ground. I've had enough bus-riding experiences in Central and South America to last most of this lifetime and they were invariably on narrow mountain roads undefined by anything so practical as guardrails. As a result you feel to be hanging by a few centimeters of bald rubber to the edge of precipe and canyons, cutting sharp corners with a precision guaranteed to come splat to splat with anything traveling in an equally foolhardy manner in the opposite direction.

Somewhere deep in my backpack I usually carry a tiny Saint Christopher pendant presented to me by my grandfather, who realized that he was largely to blame for releasing the wanderlust in me during my formative years (he was a *National Geographic* nut and made me one too). He felt a need, I suppose, to assuage his guilt by giving me this token of saintly protection. Usually I don't wear the thing. I have a distinct aversion to men draped in chains and trinkets. But always—on Latin American mountain highways—I make an exception and slip it around my neck, under my shirt. I've read countless and very bloody accounts of busloads of peasants and adventurous backpackers being pulped in remote valleys after vain attempts at flying, off and over the edge of these notorious roads. But this time, as I said, we were on level ground and somehow Zolo's attempts to become airborne seemed far less threatening.

Then he became a mere mad mortal again as we hit the first mud hole and sank below the wheels in a pool of thick gooey liquid that stank of festering vegetation and ripe sewage.

Zolo took the incident personally, cursing and raving at the track as the undercarriage of the bus steamed and the engine stalled and we sat for a few moments of silence in the sweltering heat.

Then he must have said—rather shouted—some magic word at the passengers, for one by one they began to leave their seats and their bundles and baskets (and a cage with three cocks in it) and shuffle down the aisle, out of the door, into the mud pool. They were like automatons. They didn't even try to leap for the dry high ground at the edge of the track. They just stepped right in the goo as if paddling into the ocean. A few rolled up their dusty, stained trousers, but most didn't even bother with that meager refinement.

The hell with it. I was damned if I was going to get out of the bus into that stinking morass.

Then Zolo directed his anger toward me, as I was the only passenger left sitting, holding tightly onto my backpack. And— surprise, surprise—I obeyed unquestioningly just like the others, shuffling down the aisle, trying to leapfrog the mud hole and failing miserably. I sank up to my knees in the stuff. The other passengers, who had been sitting mute for the first three hours of the journey, now decided it was time for a little light relief at my expense. Their laughter and giggles and ribald comments could have turned me into a raving nut case, like the driver, but after a second or two's reflection I began to see the situation from their point of view and decided that we all looked pretty silly wallowing about in the goo, wondering what to do next. So I laughed along with them.

Zolo took charge again, replacing his anger with a fascistlike dictatorial role as he instructed where, when, and how to push the bus forward through the mud hole. And as we gave it our all, heaving and huffing like pyramid-building slaves, he stood dry and detached at the top of the steps issuing more orders and disappearing every so often to try to restart the recalcitrant engine.

160

Slowly—very, very slowly—we pushed two tons of dead-weight machinery through that fifty-foot-long swamp of brown molasses until, ten long minutes later, it stood dripping and decorated in a Pollock frenzy of splattered globs on top of a dry stretch of track. Zolo managed to get the engine roaring again, spraying most of us with jets of steaming liquid earth and exhaust fumes. Then, rather than wait for us, he began to move the bus down the road, leaving us to chase after it and haul ourselves back on board in a Keystone Kops scene of utter confusion.

Strangely, rather than tear the driver limb from limb as any normal load of New York bus riders might understandably do, the mud-caked passengers returned morosely to their seats to await the next disaster. Which, of course, occurred within minutes of the first and required even more exertion on our parts.

After the third mud hole we were all beyond hope. Fatigue and frustration had eradicated any hint of protest. Our only link to sanity was to seal our thinking, feeling minds and set our mutual goal on getting through this series of morasses and into Yaviza before the cantinas closed. For every time we shuffled out of the bus and into the mud and then back into the bus again I mentally added another two frost-coated bottles of beer to my table at the first cantina I came to at our final destination.

By the time we arrived, late in the evening (after ten hours to cover 140 miles), I had accumulated a total of twelve frothy promises and actually managed to get through five of them before going to look for a place to stay in this village on the edge of nowhere.

Yaviza truly feels like the end of the road. A place where the dreams of its nine hundred mainly black inhabitants come to die and to be buried in the humid torpor and boozy languor of terminal apathy and hopelessness. I rarely saw anyone smiling in this ramshackle town of pastel-painted, mold-flecked shacks and weed-strewn streets which ended abruptly on the edge of the mangrove-fringed Tuira River. If this had been in Haiti I'd have been tempted to wonder if the residents had been zombied into catatonic trancelike states. I felt I was walking among the living dead and after a day or so I even gave up walking. At least Panama City had energy and verve; Yaviza had unbearable heat, mosquitoes, cheap beer, and little else. According to historical records

161

Balboa is said to have constructed a boat-building facility here in 1514, using the tidal Tuira to carry his craft down to the Pacific. From the look of the lethargy of the place it was hard to imagine anyone having the energy nowadays for such an ambitious undertaking.

I needed a canoe and a couple of guides. Nobody, except those seeking an early end to their lives, enters the Darien without some kind of local help. And I was lucky enough in that respect. After two days of increasing desperation I was introduced to a couple of Cuna Indians who had come to Yaviza to transact some mysterious trading arrangements involving a boatload of bundles wrapped in banana fronds and tied with hairy hemp ropes. I have seen such bundles in other parts of the tropical world and decided not to inquire too intensively as to their contents. "Medicine" seems to be the popular euphemism and I left it at that. I've seen "medicine" in many different forms and, who knows, maybe the Indians were delivering a new jungle-harvested panacea for cancer or AIDS. I'd like to think it was something like that.

But at least their boat, a native piragua hacked from a tree trunk and powered by a rusty outboard motor (but more often by pole), would leave empty, relieved of its bundles, and the two men agreed to take me with them through a part of the Darien as far as their destination, somewhere deep in the jungle.

First impressions of the region were not encouraging. In spite of strict government regulations forbidding logging and the decimation of the jungle for cattle ranching, no one seems surprised by battered trucks hauling enormous loads of old growth lumber out of the wilderness. Panama's land-hungry *campesino* peasants also see this as a promised land, a place to "slash-and-burn," to stake a claim to their own patch of earth and wrench themselves free from Panama's poverty cycle.

Far more exotic claims of "golden cities" and "all the wealth of the Orient" led such early explorers as Cortez, Balboa, Columbus, and Drake to this tangled land. Columbus is said to have had "a most strange attack of madness" here during his fourth "New World" exploration. Drake had a petulant fit here in 1596 when his "world treasury of gold" once more proved elusive, and Balboa was hanged in 1517 from a banyan tree shortly after discovering the Pacific Ocean on the west side of the peninsula.

Ironically, gold was discovered much later at Cana in such vast quantities that it became known as the El Dorado of the New World. Remnants of old mining machinery and a steam locomotive brought in from Britain more than one hundred years ago can still be spotted among the turbulent scrub of the forest which, as is its nature, was struggling to reinvent itself and obliterate all evidence of prior rape and pillage.

But once in the piragua and moving southeast against the flow of the Tuira River, we soon entered a tumultuous world of thick rain forest entangled in vines and creepers. The river was full following a recent series of storms in the distant mountains along the Colombian border, but the two Indians had an uncanny knack of avoiding the strong currents of the outer bank and easing us through the shallow stretches where the water trickled over boulders and rocks clearly visible in the crystalline stream.

At last I'm really off, I thought, as clouds of bright blue and yellow butterflies flurried past. Into the deep unknown, I thought. Maybe even retracing some of the routes of fifteenth- and sixteenth-century explorers. . . .

But my thoughts and elation were premature. We had barely begun, a mere two hours on the river, when I heard, boomboxing through the forest, the sound of salsa music once again. And as we rounded a bend I saw another forlorn little village perched high on the riverbank.

"El Real!" my two guides shouted at me excitedly as if I'd be delighted to find a rest spot so soon after leaving Yaviza.

In a form of communication we had developed during our short journey—a haphazard mishmash of winks, nods, and other gestures coupled with a dozen or so words that sounded vaguely Spanish—they explained that they had business to conduct in the town and that we would be staying overnight. They suggested that rather than pitching my pathetic little pup tent I might want to stay at the local hotel, and insisted it was not only inexpensive but well served by ladies whose attributes (if their gestures were anything to go by) were generously endowed, and whose ardor would not be daunted by the appalling heat.

A line of naked Indian children with faces painted in odd black markings, particularly around the eyes, stood mute and motionless at the top of the steep bank and watched us closely as we ascended a precarious staircase formed of crudely notched tree trunks. As soon as I arrived at the top, puffing with my overloaded pack, they squealed and scattered.

Ahead of me were groupings of simple timber and thatch huts raised on stilts. Some had roll-up walls of bamboo slats that were kept raised during the day, Samoan-style, revealing all the intricacies of Indian domestic life.

These were Choco Indians, my guides told me before vanishing off among the huts to transact their mysterious business. "Not like our Cuna people. They do not wear clothes and they still hunt with bows and blowpipes and arrows of poison. Be careful," they warned.

Two elderly men, sprawled in hemp hammocks, watched me sleepily. They wore loincloths and little else while women were more modestly dressed in old T-shirts (and some not) and sarong-like skirts. Most of them were cooking on open fires. The smell of frying plantains wafted through the scrub surrounding the village. It was hard to believe that we were only 150 miles or so from the raucous din of Panama City, although the crackly salsa music from behind the thatch-roofed huts reminded me that twentieth-century urban influence spreads rapidly even into the remotest parts of the globe. My previous travels have revealed VCRs in the wilds of inner Mongolia, Bruce Springsteen posters in the almost inaccessible tribal settlements of Zaire, Big Apple sweatshirts in unmapped Himalayan hamlets. Our global village is no longer a McLuan fantasy but becoming more and more a reality of life with every new electronic innovation. And I—an incurable romantic—usually resent it.

In spite of its sleepy spirit today, El Real has a remarkably dramatic history which began three centuries ago when the town became the key shipping point for gold mined in the region. Boats carried the valuable cargo down the Tuira out into San Miguel Bay and up along the coast, past the Perlas Archipelago, to Panama City. A tempting prospect indeed for pirates and buccaneers who plagued the region. English privateers burned the poor little town to the ground in 1680 in frustration when they realized they had missed the shipping of over three hundred pounds of gold to Panama City by a mere three days. Then came more raids by other European pirates, rebellions by local slaves transported here from Africa long before the notorious American slave trade, and attacks by Choco and Cuna Indians, who resented the intrusion of strangers into their tribal territories.

The El Real of today is a far more tranquil place and I even found the hotel—a hotel that boasted a restaurant with no furniture and no food, a bar with no beer, a toilet with no toilet, and rooms with no keys. Decoration consisted primarily of pinup photographs, four of which had been elaborately framed like old masters.

"There are no other guests here, so your bag is very safe," I was assured by the young boy at what I took to be the reception desk. He inspected my passport with the overblown seriousness of a border guard waiting for his "tip" and said my photograph was *muy* something or other, which didn't sound at all complimentary.

After a wash in a sink with a single tap that released pallid brown water in a hesitant trickle, I decided to go in search of the salsa music. Not really because I wanted to but because it seemed to be the only source of life in this odd little place.

"Main Street" was a pleasantly haphazard mix of more huts on stilts topped with untidy fringes of palm-thatched roofs interspersed with gardens and flowering trees. Aromas intermingled in the dusky air—more frying plantains, strong cigar smoke, and a couple of stalls selling plantains (of course) and some soupy concoction of maize, vegetables, and oval chunks of white meat. Three discarded and still bloody snakeskins nearby may have been the source of the meat, but I never tasted it to find out. Families sat in the shadowy recesses of their verandas and smiled at me as I wandered by, following a flow of villagers making their way to the source of the music. There seemed to be considerable activity for such a small community. Then I realized it was Saturday night. Time for the weekly *pico-pico* dance.

Illuminated in Christmas-spirited garlands of pink, blue, and yellow lights, the dance hall was already a sweaty crush of churning bodies dancing and stamping to the ceaseless surge of salsa. As the crowd thickened they turned up the volume to such a pitch it was hard to distinguish the instruments from the crackles of overloaded speakers.

I edged over to the bar and bought a lukewarm beer. So far I'd felt pretty inconspicuous in the mélange, but as I lolled against the counter I became aware of a group of men gathering around me.

"You got cigar?" one of them asked me.

I was smoking quite an acceptable Panamanian brand of cheroot and saw no reason not to share them. My generosity brought me instant popularity.

"An' my frien's. They like cigar too."

Five cigars vanished in as many seconds. Apparently I had now bonded with the group and they pinned me against the bar, puffing away happily on my cheroots and asking me a rapid-fire series of questions in a Spanish dialect I hadn't yet learned to decipher.

After a while the gist of their queries became clear. Every time a woman passed with anything approaching passable features, they would gurgle and grunt and gesticulate their hips in a manner so suggestive that even Elvis would have blushed.

Then one of the men vanished and returned a minute later with a large Indian lady, possibly in her early thirties, wrapped in a flowery sarong and showing distinct signs of wobbly intoxication.

"You dance with?" he asked, nodding rapidly. I had no wish to offend, so I took the outstretched hand of the unsteady lady and found myself being dragged into the thickest churn of bodies.

Now, I'm more of a foxtrot and quickstep dancer myself, and quite a good one, or so I've been told. The lady quickly realized that I had no idea of the subtleties of salsa and, having clutched me as tight as a boa constrictor to her ample figure, swirled and spun me like a bag of lumpy laundry. I tried as best I could to avoid her feet and flow with the incessant beat, but it was just too fast and too hot and I could feel my interest fading fast. *"Bueno, bueno,"* she cooed as she pulled me closer and rotated her broad hips across my torso. I tried to smile and keep up with her. *"Bueno*—ooh. Chi-chi-chi. *Bueno, bueno*, cha-cha-cha." Her endless endearments somehow kept me going. I couldn't escape anyway. There were gyrating bodies doing the most evocatively erotic things all around me. Although my smile was rapidly becoming a grimace, I persevered, hoping there might be a quick end to the tune when I could escape, back to the benevolence of my beer. But salsa is endless. Maybe it's all on loop tape that just keeps playing until bodies collapse in utter exhaustion. Except that no one else looked exhausted. As the music pounded on, the faces of the dancers became ecstatic. Eyes were closed. Heads, bodies, arms, and legs—all moved faster and faster. The room was Hades hot, but no one noticed. The dancing went on and on like some kind of African tribal rite and I was trapped in the middle of it all, belly-to-bellied by this buxom matron with her endless *bueno, buenos*.

Somehow, eons later, I staggered back to the bar, only to find that someone had finished my beer for me. I ordered another and my dancing companion, whom I thought I'd managed to escape, rubbed my arm and made it clear that she felt entitled to a bottle too.

One of my previous male companions returned, still smoking my cigar.

"Good, no?"

I nodded and tried to brush away the sweat that was now tumbling off my forehead in waterfalls.

"She likes you," he said, and began his nodding antics again. "You want?"

No, I really didn't want. I didn't want the Indian lady, I didn't want any more dancing, and I didn't particularly want his company any longer.

"No, no," I said. "I go now."

The nodding stopped and he looked horrified and confused.

"No want? To hotel. She go with you."

"No—honestly. I think I've hurt my leg." I tried to demonstrate my limping technique in the press of bodies at the bar, but he didn't seem to understand.

As if by magic another Indian girl appeared—younger and obviously pregnant. She looked as sullen and dejected as I felt.

"You like this one?"

"No—no. Listen, I really have to go."

He was nonplussed. Obviously his role as pimp or whatever was being maligned. Two other men—big men—were pushing their way through the crowd with their eyes very much fixed on me. This, I realized, could become a little unpleasant.

"Well"—I tried to sound cheerful and nonchalant—"thank you so much. I've enjoyed meeting your friends. I must go back now. My leg is very bad. *Muy, muy malo. . . .*"

He muttered something menacing as I turned to leave and I felt his hand grab my arm. Oh, well, I thought, here we go again. Time for another beer-hall brawl. I swung around quickly with my ready-for-battle look, expecting the worst. Fortunately, he backed off, uncertain what to do next.

I smiled and gave him another cigar, hoping that would repair his injured pride.

He grunted something but took it anyway and I left him standing with his two ladies.

I made it through the throng to the main door and regained the relative sanity of the street. I half expected the men to follow me and was very relieved when they didn't.

The cool night air brushed my wet body like a gentle fan and I made my way back to the hotel, acknowledging the quiet *olas* from the families on the verandas and whistling a little to suggest a nonchalance I didn't really feel.

True to their word my Cuna Indian guides arrived early the following morning before the heat hit and we strolled down to the river past the debris of last night's antics. Salsa was still playing somewhere back in the village and a few inebriated souls sat on the steps of their stilt houses or wandered the streets like lost dogs.

I was happy to say good-bye to El Real and hoped that finally we'd leave these last remnants of questionable civilization and enter the Darien proper.

And we did. Quite abruptly too. Five minutes after waving farewell to another straggle of children on top of the steep riverbank, we were skimming up the Tuira through a tunnel of vine-festooned forest. Back in the shadowy recesses behind the riot of river vegetation, I could hear monkeys calling to one another. Butterflies bobbed about us again—red and black ones this time—and the cries of unfamiliar birds echoed in the canopy.

In the shallower sections of the river the motor was turned off and the two Cunas poled us through with the grace of straw-boater-clad punters on the streams of Cambridge University in England. At one point the river broadened and, as none of the channels seemed deep enough even for poling, we all hopped out and pushed the piragua through the gentle current. Sand trickled between my toes and the water felt warm and silky. I expected onslaughts of mosquitoes on our exposed bodies, but strangely, there were none.

The pushing was easy and I felt a surge of special pleasure again that comes to travelers when they sense the adventure they longed for beginning to happen. I think the two Cunas picked up my mood and they smiled too as we eased the craft up the soft river bottom.

The day drifted on, punctuated by periods of poling and pushing. The forest grew thicker now, although we saw occasional clearings of Indian gardens and, more ominously, the smoke from slash-and-burn fires that plague the western fringes of the Darien.

You can hardly blame the peasants for wanting to be pioneer-farmers in this nation of go-nowhere poverty. But, in their thousands, they are decimating one of the last of the earth's great wildernesses (great, that is, in ecological values, not size). And, as research has proven over and over again, they end up no better than before they began their machete-felling and burning and creation of small but very short-lived farms.

It may seem odd, but in this fetid environment of teeming plant life, the soils are invariably ill-suited to intensive agriculture. The story goes as follows: Peasants are often driven out of other small farms well away from the rain forests by avaricious cattle ranchers who acquire their lands by fair means or foul to raise thousands of steers to satisfy the ever-increasing worldwide demand for beef. Driven eastward in their search for new land, they slash and burn into the forest perimeters and plant their subsistence crops of bananas, corn, and maize on poor soils nourished for a short while by the ash from the burnings. Within three or four years the soil nutrients are used up by the cultivated plants or are washed away by the two hundred inches of rain a year received by this region. So in desperation the peasants turn to

169

creating small grass pastures, which they then sell to the land-hungry ranchers. Invariably this second phase ends with over-grazing. The leached soils are then abandoned as the process moves ever eastward, even into the foothills of the Darien and San Blas Mountains which form a four-thousand-foot-high wall between the threatened forest and the vast liquid landscape of the marshes fed by Colombia's Atrato River and its tributaries.

Denudation of forest in these foothills, plus overgrazing, leached soils, and ultimate abandonment, invariably results in unchecked erosion. The meager soils are rapidly washed down newly formed canyons and out to the Pacific via the Tuira River. It's a sad and stupid cycle. Predictable, preventable—yet perpetuated by short-term interests driven by a desperate search for land by the peasants and easy profits for the ranchers.

On a global scale, over two billion acres of tropical forest are being destroyed at a rate approaching fifty million acres a year (or almost one acre a second, if you prefer statistics in manageable form). The implications of this terrifying rape of the planet have been studied for decades. A recent U.S. government report, *Global 2000*, not only warned of catastrophic climatic changes as a result of forest denudation, but also the elimination of a million species of plant and animal life by the end of this century. Over half the world's estimated five million species are to be found in these forests and the destruction of this enormous gene pool, vital to the future cultivation of new food sources, fibers, and natural medicines, is increasing every day throughout the developing world.

To some, all this may seem like another one of those false alarms caused by the overanxious Birkenstock-and-bean sprout crowd whose frantic warnings of "greenhouse effect" and other headline-grabbing harangues eventually engender a "cry-wolf" attitude on the part of a generally confused public. Surely a few little fires in this remote wilderness of Darien could hardly be prejudicial to the future of mankind on the planet?

I think back to the first time I flew down to Central America from the United States four years ago seeking out the magical cloud forests of Costa Rica's Monteverde. We were skimming over Guatemala at the time and I became aware of a heavy haze across thousands of square miles of seemingly untouched jungle below me. When I looked closer through my binoculars I realized that this was no climatic quirk. It was a vast smoke haze, two or three hundred miles in length, caused by countless "controlled clearances" (*milpas*). I could see the forest quite clearly in places where the smoke haze was less thick. In fact it looked like an enormous patchwork quilt of dark untouched jungle broken by thousands of lighter slash-and-burn squares. Others on the plane saw it too and soon the sound of horrified gasps broke the martini-and-macadamia mellowness of the flight. People struggled to peer through the tiny windows and then pulled back in shock. Even the plane's captain felt obliged to confirm what we were seeing. I'll always remember his words:

"I am from Guatemala. My family lives in Guatemala. Every day this haze hangs over our country and every week we lose another ten thousand hectares of forest. I see this every time I fly this route. I am sorry you had to see it too. It is hard to forgive the government for allowing this. I am very sorry."

I remember something else I once read which had in it the seeds of a solution. It was one of the other reasons I wanted to come to the Darien and to meet the Cuna tribespeople, whose attitude toward land and forest preservation is exemplary in an age of blinkered "progress," a.k.a. planet pillage.

The Cuna are one of the last tribal groups in Latin America to withstand the scourge of conquistadores, colonialists, and modern-day capitalists in a relatively unscathed state. Once rulers of most of the Darien region between the two oceans, they have gradually been corralled into a 150-mile-long strip of mainland and islands along the Atlantic coast, encompassing parts of the Darien Mountains.

They have been labeled by anthropologists as "the last original democracy on earth" and still conduct their affairs in the heat of community debates, similar in many respects to the United States' time-honored town meetings. Among their notable characteristics is an ancient and abiding love and respect for the forest in which they live.

One story, which has now taken on an almost folkloric significance in Panama, illustrates their beliefs and principles. The notorious doyen of development and one-time ruler of Panama, the late General Omar Torrijos Herrera (the man who negotiated successfully with President Jimmy Carter for the return of the Panama Canal) once flew over the virgin rain forest of the Cuna reserves on his way to a meeting with tribal officials. When he rose to speak later in the day he is reported to have demanded angrily: "Why do you Cunas need so much land all to yourselves? You don't use it. You don't do anything with it. And you are always complaining if anyone does so much as fell a single tree."

After a short pause, one of the Cuna leaders rose to reply: "Please tell me this, General. If I come to Panama City and break the window of a pharmacist's store because I need medicine, would you not arrest me and put me into your jail?"

"Of course," said the general.

"Then I ask you to understand that our forest is our pharmacy. If we are ill, the forest provides all the medicine we need to cure us. It is also our pantry. The foods it gives us are bountiful and fresh. We Cuna need our forest, even though it is much less than we once had; unlike your people, we can take what we need without having to destroy anything."

Then there was silence in the meeting hall. Torrijos stared at the Cuna leader for a long time, saying nothing. Then he finally strode across the floor and hugged him like a long-lost brother.

It makes a good story, although it didn't altogether solve the Cuna's concerns, especially when the general later became enthusiastic about a coastal road right through the heart of their reserves. So they reached out to international agencies for help and advice and were instrumental in establishing areas of perpetual preservation, both to protect their homeland and to enable outsiders to study these sanctuaries for medicinal, ecological, and biological purposes. A unique partnership is in the process of being established here linking an indigenous culture and informed international interests.

And so, as we pushed and poled up the Tuira River, through the forest and eventually—if I was lucky—into the foothills of the Darien range, I looked forward to my meeting these wise (and wily) Cuna Indians, who may have found a way to slow the seemingly unstoppable surge of slash-and-burn enthusiasts and land-lusting ranchers. Our last "lost worlds" are such frighteningly fragile places even though, from within their wildernesses, it is often hard to imagine their imminent demise. We urgently need more ideas and action to protect them—from ourselves.

As I was to discover later in this journey, we have much to learn from these intrepid Cuna.

Another eight hours of piragua travel through the increasingly dense forest brought us to the village of Boca de Cupe. Once again we were greeted by a bevy of shy children with painted faces and a generally disinterested populace.

"*Estampa*," one of my guides told me, and pounded his fist into the palm of his other hand. "*Estampa. Muy necessario.*"

It turned out that the village was the place to get my papers stamped for entry into Colombia, even though the border was more than thirty long miles away, high up among the ridges of the Darien range.

We decided to make camp here, and after my tent was pitched I went off to find the stamp man, who turned out to be a mul-tifaceted official—mayor, chief of customs operations, military at-taché, and local grocer. He was sleeping in a hammock outside his store but rose with dignity, shook my hand, and performed the necessary formalities in a friendly—if sleepy—spirit.

"You are going where?" he asked.

"To the mountains. To see the Cuna people and then down to Turbo."

"Ah, Turbo." He sighed and shook his head. "Bad place. Much gambling, drugs, women. You must be careful in Turbo. It is like your American Wild West."

"I don't plan to stay there long. It's just the place where my journey ends. Where the Pan American Highway ends too, I think."

He laughed. "And I hope it always end there too. They say they will build the last piece through the Darien in ten years, but that will be bad. Too much people. Too much drugs. Too much bad cattle."

"How do you mean, bad cattle?"

"That is one reason we do not want the highway. The cattle from the south—from Colombia and other places—they have dis-eases and they kill our cattle."

"I hadn't heard that before."

"Ah." He smiled, sliding back into his hammock after performing his official duties. "Maybe there are many other things you have not heard also."

I wondered what those "other things" might be, but it was obvious that he was anxious to return to his reveries. He had also noted the word "writer" on my passport and possibly decided that caution on his part might be preferable to revelations or comments on the post-Noriega government, still sensitive to overt criticism.

We were off again early the next morning, as the gold dawn light filtered through the trees, turning drops of dew into diamonds necklaced along the edges of fat green leaves. Roosters croaked as if clearing their throats before letting blast with the full force of their morning oratory. Dogs barked sleepily and without rancor. A few pigs—small peccaries—grunted around the bamboo and thatch huts, and my two guides chuckled together about something that had happened the previous night. I was tempted to ask details, but, although they were friendly enough to me, we hadn't established the camaraderie I often found with other guides in remote places. Possibly they knew our journey was relatively short and they'd never see me again.

In other places—India, Thailand, China, Nepal—I'd felt that a significant spur to friendship with guides was their hope of future assistance from me. I was a "bankable" item—someone to help them if they ever realized their dreams, usually expressed in the phrases "I would very much like to come to your country" or, more ambitiously, "*When* I arrive to your country I will come to you."

My two Cuna Indians seemed to need nothing. Their mysterious trading activities and their lives deep in the forest provided all they required. They were not at all curious about my travels. They expressed no interest in the United States or any hope of one day moving there or anywhere else. I sensed a completeness in their lives and an almost European reluctance to reveal much about themselves.

I accepted their polite reticence and enjoyed their quiet company anyway. And their cheerful endurance too, during what was becoming an increasingly arduous pilgrimage for me into Cuna country. The river had narrowed now and became petulant in the shallow places, putting large boulders in our way, making us get out and push the piragua for much larger distances in the increasing heat of the forest.

If only there was a breeze once in a while. Anything but this perpetual, energy-draining steam-room humidity. Occasionally a wind high up in the overhanging canopy rustled the upper branches and vines and sent birds and monkeys into cacophonies of screeches. But down here, among the roots and dead trees and leg-scratching snags in the stream, nothing moved except the water itself. No breeze. Not even a scintilla of a sigh. Just thick gooey rot-reeking air that oozed out of the shadowy recesses and hung like a shroud—maybe for weeks at a time, who knows?—over the river.

Hour after hour we edged our way upstream. And now there were mosquitoes too—big brazen bastards with proboscises like knitting needles—leaving trickles of bright red blood running down my arms and legs. I sprayed on the familiar range of Deet-laden repellents, but those spitfires of the sky always managed to find an untreated spot or merely waited in a hungry haze of buzzing wings until a combination of sweat and river water had washed off prior applications and opened up my bodily territories again to their pernicious probing.

Why? Why do you do this kind of thing? I heard the old hedonistic me again—the one who is not at all averse to long, lazy days paddling aimlessly about on the lake back home, letting the hours pass languorously while I read about other people's tormented travels, and break off to drag my poor overworked wife down from her studio to the decadence of frosty cocktails on the deck as the sun sinks down behind the purpling mountains. . . .

Why do I keep coming back to this kind of masochistic mess—pushing my overpampered body to its limit and beyond, inviting perils that are undoubtedly prejudicial to a healthy longevity?

Because you love it, my better half responded.

Oh, yeah! Sure, I love it! The lousy food; languages I can't even begin to understand; bugs, bites, and biliousness. Banging

175

my head against padlocked doors of self-discovery and self-knowledge. Seeking wisdoms and insights that would lift my life onto a higher, more ethereal plane—yet invariably coming back to the limitations of my own psyche and my prejudices and my low resistance to pain. Yeah—sure, I love it!

Something smiled inside and nodded with the annoying certainty of an understanding father—or a personal sadhu. Do we all carry our sadhus within us, our "better selves," our inner god, our "soul"? I suppose we do. I've come to know mine pretty well during the craziness of the last twenty or so years and I suppose I love him dearly. Only why do I have to keep grappling with this other me, or me's? Why can't I just soar into a permanent sadhu state and remain there forever—centered, focused, all-knowing, all-understanding, all-accepting?

Because you're a human being, the voice replies with a gentle giggle. And because you're you.

Fine. But there are times like this when I'd like to be a different me. I get tired of all this tiredness.

Just look around, you dummy, my sadhu says. So I do and he's right again. It is so incredibly splendid. This whole trek: the forest, the river, the guides, the rough-edged tree-trunk boat, the sounds, the great extravaganza of emotions and beauty and insights and pain and—yes—even the itchy mosquito bites. All of it. It's all as it should be!

And just look at it! Behind the delicate groves of bamboo that edge the river are towering guilpa trees, whose smooth trunks soar from a tangled ground cover of roots and rotting branches into the canopy to explode in a riot of stubby leafless branches; snakelike lianas and vines are curled and coiled around trees or hang like guy ropes, holding upright the vegetation they had killed in rotting splendor; evergreen palms, wild banana trees, mango bushes, six-foot-long elephant-ear leaves, spiny palms, all creating an impenetrable mass that no one in his right mind would think of entering. A wonderful wild place!

And yet it's sometimes hard to keep a right mind in this place. During the day it isn't so bad. The forest broods; sounds cease as the heat increases, unless we disturb a gathering of banana-billed toucans, bright green and red parrots, or howler monkeys, whose racket echoes through the gloom for a while and then fades as the threat of our presence diminishes. However, as night eases into the thickets and we make camp beside the chittering stream, the symphony of insanity begins again. First come the birds, thousands of them, each presumably declaring its occupancy of territory; then the cicadas, whose leg-scratching racket rises and falls with a surflike rhythm; and finally the invisible tree frogs, whose high-pitched chattering hits a shrieking crescendo and never seems to waiver. Even plugging my ears with cotton wool pulled from the top of my ubiquitous aspirin bottle only serves to reduce the intensity of the sound but not its nerve-shattering pitch. Fortunately, I am usually so worn out by the day's boat-pushing activities that I slip into a deep sleep before insanity finally hits.

Oh, yes—the little sadhu inside keeps telling me—but it's still wonderful and you'll miss it all so much when (if) you leave this wilderness and return home to your quiet lake. . . .

After a meager breakfast of fried plantain and mangoes gathered from bushes around our campsite, we set off on what my Cuna companions told me would be our last day together.

The biting *bichos* were out again in the early morning. Nipping spiders, ticks, ants, chiggers, mosquitoes, and little black gnats somewhat similar to Maine's no-see-ums. Sweat ran down my body and the salt irritated every bite.

As we edged up the stream, vines and spider-webbed branches caressed us like living things. Some of the vines were so snakelike that I found myself inspecting each one carefully, dreading the intrusion of Panama's corals, bushmasters, or fer-de-lance, three of the deadliest snakes on the planet. We entered the damp world of greens again—more greens than I had ever thought possible from the limited palate of my landscape painting activities back home.

We maneuvered among whole trees uprooted and thrown aside like twigs in a recent mountain downpour that must have turned this modest stream into a roaring cataract. The banks were mustached with hairy roots of bushes and ferns, newly exposed. Even the delicate clusters of bamboo, lit by filigreed light through the canopy, had been beaten and broken into piles of hollow detritus, their delicate thin leaves dying in the shallows. Yet, even a few days after the storm, new bamboo shoots were emerging from the mulch. The eternal cycle again. Life begetting death begetting life. A valuable reminder of my own mortality. And knowing that soon I'd be on my own in this jungle, my senses of vulnerability and mortality were particularly pronounced.

I assumed our farewells would take place in a village or riverside camp with maybe some food or fruit or rum to assuage the sadness I felt. They had been good, strong men and I would miss their humor and their endurance, particularly as I had been warned back in Yaviza that the path I would now have to follow, away from the stream, was difficult. Difficult in this territory may mean impossible for this weary wanderer with overloaded backpack and bug-bitten body.

But there was no village or camp. We simply arrived at a point where the stream made a sharp bend to the left and they pointed to a semblance of trail that disappeared into the green gloom. Then they smiled, touched my shoulder, waved, and within a minute were gone around the bend, poling their piragua to another one of their mysterious destinations. Maybe to pick up more of those frond-wrapped bundles of whatever. They didn't say and I didn't ask.

Okay. Now begins the real test, I thought. And I was right. What is so frustrating about this place is that, on the map, distances look so small. But on the ground, which was now beginning to rise slowly into the foothills, a mile feels like ten and I had at least fifteen—maybe twenty—more crow-flying miles to go until I reached that "peak in Darien." Many more in wiggle-waggle, up-and-down, jungle-trail terms.

It was hard and sticky going, but slowly the disappointment at losing my friends so abruptly was replaced by a growing excitement. This was *my* adventure now. If I failed, it would be my fault. If I succeeded, then I'd turn the town of Turbo upside down in celebration. Frosty beer bottles began to accumulate again in my mind. Every five miles, two bottles, and an extra two when I reached the high ridges. Good deal, David. Go for it.

Another raucous night in the jungle. This time alone, but I was beginning to get used to the place now. Fears of being attacked in my pup tent by shadowy forest creatures or eaten to the bone by those big black ants I saw all day long faded. The Darien no longer felt dangerous. Challenging, certainly, in its own fetid and feverish way, but also charming. A riot of nightlife (particularly those damned tree frogs) but a riot that had occurred like clockwork over eons of time and was in no way caused by or threatening to me. It was the forest. Eternal and unchanging—unchanging, that is, if the Cuna have their way and protect its completeness, its wholeness, uninvaded by the Pan American Highway or any other panderings to so-called progress by the Panamanian government. Just let it be, I prayed that night. Let it remain as it is for the Cunas and for all of us. Eventually even those who never venture here (and I hope not many do) will sense its presence as the earth's last untouched places become increasingly scarce and valued. We'll know it in the air we breathe and in the rains, maybe even in new medicines and foods. Maybe some will even know it because of the journeys made by individuals of questionable sanity, myself included, and in the words we carry back from peoples like the Cunas. Maybe.

Sleep came quickly.

Somehow, along the trail during the following two days I missed a village the Indians had told me about and finally dragged myself into the ancient community of Paya, a Cuna tribal cultural nexus, around dusk. I was hungry, worn out, drenched in sweat, and in need of human contact and comfort.

A narrow river flowed by the village of bamboo and palm-frond huts. The river was a tributary of the Tuira. If only my two Indian guides had kept on going to Paya as I originally thought they intended, I would have been saved almost three days of hard hiking.

It was the women I noticed first. Compared to the simply adorned and often bare-breasted Chocos I had met during the earlier part of the journey, the Cuna ladies strutted proudly in all their finery—bright red and yellow scarves framing heads liberally adorned in huge silver and gold earrings, nose rings, and necklaces of pearls and coral, all in a rich display of wealth and status. But most dramatic were their red *mola* blouses, hand-decorated in ornate geometric and animal patterns. Even in the dusky light

179

the colors of their clothes and jewelry glowed and flashed in the light of cooking fires.

The men were far more modestly dressed—old jeans, rag-bottomed shorts, and loose shirts. As Paya was supposedly one of the most important mountain villages of the thirty-thousand-strong Cuna tribe, I thought at least the headman might come decorated in appropriate regal accoutrements. But he wasn't even there. One of his sons explained that he had been called "off the mountain" to attend a council meeting with members of the tribe on the San Blas Islands, that scattering of miniature paradises off Panama's Atlantic coast.

The son was not altogether unfamiliar with strangers entering his father's domain in this condition. Since a National Geographic expedition attempted to cross the Darien by Jeep back in 1960, he has seen a handful of curious travelers like myself trying to accomplish the same feat by piragua and trek.

"You have come a long way." He smiled and spoke slow, clear English while offering me a banana-frond plate heaped with succulent fried plantain. The women watched and giggled as I devoured slice after slice. I tried to be polite, but the food—any food—was so delicious that I'm sure I broke all the rules of protocol and munched away blissfully as the chief's son talked to me about his father's journey.

"He is trying to protect our homeland. It seems every year it becomes more and more threatened. There have been so many plans to take our trees, make our islands into places for tourists, build roads through our forest, and bring cattle into the lowland along the coast."

"Yes, I have heard of many of these things," I said. "But so far you seem to have been able to stop the government. Someone told me that tale of General Torrijos at your council meeting when you explained how precious the forest was to you."

"Ah, yes. That was Rafael Harris, one of our leaders, who said those things to the general. And for a while things became quiet. But"—he shrugged—"now we have a different government."

"What about all those organizations that are now working with you to keep the forest and the islands as permanent sanctuaries?"

180

"They have been very helpful and more people are joining them. But—well, we will have to wait." Then he laughed. "I can see you are very hungry."

I hadn't realized that I'd eaten all the plantain slices.

He waved and another banana-frond platter appeared, brought by a young girl dressed in one of those finely embroidered *mola* blouses.

"You are very kind. I didn't know I was so hungry. But now it's my turn. I would like to give you a gift."

I had noticed his eyes following my pen as I scribbled notes of our conversation. "May I give you this pen? I know your people are among the best-educated tribes in the Americas—I'm sure this may be useful."

He smiled and pointed proudly to the school building across the clearing. It was in the process of being extended.

"We believe education is very important. The young people must be taught the ways of our tribe, but also we must understand the ways of others. In that way we can survive."

"Well—from what I've read, you've done pretty well so far. And you've still got your land."

"Much less than we once had."

"Yes, I know, but maybe you can show us how to solve some of the problems that the world is only just beginning to face."

"There are many maybes," he said, and smiled. "You see, our people—our culture—it is very ancient. Many things are hard to explain, maybe hard for you to understand. *Preservation* is a word you might use—a word many of the people who help us use. It suggests the possibility of alternatives . . . but to us, such alternatives do not really—truly—exist. You see—we are the people of the Golden Time. We believe in the Great Mother—the creator. We believe the forest is part of that Golden Time when the trees, when the houses, when the rivers—all were gold. Then that paradise—the place that was our place—became corrupted. It became a dangerous world of creatures—spirits that are dangerous to us. We call it 'The time of the half man–half animal.' A time when snakes had only to look at their victims to bring instant death. Poisonous plants appeared—trees grew thorns. The paradise was being lost . . . you understand me?"

"Yes, I think so."

He laughed softly. "It is difficult to understand unless you are Cuna. You see, to us the spirit world and what you call the 'real' world are not different things . . . they exist together . . . one is a shadow of the other. Our legends have many uses—they teach us our history, morality, even what you might think of as 'natural science' but—more important—they tell of the central way, the way of the Great Mother . . . the balance of forces. For example . . ." He thought for a while. "All right—for example, the waters, the streams. When the rivers flood it is a sign of the guardians—the spirit guardians—of the whirlpool, releasing the power of water so that things will be brought into balance. When the waters—the streams—do not produce as they should, the guardians of the gates that lead from the spirit world to the earth world may act for us—they will open the gates and release the fish—whatever we need—into the waters for our use. We live in this—how you say?—a two—no, a dual world—where the spirits travel freely and can do much harm to us or protect us. It depends on how we treat them. Do you see?"

I nodded.

"Have you enough food?"

"Yes, I'm fine. I'm trying to understand."

"Well, you see, when the people came after the Golden Time they had to accept many dangers. Some of the dangers have been reduced—but our earth—our place—it is still a difficult place and we must protect what we know—to keep the balance. In the forest we have places where there are many spirits—we call them Kalucanas—sacred places where only the wise men know how to enter and what things to say to the spirits. If someone who does not know these things comes too close to these places, he will feel as if a net has been thrown over him and he cannot get out. If he does not run away—if he goes on, he will face many dangers—an invisible door will open and the bad spirits will come out. He will be attacked by the man-animals—the jaguars, the snakes—they may kill him. Eat him. Anything."

He paused and looked at me to see if I understood.

"So that is why the forest is so special to you."

"Yes. You see, as Cuna, the spirits are part of our lives, every day. The sanctity of the Kalucanas has protected us ever since we were born. You are concerned with things like 'environment'—

'ozone'—things like that. And that is good. You too are hoping to keep the balance of things. But to us it is different—it is part of the sacredness of our place, part of the Golden Time. And for this reason it must remain as it is. Forever. That is what Rafael Harris was trying to explain to Torrijos, but of course he had to use words the general could understand."

"Well—I think I know what you're saying. When I watch you speak I can feel how important this world is to you. Maybe the way I see it is a little different from you—but I think the result is the same. To understand the balance and keep the balance."

"Yes. Keeping the balance. In that way we have our world. And you will keep the things that are precious to you too. So we all . . . win? We give to each other."

"And you are giving many things to me. This is my fourth plate of plantains! That's why I'd like you to have this pen," I said. "It belonged to my father and I'm sure he—"

"It is your father's pen?"

"Yes."

"Then I cannot accept. And you should not offer it."

He was right. I was reluctant to part with it, but gift giving, I knew, was an important part of Cuna tradition and I had so little else to give.

"May I see your notebook?"

I handed him the damp dog-eared pad in which I recorded the journey and kept sketches of people and places I'd seen.

"You did these drawings?"

"Yes. They're only rough."

"They are very good." He flicked through the pages and paused at a sketch I'd done of one of my Cuna guides.

"You draw people well," he said.

"Thank you."

"And I thank you for your offer of a gift. I cannot accept the pen of your father, but I would like you to do a drawing of me." (Memories of Juan in the Venezuelan Andes!)

"I'd be delighted."

"Good. In the morning we will meet and you can do the drawing. And tonight I would like you to sleep in one of our houses. Many of our village have gone with my father and their houses are empty. This man will show you where to go."

A young boy was beckoned. The chief's son said something quietly and I was led across the clearing to a small bamboo and thatch hut on the edge of the village. Except for two crudely carved stools, a pile of wooden bowls in the corner, and a bamboo mat, the place was empty. The supports consisted of thick lengths of bamboo tied together with hemp rope and topped with an elaborate roof of folded palm leaves secured by more rope. The boy vanished and returned a few minutes later with yet another banana-leaf plate of fried plantains and chunks of fresh avocado.

I spread my tent as a groundsheet over the mat, used a pile of my sweat-stained clothes as a pillow, and proceeded to eat yet one more evening snack. Outside was dark and the jungle chorus began on schedule. People moved about, their shadows flickering against the huts behind the cooking fires.

But once again, sleep came too quickly. Possibly in midbite of a particularly succulent slice of plantain, because I woke briefly at one point during the night and discovered my arm smeared in squashed banana pulp.

The next morning, after a breakfast of—you got it—fried plantain I sketched the chief's son, who wore a feathered headdress and long necklaces of monkey teeth.

"To the Cuna, these teeth are very important," he told me as I sat cross-legged outside his house. "Like the Christian peoples, we believe that after death we enter another life. There are many levels in this life and one thing that helps a man reach a high level is the number of his necklaces. These are the teeth of what you call the white-faced monkey. These monkeys are quite fierce and to kill such a creature is considered brave. So—the more monkeys you kill, the longer becomes your necklace of teeth, and the more honor you will have in the next life."

He smiled as he talked, as if he didn't quite believe in such ideas.

I was pleased with the sketch and handed it to him. He stared at it for a long time and then laughed.

"Yes. This is a fine gift, my friend. I will keep this in my house."

184

Other Cuna clustered about, but he shooed them away and held the sketch to his chest.

"And I have something for you."

He took off his headdress, reached around his neck, and lifted one of the necklaces over his head.

"Come here. Take off your hat."

I removed the soggy, tattered canvas remnant of what started as quite a smart bush hat back in Panama City.

He placed the necklace gently around my neck. "Now you too will have good life in the next place!"

"But I didn't kill these monkeys."

"Ah—that doesn't matter. I gave it to you, so it is the same thing."

He winked as if to reinforce again the idea that he didn't take all these beliefs too seriously.

"This is a wonderful gift. I shall keep this always," I said.

"And I will keep this too," he replied, holding the sketch like a precious piece of porcelain.

I spent the day wandering around the village, talking with the people and visiting their carefully nurtured gardens of bananas, mangoes, papayas, and avocados. With the exception of a few chickens and peccaries, the Cuna seemed to depend on a largely vegetarian diet. They looked fit and happy, proud of themselves and their reputation as of one of the most advanced of all Latin American native people.

I had hoped to watch one of their community meetings, a centuries-old practice of equitable democracy in which all tribal issues and disputes, including the selection of the chief, are resolved by discussion and consensus. But, with the present chief and many of his associates away on the San Blas Islands, the sturdy bamboo and thatch community house remained empty.

His son outlined some of the strict protocols of these community meetings. "They can be very complex," he said. "The number of these meetings in a village tell you how important that village is. There are two main types—the chanting and singing meetings, where all the villagers come. The men who know the correct chants and songs are very important. Usually we vote them to chiefs. And then we have the special meetings for only the men when the conversation and discussion is very—what do you say?—like a church ritual—yes, like a ritual. We discuss something and when no one has any more to say, we reach a decision without voting."

"By consensus, you mean?"

"Yes, that's the thing—consensus. All together. About all kinds of things—about the things we grow, about government plans, about new schools. All kinds."

"What happens if a meeting can't reach consensus?"

"Well—if it happens very often, then the community will divide. A new village will be built and those who do not agree will live in the new place and have their own meetings."

"So everything happens at a village level."

"Very much, yes, but a few times every year we have congresses of all the villages. That is where my father is now. He has gone with some others to the islands where many of my people live, and they will discuss things that are important for everyone."

"It all sounds very organized and very serious," I said.

"Well, yes, I think it is. But we have many times of fun too. Many celebrations when people give gifts and have big hearts. If a son completes his education or marries or has a child—his family will have a big party and give away many things. We like to be generous. We do not like people who do not share what they have. That is not the Cuna way."

"And the government allows you to live in this way—the way you choose?"

"Yes. They must. Since 1938 we have always had our own lands, the Comarca de San Blas, and since 1953 we have been allowed to run things—most things—by ourselves. That is why we can do things like protect our islands from hotels and other things, and keep our forests by working with people from other countries."

"We talked a little last evening about the project you have for preserving the forest."

"Well—for us it is very important. This is our home and no one really understands how valuable the forests are. There are lots of scientists all over the world trying to understand how the forests live. Maybe in the future we can have a balance between people and land, but first we must know how the forest lives and what is dangerous for it."

"You sound as if you love this land very much."

"How I cannot? It is my home and it is very beautiful—and very special for all of us."

"Well—if you're the next chief, the forest will be safe."

"Aha! Maybe I would like to be chief one day. I have taken much time to learn the rituals and the chants—but, we are a democracy and even though I am the son of a chief, they may decide to have another person. That is the way it works with us."

"I wish you the best of luck."

"That is very nice for you to say to me. But whatever happens I am happy to be here. Being Cuna is very good!"

"I can see that!" I said, and our sudden laughter scared a couple of baby peccaries rooting in the scrub nearby and sent them scurrying across the dry earth in flurries of dust.

The following day I packed and was ready to leave when the chief's son approached me again.

"I am sending a guide with you. There is no need to pay him. When you reach the Atrato River you must find someone in a piragua and he will take you maybe to Turbo." He laughed. "Although I don't know why you want to go to Turbo!"

"It's the only way out once I cross the mountains into Colombia."

"And you want to go out?"

"Not really. It's so beautiful here."

"You know you can stay if you wish."

God—how many times have I been told this by people in quiet and peaceful places, all around the world. And I always feel the same way—torn between the flow of the journey itself and the temptation to stay and become a part of such places for a longer period of time.

I always remember something the notorious explorer-writer Richard Burton wrote: "If we stop moving and try to explain everything, we truly die; if we pause, if we take our gaze off the shimmering horizon for an instant, if we abandon the path in order to reflect or to plot our silly course, we go into exile."

A CUNA VILLAGE
— in Panama's Darien

The impatient, impulsive Burton believed in movement for movement's sake and some of his travel journals reflect a distinct lack of reflection. I know the temptations—the weighty momentum of the journey itself—but I also know the joys of staying awhile. And even if I don't stay, in my heart I always promise to return after searching out the next lost world.

And, who knows, when all my wanderings are over, maybe I'll return to this little village deep in the Panamanian rain forest.

It's just that "maybe" that concerns me. . . .

The next two days were hard going, climbing ever upward into the Darien ranges. At the highest point they reach over six thousand feet, but my guide insisted, in a Spanish dialect I could barely understand, that we were taking "the lower way." Only it didn't feel like that. The track, barely distinguishable among the riot of ferns, palms, and vines, wriggled like an inebriated snake up the endless muddy slopes. His panga was a useful instrument for clearing scrub in the thickest places, but we still had to somersault over enormous moss-covered trunks that had fallen across the track, and crawl in rotting slime up the steepest inclines.

Somewhere along the way we entered Colombia and paused in a small clearing at the top of the ranges to celebrate the views from our "peak in Darien." Unfortunately, low clouds hid the view of the Pacific sixty miles or so to the west, but I could vaguely make out the Atlantic coast twenty miles to the east.

Between the coast and our aerie lay more jungle, which eventually merged into the vastness of Colombia's enormous and little-explored swamplands. There was no sign of human habitation anywhere. The liquid landscape of this region would be an ideal candidate for "lost world" journeys—a mysterious green wilderness, through which silver-flecked streams wriggled into flat hazy infinities.

Maybe I'd do some exploring there after a little R and R in Turbo. (Another one of those damned maybes.)

The descent was almost as bad as the climb. Not quite so strenuous but leaving both of us like swamp creatures as we skidded and slid down through the tangle of vegetation, searching for a tributary of the Atrato that would carry me safely by piragua to the coast.

On the third day after leaving Paya we eventually found a stream, full and navigable following an overnight rainstorm that had battered my tent into a soggy, matted mess by morning.

My guide left me sitting on a pile of newly exposed roots by the water's edge and went upstream to see if he could find someone willing to take me to Turbo.

Three hours passed which I had hoped to spend musing on my journey but was so plagued by mosquitoes and other biting *bichos* that I ended up wrapping myself in my wet tent and dozing in the sticky heat.

Luck was with me, though. My Cuna guide returned in a piragua with a man who looked far too old for paddling and poling. We said our farewells and I gave my guide the gift of a knife he'd admired when he watched me cut the fruit we'd been eating for the last few days.

Once we reached the Atrato the journey became relaxing. The old man was on his way to trade in Turbo (more odd bundles wrapped in banana fronds and tied with hemp) and we eased down the river through the northern swampy fringes, out into the vast delta, and across the shimmering Gulf of Urabá.

Turbo was as bad as I'd been warned. Its Wild West flavor had none of the charm of the old gold-mining towns of the United States. It was a seedy, forlorn place full of street gamblers and cheap-beer saloons and slouching *campesinos* who had come to this terminal point of the Pan American Highway in search of something they couldn't seem to find and didn't know what to do next. I celebrated the end of the journey by drinking my first cold beers in almost ten days, but they didn't raise my spirits much. The place had an end-of-the-earth feel and I quickly set about making arrangements to travel by ship to Colón.

I couldn't forget the invitation of the chief's son in Paya—"You know you can stay if you wish." Why the hell didn't I stay in his tranquil village eating plantains and sketching the Cuna, at least for a while? Why all this constant movement? A glut of good-byes and not nearly enough "Thank you—I'll stay."

I'll work it all out one day. Maybe. . . .

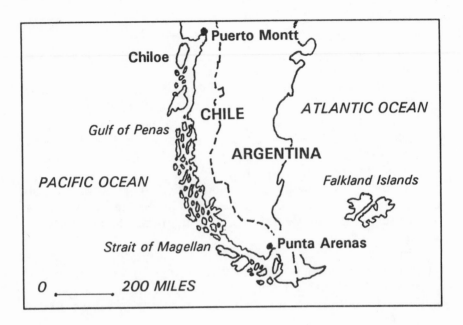

Puerto Montt

Chiloe

CHILE

ATLANTIC OCEAN

Gulf of Penas

ARGENTINA

PACIFIC OCEAN

Falkland Islands

Strait of Magellan

Punta Arenas

0 _____ 200 MILES

6. THE CHILEAN FJORDS
Killer Waves, Williwaws, and Other Wonders

I'm definitely not a sailor. Never have been, and by the look of present circumstances, never will be. I might not even be me much longer. Rarely have I felt so utterly vulnerable—helpless—at the questionable mercy of unfamiliar elements, dependent upon the skill and endurance of someone I hardly know. Oh—and facing the voids of self-doubt as my little backup security bungee ropes snap one by one, leaving me tumbling headlong into utter unpredictability—and terror. I don't even know why I'm here. . . .

An almighty crash!

What the hell was that?

The boat seemed to somersault in the heaving spray. We must

have caught a side wave again. Much bigger than any of the others. Water poured over the rail like a miniature Niagara. I was hanging on with both hands, but I could feel my grip weakening.

Why doesn't the thing bob back up like boats are supposed to? I'm looking into the waves now—I mean *into* them. They're directly *below* me. They shouldn't be there. If I lose my hold I'll just tumble down into the maw of the maelstrom. And that'll be it—one second—less than a second—and it'll all be over and finished. No more heaving like a cork in a cataract, no more of this bone-jarring roller-coastering. . . . I'd be at peace. Drifting gently down, far beneath the churning waves. Drifting into silence. A lovely, benevolent, eternal silence. . . .

It's almost tempting. I'm sick of all this clutching and crashing and grabbing and churning. Is it wrong to ask for a little respite? I mean, how much more is this poor battered body of mine supposed to take? Dammit, it's summertime down here. It's not supposed to be like this. No one had warned me. . . .

There are far easier ways of exploring the curled southern extremities of Chile. They've even built a new road through the Andes all the way down to the Patagonian and Tierra del Fuego peaks. A nice safe one-lane graded highway on the other side of the mountains, where skies are occasionally blue and winds only bend trees a little, not whole landscapes. There are even towns that boast 310 days of sunshine a year. The Chilean coast, on the other hand, is lucky to get 40! It would have been a beautiful quiescent journey—just me and the condors and the mountains and the vast Argentinean pampas to the east. I would have actually been able to see something. These impenetrable fogs and notorious "williwaw" winds and days of nothing but sodden grayness would have been as unlikely as glaciers in the Grand Canyon.

I could have slept on solid, unmoving earth or even in little roadside inns, eating the good stolid beef 'n' beef breakfasts and dinners of this rolling cattle country. I could have had days of quiet meditation and relaxation—sketching a little, catching up on my travel notes, and polishing my soul. Generally mellowing out and bestowing a few modest indulgences upon my weary body and mind.

193

And lots more "could haves" too.

Only I didn't.

I didn't do any of that. Instead, like a jolly gigolo, I allowed myself to be seduced by the idea of new experiences, new conquests, new adrenaline stimulants—the new aphrodisiac of a sea journey. On a boat. A small boat. Skimming across a purple ocean. Exploring the most magnificent (and undiscovered) fjord coast in the world. Forget the Norwegian fjords. The fjords of Chile are twice, three times the size. The whole Andean range rising up from jungle-clad bays and clefts to soaring snowbound peaks necklaced with glaciers that sparkle and wink under huge blue skies. . . . Oh—I'd done my homework. I knew that this part of Chile, only six hundred miles west from the South Shetland Islands of Antarctica, was a region notorious for its climatic idiosyncracies. Month after month of storms and gales from Cape Horn. All the way up the nine hundred miles to Puerto Montt. But I also knew—well, at least I'd been told by people who knew—that November was summertime here in these southern latitudes. A time of tranquility and restoration. A period ideal for easy exploration.

"Nobody's written about this area," I'd been told. "It's one of the earth's last real undiscovered regions," I'd been assured. "You'll be one of the first."

I should have known better. The lure of "You'll be one of the first" is always guaranteed to hook this particular fish. Brighter than an Apte Tarpan fly, as deadly as a Jock Scott or a Royal Wulff, the lure of those words always hides a barbed hook and I've had those barbs stuck deep in my psyche before as I've grappled in the soaring *tepuis* of the Gran Sabana of Venezuela, the treacherous terrains of Scotland's Torridon, the fickle terrors of the Sahara. And all because of that damned phrase "You'll be one of the first."

You'd think I'd have learned to be a wise fish by now. Keeping to the deeper places. Ignoring the clever illusive flashes of bright lures. . . .

Another crash!

Just as we were coming up to horizontal. And here we go again. Another Niagara. Another eye-to-eye meeting with that horrible green-gray morass of seething ocean directly below me.

194

I'm really fed up with this now. Honestly—I'm not kidding. I've had it. Sailing is for suicidal nuts. Men aren't meant to sail. The snide, grinning dock hands at Puerto Montt had known it would be like this. All that nudging and nodding—they knew what it would be like. They may have even tried to warn me in their cocky supercilious way—but I wasn't listening. I was off on another adventure. I only heard that damn phrase "You'll be one of the first" and everything else was mere maunginess and mean-spirited pessimism. . . . I was deaf to defeatism. Hell—I may even have sniggered at them—laughing inside at the landbound. Poor unimaginative buggers—living their dull safe lives among the cranes and capstans and old warehouses. Never knowing the thrill of discovery. Never even catching a glimpse of the towering fjords.

I wish I was back with them now. They were the wise ones. I was the jackass. Just another arrogant ignoramus off to his doom among the unnamed islands and whirlpooling channels of this topographical tumult. This time I'd gone too far. There'd be no lucky hand of fate to lift me lovingly out of this seething mess. . . .

It had all begun so calmly in Puerto Montt, where I'd come to satisfy a nagging curiosity about this strange remote region at the bottom end of the world that nobody seemed to know anything about.

As usual I'd made no prior arrangements, trusting to luck that there would be boats of some kind easing their way down the coast, through the narrow channels, across the notorious Gulf of Peñas and on down the Strait of Magellan to Punta Arenas.

I'd be following the historical wake of Ferdinand Magellan, who sliced through these seas for the first time in 1520 aboard his caravel *Trinidad*, or Sir Francis Drake, who, sailing his famous *Golden Hind*, discovered a safe if choppy route between cliffs and storms. Or even the poor Captain Sarmiento de Gamboa, who established some of the first communities in these southern extremities of Chile and later saw them desolated by isolation and starvation. Ah—what a journey. What a dream!

Of course I expected to hang around the docks and cafés of Puerto Montt for a few days looking for a lift. After the noise and

195

swelter of Santiago, seven hundred miles to the north, this quiet Bavarian-flavored, end-of-the-line port town founded by German immigrants in the 1850s is a pleasant place for dallying. In this capital of Chile's famous Lake Region I envisaged a couple of trips into the mountains playing tourist, but luck suddenly appeared abruptly on day two in the form of Peter Swales, an Australian sailor who, in his words, was attempting "a half-assed 'round the world thing with lots of holdovers!"

"Is Puerto Montt a holdover?" I asked him.

"Not from what I've seen. Don't think there's much point hanging about. Too quiet."

"So where are you heading next?"

"South—down the coast. See the fjords. Have a look at the Magellan. They say that's beaut sailing down there!"

Well—time to go for it, I thought.

"Do you need a deckhand? I gather it gets a bit rough."

He looked at me and I looked at him. He was a wiry, short man of around forty with sun-frizzled hair, a deep tan, and unusually large brown eyes. He seemed honest and direct, like most Australians I've met on my travels.

"Who you pitchin' for—yourself?"

"Sure. Who else?"

"Sailed before?"

"Not much."

"Get seasick?"

"I expect so."

"D'you know what a halyard is?"

"No idea."

"Can you cook?"

"I'm a great cook."

"Got some spare cash to share costs?"

"Not much."

A brief pause, then a quick laugh from Peter and an extended hand, deep brown and laced with rope burns.

"Six in the morning we leave. You can sleep in the boat tonight if you want. I'm not going to get a girl in this place, anyway. 'Least, not for free."

And that was that.

At six the following morning, as Peter had said, we left the harbor in his small boat, *Christine*, and began our nine-hundred-mile journey south through one of the wildest lost worlds in the Southern Hemisphere.

Just looking at a map of the world makes you curious about this ragtag coastline at the southern end of Chile. There are islands, hundreds of them, and deep gashes into the Andean spine (much deeper than those Norwegian fjord incisions). It's been called "a topographical hysteria" and "the wettest place on the planet," but on that first morning, as we drifted through light mists out of Puerto Montt, the thrill of new discoveries overwhelmed any sense of foreboding.

Unfortunately, the mists stayed with us most of that first day and well into the second, but at least the wind was "tame," hardly twenty knots according to Peter but quite frisky enough for me.

We had planned to rest over in Castro, on the Isle of Chiloé (the last town of any size for hundreds of miles), but Peter had lost a key navigational map and didn't fancy feeling his way through the shoals and islets in a fog.

"Listen, Peter," I said, "let's just give it a couple of hours. Maybe it'll lift, and I'd really like to see Chiloé. After this, according to the map, we're on our own. How about a few beers and a decent steak?"

Peter looked uncertain. There was something inside him—impatience, maybe—driving him on. I know those sensations well and find I have to fight them fiercely, otherwise my journeys would become nothing but mere mechanics of movement. I played an ace.

"I'm buying."

That did it. He smiled and nodded.

"Ah—well, that makes all the difference. Now what I see is one of those gigantic Black Angus steaks falling off the edge of the plate, barbecued to a crisp on the outside, blood red in the middle, with a great pile of . . . "

So we waited and the fog lifted for us. Darwin cursed this place for its appalling weather, the Spanish explorers loathed it, but we'd been granted a period of grace and decided to make the most of it.

Three mottled brown pelicans, saggy-beaked and with enormous wingspans, kept us company as we sailed for shore watching the twin orange and lavender towers of Castro's cathedral, the Apostal Santiago, rise up among lush green hills flecked with fields, orchards, farmhouses, and swirls of forest.

In such a fogbound, rain-scoured part of the world and on the edge of one of the most chaotic landscape and seascape combinations known to man, it was a delight to see the brightly colored little town edge closer. Startling canary yellows, vivid greens, turquoise blues, pinks, and mauves covered the tiny cottages, scale-clad like fish in wooden tiles, or *tejuelas*. They use the trunk of the local alerce tree to make these tiles and tradition has it that they bend outward every time it rains to keep the cottages dry and cozy.

The boats—even the people—were clad in the same array of brilliant colors. Chiloén women are notorious knitters—every spare minute they're sitting on the doorsteps clicking away with their needles, catching up with the local gossip, and producing a boy's sweater before dinner, when they vanish indoors to prepare their famous empanadas and strange dark stews (*cochajvja*), whose main ingredient seems to be black Chiloé seaweed, and the most traditional of their island dishes, *curante*, an odd blending of layered meats and seafood baked traditionally on heated rocks.

We tied up the boat near the harbor, close to a ragtag composition of *palafitos*, little cabins and houses built on high stilts to compensate for twenty-foot tides. At a dockside bar (bright pink shingles and violet-framed windows) a plump, apple-cheeked waitress was serving huge bowls of soup brimming with clams, mussels, scallops, and fish chunks, served with crisp seaweed cakes. Peter nudged me. "Stop gawking at that stuff. We're in here for steaks. And you're buying, right?"

"Right," I said. He was a stickler for protocol.

We passed a small town market. All dressed in bulky sweaters, the women were prodding through piles of homespun scarves, mittens, and caps spread out on the ground. Others were selecting from fifteen different types of seaweed tied, compressed, bundled, or packaged in plastic bags, depending on the type, and all looking like some illicit haul of exotic jungle drugs.

One old man in a thick drooping leather hat and a woolen

poncho sat on a stool presiding over his library of secondhand books and parchment-colored pamphlets. I picked one up with garish illustrations depicting the famous Chiloén legends of sea serpents, phantom galleons, boat-wrecking mermaids, forest trolls, a Dracula-like snake with a hen's head that lives on human blood, and an enormous plumed horse said to be the favorite form of oceangoing transport for island witches.

On the last page was Chiloé's most notorious spirit, El Trauco, an evil-eyed and bent-bodied goblin who turns modest maidens into passionate lust-crazed vamps and has been blamed for countless illicit unions and unexpected offspring among the island's nubile nymphs. One gentleman with a large walrus mustache and wearing a felt Hamburg hat paused to peer over my shoulder at the page, winked, and muttered something that sounded rude in the local dialect. I felt as though I'd been discovered peeping into a pornography bookstore and hastily replaced the book.

We finally found our steaks in a café overlooking the ocean and ate like kings under an unfamiliar blue and almost cloudless sky. Across the scattering of outer islands we could just make out the hazy, ice-flecked summits of the Andes and the volcano of Minchinmávida fifty or so miles to the east.

I could stay here for a while, I thought, exploring the other little towns on this lovely island, each with its church founded by the Jesuits, who maintained strict religious discipline here for two centuries until being harassed and then exiled by Spain's Philip II. I'd read about the old steep streets of Chonchi, the great Pacific beaches of Cucao, the Spanish fort at Ancud, and the delicious sea urchins of Quellón. Maybe if I could lure Peter on with more promises of steaks and Chilean *pisco* to wash them down.

But Peter was pining for the ocean again. "Just look at this weather," he said. "We'll really zip along in this breeze." So, reluctantly, I left Castro and "zipped along" with my impatient companion into the Gulf of Corcovado and headed due south toward the Moraleda Channel, the main channel through the Chonos Archipelago Islands. The weather was still kind to us and we meandered through a maze of sculptured islands dotted with coves and secluded beaches. I would have happily stayed for a week or two in each one, but Peter needed to feel movement and the wind in his sails. So we moved on.

It was strange—almost eerie—to see such beautiful places totally uninhabited.

"This should satisfy your lost world lust," said Peter as we passed by soaring cliffs and through bays edged by straggly woods and tundralike patches of emerald-green moss. (We were to learn much more about these "moss moors" later in the journey. They are not as benign as they look.)

We did spot a small fishing camp on a particularly idyllic stretch of beach at the southern end of the archipelago. Peter agreed to slow his southward rush and we sailed in closer to the island, hoping for an offer of a free meal and maybe even a night's lodging on firm ground. There were three big tents, ex-army types made of thick canvas, but no sign of boats, people, dogs, or anything. We called out, hoping there might be someone inside the tents, but our voices echoed on the cliff walls and received no response.

I was disappointed. A little relaxation in this lovely camp would have been ideal for this untrained sailor, but Peter was not prepared to invade uninvited. We reset the sails and moved back into the currents of the channels.

Ten days later I wished I'd followed my instincts and remained in the balmy harbor of the Chonos.

The first gale struck us as we sailed alongside the Taitao Peninsula down toward the Gulf of Peñas and it was then that I realized I'd always be a landlubber. If only I'd taken that highway back behind the mountains.

On the second day of fifty-knot storms, broken by strange ominously still periods that only lasted for an hour or so, I was seriously questioning the sanity of this adventure.

It was becoming all too familiar now—the wind shrieking in the rigging, everything soaking wet and with little chance of really drying out, the little craft leaning at a forty-degree angle, and Peter back there at the stern always adjusting the self-steering device, which, in spite of all his innovations, slammed noisily from side to side, threatening—so he kept telling me—the "main casting" (whatever that was).

We always had some jobs to do—tightening the preventer

lines, lowering (or raising) the pathetic little pocket-handkerchief-sized storm jib and the more difficult treble-reefed main, and checking the speed indicator, while in the distance marched that endless series of gray-black waves topped with blowing spindrift and angry breaking crests.

Up we'd soar like surfers as the waves hit, and then run down into twenty-foot, sometimes thirty-foot troughs, looking just like those bleak boggy valleys I'd once hiked across on England's Pennine Range. All around were moving mountains of surging water. A brief lull in these valleys, a passing moment of calm not dissimilar to an eye-of-a-hurricane sensation, and then the sudden soar up the heaving ridges which left us momentarily perched delicately on the crest, with broad vistas of white angry peaks and ridges all around us.

If only the sequencing of trough and crest had come a little more slowly I might have even enjoyed the calm moments when I felt suspended—weightless—in limbo. But the rhythm was just too aggressive, too rapid. I longed to hang on to a crest and admire the power and monotone beauty of the surging, screaming scene.

But no. Off we went again, roller-coasting from the tops and down into the next trough. And hoping—praying—that we made the subsequent crest before the damned wave broke, blew apart, and crashed down on us like an avalanche. These were the worst moments of all. Waiting for the pounding we'd get as tons of water hit us, the rigging, the deck. And not only did we have to withstand the sudden blows, but we had—somehow—to estimate the extent of the boat's keeling so that we could try to maintain a relatively perpendicular profile against the tearing, clutching water.

Fortunately, Peter's little boat was a canny creature. Twenty thousand miles of ocean sailing under his capable supervision had taught her a trick or two. I—nonsailor that I was—always dreaded the out-of-synch wave, a bloody-minded fiend that would crest too soon and hit us broadside before the boat had a chance to heel and shake off the deluge. Or one that would roll or toss her unexpectedly into a trough. Or maybe (my biggest dread of all and one that, to my untrained eyes, seemed almost inevitable) that we'd perform some kind of aquatic somersault as a gang of waves attacked together in a flurry of foul play.

But they never did, and we never did. Somehow that wily little craft seemed to psyche out the spirit and intent of each surge and, except for brief dousings of the cockpit and a back-wrenching lurch or two, she soared up and over and down and out again with the tenacity of a cork in a cataract.

Peter told me later, during a well-earned respite, that he preferred the big storms and waves to the "smaller seas." "They're sneakier. The rhythm of waves isn't so distinct. They get frisky and cheeky—like kids—and you get tossed into troughs so fast the boat doesn't have time to line herself up for the next bashing. Give me these big sods any day. She always knows how to get through those!"

For three of the last five days we'd been like this—bouncing through the "big sods"—and I could feel the strain beginning to tell on Peter. I always had the option of going below, locking the hatch and lying on the bed. There was nothing much to do aloft anyhow except get soaked, worry about the steering gear and the preventers, and watch for that one rogue wave that might finally do us in. But—in spite of the temptations of the warm and dryish cabin—I normally stayed on deck with Peter. It just seemed impolite somehow to leave all the tension and worry to him.

And as it turned out, it was good that I did.

"Hell 'n' fuckn' damn 'n' shit," I heard him shout (his most extensive use of expletives to date, so I knew we had a problem). "Support struts are going."

"Is that bad?"

I think if Peter were more used to hurling four-letter expletives about I might have been at the receiving end. Instead all I got was one of those belittling "Why the hell are *you* here?" looks and a rapid-fire rush of technicalities about the preventer lines pulling too hard and the main castings being cracked and goodbye self-steering. He started pulling on tiller lines to reduce the swing and lunge of the gear.

At that moment we had that sneak attack from a wave we hadn't even noticed. Coming in and cresting prematurely, it caught us both unawares and sent me skidding across the deck until I managed to clutch at a section of rail. Peter wasn't quite so lucky. He lost his hold on the tiller lines and fell sideways across the stern, hitting his head on some brass fixture near the sail. He reached out in a kind of halfhearted way to grasp for a rail, but then came another crash of seething water and he was spun completely around and sent skittering on his back, blood streaming from a cut above his ear, and down the deck toward the bow . . . just at the split second that we surged over the crest and down into the next wallowing trough. He was out of control, like a thrown rider in a rodeo, heading so fast for the bow that it seemed he'd go straight through the rail and into the ocean.

Then, like magic, the old slow-motion mind game snapped on like someone had pulled a switch. All this was happening in nanoseconds—it can't have been more than a moment since the wave hit—but in my head everything became so blissfully calm and silent that I thought I'd suddenly gone deaf. I could see Peter quite clearly even in the thrashing spray, waving his arms, trying to catch hold of something as he slowly spun toward me down the sloping deck. I was clinging to my bit of rail with both hands but felt no strain at all. A moment before I'd been convinced that unless my hands hung on with every sinew I'd be tossed overboard as quickly and neatly as an empty bucket. But now I suddenly felt balanced and perfectly centered in the storm—a sensation I used to get back in high school when I indulged in my favorite sport, discus throwing. There was that wonderful surge of utter certainty, just before a good throw, that everything was perfectly in synch—the speed of the spin, the balance of the discus in my hand, the angle of my arm, and the centrifugal force that would set the discus free, cutting the air like a scimitar, keeping its finely arced flow as it soared toward its apogee and then gracefully spun down through the air to skim the ground in the lightest of landings.

And when the picture in my mind and the reality of the actual flight coincided, I remember the most overwhelming sense of almost spiritual joy, a sense of having become one with that beautifully formed, flying saucer-shaped instrument of mahogany and bronze. . . .

It was the same sudden sensation that I experienced on that chaotic deck. I no longer seemed to need to fight the boat's surging antics—we were working together, almost glued together, and I was as safe and centered as I would be on my patio back home.

Next thing I knew—and I think I only really "knew" it later—

I had let go of the rail not just with one but with both hands and stepped out across the deck, caught Peter's swirling body by one of his outstretched arms, pulled him easily back to the rail, and fastened his fingers around the steel bars. I helped him stand and spread his legs and then casually reached out for my section of rail and resumed my original position.

The blood was still flowing from the gash in his scalp. I wiped it away and turned to see what the waves had in store for us next. They were still churning and surging (it was hard to imagine them ever being calm again) but they seemed to have lost some of their demonic nature. I was no longer frightened of them. Frustrated, maybe, annoyed by their mindless pounding, but accepting and curiously calm. Again, that similarity to the discus memory; the better the throw—the closer it came to the mind picture and my projected will for its flight—the calmer and more accepting I became. A sense of inevitability surged through me—the discus had flown the way it did because I'd been with it—a part of it—every inch of the way.

And that's what I sensed about our predicament in those malicious straits. I was no longer fighting, no longer placing myself as adversary. I was a part of it now, as I had been from the beginning but just forgot for a while, that's all. And we'd be okay. Peter was fine. I was feeling fine. Tomorrow the storm would die down, or maybe not, and either way we'd come out of it and move on to the next series of experiences—as an inevitable and willing part of those experiences.

Then came an odd little bonus. As all these thoughts, sensations, and actions took place in a minute, two at the most (it's taken much longer to write them down), I felt something else stir deep inside. It was almost like a chuckle, then expanding into a great gush of giggles—not just "mine" but from someone, something, some other essence within. And a voice—a voice I realized I'd only heard twice, maybe three times before in my life—saying "You have always known this." And a feeling, like a rush of hot lava, that a valve had been opened, a switch switched, and that the little insight I'd gained from these acquatic antics had been here all along—who knows, maybe even prebirth, deep in the genes or in some implanted library of eternal truths hidden somewhere in the recesses of the brain. The library that we all, to one extent or another, know is there and spend our lives seeking to find and understand, using all manner of exploratory devices— religions, meditations, drugs, "altered-state" exercises—you name it.

Peter must have thought the ocean had finally gotten to me. To him I was a giggling, grinning jackass who'd just done one of the dumbest things you can do on a bucking boat in a maelstrom, which is to let go of a firm hold. But the laughter continued on inside as I listened to my mind and this other new voice chatting away like two old and dear buddies. The inner laughter occasionally turned into outward giggles as the waves crashed down on us and poor Peter nursed his gashed scalp and kept giving me the most curious of glances, which started the giggles all over again.

The storm finally died. A few more hours of declining fury and then the calm of a gray-pink evening while I cooked our first real meal in two days and Peter fixed the struts of the self-steering assembly and grumbled about his cracked casing and broken preventer lines, mumbling things like "One more go-around like this and we'll really be in trouble."

He tried to explain what he meant by "trouble," but it all became too damned technical—all that gobbledygook about mainsheets, cam cleats, halyards, lifts, guys, reefing lines, winches, jibs, vang tackles, spinnakers, stanchions, bilge pumps, goosenecks, binnacles, luffs, clews, daggerboards, gilguys, gunwales, jumper struts, roaches and leeches, mizzens, mousings, boom vangs, and whisker poles. Another language—another level of communication—complete with such strange expressions as aback, abaft, broach, bear away, close-haul, full and by, heave to, kedge off, yaw, and, one of my favorites, wing and wing (which another colleague explained as "sailing before the wind with a jib and mainsail set on opposite sides" and left me even more confused).

My past sailing experience has done little to endear me to the practice. Back in my days as a city planner in Los Angeles I had once been invited by a more affluent colleague to join him for days on the ocean out of the Santa Monica marina. He was a tall, trim individual from an "old money" family whose ability to breeze through life and work in our office always amazed me. I even think I was envious. Prior to any meeting or major presentation I'd be sweating the details in my cubicle, checking the plans and schedules, rehearsing recitations of data and strategies, yellow-marking key phrases and buzzwords in my notes, and caffeining myself up to knife-blade sharpness.

John, on the other hand, would be bumbling along the highway somewhere in his souped up MGTC sports car, top down, music on, his tan deepening in the bright sun and sea air, always an hour or two late for work and barely aware that he had a job to go to at all. Little pink message slips would pile up on his desk (which was always empty—mine invariably looked like a garbage dump). And when he finally arrived, glowing with health and newly bronzed skin, he'd find a way to waste the last hour or so before lunch chatting with the secretaries and telling a few ribald tales to the technicians and draftsmen in the office, who were always eager for distraction and a good morning belly laugh.

"Just wing it," he told me once before a particularly daunting presentation to a client known euphemistically to be "difficult" and a real "nitpicker." "You know the stuff—don't sweat it," John told me. "Just get up and give 'em a smile and let it rip. If you don't know the answers, wing those too. Most of the time they don't know the difference. It's all in the attitude!"

And he lived up to his philosophy. Five minutes skimming through a day's worth of heavy technical treatises was all he needed and he was off to his meetings, shaking hands, patting shoulders, rattling off his spiel like a Baptist preacher, full of conviction and confidence, seducing his clients with brilliant word-pictures and leaving them breathless and begging for more.

Yes, I did envy him and I never learned his apparently easy knack of "winging it."

But (and here comes the rub) on his boat he became a different kind of character altogether. Talk about chameleon psyches. There was no "winging it" whatsoever on the burnished teak deck or around the overpolished brass sailing gear or even in the galley, where every item had a carefully defined place and lord protect the guest who forgot that. He was a tyrant indeed on his beloved *Evangeline*. He strutted about like a Captain Bligh shouting out orders to his "crew" (usually inexperienced colleagues who he'd lured to his boat by promises of easy days out on the ocean— with girls), complaining of lines not properly laid, greasy finger-prints on his brass fixtures, and sails sloppily raised.

A day at sea for John was like a campaign of war—exactingly planned, executed to the smallest detail, and with names taken of any errant crewperson who mistakenly thought he or she had come along for a little pleasure and play. There was hardly a moment of rest on John's cruises. Even when the wind died and we'd float in the calm seas, ideal for a bit of splash 'n' frolic, he'd seek out the faintest of breezes and have us all hauling and lowering sails, just to keep us moving, no matter how slowly, through the doldrums.

And when we returned to dock, worn and washed out, there'd be no escaping the boat until everything was packed, rolled, tied, repolished, and shipshaped to pass his exacting inspection.

Needless to say, I didn't sail too often with John.

So why am I here with Peter? I kept wondering. Although I felt far more confidence with this stranger than I'd ever felt before in a boat, our journey through the treacherous channels was testing us both to the limit. And his craft too. I wondered how much more it could take before the gear broke or something snapped and the sails were ripped to shreds and we'd be left floating helplessly, waiting for the sea to smash us against the cliffs of one of those fogbound little islands or against the black shore of the fjords.

But then came miracle-time. The wind suddenly dropped. The seas eased down to a choppy roll, and the mists began to lift up from the fjords like the rising of a stage curtain on some magnificent set for Grieg's *Peer Gynt*. Layer by layer the hills slowly rose from the shadows. Sea-level forests, rising higher to brittle-edged ridges and arêtes, higher and higher through sun-splashed snowfields, up past the gleaming blue-gold glaciers, to the sparkling peaks and domes of the Andes themselves.

The boat was barely moving now and we stood together, mouths open, as the scene emerged and the mists evaporated, leaving little serpentine strands floating in the high dark clefts.

FJORDS & GLACIERS
— Chile's Southern coast

"Unbelievable," I said (or some equally inadequate expression of wonder).

Peter didn't speak at all but opened a couple of beers and handed one to me. It was then I realized we'd hardly eaten or drunk anything in the last twenty-four hours. The storm and our concern for the boat had removed both appetite and thirst. Now I felt ravenous.

"Where's the canned tuna? I'm starving," I said.

"Yeah," said Peter. "Time for celebration."

And so we celebrated as the grandeur of the fjords continued to expand in all directions. Even the dumpy islands behind us, wet, mossbound, and uninhabited, took on a more appealing appearance as the sun splashed them with dapples of light.

This is what I'd come looking for—the magnificent loneliness and majesty of this remote place where no one lives and only the birds and the dolphins and the small creatures of the rain forests are companions.

And, as if on cue, we spotted three different species of albatross (the royal, sooty, and brown) circling us, followed minutes later by half a dozen shiny-skinned dolphins, who paused in their rolling ride north to put on a display of somersaults and leaps and birdlike calls especially for us.

"They used to give special decorations to sailors who crossed this Gulf of Penas in wintertime," Peter told me.

"Who was Penas? Some explorer?" I asked

"No, no. It's Spanish for 'tribulation.' Maybe 'misery' is more accurate."

"Very accurate."

Way, way to the north behind us we could see the faint outline of the Taitao Peninsula and the entrance to the more sheltered channels that had carried us south from Puerto Montt.

And then we saw the glacier.

We'd noticed it marked on the map in the northeast corner of the gulf, but Peter had decided the weather was too bad to go looking for it. But now with sunlight bathing the whole mountainbound bay we could afford to dally awhile.

And thank God we did. What we saw and experienced in the next day or so made the whole journey worthwhile.

As we edged in closer to Lake San Rafael we watched as the

great San Rafael glacier, a ten-mile-long, one-and-a-half-mile-wide river of ice, soared higher and higher in front of us. Thousands of feet above were the shattered peaks of 13,310-foot Mount San Valentine and a string of lesser mountains cloaked in snow and ice fields.

We met our first ice floes, heading out to the gulf, followed by icebergs of increasing size.

"She's calving," said Peter.

"What?"

"The glacier's calving. The ice walls are cracking. She's breeding baby icebergs—calves."

Soon we had to start edging our way cautiously between the "calves." Many of them had large horizontal shelves of ice under the surface and they could be hazardous even for small shallow-draft craft like ours. There were lots of them now, some less than twenty feet high and still showing the fracture marks where they'd broken from the mother glacier. Others towered above us in the still, mirrored water, more than a hundred feet high, bright white on the outside but with blue cracks and fissures, the blueness deepening with their depth. At one point we were surrounded by these enormous creatures, unable to see the mountains or the forest-covered shores. A lost world in miniature, bound by soaring carved walls and towers and broken jagged peaks of crystal ice, always moving in relation to each other, creating new patterns, revealing new silhouettes, rounding in on us, then offering us narrow channels of escape between walls of turquoise and royal blue ice.

And all in total silence. For some reason I'd expected groans and cracks and creaks (memories of books on Arctic expeditions when the ice always seemed to be alive?), but beyond the slight hum of our diesel engine these enormous edifices, rounded in places like great Henry Moore sculptures, others roughly hewn, Rodin-style, moved past us with no noise whatsoever.

Crack!

Followed by a tearing roar and then the echo of a huge splash.

We rounded the delicately shaped edge of an iceberg and saw the ice wall of the glacier immediately in front of us, hardly more than a mile away. All two hundred vertical feet of her. Torn,

211

broken, and bruised-blue up her vertical face, then gold-flecked white on top where the sun sparkled on her broken surface.

We had just missed a "calving." An avalanche of ice shards followed the collapse of a hundred-foot tower of ice into the ocean and a small tidal wave was heading our way, bouncing the icebergs like galleons in its path. Fortunately, its ten-foot-high cresting wave diminished to a rolling ripple by the time it hit our boat, but Peter was cautious. "I think that's far enough. If we move too close we'll be swamped."

I was disappointed. I wanted to ride right up to her slowly collapsing face, see the towers topple, feel the crash when they hit the ocean, be bounced by the tidal waves.

But Peter was the captain and I a very subsidiary deckhand. So I watched with him from a safe distance as the glacier cracked like cannon shot and towers toppled and new icebergs arose, at first shakily from the ocean, then, having found their balance, holding themselves in a haughty manner, waiting to be carried slowly by the water out into the gulf.

We spent hours floating there as the breezeless afternoon eased on and the colors began to deepen on the mountains across the lake. Finally we decided it was just too beautiful to leave and sailed to the northern shore, well away from the floating ice, and found a cove bound by blankets of thick moss for the night.

And as the sunset waned, bathing the glacier, the icebergs, and the towering peaks in a golden-pink light, we watched for the moon and, much later, tried to identify all those new and very unfamiliar star patternings and constellations. If only the sky would stay clear and open for the next few days we'd have the sail of a lifetime down through the mysterious uninhabited channels to the south, down the notorious Strait of Magellan, all the way to the rowdy urban distractions of Punta Arenas, six hundred miles to the south of the Gulf of Penas.

But luck only gives of itself sparingly here.

When we climbed on deck the following morning at five A.M. everything was cold and damp and gray.

"Bloody fog again!" said Peter.

"It'll lift!" I said in what I hoped was a cheerful voice.

"It'd better bloody lift. We can't move until it does. It'd be suicide with all those 'bergs floating about. We'd never make it back to the gulf."

After an hour or so the fog thinned enough for us to raise anchor and ease slowly down the northern shore of Lake San Rafael. We spotted a couple of monster icebergs to the south and a few smaller floes, but they were well away from us and after a couple of hours we were back in the ocean again.

Peter was still not happy.

"I'm not sure we should have left, y'know."

"Why? What's wrong?"

"The wind's coming in from an odd angle. The sea's got a pull to it. I don't know. Something just feels odd. Might be nothing. . . ."

It was rare for Peter to share his uncertainties like this. Usually he'd wait until his suspicions had been confirmed and then describe the accuracy of his silent predictions with the cocky confidence of a soothsayer.

For the first few hours it appeared his fears were unjustified. We sailed south in a light breeze as the fog and morning mists continued to clear, revealing once again the grandeur of this fjord coast. The soaring Andean ridges appeared again; sunlight gilded the snowfields and glaciers, and the lower rain-forested slopes looked so inviting that I wanted to leave the boat for a while and go off romping among the tangled vegetation, discovering the cool shady mysteries of their depths.

But I knew Peter was anxious to get farther south, away from the treacherous currents and fickle storms of the gulf and down into the naturally formed canals between the fjords and the Pacific islands, down the Mesier, Inocentes and Smyth channels, past the Archipiélago de la Reina Adelaida, and on into the Strait of Magellan.

So I became content just to watch the mountains and the deep shadowy cliffs of the fjords and the shimmering waterfalls that plunged in steps, thousands of feet down from the ice caps to the forests and the roiling ocean.

And the albatrosses. How I loved their flight, stretching their great six-foot wingspans and skimming only inches above the water, rarely flapping, allowing the air to cushion them effortlessly. The slightest adjustment to their wing profiles enabled them to soar gracefully or turn slowly to follow us, watching us with indifference in their dark eyes.

Closer into shore were the steamer ducks with their bright lemon-orange bills, floating in small clusters of a dozen or so and then vanishing together in unison below the waves, where they propelled themselves with their stubby wings as rapidly as cormorants. When it comes to flying, though, they're useless creatures. Their wings don't seem designed for liftoff and when alarmed they flail away at the water and vanish in rainbowing sprays, half running, half kayaking across the waves.

On the rocky shoals close to shore I spotted seals, scores of them, basking in the brilliant morning sun. In such a desolate setting, two hundred miles now from the nearest village or fishing camp, it was reassuring to see such amiable creatures who seemed curious about, but in no way alarmed by, our intrusion into their secret world.

As the day slowly eased into late afternoon, Peter decided we should put in early so he could perform some technical tasks on our battered craft. He selected as our anchorage a calm broad fjord, edged by dense rain forest, and was soon working away at the steering gear again.

"Sure you don't need any help?" I asked, hoping he'd say no.

He said no and suggested I might want to go ashore for a while.

"Bring back some mussels if you find any. They're supposed to be the best in the world."

We were anchored only fifty feet offshore, so I jumped into the water. . . .

I'd never thought the ocean could be so cold. Somehow, as we'd battered the tempests over the past few days, the waves that soaked us had always remained on the tepid side. But this particular cove contained water on the verge of turning into ice. By the time I struggled over the slippery rocks and onto the shore, I was blotched blue and shivering, my teeth chattering like a woodchuck. I started flailing my arms about to jump-start the blood circulation and promptly collapsed on the pebbly beach. I stood up again and found I had almost no sense of balance. My body had become so used to being bounced around on the always-moving deck of the boat that it had apparently forgotten how to deal with the solidity and stability of terra firma.

For a while movement was limited to crashing around on all fours. I could hear Peter laughing back on the boat.

"What are you, some kind of bloody bear?" he shouted.

All I could manage was a distinctly explicit finger gesture as I wobbled about trying to find some way to stand on my feet for a few seconds.

"Just sit down for a while—you'll be okay in a while," he bawled, still laughing.

Peter's advice was sound, but I could do without all the levity at my expense.

I decided to rest and enjoy the scene.

Late afternoon shadows were moving into the fjord—the ice-capped ridges thousands of feet above me were turning a burnished gold, edged with pink. A short distance from the rocky beach strewn with driftwood were enormous mounds of moss, like rich green lava. Beyond I could see patches of brilliantly colored wildflowers, none of which I could recognize from this distance—orange, vermilion, turquoise, crimson, and white. And behind these, the shaggy, moss-coated mass of stubby trees rising from a tangle of roots to a height of twenty feet or so. It was at once tempting and eerie. The openings between ferns and dead tree trunks and twisted branches beckoned, but the sinister gloom beyond made me hesitate. It was so black in there. No light seemed to penetrate the thick green canopy overhead. But c'mon, I told myself, you're perfectly safe. The boat's only a few yards offshore. All you've got to do is get across the mossy fringes here and you'll be able to see how safe it really is.

Two emerald hummingbirds flashed by, hovered for a while over tiny flowers in the moss, and vanished. I was hoping to catch a glimpse of hare-sized pudu—the world's tiniest deer—which I'd read was a resident of these moist forested places. And maybe a guanaco, cousin to the llama, although I associated these creatures with higher, drier Andean mountainsides.

Okay, up and off. My balance seemed to be recovering. I was ready to explore the forest.

Only it wasn't that easy. The maze of mossy mounds into

which I stepped were not mere coverings of piled rocks and boulders as I'd thought, but enormous independent entities, three or four feet deep, and covering the thickest, blackest, stickiest goo that it has ever been my misfortune to encounter. Far worse than the peat bogs in Scotland, which at least gave off a pleasing earthy aroma when punctured by boots, this stuff reeked of dead fish and rotting matter, eons old. And the more I struggled forward, the deeper and smellier it got. I was soon up to my thighs in the mess. As I tried to press down with my arms to move forward, they too sank beyond the elbows and were difficult to extract. The moss seemed to suck them in and if I moved too quickly my whole body sank deeper. I could feel no rock base under the moss; it was obviously a much thicker covering than I'd thought and I gave up all attempts at trying to move any farther through it. The primary challenge now was to get back to where I'd begun at the pebble beach, and the only way to do that was to literally lie on the stuff and pull myself across its gelatinous surface using hunks of the green and ocher-colored moss as handholds.

What emerged from this morass much later was a mud-covered Paleozoic monster, stinking and miserable. Peter's laughter from the boat was now reaching the point of wild hysteria. "What the hell are you doing?" he yelled.

I daren't shout anything back in case some of the goo dribbled down from my caked forehead and into my mouth. Another extremely vulgar finger sign sufficed as a response as I lumbered across the beach and flung myself into the ocean to scour my body of the odious slime.

I would not be defeated. There had to be another way into the forest.

I walked farther up the beach, keeping well away from the moss mounds, until I came to a spine of smooth gray rock that rose up from the morass like the back of an enormous hippo and ended a couple of hundred feet away at the treeline. That would do it. And it did. I strolled easily along its arched profile and at last eased between wind-broken trees into the darkness of the forest.

All was silence. Even after just a few yards in, the splash of the waves and seething of breezes along the shore vanished as if I'd closed a door behind me. But as I moved farther into the gloom

I became aware of a sound I'd rarely heard before. As if something were breathing. Something large that seemed to be all around me among the twisted trunks and tangled branches of this strange place.

I eased deeper in. The forest floor was a pulpy carpet of moss-shrouded limbs and decayed trunks from which new growth emerged in tendriled profusion. Broken branches writhed like pythons, sheened in moisture from the mists that constantly crept under the canopy, wraithlike, from the fjord. Vines and tentacled fronds brushed and clutched at me like living things; roots wound out of the damp earth in tortured convulsions before disappearing between cracked boulders; rare strands of sunlight at first glowed green and then broody-bronze through the tall ferns. I walked deeper into the gloomy hollowness under the thick roof of leaves. Within minutes I was scoured with branch scratches and tacky with torn spiders' webs. It was warm—a thick and porridgey heat—and glints of dim light flared in swampy patches.

But for all the discomfort, I sensed a pleasure, a rich joy somewhere deep inside. I felt I had entered a sanctuary—a throbbing place full of life and that endless cycle of re-creation. I moved more easily now as if in a sacred place, burying my feet in the softness of the forest floor, touching the moist branches and feeling their life and—hardest to explain of all—feeling them somehow touching me back, embracing me, welcoming me as a distinct entity in their quiet place. I was not alone here. I was part of its mystery, having come with no intention other than to look, to touch, and to sense its wonder. And that breathing came again. That slow steady rhythm which I now realized must be collective movement of the canopy high above in breezes I couldn't feel. But it felt like much more than that. It was the primeval forest itself—growing, dying, changing, and yet hardly changing at all. Just being. Alive and eternal in this remotest of remote places barely known to man. Complete and whole within itself. Needing nothing other than what it had always possessed among the ice-bound peaks and shadowed ravines of these fjords.

After an hour or so of slow walking uphill through the forest, the trees thinned out and I emerged on grass- and rock-strewn slopes with the black granite walls of the mountains towering above me. Thankfully the only moss I found now was mere delicate ground cover between lichen-flecked boulders. The goo was gone and I was happy as I found a sheltered ledge and paused to look around at the immensity of the vista.

Far, far below was little *Christine* reflected in the still purple water of the fjord. She looked fragile and delicate, such a vulnerable thing against the rigors of the williwaws and waves of the Gulf of Penas.

Across the narrow cleft of fjord the striated forest-strewn slopes rose into an enormous rock bowl edged by jagged ridges and laced with a filigree of waterfalls. And higher up, the crisp white cliffs of ice and blue-sheened glaciers culminated in sparkling peaks and domes against a cloud-flecked evening sky.

I wished I'd brought my sleeping bag to spend a night up here. It was too beautiful and majestic to leave—it seemed to be inviting me to stay and, once again, I sensed a silent communion with this place that was revealing more of itself to me with every minute I spent here.

When I finally returned slowly through the forest to the pebbly beach, it was almost dark. Peter had turned on the lights in the galley; reflections of gold dazzled across the rippling water of our cove. At first I heard nothing; then came the occasional clink and clang of pans.

Oh, God! He's cooking!

Now Peter had left most of the cooking to me (when it was possible to do any) because he was, as he'd explained at the start, the world's worst chef, hardly capable—no, correction—incapable of boiling a pot of beans without reducing them to popping cinders.

I swam back to the boat, dreading the worst. He heard me hoisting myself up the side and appeared at the top of the galley steps looking very morose, with grease stains across his arms and forehead.

"Listen, Pete," I began. "I told you I'd do the cooking—"

"David," he replied in his "Now, let's be real serious" tone. "I've got bad news and I've got badder news."

"Okay. Bad news first."

"The bad news is that dinner is ruined."

"You surprise me!"

"There's no need to get all pommish!" (He'd recognized my British accent back in Puerto Montt and reminded me every once in a while that the British were occasionally known as "pommie-bastards" back in Aussieland.)

"And the badder news?"

"The badder news is that we aren't going to make it down to Punta Arenas. It's another five hundred miles and the steering gear's a mess, plus there's a crack in the —"

"We've got to go back? To Puerto Montt?"

" 'Fraid so, mate. And even that's going to be a bugger if we get much more of that williwaw crap."

There was a long silence. At first I felt angry, even betrayed. But then I realized he must be feeling much worse. His planned sail of the Strait of Magellan was to be one of the grand climaxes of his around-the-world voyage.

"Hell, Pete—I'm sorry. That's lousy luck for you."

"And for you too, mate."

"Well—at least I've seen some of this country. I can always come back."

"Maybe when I get it all fixed—shouldn't take more'n a week or so, with luck—maybe you want to try again?"

"Maybe. Let's just make sure we get back to Montt first!"

"Yeah. It'll be tricky. No bull."

More silence. We were both feeling very dejected.

"Pete, listen—you're in no rush, right? A day or two doesn't make any difference?"

"Heck—no. I've got no cash, not much of a boat at the moment. But time I've got. What d'you want to do?"

"I want to stay here, if the weather holds."

"Here?"

"Yes. I think there're a few more things I can learn. Y'know, just walking around and watching?"

I could tell he was uncertain. The weather was good and he seemed anxious to make it back before his poor *Christine* got battered again by those coastal storms.

I think he was about to say no, but then something very odd happened. An old albatross with the broadest wingspan I'd seen

219

yet circled us slowly, then gently landed on the bow and stood looking at the two of us with quizzical eyes.

"Hey," I whispered. "Isn't that an omen or something?"

Peter chuckled. He was a hard-nosed Aussie. He didn't believe in that kind of stuff. But then he started looking around—staring at the forests and the dark granite walls of the fjords, the blue-purple glint of the high ice fields, and the crimson-tinged tips of the Andean peaks, and that vast evening sky. The whole wonderful totality of this magic place.

"One day do you?" he asked.

"One day's fine," I said. "Just fine."

We made it back to Puerto Montt without any more dramatic incidents or major storms. We were lucky too. His boat was in worse shape than I'd realized—it was going to take much longer than a week to fix. I decided to continue on in search of my next lost world, vowing to return one day soon to this amazing region. The last I heard from Peter, he'd postponed his journey through the Strait of Magellan and gone off sailing with a girl through the Galapagos Islands.

Best of luck—mate. Wherever you are.

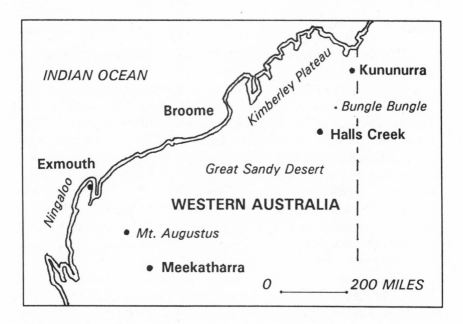

7. NORTHWEST AUSTRALIA

Bungle Bungle and the Never-Nevers

"Hey!" I shouted.

I had no choice. The whine, roar, and wind blast of the helicopter rotor blades made any kind of decorous conversation difficult. Something in my brain suggested I forget the formalities and cut, as they say, to the chase.

"Where's the doors?" I shouted into the maelstrom.

Colin, the young, frisky-eyed pilot, turned, smiled, and mouthed a big Australian "Whaddayasay, mate?"

I bawled out the question again. Actually more of a screamed plea. He continued smiling. One of those cocky Crocodile Dundee "born in the bush and proud of it" kind of smiles.

"No doors, mate. Fasten the belt and stick your foot outside on the skid."

I tried to smile back, but the grin got stuck in a grimace. No bloody doors? Foot outside on the skid? A seat belt that looked like an old piece of frayed rope? You've got to be joking. This is some kind of macho measuring test, right? Some weird form of outback initiation rite before I become a fully participating member of the beer 'n' barbie club, a fair dinkum, roustabouting, good ole g'day-ing, good-on-yer-boyo-of-the-bush, ready to down his stubbies and steaks with the rest of the lads at the pub, admiring attractive "sheilas" and talking of nothing but cattle, cars, and carousing escapades.

Apparently not. This was no initiation.

"Hang on!"

Colin's voice was lost in the screech of rotors and tornadoes of red dust that whirled around us as we lifted—no, that's not the right word—*catapulted* ourselves into the air, at a force that placed my stomach somewhere between my feet, and my brain where my stomach once was.

And then the turn. No—wrong word again. More like a somersault as he banked the tiny doorless glass bubble and sent us, virtually at right angles to the ground, skimming over the scraggy tops of the eucalyptus trees, over the dry creek beds, over the spotty desert spinifex scrub and the thorn trees.

My leg (the one resting outside on the skid) turned to jelly as the wind roared past, trying to disengage my tenuous toehold on a hollow tube of metal less than an inch in diameter.

I'm going to fall . . . any second now, I'm going to fall right out of this damned thing. I saw a body tumbling . . . spinning rapidly earthward, leaving behind a frayed seat belt and a shiny spot on the skid where its foot had been, and a pilot smiling his outback grin and mouthing such traditional Aussie inanities as "She'll be right, mate, she'll be right."

Ten minutes later I felt as if I'd been riding helicopters all my life. The fear was gone. Colin, who spent much of his time rounding up steers on Australia's vast cattle stations, skimming the scrub tops, going *under* the lower branches of trees and missing desert boulders by heart-stopping inches (or so he told me), had given me a comprehensive display of his acrobatic skills. And I was still intact, leg on the skid, seat belt still miraculously fastened, and head and stomach comfortably back in their appropriate positions. I decided that a combination of fairground-thrill centrifugal forces and the benevolent watchfulness of higher powers had determined that I would live to fly another day. And so I relaxed and began to enjoy the experience and the scenery. . . .

Once again I seem to be using the wrong words. "Scenery" hardly does justice to the Bungle Bungle—a unique, only recently discovered region of western Australia that contains some of the most remarkable and otherworldly rock formations on earth. We dallied awhile over the western flanks of this enormous twenty-by fifteen-mile red sandstone massif somewhere on the outer eastern edge of the Kimberley Ranges. I peered down into canyons, hundreds of feet deep, incised in the soft red rock. In some places they were a quarter of a mile wide, with palm trees and small spring-fed ponds reflecting the purpling evening sky. Elsewhere they were mere cracks, maybe a couple of yards across, that vanished into deep shadowy depths.

The top of the massif was basically a worn plateau, undulating in places, scoured and etched by the storms that scream across the barren plains of northwestern Australia. In crevasses and wind-carved bowls, a few hardy trees and bushes grew, their roots radiating like restless serpents seeking hidden pockets of moisture. Elsewhere was just more rock, rust-red sandstone, easing out in all directions before ending abruptly in enormous cliffs and crags, where birds circled on the updrafts and the summit dropped away suddenly to the dun-colored desert floor far below.

"Fantastic!" I shouted.

Colin turned and, giving me a "Y'aint seen nothing yet" smile, veered off abruptly to the eastern edges of the massif, where eroded formations, previously hidden, slowly emerged in the dusk light.

"They call 'em the Beehives," he said nonchalantly as we hovered above a most amazing sight—hundreds upon hundreds of interlocking pinnacles, ridges, and domes, perfectly rounded and smoothed to beehive-shaped formations, rising from gently curling stream beds that gave a jigsaw-puzzle appearance to their intricate patterning. Each pinnacle was striated with evenly layered horizontal strata ranging in color from the lightest ocher to

THE
BUNGLE-
BUNGLE
— Northwest
Australia

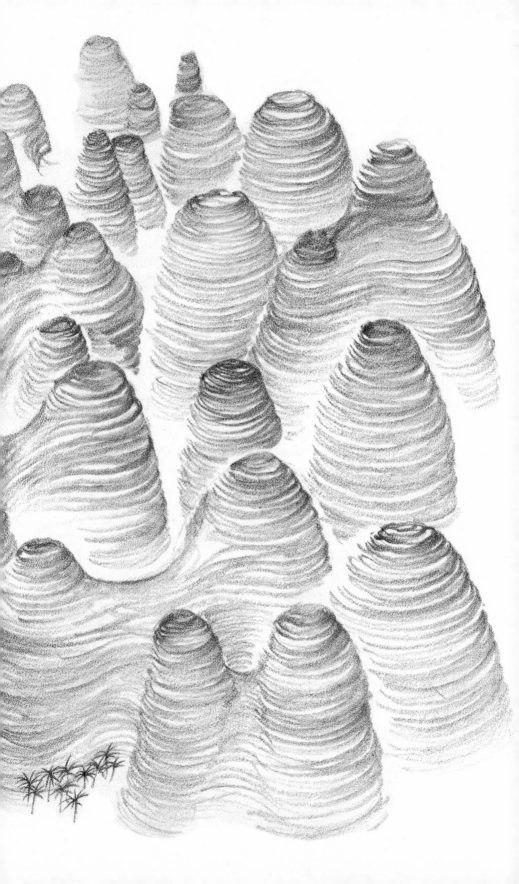

the darkest of bronzes and blood reds, as if some master artist had carefully painted every one with exacting precision over the long centuries of slow rounding down.

I'd never seen a sight like this before. I was entranced by the swirling complexity of the shapes and the unity and colors of the grouped forms. We floated over and between them like an eagle buoyed by thermals. I was no longer aware of Colin's doubtlessly clever looping antics. The magic and mystery of this place, only officially "discovered" in 1983 and still not accurately mapped, enveloped me. I had come a long, long way to be here, and it was everything that the world wanderers' grapevine had said it would be. A true lost world, offering its power and its beauty to only a fortunate few who had sought to learn its secrets.

The Bungle Bungle—or, to give it the correct Aboriginal name, Purnululu—has been known to only a handful of secretive outbackers since 1879. However, following Roger Garwood's photographic assignment in 1981 for the Western Australian Department of Tourism to "find additional places of interest around the Kimberley region" and a special TV documentary on the area in 1983, the Bungle Bungle was acclaimed as "one of the most fascinating sights in the undiscovered northwest."

This vast maze of multihued sandstone domes and incised canyons is indeed one of nature's most spectacular masterpieces. Occupied on the fringes by the Purnululu Aborigines for over twenty thousand years, the region emerged initially over three hundred and fifty million years ago as the Kimberley Ranges to the west were eroded by streams that carried the sand and quartz sediment eastward into the vast Hardman Basin. What began as a huge depository plateau was gradually striated by sudden and torrential rains and streams that dissolved the binding quartz and quickly cut down through the soft sandstone. Had it not been for the coating action of quartz, iron ore grains, and lichen that created a protective "skin" over the soft sandstone, the region may already have been eroded down to an ignominious peneplain.

The vicious scouring action of sudden floods created canyons sometimes more than three hundred feet deep but in places less than four feet wide. Hundreds of rounded "beehive" pillars were left as the canyons on the southern and eastern extremities were broadened to form today's fantasy-land jigsaw shapes, ribbed with bands of gray and iron-red strata.

Altogether one of the most unusual landscapes in the world.

My long Australian outback odyssey began in Sydney on a bright cool October day on the cusp of the Southern Hemisphere's summer. I'd only paused for a brief stopover in the city to recover from the long—far too long—flight from Los Angeles. But when I took a cab into the city from the airport, I decided to stay awhile longer.

"Do y'wanna bit of a tour, mate? Won't cost y'much."

"Sure."

It didn't cost much and I was entranced.

A city magazine masthead boasts "Sydney—best address on earth," and I quickly began to understand the immodest claim.

The 1778 birthplace of Australia is today a cutting-edge colossus of almost four million hurry-scurry inhabitants (more than a quarter of the entire population of the country!). From its gleaming downtown towers and booming waterfront extravaganzas, its endlessly varied ethnic restaurants, its iconoclastic wing-roofed opera house, and its burly landmark harbor bridge, to the delicate brick rowhouses (still with red tin roofs), huge swaths of gumtree-shaded parks, and the erotic delights of King's Cross, Sydney (known as "The Big Smoke") booms and swings and shimmers and shows off its charms with all the wild exuberance of Tina Turner struttin' her stuff at a bacchanalian birthday ball. Despite the decorous undertones of a city proud of its long history, its cultural institutions, its palatial waterside homes, and its intellectual underpinnings, the place is a frenetic flavor-of-the-month enclave. It has "party time!" plastered all over it and you can't help but go with its vivacious flow, from brilliant golden dawns across the harbor to nighttime frolics at rock clubs and waterside pubs and along the funky surfside hub of Bondi Beach. Sydney is a place you don't forget—a place that entices you to stay on, to live there awhile, in style, in its brilliant clean light, riding the roller coaster of the new Australia, with its nouveau riche heroentrepreneurs (Kerry Packer, Alan Bond, et al.); its new melting pot ethnic ethos; its cultural renaissance sparked in good Aussie movies, the landscape paintings of Sidney Nolan, the novels of Patrick White, the poems of Ian Mudie, even the sexy sassiness of Olivia Newton-John—and its wholehearted celebration of leisure and blithe-life living.

I left tired, but reluctantly, after two days of nonstop gallivanting in this gregarious, full-of-gusto place. I wouldn't be seeing cities for a while. Urbane urges would have to be sublimated and exchanged for the echoing drone of Aboriginal didgeridoos and the howl of wild dingo dogs and the "meat pie and g'day, mate" fellowship of bush bums in the great red outback that is most of the rest of Australia.

No worries, I told myself in the Strine dialect I was rapidly learning, she'll be right.

And—all in all—(allowing for a couple of near-death experiences) she was.

So—off I soared out of Sydney on yet one more crystal-clean late spring morning, heading northwest via Alice Springs to the recent earthquake-decimated (now rebuilt) town of Darwin, way up on the tip of the northern territory.

The last leg of this long series of flights would bring me down to the town of Kununurra in western Australia, start of my desert odyssey to the Bungle Bungle and the "never-never" nothingness beyond.

Writers and artists—even composers—have often tried (usually unsuccessfully) to express the vast scale of this empty land— the endless, unpeopled redness, and the flat, worn-down, and oh-so-ancient remnants of ridges and ranges that are now mere stumps and eroded humps, hardly noticeable at all from thirty-five thousand feet against Australia's hazy hugeness.

There was something frighteningly indifferent, inhuman, in the land below. Even the Sahara from above displays an ever-changing repertoire of textures and colors with occasional welcoming clusters of palms around scattered oases. But I saw few such subtleties here. It looked like a dead and utterly alien place. Like the surface of some lost red planet out in the eternal silence of the cosmos. I only hoped that on closer acquaintance, I might find more comforting signs of life and growth and the presence of people, most of whom now cling to their coastline cities and towns and leave the outback to the scattered swagmen and stock hands and the relentless scouring of a cruel and vicious climate.

I never discovered the reasons for all the delays at Darwin, although everyone seemed to accept them as a matter of course— a regular dues-paying ritual for those crazy enough to be flying so deep into the outback.

"Y'should've bin here last week, mate." A big burly man in jeans and floppy sweat-stained leather hat spoke to me from a nearby seat in the terminal. "Talk about bloody chaos. Two flights canceled back to back. Storms more'n likely. You're in the storm season now—the wet—so y'gotta expect anything. Four hundred stuck in this bloody terminal. Fans not working right, Coke machine empty. No food. No grog. Tell y'mate, place was like a bloody stockyard—full of stinkin' mad bulls."

The whites mulled around the hot terminal in search of cold beer "stubbies" and a breeze. Family groups of Aborigines sat like Henry Moore sculptures, huddled close together on the floor of the terminal (the whites had taken all the seats), unmoving, unsmiling, silent. They seemed to exist in another place, another reality. All the shuffling and back-slapping and stubbie-swilling and impatient restlessness of the whites swirled around them like so much gritty wind, leaving them untouched, uninterested, wrapped in bold familial folds of molded flesh and baggage. Stoic and still.

We flew out of Darwin five hours late.

"Big storm around Wyndham" was the pilot's only explanation, and the passengers nodded contentedly as if somehow pleased by this reaffirmation of the fickleness and sudden furies of their enormous, empty land.

"She's done it to us again," murmured a rough-cut bushman sitting beside me dressed in dust-coated dungarees and a worn denim shirt. "Bloody country. . . . " But he was smiling along with all the others.

D. H. Lawrence, in his book *Kangaroo* (one of his lesser-known works, written in 1927 after a rather rapid tour of Australia), spoke of "the peculiar, lost weary aloofness of Australia." But there is nothing weary about her notorious storms and the torrential "wets" that wash out everything that moves and a few things that shouldn't.

Our conversation—rather, the bushman's conversation—rambled on. He was a true Aussie "yarner" who used a colorful repertoire of words and phrases to describe his outback shack with a "dunny" (outside toilet) in the back; his penchant for good cheap Aussie "plonk" wine and beer served up as middies, tinnies, and stubbies in ramshackle pubs; his low opinion of Aboriginal "corroborees" (ceremonial gatherings); his favorite "billabong" campsites; and his constant amusement at the persistence of outback flies that smother your face and seem immune to swatting.

Marcus Clarke had predicted in 1877 the basic character and outlook of the "New Australian" following the demise of the notorious British penal colonies that were the founding stones of early colonialization: "The Australiasian will be a squareheaded, masterful man . . . his teeth will be bad and his lung good. He will suffer from liver disease, and become prematurely bald. . . . His religion will be a form of presbyterianism; his national policy a democracy tempered by the rate of exchange."

Precisely right. I'd just met one. His aggressively independent yet patriotic spirit is now labeled "ockerism"—a celebration of all things Australian, and watch out for your chin and your teeth if you show any signs of arrogant colonial-tinged "knockerism" that purloins the pride and spirit of the New Australia.

My tape recorder was on the blink; otherwise I would have captured far more nuances of his long monologue. Suffice to say, it was an entertaining and enticing prelude of things to come.

We landed in Kununurra to great sprays of water spuming up from the short runway. It was after midnight but the thick cloying humidity of the air tumbled in as the doors hissed open and we stepped down onto the wet tarmac.

"Collect your car rentals now. Desk's closing in five minutes," came an announcement.

Mine was waiting for me.

"How long will it take me to drive to Halls Creek?" I was very weary but had to make the 250-mile drive by nine A.M. or lose the only chance I had to visit the Bungle Bungle before this newly discovered wonder of the outback officially "closed" for the summer when temperatures soared to 130 degrees and the "wet" cut off access for most of the season.

"Normally 'bout five hours, but the creeks'll be rising, so y'better say eight, m'be nine."

"Are the roads okay?"

"Pretty good, mate. Least for the first hundred k [kilometers] or so on the Great Northern—they've made a nice job of that first bit . . . but . . ."

"But what?"

"Depends on the rains. You've got quite a stretch of dust road. Maybe mud now. . . ."

"You think I can make Halls Creek by nine A.M.?"

"No worries, mate. Get yourself a six-pack of Coke to keep you going."

"Great—thanks."

"And watch out for road trains."

"What's a road train?"

He gave me a strange look—a mix of suppressed mirth and pity.

"Aw—you'll find out soon enough, mate. Pull over far as you can to the left—don't forget we drive on the left or you'll never make it—jus' pull over before the lights blind you and let 'em go by."

"Big trucks, right?"

"Bloody big, mate. Jus' keep out of their way and she'll be apples."

I obviously hadn't done enough reading on the hazards of night travel in the outback.

"Anything else?"

"Well—watch for 'roos. They hop around a bit at night. And the cattle. They like a nice warm road to sit on."

"Wish me luck," I said uncertainly.

"Naw—no worries. You'll be fine."

And I was fine, for a while. The road was fast, the Coke was doing its magic, and for the first sixty miles or so I'd not seen a single 'roo or cow.

Then the road vanished.

Just like that. No signs. No warnings. The smooth blacktop highway suddenly came to an end and I found myself careening down a red dirt road with ill-defined edges. The Great Northern Highway—pride of northwestern Australia—was, as I'd been warned, still under "improvement" and I was now well and truly on the unimproved bit. A long bit.

In my full beams the wet red earth track stretched ahead with occasional wiggles to keep me awake. I was feeling really tired now. Being mesmerized by my own lights and constantly on the lookout for kangaroos and cattle was sending my brain into a sullen stupor. The car radio no longer picked up anything but crackle and static. And it was very black out there. No stars, no moon. Just endless grass and scrub at the roadside. I had no idea what kind of landscape I was driving through. It was just me and this interminable red track.

And the rain.

The rain began again around two P.M. Not a real outback downpour but enough to make the dirt road slick and my windshield greasy. My watch urged me to keep up the speed; otherwise I'd never make Halls Creek in time. My mind warned me of the nasty repurcussions of braking suddenly on this mud-coated track to avoid an errant 'roo or comatose cow.

I'd heard all about the damage a big 'roo can do. No wonder most outback vehicles come equipped with enormous waist-high fenders, big enough to buck an elephant.

"Six-foot 'roo'll finish off y'front end, no problem," my flying companion from Darwin had told me. "Likely finish you off too if it hits you dead square and goes through your windscreen. They're silly buggers, those 'roos. See you comin' and they decide they're gonna fight. They just stand there likely as not waving their fists and then it's . . . b'jeeze, well—it's a hell of a mess. . . . "

So I crouched forward over the steering wheel, peering through the slime on the windsheld, hoping and praying I wouldn't be faced with a big boxing-crazed creature ready for a fight.

What made it even more difficult was that the topography had changed and I was now roller-coasting between creeks and gullies with hardly a flat stretch of track anywhere. Fortunately, the creeks had not risen above a few inches and I sprayed through those easily, coating the sides of the car and the windows in runny red mud, but never in any danger of stalling.

That was my other fear. I'd heard lurid stories about the characteristics of creeks in the wet. One of the passengers in Darwin, with whom I'd shared a stubbie or two, described an experience he'd had as a trucker on the Great Northern: "That was a real bastard road, few years back. You'd get a big storm backways in the hills—sometimes last for days—and down on the road everything'd be just fine. Nice n'dry. Good driving if you didn't mind the dust. But there's one stretch near Turkey Creek that's real bad—six, m'be seven creeks in fifty k—comin' right down from the Duracks. Big storm in them ranges and an hour or so later them creeks'd start fillin' so fast it was like a dam burst. Four, five feet, m'be more in an hour. From nothin' but a dry creek bed that ain't seen rain in six months to these bloody great thrashin' rivers that'd sweep you off the road in no time flat."

"Problem was you had to make up your mind. If the first creek was rising, you'd got time to turn back and rest up awhile. Even drive back to Halls Creek and get a room and a bunch o' mates and have a high old time.

"But if y'were carrying stuff that'd spoil, you'd think, what the heck, I'll get through. So you'd get her all revved up and try to make it through the other creeks. When you got to Turkey you know you'd be okay. An' likely you would if it was just startin'. But you couldn't tell for sure. Best sign was if trucks was still comin' th' other way. Then you'd be okay. But—anyway—this one time I was carrying cut steer and the 'frigerator was on the blink and I passed that first creek and everything was fine. 'Bout a foot or so—no worries. Second one, three feet. Up around th' axles. No worries. Third one, around the door. And I'm thinking, I've got three more to go and it's not lettin' up. And there's no traffic. Nothing. Few fellas behind me, way back, but nothin' comin' from up ahead. Now tha's bad. So I'm thinking, do I go back or what? But I know them cut steer needed to get to the warehouse in Wyndham, so—I had a good truck—real good truck. So I kept going.

"Fourth one's a bit of a problem. Bit of spluttering in the engine, but I'm through. Then comes the fifth. I knew it was all over by then. I could see them trucks, m'be twenty of 'em in front

233

of me. Long line of 'em and I knew we was stuck. So—I got in line and walked up to the front—to the creek. Most of my mates was there—Larry Thompson, Jeff Bakely, Dave Williams. They was all standin' watchin' this damn creek. Like a bloody great river now—hundred meters 'n' more across, going like the clappers, trees crashing by, boulders, the lot. Never seen nothin' like it. And gettin' higher by the second. You could see it creepin' up—like watchin' dough rise. Mean as a bitch. Pullin' down the banks like they was cotton candy. Great slabs of soil and rocks come tumblin' in and they'd just disappear—trees, fence posts— a bloody great boab tree—roots stickin' out for twenty, maybe thirty meters—just came tumbling down with a bloody great crash, branches all smashin' up, bobbin' about like a great fat whale . . . took the whole bloody lot away in seconds."

"We all pulled the trucks back up the hill far as we could. This thing looked like it wasn't going to stop . . . and it didn't. Rain kept comin' for three days . . . never seen anything like it. Three solid days. Even then it took another two days to get so's we could think about crossin'."

He paused in his long monologue. I could sense him reliving the experience; his eyes were bright and his hand was shaking as he tried to capture the enormity, the power, of that raging, if short-lived, river.

"So what did you do for five days?" I asked.

He let go a huge bellowing laugh. "What did we do, mate? We lived like fuckin' kings is that what we did. Set up a kitchen in one of the empty trucks. I dragged in some beef—we cut it up and roasted steaks, played cards, one fella was a beer trucker— Foster's man—so we got plenty of stubbies—'nother bloke had his guitar. . . . I tell you, we had a real party. Fellas on the other side of the creek were partying too. Couldn't get across, but we could see 'em well enough. . . . We had a great old time. Made a few bob on the cards, so—no worries. Beef was gettin' a bit high, but nothing I could do 'bout that. W'ate as much as we could. I drove the rest of it to Wyndham. Don't know what they did with it there. Couldn't care less. I tell y'mate . . . in Australia you get used to making do . . . get yer billies out, get the beer out, get y'self a good steak three, four times a day . . . won't get no crook in the gut that way. S'not such a bad life."

Replaying the mind-tape of our conversation I may have lost concentration. The rain was still falling, the windshield was getting a thicker coating of goo, and I didn't spot the headlights approaching until it was almost too late.

I'd just topped one more rise on the track when my vision vanished in a thwack of brilliant silver light. I couldn't see a thing. But I knew something was coming straight at me . . . and it was coming fast. My brain screamed at me, pull over, pull over!

I had no choice. I also had no idea where the side of the track was. All I knew was that the road was a quagmire and I'd been driving close to the center to avoid the ominous headlight gleams of mud and rainwater pools.

I braked hard (not a good idea), pulled the wheel violently to the left, and felt the car fishtail and slide into the morass.

A horn, far too loud for any normal vehicle, blasted through the silver miasma, lights flashing furiously, and something like a herd of mad rhinos tore past, sending surf waves of red mud and gravel surging over the car, which rocked and quivered like a frightened rabbit in the howling slipstream.

The noise took a long time to die. I sat frozen in the driver's seat; the bones in my fingers seemed reluctant to release the hard security of the steering wheel. I had missed a very messy and ignominious demise on this hell highway by inches. In fact the buffeting from the slipstream had been so furious that I was convinced the side of the car had been ripped off like a microwave dinner wrapper as the whatever-it-was tore by.

But of course I knew what it was, even though I hadn't actually seen it.

It was an all-Australian, drive-through-the-night, stop-for-nothing road train. A remorseless wall-of-gears monolith, twice the size of anything allowed on the roads in the United States, tearing across the empty outback like a low-skimming B-52, a roaring juggernaut going straight for the jugular of any unsuspecting, half-asleep, remember-to-drive-on-the-left novice of the highway like me.

My body began to shake. First the legs, then stomach muscles, then arms and shoulders. I reached for a can of Coke, but nothing remained on the passenger seat—cameras, notebooks, pens, films, the Cokes, and God knows what else were scattered around the car like so much flotsam and jetsam after a boat wreck.

Finally I found a can. The sneezy-wheezy pop of the flip-top was reassuring. The geyser of warm brown carbonated syrup that shot straight up to the roof and then immediately cascaded down again, drenching me in sticky fluid, was not. But at least it allowed me to hurl epithets by the dozen at the mud and the goo and the black, sodden night outside.

I felt a little calmer until I realized the car was tilted at a rather peculiar angle.

Of course. I was in mud. Hopefully still on the road, but certainly in mud.

I crawled out of the door onto the—thank God—slick but hard surface of the track.

It was cooler outside than I'd expected, unless my body was playing odd tricks with my senses. In fact it was decidedly chilly—that strange chill of the desert night that follows blazing hot days. There were stars too. The rainstorm must have passed over. Unfamiliar patternings of stars. Everything seemed upside down. Southern Hemisphere, dummy, said the quietest part of my brain. Right. I kept forgetting I was now at the bottom of the globe. And a moon. Low and scimitared, just above the horizon. And light. Enough lacy light to see the tracks left by the road train. I traced them a ways over the brow of the hill and noticed that they hadn't veered an inch to avoid me. Road train drivers just expect all other puny gas-pedal-pushers to pull over far enough to avoid being pulped while they continue their endless odysseys, straight down the middle of these wild, empty roads.

I turned to look at my car. The shiny black Australian Holden (the rental agent had been so proud of it: "Only a thousand on the clock; we saved a brand-new one for you") was now the same color as the road, a sort of tired earthy red, decorated in streaks and globs and meandering mud trickles.

And leaning at this very odd angle.

Shit! I'd never make Halls Creek unless I got the thing out of the mire.

It looked hopeless but I had to try. So—back into the driver's seat, start her up, down into first gear. Gentle steady revs at first . . . then accelerate gradually as the wheels gain traction . . . only they never gained traction. The more they spun, the more the car eased itself over into the mud. Much more of this and the driver-side wheels would be off the track and spinning uselessly in the chilly night air.

What happens if another road train comes and doesn't see me stuck on the brow of the hill? I turned on the headlights and the flashers, which seemed a little redundant on this deserted highway . . . but I wasn't in the mood to take chances.

An hour passed. A long, slow, cold hour. I'd decided not to use the heater in case I drained the battery. So I sat in the passenger seat, lonely, dejected, and scared.

Another thirty minutes. Not a single vehicle had passed. Not a light or a sign of civilization anywhere. Hardly surprising at three-thirty A.M. in one of the emptiest regions of Australia.

I must have dozed off. The next thing I heard was a rasping voice off to my right.

"You got y'self in a right fuckin' mess, mate!"

I awoke to find a pair of wild, laughing eyes staring into mine from a car drawn up alongside.

"What happened?"

"Bloody road train," I mumbled, and then smiled. At least I had company now.

"Yeah—I saw him too. Y'don't mess with those buggers. Y'pull over and hope the hell they see you in time."

"This one missed me by inches. Crazy sod."

The young man with long, straggly hair seemed to consider the whole thing highly amusing. I could smell the booze in his laughter. He'd obviously enjoyed a big binge night in town. But which town? Surely not Kununurra? That was well over a hundred miles to the north—the last sign of human habitation I'd seen.

"Don't think I can help you with this." He gestured at his own small, battered car. "You'll need a four-wheel to get you out of that."

"Yes—I know."

There was silence for a moment.

"Listen. Lock this thing up and come on with me. I'm at a cattle station few *k* down the road. We'll get the truck. Leave your flashers on."

We drove together in his rattletrap car for a "few miles" (actually twenty-seven), then suddenly pulled off the road through a patch of wild scrub and parked by a ramshackle tin shack.

"Hold on a second," he said, and vanished.

Dogs barked. Doors slammed. Lights went on and then off. He was back.

"Okay, mate. Get in the truck and let's get that bloody machine of yours moving before you lose it. Wanna beer?"

"Sure."

We drank and talked on the twenty-seven-mile return journey. His name was Dan Peebles and his checkered career since school had run the gamut from shrimp fisherman to garage mechanic to stock hand to truck driver to gold prospector and back to stock hand. Two marriages, three children, a bout of detox in a Wyndham clinic for alcoholics, girlfriends galore, a brief stint in jail ("th' got the wrong bugger, but it took 'em two months to find out. . . . "), and now a lonely spouseless life with his dog at this cattle station in the middle of nowhere, with weekend bottle bouts in Kununurra or Halls Creek. (I was to hear this kind of life profile many times from "bush bums" I met in the northwest outback.)

The car was where we'd left it, flashing weakly in the night.

"Okay—hop in. This your own car?"

"No—it's rented."

"Fine. Coupla dints won't matter, then."

Back in the sloping driving seat, I felt Dan nudge the rear of my Holden with his enormous steel-grille fender. He revved hard. There was a crunching of metal and the splinter of broken plastic (my metal and my plastic), then I was shot forward like a cannonball out of the mire and sent skidding down the track. I drifted down the hill, away from the dangerous brow, and then got out to inspect the damage.

"She's okay now. One of your rear lights gone, but y'should be fine. Where y' going?"

"Halls Creek."

"Still a way to go, mate."

"I've got to get there by nine."

He whistled. "Might just make it if you thump her. Here . . . "

he reached down and picked up a couple of beers from the floor of his truck, "take these."

I thanked him and tried to offer a fistful of rainbow-hued Australian dollars for his timely assistance.

"Naw—tha's fine. Happens all the time, this kinda mess. You'd do the same for me."

"I'm glad I met you, Dan. Very glad."

"No worries, mate. Say hello to Halls Creek. I'll be down there next week. May see you. Have a few beers, right?"

"Right."

"Good on yer. An' mind them road trains. Nasty buggers."

And he was gone. Tearing off into the night, back to his tin shack and his dog and his life among the cattle.

Dawn eased in strips of mauve and lemon over a line of brittle-edged mountains. What had previously been a dark mystery now became a landscape—a most unusual landscape—of scattered, shaggy clumps of eucalyptus trees and low bush stretching endlessly across a golding desert plain. Bulbously fat boab trees rose from the cracked earth. Their bloated trunks, textured like elephant hide, exploded in a profusion of stubby branches, and white cockatoos swooped between them or perched on the top of man-high mounds of red mud—hundreds, thousands of mounds—scattered as far as I could see across the desert floor and up the dry foothills of the ranges. Termite mounds.

A young botanist in Darwin, a fellow passenger on the flight to Kununurra, had described the amazing ecosystems of these mounds as we'd sat during the interminable flight delay, swapping travel tales. Each one apparently is an infinitely complex honeycombed structure containing millions of tiny termite ants whose primary functions in life consisted of constantly expanding the mounds and guarding the vital fungus gardens inside to feed their queens—those portly, four-inch-long sluglike creatures, thick as a thumb and discharging eggs at a rate of thirty thousand per day for up to fifty years! Perfect breeding machines.

"I've seen them higher than twenty feet in the northern outback," he told me. "Given your average termite size, that's the equivalent of a building two and a half miles high. Frank Lloyd

BOAB TREE
& TERMITE MOUNDS
—Northwest
Australia

Wright would've been envious—he chickened out at a mile. And it's fully air-conditioned. Air holes near the base and ventilation tubes that stretch up from the nurseries and fungus gardens and open up near the top of the mounds. Problem is these tubes are also nice places for lizards and snakes—sometimes birds—so they keep having to carve out new ones through the mud. If that doesn't work they go off and build another mound."

"It still must get pretty hot inside."

"In the outback they're real nifty. It gets hot as hell, as you know—sometimes up to a hundred and thirty degrees in summer—so they build the long axis of the mound in a north-south alignment to cut down the direct burn of the sun. The fungus only grows well in a narrow temperature range, so they close off or open up the vent tubes to suit the season."

"The fungus just grows on the dried mud inside?"

"Oh, no—it's much more complex. The workers' job is to gather grass and stalks—anything with cellulose in it—chew it up for food for themselves and the soldiers who defend the mound, and then construct slabs of the stuff, coat it with their droppings, and cultivate the gardens for more food. They also use a similar mix of wood fragments, cellulose, and fecal droppings to make 'carton'—a bit like cardboard—to build all the internal galleries."

"What happens when the mound reaches maximum size?"

"Well—that can take a while, sometimes up to sixty years. But as it fills up and the colony gets established, the queen suddenly breeds a new kind of termite—the alates—they've got wings and they fly off at set times of the year to breed and establish new colonies. I've only seen it a couple of times. Usually at night. They come out up the tubes and cover the outside of the mound in this sheen of bodies. Thousands of them. Then they fly off, usually not very far—their wings only last for a day or so. They mix and match fast into couples, dig small holes, seal themselves in, and mate. Eventually the females become full-blown queens, pumping out the eggs every day like a conveyor belt, and the mound grows. Somehow she knows just the right balance of workers and soldiers to produce. If some of the soldiers get massacred in a battle, she lays a new mass of soldier eggs; if the workers aren't producing enough carton and fungus, she produces more workers. They're all carried to the nurseries above the royal chamber and in around three weeks or so you've got enough of each to keep the whole colony balanced and healthy. It's a fantastic system. I've been photgraphing mounds for years—they're really beautiful pieces of desert architecture."

I paused to photograph them too. Some were thin, spirelike constructions, their outer red surfaces eroded by sudden rains to form towers and pinnacles; others were fat, ungainly edifices with rotund protrusions, rather like gigantic scoops of melting strawberry ice cream.

And then—at last—came Turkey Creek, a ramshackle roadside rest stop offering a sun-bleached straggle of motel rooms, a gas station, store, and restaurant selling strong coffee, sandwiches, and a droopy selection of Australia's deep-fried delights—potato and bacon croquettes, fried dim sum, shrimp toasties, battered sausages, meat rissoles, and battered "veggies." Oh—and meat pies ("dead 'orse")—the ubiquitous Aussie snack of finely ground meat and other indistinguishable items wrapped in a pale pastry crust. Filling, fattening—but otherwise a flop as a tasty snack. Altogether not a particularly enticing collection of edibles but fine for a weary traveler who had escaped a messy demise under the wheels of a road train.

And there they were. Two of those enormous creatures, parked by the gas station and taking up most of the dusty forecourt with their mud-splattered and awesome bulks. A driver was dismounting from the cab of one of them, a Mack truck monolith. Somehow I had imagined such men to be Mad-Max demonic crazy-eyed giants, rippling with Schwarzenegger muscles and clad in tight rivet-studded leather outfits trimmed with the token scalps and bones of decimated occupants crushed in puny little passenger automobiles.

Eddie Simpson was nothing like that. Under a floppy baseball cap printed with small gold letters that read GASCOYNE TRANSPORT, a pair of smiling blue eyes peered up from a skinny five-foot frame clad in a grubby tartan shirt, jeans, and a pair of torn sneakers.

"G'day to you, mate. How's it goin'?"

I told him of my narrow escape and he smiled even wider while nodding sympathetically.

"Yeah—y'gotta be careful on the Great Northern. Big zinc oxide and cattle transports—up to maximum length, over a hundred and seventy feet. Usually, though, it's not car drivers that give me problems—its those bloody 'roos and cattle. All over the bleedin' place some nights. Make a real mess of me front end."

He gestured toward a six-foot-high steel-beam fender liberally splattered with dried blood and bits of gore.

"Gotta couple a 'roos during the night. Just outa Halls Creek. Nothin' y'can do." He shrugged his shoulders. "Here—let me get you something."

He clambered back up the three steps into the towering cab and came back with a baseball cap identical to his own, and a pamphlet.

"Here y'are. Wear this and read this."

I thanked him and he vanished into the cool of the café with a final "You'll be okay to Halls Creek now. Good road."

It was getting hot even so early in the morning, so I put the GASCOYNE TRANSPORT cap on and read his pamphlet with increasing amusement. It was entitled *Mixing with Monsters* and contained the following valuable advice:

Large road vehicles play an important role in the economic development of Western Australia.... long distance travellers are certain to encounter these vehicles sooner or later in the North West and Kimberley regions.

A typical road train can be travelling at 90 km/hr (60 mph) though capable of far higher speeds ... an overall load can be up to 7 metres wide (23') ... they can be unforgiving of CARELESSNESS, IGNORANCE and IMPATIENCE ... Don't think accidents only happen to other people. They can happen to you.

My favorite paragraph read as follows:

When meeting a road train on a narrow bitumen road you have two options—(i) retain your 50% of the bitumen (which the law provides for) or (ii) pull off the bitumen and leave it for the larger vehicles. Once you have made your choice, act immediately. If you chose (i), slow down and move over, keeping your nearside wheel on the bitumen. (Prepare for flying stones and dusty conditions!) If you chose (ii), slow down, pull right off the bitumen and allow the large vehicles to pass. THIS IS THE BETTER OPTION.

Not when there's three feet of mud at the side of the road, it's not.

Eddie was right. The rest of the drive to Halls Creek was on smooth blacktop and I rode, without road trains, across more desert plains liberally sprinkled with termite mounds and boab trees. I saw not a single kangaroo, and cattle remained at a safe distance from the road, turning their skinny torsos and bony heads to watch as I skimmed by.

Around nine-thirty A.M. I finally arrived. My clothes were mud-stained, my stomach a churning mess of meat pie and deep-fried sausages, and my mind was begging for sleep in a quiet, cool motel room.

Halls Creek offered a straggly street of gas stations, small stores, a bakery, bungalows shaded by verandas and huge hedges, and a sun-scorched park with somnolent groups of Aborigines sitting or lying in the shade of stunted eucalyptus trees. Not much of a place, really, but it felt like a razzle-dazzle metropolis after 250 miles of nothingness.

If I could just sleep for an hour or two. . . . but that was not to be.

"Well, g'day, Dave—my God, we thought you wouldn't make it—called up Kununurra and they said you left 'round midnight, so we expected you seven, seven-thirty, mate."

A smiling bespectacled face atop a small wiry frame addressed me through my mud-splattered window.

"Name's Graeme Macarthur, Dave—cattle dealer, station manager, gold speculator, windmill agent, cattle trough designer, tour operator, and general all-round nice bloke. Me mates call me "The General," but Graeme's fine. And . . . this is Murray, my camp manager."

Murray was all an outbacker should be. A broad-shouldered bulk of a man with a sun-bleached straggly mass of hippie-length hair tumbling from a large sweat-stained leather hat. Big bushy beard, big beer belly, big earth-engrained hands, and a big boozy grin exposing big, yellow, and very chipped teeth.

"Good t'meet y'Dave. Y'ready to move?"

"I guess so. A wash and a nap would be nice, but—"

"Naw—you'll have plenty of time for that at camp. We gotta get movin' . . . this is our last trip out to the Bungle. We've gotta close down. Best we get there soon as possible. . . . I'll get y'some coffee. You'll be right, mate."

Five minutes later we were off, my backpack loaded in the rear of Graeme's Land Cruiser, hot coffee in my hand, and two lively up-and-at-'em Aussies for company.

Graeme was the raconteur and jokemaster—a real Aussie "spieler." We rolled out of town ("Give you a tour, Dave, when we get back—okay?"), passing the Aborigines again under the trees in the park. Some were sleeping. Others were decidely drunk despite the early morning hour.

"Same as everywhere," said Graeme in his high, fast-talk voice. "Bloody shame. Wasted by thirty—dead by fifty. Y'heard many Abo jokes yet?"

I shook my head.

He grinned, knowing he now had a new, open-eyed, open-minded novice as grist for his gusto.

"Well, there were these engineers—oil well men—way out in the desert and they was dancin' 'round and 'round and the black stuff was spurtin' out the ground and they was laughin' and singin' 'cause they'd found this new oil well. Now, up on a hill, lookin' over the desert, were two old Aborigines, starkers, just sittin' there watchin' 'em.

"One of the Aborigines says, 'Looks like them white bastards've found some more oil down there, mate.'

"And the other Aborigine says, 'No. Looks like we just found us another sacred site, mate. . . . ' "

He waited for my laughter.

"Another sacred site. Y'get it, Dave? . . . Another sacred site."

Murray rolled about in the back of the Cruiser, chortling and spluttering, "Graeme—Dave's only bin 'ere couple days. He don't know all this stuff about the boongs."

"Tha' right, Dave? Y'only been here two days?"

"Four, actually."

"Aw, well—you've gotta bit of catchin' up to do, mate. We'd better fill y'in 'bout things the way they are 'round here."

And so for the next half hour or so Graeme gave me his potted-history version of the Aborigine versus the white Australian. It was a long, tawdry monologue, amusing at times, but basically the familiar "surely we've done enough for them now" kind of diatribe one hears at home from staunch right-wingers.

"I mean, it's gettin' crazy, Dave. They've got these sacred sites everywhere. Any bloody rock or stream or mountain you look at—it'll be a sacred site of some kind."

"Well—isn't that the 'songline' concept?" (I had decided it was time to say something.) "The Aborigine idea that Australia was 'sung' into existence and only keeps that existence by constant 'singing' along invisible trails that link all landmarks—all those sacred places—lakes, rivers, ranges—whatever." (I'd just finished rereading Bruce Chatwin's beautiful book *The Songlines* and was feeling a little professorial).

Graeme gave me a frowning sidelong glance—a rather diffiuclt thing to do, as we were now crashing and bounding along a five-foot-wide dirt track that disappeared with increasing regularity into creek beds and thickets of spinifex, dwarf palm, and thorn trees. It looked like the African savanna.

"How long y'say y'been here, Dave?"

"Four days—and mostly without sleep." (God—was I looking forward to a quiet campsite and a bed on soft earth, hummed to sleep by choirs of cooing doves and whistling cicadas. . . .)

"Y'been doing some readin', then?"

"Oh, some. But it's interesting to hear your viewpoint."

"Yeah, well," growled Graeme, his voice a little lower now, "you'll be hearin' plenty more as you travel around. We're gettin' really fed up with the whole bloody thing. Y'know what they done now. They've gone'n claimed Ayers Rock as a big sacred site and they're stoppin' ordinary people takin' photos and they're chargin' journalists and that kind a flippin' fortune."

"Yes," I said. "I'd heard something about that."

"Yeah, well—it's getting worse all the time. We jus' keep throwin' money at 'em and they just keep grabbin' for more. And then they waste it all. We buy 'em bloody Land Cruisers—brand-new, twenty-five to thirty-thousand-dollar machines—and what do they do? They run out of petrol and think the bloody thing's gone 'n' conked out on 'em, so they ditch it and say it's no good and ask for another!"

(Memories of all the old tales back in England about the uselessness of building public housing for poor slum families—"What do they do? They've never seen a bathtub in their lives before, so they use it to keep coal in . . . and pigs in the back garden . . . and . . . ")

Graeme must have read my thoughts. "I mean, take Halls Creek. My town. Only a little place. I was on the council. We built brand-new houses for 'em—lovely, they were—painted 'em up pretty—new kitchens, bathrooms. Planted trees and bushes 'n' that. An' jus' look at 'em now. Five years later. Bloody great holes in the walls, windows knocked out, wiring and pipes gone. They're out there in the garden where the grass was, burnin' up their trees 'n' bushes in campfires. We had to move them. You'll see when you get back. Most of 'em's empty now. They were wrecked! They said they wanted to go back to the bush. So we gave 'em some concrete floors, a well, some toilets—in the hills jus' out of town—and some sheets of corrugated iron 'n' stuff, and let 'em build whatever they wanted—and they built what they've built for thousands of years, little humpies, like open Quonset huts with sidewalls of spinifex and bushes. They're happy now . . . but all them houses are just wasted. I mean, it's bloody criminal, Dave. I tell you—we've had enough."

I nodded. There didn't seem to be much point in arguing fine details at this time about the slow pace of societal evolution and imposing Western values on ancient indigenous cultures that weren't particularly enamored with us—or our material trappings.

"I hear what you say. I've seen similar problems in the Indian reservations back home in the United States."

"Yeah, well, I heard America's got plenty o' problems. But I think we've just gone too soft. We give 'em everything they ask for and hope they don't make any more fuss. Y'just can't keep doin' that, Dave."

Murray added his assertions and affirmations in the form of strings of expletives and graphic threats of confrontations and retributions to come.

Then there was silence for a while. We seemed to have got

through the diatribe stage and I was glad they'd let off steam so early in the journey. Now perhaps we could move on to other things—like the journey itself.

"Wallaby there, Dave—y'see it?" Murray was pointing to a hillside of bare boulders. I couldn't see anything except rocks.

"Y'gotta keep your eyes peeled," he cautioned. "They move like the 'crackers 'round here."

And so did we. The Land Cruiser seemed an old exponent of buckled, rockbound track travel as we crashed and thrashed our way through more creek beds and over boulder-strewn ridges. The land was cracked and brittle despite the recent downpours. Heat hazes shimmered along the horizons. The sky was a searing silver which stung the eyes. Hot dry air full of dust and grit tore through the open windows.

"Doesn't look like this track is used much."

"Naw, y'right, Dave," said Graeme. "The Bungle's still a pretty remote place for most folks. Some of 'em start out all right, but after the first puncture or a sideswipe from a boulder they decide they'd rather keep what's left of their car than chance it any further."

After a couple of hours driving deeper and deeper into the buckled, broken desert, we paused by a spring-fed pool shaded by white-trunk eucalyptus—aptly named "ghost trees." After the din and dust of the trail it was wonderful to lie on warm soft sand, dangling my legs in cool water, and listening to the silence of the desert. Even Graeme and Murray seemed moved. All the aggressive belligerences of their earlier outbursts seemed to have faded away into the peace of the place and they lay back in the shade, smoking cigarettes, sipping the cool water from their billy-cans, and saying nothing.

Our break was only a short one. The driving continued and the track got worse, and I began to realize why the Bungle Bungle may have remained an elusive secret for so long.

Then we topped a high, barren ridge and Graeme paused on the crest. As the red dust dissipated he pointed across the spinifex plain below to a hazy gray-red rock massif.

"There she is," he said.

At first sight it was not a particularly entrancing scene.

"Where are all the beehives?" I asked. It looked like a poor man's Ayers Rock.

Graeme laughed. "You're looking at the west face. The beehives are all on the other side. You'll see 'em!"

I was still not convinced it had been worth all the effort. Many of Australia's "sights" are notable for their subtle modesty—enjoyed more in microcosm than in breathtaking macro-vistas. There are no great alpine ranges or Grand Canyons in the vast red and ancient plateaus that form most of the nation's endless outback. This looked like just one more rather anticlimactic attraction.

"You wait on, Dave. You won't believe this place." Graeme smiled and slapped my shoulder. "No place like it—anywhere."

I smiled back, a little weakly, and hoped he was right.

After more interminable bone-battering driving we arrived at "camp," which consisted of a series of army-gray tents and a cookout area on the edge of a dry creek and shaded by white brittle range gum and river redgum trees. "Shaded" is perhaps the wrong term. Eucalyptus trees are notorious for their lack of shade. Sparse narrow-leaf coverage creates at best a lacy semblance of shadow but no real protection from the heat, particularly at this time, the approach of searing summer and the great "wets" which last from November through March.

Graeme possessed a remarkable love for the scraggly, bark-dripping gum trees of the outback and, after unloading supplies, took me on a tour of the campsite. He rattled off the names, both in colloquial Australian and loquacious Latin: "Now that's a *Eucalyptus papuanti*, the famous ghost gum that you see in a lot of paintings, and there's your *Eucalyptus confertiflora*, the cabbage gum. Now here's a nice little snappy gum, the *Eucalyptus brevifilia*, and your silver-leafed box, the *Eucalyptus pruinosa*. . . ."

Someone told me that Australia boasted over two hundred different species of gum or eucalyptus trees and it looked like Graeme was endeavoring to find an example of each around our dusty camp.

Fortuntately, he noticed my sweaty, tired face.

"Jeez, Dave, y'look bushed, mate. Listen, we've got things to do for a while. Why don't you just kip down and we'll take a drive later on when it cools?"

If I was in the habit of doing so I would have hugged him. But I compromised with a grateful smile and a weary nod.

He suggested a place shaded by the trunks of a group of trees and gave me a hefty canvas "Kimberley Swag."

"Y'see one of them before—right?"

"No—I don't believe I have."

"Aw, these are great. Real outback kit. Here let me show you. . . ."

He carefully undid the leather straps and buckles and opened up a broad piece of green canvas, around nine feet square, to reveal an instant bed—pillow, thin foam mattress, two Velcro-sealed pockets for valuables, and a long, sewn-in mosquito net.

"Okay, mate. Get a bit a kip and I'll wake y'up with a cuppa later on."

I didn't believe it. I was actually being invited to sleep after three days of almost constant movement. As soon as my head sank into the little foam pillow I was gone.

Evening was all an outback evening should be. A great crimson ball of sun sinking slowly toward the western ridges, stroking the plains in a translucent orange light and casting long, thin shadows of spinifex and thorn tree. The bulk of the Bungle Bungle looked more majestic now, its towering sandstone cliffs glowing with such violent intensity it seemed that the light came from within the ancient rock itself.

I remembered something else I'd read in D. H. Lawrence's *Kangaroo*. He wrote of "a subtlely remote, formless beauty, more poignant than anything I've ever experienced before." I was beginning to understand the feelings behind his words.

Something was watching me. Something quite close by. I lifted myself up slowly from the swag and saw a four-foot-high rotund ball of fur with a face something like an interbred deer and rabbit with delicate little front paws clasped together as if about to make a speech, and a rotund haunch, ending in a long, leathery, wormlike tail.

A young wallaby. At last!

My eyes were still full of sleep and I must have moved a little

251

too clumsily trying to reach for my camera. The creature gave a kind of frustrated sigh—and vanished.

"Did y'see him?" asked Graeme, carrying a huge enamel mug of hot tea over to my swag.

"Only just. He didn't seem to want to hang about."

"Aw—he'll be back. We've seen six already. They're always a bit nervous at first."

I drank the tea and watched the shadows ease across the dry sandy earth. Birds fluttered and chirped in the trees. Graeme murmered their names (without the Latin this time): "Couple of willie wagtails there . . . a jacky winter . . . restless flycatcher on that branch, y'see it . . . rufous songlark . . . there's the little friarbird . . . a honeyeater, yellow-tinted . . . a young nightjar . . . there's a kookaburra out here somewhere, but I can't see it . . . two sulphur-crested cockatoos earlier on, they're gone now . . . couple of blackfaced wood swallows over on that bloodwood. . . ."

The tea, very strong and very sugary, was doing what tea does so well.

"Listen," Graeme said, "You wanna have a quick wash? Dinner'll be ready in five minutes. Murray's the bush tucker-stuffer, the camp cook, tonight so it won't be fancy. We let you sleep. You were fagged out. So—forget walking tonight. You can start early tomorrow."

Over thick steaks, mushy peas, mashed potatoes, and damper (a basic form of campfire bread made from flour and water and little else), I met two men who were very different from the angry, almost racist bigots of the early morning. Both Graeme and Murray had traveled widely across Australia and their colorful tales of outback adventures made me salivate with anticipation.

But eventually—inevitably—conversation returned to the constantly niggling "problem" of the Aborigines.

"Y'know, we really fucked 'em around," said Graeme with a gentleness I hadn't noticed before. "I mean—dammit, it was their country. For over forty thousand years—who knows?—m'be much, much longer if you believe some of them Sydney anthropologists. And then we come along . . . hell, our Australia was nothing but crooks and shysters from Britain and penal colony governors and guards who were as bad as the riffraff they carried here in convict ships. Not much of a way to start a country, eh?"

"I suppose not," I said, sensing dangerous ground ahead. "I've felt a lot of repressed anger about those early days, even in the short time I've been here."

"S'not so bloody repressed," mumbled Murray. "Doesn't take much to set us off, 'specially if there's a bloody pommie-bastard around . . ." he hesitated, "no offense, Dave."

"None taken, Murray. But the anger seems to get in the way somehow. I'm never quite sure when it's going to surface. There's a kind of in-your-face feeling . . . if I make the slightest slip of the tongue, particularly with my British accent, it's like I'd better be ready for a punch-up."

"That's Australia, Dave," said Graeme with a gentle smile. "It's the 'no one's better than me and no one's worse' attitude. We can't stand people who are stuck up, y'know, bloody pompous. We don't like 'knockers'—people comin' in and criticizing the country. We're still a pretty rowdy bunch—'least some of us are—we like mavericks—guys that take on the system and win, and we like our beer—when you hear people talking about driving across the outback they'll describe it in terms of how much beer you'll need—'That's a five-stubbie trip, that's a ten-stubbie trip' . . . that kinda thing. We eat all the wrong foods, but you'd better watch out if you say so. We do dumb things like—well, like dwarf-throwing contests and that kinda stuff, y'heard of them . . . what else?—Well—Slim Dusty sings about them—he's like our Australian country cowboy—listen to some of his songs."

"No wonder the Aborigines get a bit confused," I said. "I've noticed how they just seem to sit and watch as if they're curious to see what the whites'll do next."

"Poor buggers," said Graeme with a sigh, a genuine one. "I mean, they had the whole thing all set, all organized. Maybe just like Europe was in the Middle Ages when everything was all laid out nice and neat—y'know, y'had your kings and barons and lords and bishops and priests, y'had your workers, your serfs, and then y'had God—right on top of the pile—God telling you what to do and how to keep things straight. A nice neat system." He suddenly seemed a little embarrassed by revealing that he'd obviously done some reading, and some thinking himself. "Well tha's how it seems to me, anyway. What y'think, Murray?"

"Yeah," said Murray.

How nervous Australians seem about revealing knowledge, qualities, and talents that may differentiate them from the mythical "ordinary bloke." There seems to be a deep fear or certainly suspicion of overt "tall poppy" success (unless it comes from beating the system) and flamboyant demonstrations of education or ability. An abiding assumption of equality and the ordinariness of mankind is the great unspoken leveler here. Not quite so evident as the *kerekere* spirit of South Pacific Islands, where all individual achievements and possessions are considered the property of the communal family or clan, but enough to mute men and minds and encourage the pub-bound spirit of beery bonhomie. An odd contradiction in a country that superficially glorifies the individual. "Be your own man," Australia seems to say—and then adds, "But don't think or show you're better than any other man."

"So—you think the Aborigines got a rough deal, then?" I asked.

"No kiddin', they did," said Graeme, glad to be on safe conversational ground again. "Down in Tasmania they wiped out the lot of them in less than a hundred years. Up here we shot 'em, like rabbits—pests—we pushed 'em further and further into the outback just like the Americans did with the Indians. Plowed up the sacred sites, built towns over their graves, gave 'em a few handouts to keep 'em happy, gave 'em booze to mess up their minds. . . . We really did a job on them."

"But earlier on this morning you were criticizing them for not living like other Australians."

"Yeah, I know, Dave, I know. Most Aussies feel the same way. Sort of mad and sorry at the same time. . . . It's guilt, I suppose. Guilt at what we've done and guilt that they're still around to remind us what we've done. A hundred sixty thousand of 'em, most trapped in that old poverty crunch—cheap booze, bad health, poor education, and no jobs. That's why all the money's spent on 'em, pamperin' 'em with things most of 'em don't want. We're sick of hearin' about their Dreamtime and their songs and their sacred places. . . . I suppose we wish they'd just go away. We give 'em big chunks of the outback—I mean, real big, some the size of Britain—and hope they'll just bugger off into them and stay there."

I remembered something I'd read in the reprinted 1770 journals of Captain James Cook, one of the first "discoverers" of Australia, then referred to as the fabled Southland. This hot-tempered son of a Yorkshire farmhand was not known for gushy sentimentality and yet his brief description of Australia's "noble savage" was the precursor of many later expressions of admiration for—and regret—for the decimation of indigenous cultures during that volatile Age of Discovery:

> In reality they are far more happier than we Europeans; being wholly unacquainted with not only the superfluous but the necessary Conveniences so much sought after in Europe... the Earth and sea, of their own accord, furnishes them with all things necessary for life.

No wonder there's guilt in this new land. Guilt at almost destroying a complex culture, guilt at the nation's one-time "white Australian" policy which resisted Asian and Oriental immigration with such phrases as "Two Wongs don't make a white," even guilt at the low-brow tone of rampant our-Australia-wrong-or-right "ockerism." There's plenty of guilt to go around here and you can sense it, crawling and festering behind the reassuring piles of middies and tinnies and stubbies and the buoyant cynicism and braggadocio of yarners and spielers in any tin-roofed, clapboard-walled, sawdust-floored outback pub.

Murray had been sitting silent for a long time, playing with a lukewarm beer.

"You know many Aborigines, Murray?" I asked.

"Some . . . yeah, I know some."

"You think it'd be better just to let them get on with their own lives in those reserves—whatever you call them?"

"The Lands. The Aboriginal Lands." He was thoughtful for a while. "Hell . . . I dunno. I agree with Graeme, though. They have different ways of seeing things . . . everything. I mean . . . listen to the names they give places—thousands of places. They're different from ours. They sound different. Sort of like poetry. Like they give them names that sound like how they look. We call our places after people—like Geraldton, Darwin, Sydney, Melbourne, Gladstone, or after towns back in Britain and Ireland . . . they have names like Kambalda, Yalgoo, Cooloomia, Ningaloo, Kalkariaji, Kununurra, Nulunbuy."

"Beautiful names," I said.

"Yeah," said Murray. "Different."

I could see he was still hesitating, not sure how much to say. "Tell me about the Dreamtime."

"Aw, I dunno, Dave . . . it's not easy. . . . Graeme knows much more."

"C'mon, Murray," said Graeme. "You've been in the outback all your life. . . . You know it."

"Well," said Murray slowly. "It's just a story. Sometimes I think they just made it up to get us riled."

"You really think that?"

He laughed a kind of naughty-boy laugh. "Naw—not really. But y'wonder sometimes. . . . I mean, it's just so . . . well, it's different thinking, different way of seeing things. . . . They see everything as kinda alive, y'know, rocks, mountains, rivers. . . . They're all like living things and they're sort of in there with them . . . y'know, like a part of all this living land. They believe that their ancestors who'd come up out of the ground had 'sung' the earth into life. . . . They'd made it perfect but told the people, the Aborigines, that if they wanted to keep it that way they'd got to keep 'singing' it. . . . They'd got to walk along thousands of invisible lines that kept everything together—they called them the songlines—and they'd got to remember special songs, chants, and remember all the places, the landmarks, places where the ancestors, who were like early animals, had passed and made the land. And where they're still sleeping under the ground. That's what the Aborigine 'walkabout' is. . . . We used to think it was just a bunch of boongs goin' off for a booze-up in the desert . . . some of 'em did . . . but for the others, it was more serious. Like a way of keepin' the world right. They'd walk sometimes hundreds of miles, singing the chants and that. And all those special places . . . they call them strange names—a big pile of round rocks they'd call eggs—the eggs of the Red Snake, or a mountain with a pinnacle—that may be the tail of the Golden Lizard . . . things like that. Other places they'd name after honey ants, kangaroos, the bandicooks, the witchetty grubs, cockatoos, fire, wind . . . what else, Graeme?"

"Something I once read, Dave," said Graeme. "It said, 'They wrapped the whole world in a web of song.' That's nice. Forgot who wrote it."

I looked around, through the lacy filigree of the ghost gum leaves, out across the vast emptiness of the desert, falling away to horizons sheened in a soft dusk light. What to me was a beautiful but featureless flat plain would be, to many Aborigines, an infinitely complex interweaving of invisible songlines and sacred places, each one a vital part of a huge complex whole. Their earth, as they knew it.

Was it just one more way for man to deal with terrible loneliness of being, in a cold, disinterested universe, and particularly on this ancient, worn-down, empty land they now call Australia? The need to give a reason, an explanation, for things around us? The fear of the ultimate unknown—death—that makes us build elaborate fantasies of imaginings to convince ourselves that we are not alone, that we have a purpose, a function, a reason for being? The "walkabout" as the primary purpose of existence? All driven by that great cry of realization, bursting out with joy, fear, and hope—the eternal—"I AM."

Or was it something more? More than just elaborately defensive mental exercises against all that terrifying, screaming nothingness? Is there something within us that *knows* there is a presence, a context out there, or under or above? A shard of a once-absolute knowingness that remains implanted in our psyches and leads us, like salmon to the pool of their birth, seeking throughout our lives to reestablish contact, to regain the context, to know again the whole from which we have been released to live, and will once again return to after life?

We all sat quietly with our own thoughts as the light dimmed into night and the fire flickered and flying things buzzed and clicked around us.

" 'Nother beer, Dave?" asked Graeme.

"Sure."

"Murray?"

Murray seemed to be in another place. His eyes were closed. For the first time he looked tired, as if his short but pungent monologue had drained him.

"Murray," said Graeme louder.

"Yeah . . . what?"

"Beer?"

"Yeah."

Sleep came easily that night under a silver black sky crackling with stars.

And the next few days were all mine.

Graeme and Murray had much to do, cleaning up the campsite and removing all the gear that had hosted small groups of adventurers throughout the cooler April through November period.

"Take the Cruiser," Graeme had said, handing me the keys and a rough-drawn map of the Bungle Bungle massif. "Go and explore for a while. When we're finished here we'll try to get into the canyons with you."

He loaded the back with a large "eski" cooler full of water, soda, beer, and snacking supplies.

"Take more'n you think you'll need," he advised. "Can get damn hot in there. You'll sweat like crazy."

"Any other warnings? Snakes, biting things, poison plants?"

"Naw. You'll be right, Dave. Just get in there and enjoy yourself."

Which is precisely what I did. Day after day.

The wonders and delights of this strange, sometimes eerie place have merged in my memory. Recollections return in drops and sprinklings of color, form, shape, and sound. To be alone in these strange clefts and canyons made me rejoice once again in the stroking comforts of solitude. I could imagine—I did imagine—that I'd discovered this place myself, just come across it on some long outback odyssey, entered its passages, learned its secrets after days on the bright brittle plains.

The Bungle took me in and enveloped me. For hours I sat in the shade of canyon walls, three or four hundred feet high, listening to the soft prattle of palm fronds, watching the shadows move with the sun across the smooth striped and tiered walls, rejoicing in the occasional cool breezes that wafted down from the high, narrower places, letting the soft red sand on the floor of the canyons trickle through my fingers.

I drank from clear cold pools fed by secret springs; I shared a sandwich lunch with a pink-crested cockatoo; I watched tiny lizards scurry through the sharp, spiky grasses; I looked for Aborigine wall markings and symbols, but saw none. Even they, I later learned, were reluctant to wander within these mazelike clefts. They buried their dead here and left them in peace, among the timeless silences.

I remember the grand climax to an arduous walk and climb through Cathedral Gorge, where, after squeezing at one point through a cleft no more than two feet wide, I finally entered a vast natural ampitheater where the gorge ended in a basilicalike bowl shaded by an enormous rock archway in which was a crystal pool fed by a trickling waterfall. The place echoed like the Blue Mosque in Istanbul, wispy threads of sound rolling around the towering curved walls. Mystical. Almost magic.

I sat on a low dome of blown sand waiting for something to happen. Everything seemed set for an appearance, a celebration, an offering—something to give focus to a setting so spiritual, so silent, so majestic that it's hard to believe it existed, merely for me and the moment of my being there.

To think such a place as this has gone untouched, unmolested, unexplored for so many millions of years without even the modest intrusions of the Aborigines. . . . It gave new life to all my lost-world explorations and expectations. There may be hundreds of such places, still unknown, still unmapped in our seemingly poor, cluttered, overdiscovered, overused world. Not "may." I know there are. Some too small or fragile to mention, even to friends. Others so remote and inaccessible that they exist in their wholeness, safe maybe forever from prying eyes and inquisitive minds. Vast underground worlds of water and caves and galleries dripping with millions of stalactites; deep, jungle-hidden grottoes harboring life-forms as yet unknown and unrecorded; other canyons, other Bungle Bungles, so elusive that we may never find them and never experience their beauty and their own special solitudes.

To know that our world still remains a thing of mystery, silence, and secrets—this I find one of the greatest joys of all. It

ONE OF THE BUNGLE-BUNGLE CANYONS

gives me that shiver of pure *duende* that scampers through my body when I experience a place or a thing with new eyes and new sensations; when the mind's constant gauging, measuring, comparing, and contrasting cease and you gaze—mind-less— at something so unexpected and so overwhelmingly all-encompassing that you are drenched in the golden cascades of pure feeling. A great cleansing of the spirit, a breaking of barriers, an annihilation of "attitudes"—a powerful rush, upward and out-ward into infinite new possibilities, infinite new delights. A re-joicing in the great "I AM"—and, even more—a reinforcement of the "you are" . . . a sense of being propelled into far broader spaces and conceptions . . . and, most strange of all, a sense of coming home to a place that, somehow, deep, deep down, you always knew was there.

Maybe I'd been reading too much of Chatwin's *Songlines*. Maybe I'd been touched by Murray—that raunchy, stolid out-backer—trying to understand some of the secret world of the Aborigines he so easily dismissed in barstool lingo as "boongs" and drunken layabouts.

He knew. And despite all the bravado, he possibly yearned for a sense of the wholeness and the completeness—a Dream-time—in the confused, roustabout world around him.

He'd never say so. But neither would many of us, plowing through the clutter and distractions and trappings and little tired emotions of our lives of quiet desperation.

I come to places like this to shed the cloying skin that en-velopes us all at one time or another. I come to be cleansed. I come to learn—or rather, to be taught. Or maybe I come to be reminded of things part of me already knows. The part of me that needs air and light and solitude and silence . . . the part of me that I laid on those soft sands of Cathedral Gorge and offered, freely, willingly. And watched it soar. . . .

Oh, yes. There was magic in that place.

I found it. And it found me in many other places in this Bungle Bungle—this still-unexplored enigma. In the clefts of Echidna Chasm, in Frog Hole, in the long, winding corridor of Piccaninny Creek which ended once again in a crystal pool filled with dazzling reflections of red-domed canyon walls.

I could—maybe should—have stayed longer. Every day

brought fresh discoveries and new sensations. Each evening I would return to camp worn out but, as Graeme noted, "charged."

The last day came and the camp was gone, leaving a few worn patches of boot-marked earth between the straggly gum trees and explosions of spinifex.

"Got a surprise for you," Graeme said with his slightly secretive Graeme-grin.

"What?" I asked. One more surprise in almost a week of surprises wouldn't hurt.

"Hang on. You'll hear him in a minute or two."

"Who?"

"Just wait."

So I waited, wishing I had time to go back into the canyons for one last quiet walk.

The air throbbed way back behind the ridge, then thundered, then crackled like smashed glass as a tiny bubble-cockpit helicopter skimmed over the treetops and landed on a bare patch of dust close to the campsite.

"Well—here's your surprise." Graeme smiled.

"A helicopter?"

"Friend of mine. Takes flights over the Bungle in the spring. He's coming to clean up. Says he'll give you a ride if you like. See the other side of the Purnululu."

"Y'mean the beehive formations?"

"You got it, mate. Those are what really put the Bungle on the map. Better get on over."

I ran across the open ground. The pilot remained in the cockpit, we shouted our introductions at one another, and then I was off in that doorless Plexiglas bubble that whisked me high over my beloved canyons, across the eroded red plateau, and—well, I described it all at the outset.

Suffice to say it was one of the most enervating and exciting journeys of my life and a fitting finale-experience in this most unique of landscapes, deep in the northwestern outback of Australia. A place I was learning to love and even understand. A little.

I'd hoped for a tour around the town when we got back to Halls Creek. Graeme had told me about the abandoned gold mines, remnants of western Australia's first rush in the late 1800s. "There's a meteor crater too a few miles out, second largest in the world," he had said, "and then we could drive through some of the Kimberley cattle country." He'd also promised to introduce me to a local legend, Betty Johnson, a longtime Halls Creek gold prospector who once slept through a cyclone in the outback and awoke to find her campsite surrounded by fat, shiny nuggets.

But things didn't work out as we'd planned.

"You're in luck again," Graeme gushed. "How do you feel about a ride in a mail plane into the Never-Nevers?"

"Into the what?"

"Pilot's off to Mount Augustus—middle-of-nowhere place— and then to Exmouth on the coast. Near the Ningaloo Reefs— sort of a west coast Great Barrier Reef. Beaut place, Dave—very quiet."

"Never heard of either."

"Well—neither have most blokes. But you'll really get a feel for this part of the country. And it's free."

"Free?"

"You got it, mate. He likes company. And you're not such bad company . . . for a pile."

"And what the hell's a pile?"

" 'Nother word for a pommie Britisher. Piles come out, never go back, and give you a pain in the ass!"

"Thanks, Graeme."

"Only kiddin', mate. Good word tho', in't—we got flooded with pommies back in the sixties. Government usta pay 'em to come here. Free flights from London, free put-up till they got fixed with a job. Nice cushy little package."

"I remember that. I even thought about doing it myself."

"Too good a deal, Dave. They came out in the thousands. Had to stay two years to give it a try. Lots of 'em went back. Miserable whining bastards."

"And y'think this pilot would like a 'pile' for company?"

"He likes anyone who'll listen to him. Gets bloody boring flying around the outback by y'self. She'll be apples, Dave. Bright red ones. You'll be fine!"

264

I had other plans, but they could wait. I accepted the offer and the same afternoon left Halls Creek in a twin-engine plane sitting beside a stocky and very animated pilot whose name seemed to be either Taffy, Dick, or Walrus (he had a big black mustache that drooped walrus-fashion almost to his chin), depending on who he was talking to.

And could he talk.

Above the roar of the engine, Walrus expounded on Australian history, Australian flora and fauna, the Aborigines (of course), the perils of flying "junkers" like his, and the sexual prowess of outback cattle station wives who gratefully received their mail every two or three weeks and got "real lonely" when their spouses went off for days, sometimes weeks, rounding up the errant steers on million-acre station spreads.

Walrus seemed to enjoy his life. "Listen, Dave. My thinkin' is that life is like a big bloody orange full of juice. You peel it, slice away the crud, dig out the pips, cut it into as many pieces as you want and suck 'n' chew each piece till you get every mouthful—every drop. And if that's not enough, you can chew on the peel too . . . whaddyathink?"

Walrus liked to talk rather than listen. My responses to his rhetorical questions were usually irrelevant as far as he was concerned. Attempts to answer or argue were usually met in midsentence with "Right y'are, Dave, so anyway . . . " After a while I gave up and sort of half heard his rambling philosophies and outback adventures while watching the enormity of the desert ease by hundreds of feet below us.

The scale of this wild, empty country is staggering. Hour after hour we flew over these ancient peneplained plateaus. Hour after hour across the Great Sandy Desert, an ocher-toned infinity where the reds ranged from brilliant crimson to the deepest rust, patterned by sinuous streambeds that captured the swirl of rain torrents maybe twice a year at most.

Way to our east we caught occasional faint glimpses of the notorious Canning Stock Route that snakes eleven hundred miles across some of the most unforgiving land on earth. Surveyed and bore-holed for wells by Alfred Canning from 1906 to 1910, this legendary track provided the only way to move thousands of head of cattle from the east Kimberley cattle stations south to the teeming southern oil fields and the railhead at Meekatharra.

The endurance and determination of Canning, his men, and his Aborigine guides became the vivid stuff of Australian folk history and his route was in regular use until the emergence of the road train system after World War II. Herds made this last journey in 1958 and today it is a key element of the outback exploration dreams of most citybound Australians. To have been a "Canning Cowboy" is something very special.

Graeme Macarthur takes occasional two-week Jeep treks down the route from Halls Creek, crossing interminable swaths of dunes, pausing in the shade of rare desert oak forests, passing the vast white salt flats of Lake Disappointment, withstanding dry wells, broken axles, and even broken-spirited passengers, to end up in the isolated little one-pub town of Wiluna. He agrees wholeheartedly with Keith Willey's (*The Drovers*) description of the Canning as "unquestionably the loneliest, most difficult and dangerous route in Australia."

It remains one of the country's most celebrated outback adventures. Something I'm tempted to try next time.

My eyes were playing tricks. Staring down at the redness below I began to see patterns, strange wild patterns of white dots scattered in lines and curlicues across the desert. I blinked and they remained somehow familiar. Walrus dismissed them as "outcrops and spinifex clumps," but I'd seen those patterns before . . . in Sydney . . . in one of the museums displaying Aboriginal art. . . . Of course! They were like the ancient dot paintings. One of the most unusual art forms in Australia. Huge ocher-colored works swirled with contrasting reds (the streambeds?) and patterns of white dots (the spiniflex clumps?). But how had the Aborigines seen the patterns on their vast horizontal terrain? Were they visible in such patterned formations from hills and bluffs? Surely from that height they'd look like pretty much just what they were—scraggly clumps of dry vegetation. One could only really see their intricacy from a great height, the height of a plane flying over the land. . . .

I never resolved the mystery. A brief meeting with an Aborigine artist later in my journey only added to my speculation and confusion.

"These are the old pictures," he told me. "You can see them painted on cave walls. I'm just telling the old stories."

"Yes, but stories of what?"

"Of the Dreamtime. Of the land."

"But surely to see these patterns, those pictures, you need to fly."

"Of course. We know how to tread lightly on the earth."

"You mean—you did fly?"

A shrug, a twinkle, and a wink from under a prominent brow shadowing dark eyes.

A companion of the artist smiled and said, "Try some pituri, mate, the Aborigine chewing tobacco. You'll soon be flyin' yourself."

It was not a very enlightening exchange. But neither were most of my conversations with Aborigines. Each time I felt I was beginning to understand the ancient concepts of the Dreamtime, the songline webs, the totemic systems of the ancestors, the dread of "dead" unsung lands, the vast tomes of unwritten ritual knowledge, the tales of ancient shell middens, the "bone-pointing" rituals of sorcerers, the strange tjuringa plaques made of mulga wood that were treasured almost more than life itself . . . each time, another element would be introduced and the kaleidoscope would change once again. New patterns of thought, new perspectives, new ways of seeing all the complex interlockings of stories, songs, beliefs, and rituals.

I began to understand the frustration of your average let's-get-things-done Australian when faced with endless Aborigine claims of sacred places and talk of honey ant dreamings and lizard dreamings and porcupine dreamings. While it all entranced me and made me dizzy, it makes others angry, impatient, and suspicious of a "big con job."

Walrus was definitely one of the latter. "I'm sick of the whole bloody rigmarole. We're bloody fools listenin' to all this nonsense," he'd mumbled through his billowing mustache at one point in our flight. "It's got to stop. Otherwise we might as well give 'em them their bloody country back, pack our bags, and move down to Tasmania. They solved their problems a hundred years back there. Now all they've got are a few faggot 'Greenies' moanin' about the forests. We'd soon put 'em right, mate! No worries."

On and on and on we flew with only the occasional sand devil ("willy-willy" in Strine) to break the monotony below.

We had a brief touchdown at Jiggalong for a mail drop in a rusty, battered oil drum nailed to four fence posts. All around us was a lemon-tinted desert spotted with spinifex. A distant clump of almost leafless gum trees marked a ranch house. There was no one around. No grateful station wife, no wild dingo dogs, no birds. Nothing except a hot wind, scraggly cirrus tails in a blue-lemon sky, and a little girl's shoe, cracked and torn, at the base of the fence.

"Shirley usually comes out," Walrus mumbled, obviously disappointed by the absence of one of his "desert girls."

"Must be shopping," I joked.

"Right! Nearest decent store's four hundred k north of here. On a dirt road that's likely been washed out in the last wet." He seemed reluctant to leave.

"Shit!" he shouted finally at the vast blinding nothingness, and we took off in a rage of yellow dust and desert gravel. Looking down I thought I saw someone driving from the ranch across the flats to the mailbox, but I wasn't sure. I decided not to mention it to a rather morose Walrus.

"Mount Augustus coming up," Walrus mumbled an hour or so later. "Biggest bleedin' monocline in the world. The Ayers Rock of the west and twice the size!"

"What's a monocline?"

"Lord knows. A big rock I suppose."

Whatever it was, it was indeed a big rock, bare and bold. A 3,350-foot-high surge of billion-year-old Proterozoic sandstone, over five miles long and visible from the air for over a hundred miles. Other ridges and rifts rose through the haze to the south, but Mount Augustus stood alone in a vast red nothingness, the dying sun coating its flanks with crimson.

"At bloody last—stubbie time." Walrus smiled as he eased the little plane down through the purpling dusk light. We landed with a gentle thump on the dusty runway.

"Welcome to the middle of nowhere," he shouted as small stones crackled against the wings and fuselage. "Three hundred eighty-six *k* to Meekatharra, four hundred and fifty *k* to Carnarvon—and nothing in between."

A retired couple had recently moved to the Mount Augustus cattle station ("a million acres, give or take a few thousand") and were trying to attract outback travelers to their collection of simple "trailer rooms" billed in their new brochure as "the finest of holiday accommodation and camping facilities." With a collective bathroom and toilets two hundred yards from the the rooms, the word "finest" must be treated in its geographical context. However, after my days of camping under the stars in the Bungle Bungle and hour after hour in a hot cramped cockpit, the tiny air-conditioned room smacked of presidential-suite luxury.

I washed and joined Walrus for "a splash of neck oil and yabber" (a beer party) in the camp store cum souvenir shop cum restaurant cum occasional bust-up bar (more Aborigine tales here). Someone else was there too, a large burly man with a mop of ginger hair and a thick, phlegmatic outback drawl. I was introduced to Don Hammerquist, owner of this vast million-acre station, and the evening was filled with his tales of station life and roundups and all the intricate details of his lonely existence in the "Never-Nevers."

I learned about the work of the itinerant cowboys and cowgirls—the "jackaroos" and the "jillaroos"—during the three- or four-month-long annual musters from June through September when they use four-wheel drive Jeeps, motorbikes, and a Cessna plane to flush out the cattle from remote valleys and canyons. Even the occasional helicopter would be brought in as a kind of aerial roundup pony flying at tree height to drive the steers toward the pens scattered across the ranch at key water holes.

I heard of the rogue bulls that would charge and often overturn the Jeeps, regular visits by Australia's famous "flying doctors" to tend crippled stockmen, the days of branding when young cattle would be marked, castrated, ear-tagged, and de-

269

horned, and the older ones selected for double-decked road train drives to market.

I learned of Don's seventy windmills, each of which had to be kept in working order to fill the watering troughs; I was told of the five hundred miles of barbed-wire fences that had to be repaired and rewired constantly, and the seven huge stockyards spaced out across the vast red emptiness of the station, each with its own pens, bunkhouses, and maintenance facilities.

Surely a man who owned (actually leased from the government for ninety-nine years, like most other station bosses) such a vast spread and so many cattle—over eighty-five hundred (one head per 120 acres)—must indeed be a wealthy individual, a sort of J.R. of Australia.

"Bloody wrong, mate!" bellowed Don. "There's no bloody South Forks out here in the desert. You passed my ranch house when y'walked in from the landing strip."

I nodded. I had thought his home was part of the maintenance outbuildings behind the "hotel."

" 'Kings in Grass Castles'—that's what they call us," said Don. "And that's jus' 'bout right. You gotta work every bloody day, day in and day out, just to break even—me, the wife, the boys, the stock hands—y'never stop. Sometimes I'm off out on the bottom part of the range—the Never-Nevers—over back of Augustus—for four, five days, fixin' things, chasin' up the scrub bulls in me bull-buggy, tryin' to get everything right before the wets. Bloody hard life, mate. Wife gets down to Perth m'be once, twice a year if she's lucky, for a bit of shoppin'."

"You don't go with her?"

"Not if I can help it."

"You don't like cities?"

"No. Soon as I get there I start thinkin' when I'm leavin' . . . too many people, too much bloody commotion."

"What about retirement?"

"What about it?" growled Don. "I'll be doin' this every day till I drop."

"And that's okay with you?"

"Too bloody right, mate—that's fine with me."

* * *

Walrus decided he'd have a lie-in and "do a few jobs" the following morning so I borrowed the hotel owner's Jeep and his map and bounced along the thirty-mile track circling the base of Mount Augustus.

Below the surging ridges of this great monocline were little hidden places of pure delight: dry creek beds shaded by huge ghost gums, dark cool pools fed by springs, caves and hollows decorated with some of the earliest Aboriginal wall paintings found in Australia, clefts and gorges littered with house-sized sandstone boulders, worn and rounded to eggshell smoothness. . . .

Walrus was ready for takeoff when I returned. I was tempted to stay awhile longer in this lovely, lonely place, but transport to the nearest town of Carnarvon was rare.

"Don' be a bloody galah, Dave. Y'could be stuck here a week or more. With me you'll be in Exmouth in a coupla hours. Lovely sheilas. Beaches. Pubs. Lots of dead 'orse. You're on your own then."

"Y'know, Walrus, I really appreciate—"

"Don't piddle in yer pocket, mate. Jus' get your clobber and let's get movin'."

A couple of hours later, after more dot-speckled, red infinities, we crossed the North West Coastal Highway and eased down across Exmouth Gulf to a small, scattered town on the edge of the surfless blue Indian Ocean.

I quickly realized, after my farewells to Walrus and a brief ride into town, that Exmouth, while still a little outback in appearance, is soon destined to transform itself into a major west coast resort. A couple of new motels, a few new stores, constant rumors of offshore oil fields, and a determination to persuade the U.S. government to maintain its naval communication station in active operation nearby—all combine to give the ambitious little town a sense of concerted momentum toward a bright new future. There's even a "glass-bottom boat" operation offering trips out to the reefs on the eastern edge of the peninsula. Everything is still pleasantly amateurish and entrepreneurial. A true bootstrap spirit permeates Exmouth, at least until the nationally famous annual game fishing tournaments and boat races, when the place becomes a social hot spot for a brief spell. I liked its spirit.

"Exmouth," the colorful brochures proclaim, "where it's summer all year round." From what I'd heard of the real Australian 120-degree summers, this kind of hook seemed of questionable appeal, but Richard Agar, manager of the Exmouth Coral Coast Tourist Bureau, insisted that constant sea breezes and low humidity made Ningaloo and Exmouth "ideal resort areas."

The hell with resorts. I'll take it just the way it is now with emus pecking at the scrub on the edge of town, kangaroos hopping between the water holes on the flats below the craggy clefts and canyons of Cape Range, and utter peace and silence on the white arced beaches of the Ningaloo Coral Coast. Two ospreys floated high above us. Tiny white ghost crabs scattered like surf froth as we walked barefoot on the warm sand. Geckos darted between sprays of spinifex on the low dunes.

Richard drove me south early one morning along a rough gravelly track past the beaches to Yardie Creek, where a narrow inlet of Mediterranean-turquoise water rippled against red and gold sandstone cliffs. We ate an outdoor breakfast of steaks, bacon, eggs, and beans cooked on Richard's portable "barbie" while he pointed out the wildflowers still sparkling with late spring brilliance among the boulders. I remember some of their lovely, unfamiliar names—kangaroo paws, scarlet feather flowers, smokebushes, elegant-banksias, and deep purple sheens of mulla mullas.

In a hollow above the creek we strolled across an ancient Aboriginal midden of broken shells.

"Y'know, Australians are funny," Richard said quietly as the shells crunched beneath our feet. "They go tearing off around the world like gypsies—seeing everything—and then finally they wake up to their own country. They get the outback urge and come to places like this to find out what their own country's all about—what *they're* all about."

He pointed to the high brittle plateaus and gorges of Cape Range rising up from behind the creek. "There's so many places in there . . . some of them you have to walk to . . . hidden places, valleys, canyons. . . . You can lose yourself for days looking for striped rock wallabies, cave paintings . . . they're all in there. And if you drive the track further south to Carnarvon you'll find some of the best empty camping beaches in the country."

"What about the reef?"

"Well—they call Ningaloo the Great Barrier Reef of the West Coast, but that's not really true. It's nothing like as long—only around two hundred miles. But it's not known either, so you usually get the whole place to yourself. You can take a boat out there"—he pointed to the line of surf a mile or so out in the ocean—"and its all yours—great spreads of brain coral, cabbage, staghorn, fire coral. You'll swim out there with mantas, great fat turtles, some sharks, and whale sharks, parrot fish, marlin, eels, sailfish, humpback whales—they've recorded more than five hundred species here. . . . It's fantastic."

Exmouth is fortunate to have such an enthusiastic tourist bureau manager. Richard's love of this remote place made me realize why I was enjoying my ramblings through Australia so much. You feel the country is still largely undiscovered. You can still sense the pioneer spirit of the northwest ranchers and the people living in the little desert towns, hundreds of miles from anywhere. And you can see it in the eyes of citybound Australians from the east who come here to discover the timeless essence of their young country. There's an adolescence of spirit here, a willingness to keep options open, to keep the dreams alive, to keep exploring, seeking wide-open futures in this enormous, empty land. In an ironic way, the walkabout "singings" of the Aborigines and the bright-eyed wonder of Australians discovering their own country for the first time have a similar and complementary effect—they keep Australia fresh, vigorous, and endlessly enticing. The vast red emptiness of the northwest is laced both by webs of ancient songs and more recent anthems of awe from the new discoverers. It is alive and vital. The land sings its own spirit. And I heard it many times in my journeys. . . .

Journeys which almost came to an abrupt end in the warm floppy ocean off Exmouth.

It was my last day and I decided to join a handful of other travelers on a glass-bottom boat excursion among the colorful reefs of the peninsula's eastern shore.

For an hour or more we drifted in the shallows, watching the parrot fish, groupers, red emperors, coral trout, starfish, sea slugs, and enormous turtles among the multicolored explosions of coral heads.

After a while, seeing such sights through thick glass was no longer enough and a number of us decided to go snorkeling. We wanted to float among the fish and lose ourselves for a while in the sun-dappled shadows of the coral forests.

I lost track of time.

Coming to the surface a while later I realized that all the others had gone back to the boat. I could see them perched on the bow in a group, drinking and listening to the skipper telling tales of the reef. They all had their backs to me, music was playing, and no one seemed in any hurry to return to shore.

Five more minutes, I promised myself, and disappeared again into the cool depths, playing with the fish and watching the shards of sunlight undulate over the coral formations.

Then something rather odd began to happen. As I lay motionless close to the surface I noticed that the coral was drifting past me. Slowly at first and then with increasing speed. A rather pleasant sensation—like peering through the window of a moving train. Only I sensed I was being pulled farther and farther away from the boat.

I came to the surface again. I was indeed being carried away from the boat. I could see my fellow snorkelers still drinking and listening to the skipper's tales, but they were smaller now and the boat was a good quarter of a mile away.

No problem. Time to swim back and join in the fun.

Only the swimming didn't seem to work. I increased my pace, but the boat came no closer. Something was carrying me farther out into the ocean. The water was noticeably colder too. And waves were forming in a breeze that had not been there before. Small waves at first, hardly chin height. And then a little bigger.

Okay—power swimming time. I switched to a steady crawl, but the boat remained just as far away. And the wind became stronger, blowing directly against me. Only one thing to do. Bawl out and tell the skipper to come closer.

I took off my mask and shouted, but my voice didn't seem to carry. I shouted louder, but now the wind was blowing the sound back into my face. I tried waving, but no one was looking in my direction. They didn't even seem to know I was out here.

I opened my mouth for a real bellow, and a wave—a wave I

should have seen but didn't—crashed into my face and sent water tumbling down my throat and windpipe.

I was gagging. I swung around away from the boat, letting the waves pound against the back of my head. If I could just get my breath back and my mask on . . . the mask! Where the hell was the mask? Dammit, it must have been knocked out of my hand when the first wave hit. Now I couldn't breathe through the tube . . . and I couldn't breathe in those waves that thrashed between me and the ever-receding boat.

For the first time in my life I became scared in water. Initially it was just a little frisson of fear, a faint shiver up my spine. Water has always been my friend, something to frolic in, something to love for its buoyancy, its colors, its dappled intricacies. But now it became an attacker. An enemy. My breath was still weak as the windpipe struggled to clear itself.

Panic hit. I couldn't reach the boat, I couldn't make them see me, and I couldn't make it to the shore that was now well over two miles away. My energy was draining as I dog-paddled with my back to the waves.

Turn around again—keep your mouth shut—and wave like crazy. . . .

The waves hit hard again, angry now. White-topped, and cold. I waved as vigorously as I could with both arms, pushing my body out of the water.

Dammit, couldn't anyone see me? Bloody idiots . . . didn't they know I was here? I wasn't going to be able to do this many more times.

I felt the adrenaline surge but knew that my strength was running out fast. . . . My heart was pounding . . . my arms felt leaden . . . my breathing was hoarse, fast, and shallow. Panic grew as I realized the horrible inevitability of what was happening; it seemed to tighten my lungs so that I had almost no air.

Stange things were going on in my brain. Two entirely different reactions: one-half seemed to be a miasma of panic and pain from a body too tired now even to swim; the other half was a brilliant kaleidoscope of moving images, a series of fast-forwarding tapes, replaying fragments of memories, sensations, emotions. Friends' faces flashed by . . . a sudden picture of me crying as a child when I'd accidentally tipped my baby sister out

A NEW AESTHETIC
— The Ningaloo Reef
Western Australia

of her carriage . . . a fight I'd once had with a bully in school back in Yorkshire . . . my father's rare but always loving grin . . . my first car, a bright turquoise-blue Austin Mini, and the pride of that first drive . . . a lobster feast on Cape Cod with friends from New Jersey . . . our first New York apartment with a tiny terrace on the fringe of Greenwich village . . . a sudden taste of blinding-hot Indian Vindaloo curry . . . and then Anne, smiling, laughing . . . and a thought—Oh, God, she's going to be really pissed if I don't get home—a crazy vivid patchwork of unpatterned images.

And then from a newly emerging third part of my brain . . . something, somewhere, cool and objective . . . came a quiet, almost disinterested voice telling me, You're drowning, David. . . . you'll be done with all this soon . . . you'll be all right. . . . There are more things to come . . . things you never dreamed of. . . .

I could see—not feel—but really see myself dog-paddling more slowly now, the energy fading, the cold being replaced by a strange warm glow. I'd never had an out-of-body experience before, but that's how it felt—as though part of me, the essential part, was above the thrashing waves, maybe twenty, thirty feet above, looking down at the sad little flailing figure below, waving its arms, fighting the inevitable.

. . . there are more things to come . . .

A calm came. An acceptance. A sense that for one of the few times in my life I was utterly helpless, there was nothing "I" could do, and that me—my fate, my life, all the me's that are me—were being given over to something else, something much larger, all-encompassing, something that would take care of me.

I didn't really sense the arm encircle my neck at first. It felt, I suppose, like another wave, another battering . . . and then, with a jolt, my three free-wheeling brains melded back into a single entity screaming out one very clear message: You're being choked!

The arm was like a vise, compacting my windpipe and squeezing out the last gasps of air. I lashed out, but the arm tightened even more. Maybe fearing that my apparent panic would destroy us both, my rescuer was determined to control my movements. I managed to turn enough so that he could see my face in the final stages of asphyxiation.

" . . . Shoulders . . . I hold . . . your shoulders . . . " Somehow the words spluttered out.

Whoever my savior was, he nodded, turned, and I swam weakly with him against the waves, one arm across his back, gripping his shoulder. I still had little air in my lungs, but I knew now I was safe, and there was no panic. Just a determination to get back to the boat without making an utter fool of myself.

Faces peered over the bow, arms reached out, and I was dragged slowly on board. Someone thrust a glass of something sweet and strong into my hand. It burned like ice and fire, but it did its work, making me choke out the seawater in my lungs and sense the warming fingers of sugary alcohol ease through my body.

I was utterly drained. There was no energy left. The boat bobbed about in the heaving swell. Then I heard the motors roar and saw the shore coming closer and closer . . . hard land, safe, dependable land. . . . I wanted to be laid on warm sand well away from that pernicious ocean and just left to sleep and sleep. . . .

Peter Hillier was the hero of the day. He had seen what would have been the last of my useless frantic arm waves and had leapt off the boat, called to the skipper to follow, and done "one of the fastest racing crawls I've ever done, mate," to save this errant wanderer from an ignominious watery demise.

Peter was a charter pilot on a brief business trip out of Perth, and we became instant bosom buddies back on land. We caroused together in the local pub that evening with a crowd of other outback adventurers, sang Australian folk songs together at a crooked moon, and made plans to fly south together, back to his home and his family in Fremantle, after a day or two more in the Ningaloo sun.

I shall never forget you, Peter. You gave me a new life—a life I celebrate now with a fresh sense of wonder and gratitude. You made it possible for me to complete this book and, I hope, many others. You made my smile wider and my spirit far richer.

For this I will continue to thank you, my friend.

Every day of my new life.

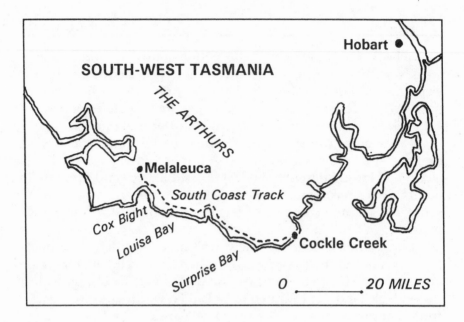

SOUTH-WEST TASMANIA

THE ARTHURS

Hobart ●

●Melaleuca

South Coast Track

Cox Bight

Louisa Bay

Surprise Bay

Cockle Creek

0 ———— 20 MILES

8. SOUTH-WEST TASMANIA

Journeys of Solitude Through a True Wilderness

"The south-west of Tasmania provides one of the finest
walking areas I have ever seen."
Sir Edmund Hillary, 1960

"Among the best wilderness experiences anywhere
on Earth."
Ken Collins, *South-West Tasmania*, 1990

"Could be a bit choppy," says Phil, the pilot.
"How choppy?" asks this nervous traveler, unaccustomed to

flying in tiny four-seater planes through clouds that crowded in at the Plexiglas windows and made it feel like we were plowing through thick oatmeal porridge.

"Hard to tell, mate. Over the Arthurs could be a bit rough."

"How high are these Arthurs?"

" 'Round about thirty-five hundred feet. West Portal is thirty-six hundred feet."

"That doesn't sound so bad." I'd flown over far higher ranges in my travels but usually in a martini haze and couched comfortably with a favorite book, lights and fan that flicked on with the press of buttons, and flight attendants anxious to respond to my every whim. (Well, for the first hour or so. After that they usually disappear. I've never found out where.)

" 'S not so much the height, mate. It's the bloody wind shear you get on those ridges—especially the first one. But—take it easy—we'll know soon enough."

Yes—I bet we will. Like we'll know when we hit one of those vertical air cliffs and gravity takes over and we end up skewered on a needled pinnacle in one of Australia's last true wildernesses.

Silence. Too much silence. Phil isn't exactly sweating, but he's certainly got a tremble in his hands unless that's just the judder that constantly rattles your teeth and nerves in this cardboard and paste flying machine.

Retrospective time.

How did I get to be here in this cloud-cuckoo land on the lowest chunk of Australasia with nothing between me and Antarctica but fifteen hundred miles of frigid Pacific Ocean?

Tasmania?

Most people have no idea where it is. Maybe vague recollections of a remote island that exports apples, fragments of irrelevant information from musty geographical diatribes given by a teacher who'd possibly never left his hometown. An island in Indonesia, maybe? Somewhere in the South Pacific? Near the Philippines?

The only image that seems to generate a flicker of recognition is that glowering, growling, slobbering Saturday morning cartoon character, the Tasmanian Devil.

THE ARTHURS
— South-West Tasmania

And ironically most mainland Australians (the "north island-ers," as the Tasmanians call them) often have similarly hazy views of the place. They know where it is, of course—that little heart-shaped blip south of Melbourne, a short air hop across the Bass Strait. But when it comes to understanding its topographical and social idiosyncracies I usually hear such offhand remarks as:

Oh, yeah, they killed off all the Abos soon as they settled the place. [Then, in a roughish mumble] . . . Just like we should've done.

Or the dismissive:

Tassie—oh, yeah—great little place. You can drive 'round it in a day.

Or the well-intentioned:

Never been there. Been to Europe, Africa, Thailand—all those places. Got to go Tassie sometime. They say it's nice.

And then come the snide jokes that I must have heard in a dozen different guises on the "north island":

What's a Tasmanian Virgin? A girl who runs faster than her brothers [or the alternative]) . . . a girl who doesn't have a father.

Ah, yes—Tasmania! Where men are men and the sheep are worried.

And much more of the same. Far too much triteness for a truly beautiful island of half a million relatively pastoral people living leisurely lives among its soaring mountains, Ireland-green mead-ows, and lovely coastal coves.

It was in a pub, way up on the western coast of Australia, when I finally decided to take a trip to Tasmania.

"Unbelievable place!" The young eager-faced sheila (Aussie-lingo or Strine for a girl) gushed as she sipped her beer and leaned forward into our group, her eyes sparkling.

"Southern Tasmania. It's like no other place in the world.

You're out there in the middle of nowhere—six days' walk from anything. No people, no farms—nothing except all this incredible scenery. Mountains, lakes, beaches—I mean beaches like you've never seen—white, empty—going on forever. . . . " She paused to take a breath. "It's fantastic!"

The group nodded. They could feel the enthusiastic vigor of the girl's experience. Most of them were your typical back-to-the-elements-crowd. Two were suntanned surf bums living a life of ease and frolic among the waves of the west coast. Another couple were from England and, by the tone of their conversation before the girl joined us, more than ready to return. Four others were true outbackers, hippielike, with long, straggly hair, flinty eyes, and of indeterminate gender. Your regular ragtag bunch of world wanderers sharing the magic of new places and undiscovered delights.

The Foster beer "stubbies" came and went as the girl described her lonely six-day odyssey along a wilderness path from a place called Melaleuca ("There's nothing there except a hut—it's just a name") to the first farmhouse near Cockle Creek. The table was a litter of all those heart-arresting, fat-filled, salt-soaked, deep-fried Aussie junk foods with such palate-pandering names as deep-fried seafood rolls, bacon and potato triangles, meat pies, sausage rolls, egg and bacon pie, deep-fried mussels, deep-fried dim sum, et al. Then she let fly with the kind of comment that is always guaranteed to hook this particular world wanderer:

You feel like you're the first person ever to have walked in these places. . . .

A week later I took the hour-long flight from Melbourne across the Bass Strait and landed with a rollicking thump in Hobart, capital city of Tasmania. As always, my plans were vague. A night in some city hotel and then off to find a small plane to fly me to the start of the South Coast Track at Melaleuca in the heart of the South-West Tasmanian wilderness.

Apparently this region is so valued as one of the earth's last temperate wildernesses that it's been declared, along with other major portions of Tasmania's western hinterland, a unique UNESCO World Heritage Area. This region, covering almost a fifth of the state, with over seven hundred thousand square miles of some of the most pristine, untouched scenery in the Southern Hemisphere, is thus doubly protected by both Tasmanian government and UNESCO resources and will be maintained in its present natural state forever.

Way back in the late 1800s, shortly after convict transport to the island from Britain had ended, this portion of "Van Diemen's Land" (as Tasmania was originally known) attracted the hardiest of adventurer-entrepreneurs. They arrived in hundreds to prospect for gold and mineral deposits, hack down the Huon pine and hardwood forests along the coast, and set up stations for whale and seal hunting. Tracks were cut through the wilderness and even small communities established, none of which exist today.

As the pine forests and whales diminished, the pioneers moved on and the South-West became a forgotten land. New maps of the territory labeled it impenetrable or unexplored and so it remained until the 1920s, when an upsurge of bush walking and mountaineering brought lost world-lovers back into the territory seeking challenge, adventure, and solace in solitude.

Much of the region has remained unmolested while the more fertile, low-lying areas to the east were transformed into pastoral havens for farmers, stock rearers, and orchardmen. Hobart became the capital and focal point of the island's pastoral and commercial economies. Today it is a pristine little place of 160,000 inhabitants or so strung around both sides of the Derwent River and overshadowed by the ominous and often cloud-topped bulk of Mount Wellington. Beyond the elegant church spires and modest glass-walled towers of recent downtown redevelopment, much of the city seems to consist mainly of typical Australian bungalows trimmed with Victoriana fretwork, topped by red tin roofs, and surrounded by privet and laurel hedges. They're dotted in the thousands up the foothills of Mount Wellington and offer their residents constant vistas of the river, the mountains, and the scraggly eucalyptus-topped hills to the east.

In recent years Hobart has become a haven for retirees from "north island" and, despite its occasional cloud-and-drizzle climate, possesses a mellow postmenopausal mood. There's none of Sydney's flash-and-flurry here, none of the sun-saturated serendipity of the mainland "Gold Coast," and only fleeting touches of Perth's cultured cosmopolitan ambience. In spite of its size and its jet-set-styled casino, you sense a small-town spirit here verging on complacency—mom 'n' pop retail outlets that close early and never open on Sundays, pretty eucalyptus-shaded parks, cozy beaches for weekend barbecues and, for the most part, careful drivers and law-abiding, respectable citizens.

Hobart's notorious nineteenth-century reputation as a place of "last exit" for British and Irish convicts seems hard to appreciate in today's green and graceful city. Admittedly the ruins of the once-dreaded Port Arthur penal settlement ("a natural penitentiary," according to Lieutenant Governor Arthur in 1830) are only fifty or so seagull-flying miles southeast of the capital, on the tip of the Tasman Peninsula. Doubtless that strange Australian obsession with its criminal origins still ripples close to the surface of psyches, but I sensed none of these ominous overtones. Even the rather maudlin tone of Peter Conrad's excellent book on Tasmania, *Behind the Mountain*, which I'd read on the flight down, failed to diminish my initial impressions of Hobart as a lively, history-aware community, proud of its new roads and glass towers, proud of its one-time whaling men and its boisterous democratic traditions.

The day I arrived the Green party claimed they'd jostled the government into a "vote of no confidence" dilemma and were demanding mass resignations and a new election. The next day, however, the "no-fleas-on-me" prime minister had turned his virulent opponents topsy-turvy through a series of postmidnight alliances and "understandings" and left the Greens gasping and gawking at his typical Tasmanian penchant for wile, guile, and political gamesmanship. Ironically, at the time of this minor political flurry, Australia was enduring a period of international rebuke for the "cowboy" antics of some of its leading entrepreneurs—Alan Bond and Kerry Packer in particular—whose widely admired, Trump-like triumphs of the eighties had now degenerated into sleaze 'n' greed reputations and public denunciations by reputable world economists. Well, apparently Tasmania's prime minister had a little of the cowboy spirit in him too.

Unfortunately, nighttime reveals another Hobart, particularly in the empty downtown streets where packs of restless, wolfish youths ramble and stagger through the shadowy alleys looking for a flurry of fists with unsuspecting victims. (Me, for example. Only the presence of slow-moving police cars kept me from a couple of roustabouts with drugged or drunken gangs.) I hoped to find respite in the pubs, but they too were filled with similar huddles of young men whose glazed eyes roamed the smoky rooms seeking easy pickings among the long-haired, cherubic-cheeked (but equally dead-eyed) girls. I sensed all the things that diatribic monologues about "our young generation" proclaim— hopelessness, directionlessness, drug-induced escapism. I'd sensed the same in small-town Australia, where rowdy gatherings at stubbie-stained tables seemed the only outlet for frustrated energies and disillusioned ambitions. The media blames unem-ployment, lack of parental discipline, inadequate education, a fascination for fast wealth, and "the constant search for instant gratification" in the form of glue-sniffing and stubbie-slurping highs, easy sex, "cool-at-all-costs" attitudes, and remnants of the high-flying eighties' "me-first" mentality.

When I returned to my small hotel I felt depressed and out of it all. Get me to the mountains, I begged of my little interior plan maker. Get me to where I'll be "the first person ever to have walked in the remote places of Tasmania."

Hence the four-seater plane, bucking and bouncing through the porridge clouds, heading west to the wilds of Melaleuca deep in the southwestern wilderness.

We were lucky.

"She'll be right," said Phil, with just a touch of relief in his voice. "No shear."

He was right. We escaped the death-defying, stomach-in-mouth plummet over the Arthurs. In fact, as we approached the first ranges, the clouds dissipated into ragged strands of mist and we peered down through scratched windows at a tortured jumble of Precambrian quartzite crags and peaks and precipices dotted with small lakes, and cirques set in mossy bowls and bound by shattered ridges of white rock.

Phil eased lower toward the cirques, reeling off names that resembled a mythical pantheon: Mount Hesperus, Mount Sirius,

Mount Pegasus, Mount Orion, the Crags of Andromeda, Procyon Peak, Mount Capricorn, Mount Taurus, Capella Crags, Lucifer Ridge—and then the little lakes: Pluto, Neptune, Uranus, Jupiter, Mars, Venus, Trion, and Mercury.

As we skimmed across the black sinister surface of Lake Cygnus, clusters of enormous tropical pandani rose like hairy alien creatures above the moss and heather ground cover.

He pointed to a faint line that serpentined through the low brush, over the peaks, and between the scoured white arêtes and pinnacles.

"That's the Western Arthurs Trail." His voice was tinged with respect.

"What's that?"

"That's about the hardest trail in all Australia. A real bastard when the weather's bad, and," he added, "its always bad in the Arthurs."

"A long one?"

"No—not in miles. Only about twenty or so. But it'll take a fit walker five days to do it. Some of the best scenery anywhere—if you ever get to see it."

"D'you get many walkers?"

"A lot of 'em talk about it and quite a few start it—but getting to the end is another thing altogether. That's real tough country down there."

Despite the clearing of the clouds and patches of blue sky, it did indeed look like tough country. Pockets of perpetual ice and snow hid in shadowy crevasses on the northern slopes where the sun never reached. There were no trees—just that thick covering of ground-hugging, wind-flattened bush out of which rose those strange giant pandani. An empty, desolate world and one I was glad to be exploring from the relative safety of our warm cockpit.

Gradually the land fell away from the high white ridges and eased out into broader sweeps of valleys, scarps, swamps, and misty ranges.

"That's the Ironbounds." Phil pointed way to the south at a range of near-black mountains, sharply profiled and sinister. "You'll be crossing those."

"I will?"

"Yeah. The coast track takes you right over the top."

"I thought it followed the beaches."

"Well, it does some of the way, but the Ironbounds come right down to the ocean. You've got to cross over. There's no way 'round."

Silence again. I could sense him grinning as he brought in yet another novice who'd underestimated the scale, terrors, and challenges of tiny Tasmania.

"You'll be okay," he said consolingly. "Just don't push it too hard. And watch the weather. It can turn fast. If it gets real bad, just make camp and stay put."

"No one lives down there, right?" I asked.

" 'Cept for the Willsons at Melaleuca. They're running a small tin-mining operation near the landing strip. After that you're on your own. Likely as not you won't see anyone for six days. Maybe longer. Depends on the weather."

Back in that northwest Australian bar with the gushy-eyed girl, a six-day hike through Tasmania didn't sound like such a big deal. In my stubbie stupor I imagined a leisurely stroll along talcum-textured sands, bathing in sheltered coves, sharing travel tales with fellow walkers, and arriving back in Hobart after a few days for a celebratory shindig or two at the local watering holes.

But now that I was approaching the starting point I suddenly felt very vulnerable and lonely. The landscape was a vast and unrelenting scene of boggy moors, treeless hills, and black ice-flecked peaks. Not a sign of life anywhere. Not even sheep. No tracks. Nothing except this endless rust- and khaki-colored land.

"Well, at least I'll share a beer with the Willsons before I set off," I said in a voice full of forced cheer.

"Doubt it."

"Oh—why?"

"They don't really take to people. They've been mining down there by themselves—husband and wife—for twenty-odd years. Took over Deny King's operation. Small-time stuff, really, but they get good ore in the peat bogs. Enough to make a living."

"Who is Deny King?"

"Was. Was Deny King. He died last year. Great guy. All the walkers loved him. Bit of a recluse, but a great storyteller when you got him going. Artist too."

"So—I guess I won't be seeing anyone."

Phil thought a bit. "Maybe Bob's around. He runs a camp in Bathurst Harbor. Outback stuff, and all that. Tents in the forest. Swimming in secret coves. Y'know the thing. Good fella, Bob."

"Is he there now?"

"Not rightly sure. Maybe. If he is he'll tell you about Deny. May be able to get you over to the Willsons too. He knows 'em."

We were starting the descent. As we sank slowly toward the boggy terrain below, patterned with curlicues of streams, the mountains rose higher on all sides. Far ahead I could see the ocean edged by white lines of surf. It vanished as the ground came closer.

"See the strip?"

I looked across the seemingly unending swath of dun-colored moor and saw nothing.

Phil pointed—"See the wind sock? Bit of a breeze down there today. Roarin' forties runnin' again."

I looked harder and finally saw a faint strip of white and green far ahead. The wind sock on a pole at the far end of the strip was stretched taut in a horizontal position, a position I associated with hurricane-force winds.

"May be a bit tricky," Phil mumbled, as much to himself as me as he lined up the plane for landing.

You could feel the force of the wind fifty feet above the strip. It was blowing us off course and into the bog. Phil made corrections so that we actually seemed to be heading away from the strip, directly into the wind. Maybe he planned to land sideways? The engine speed dropped and we were tossed and buffeted by the gale.

"Hang on," he mumbled again and I did just that, ramming myself into my seat and holding on to anything that looked secure and stable.

We hit the landing strip with a metal-crunching crash, way off center and only a few feet from the bog. The wind seemed to delight in pushing us closer. As soon as the wheels hit, Phil turned sharply away from the mud and it seemed for a second or two that we'd be cartwheeled by the force of the blast.

"Sorry 'bout that." Phil was smiling. "Had to get her down fast!" I nodded and tried to smile too. My knuckles were death-white and still gripping the seat like vices.

291

"Welcome to Melaleuca," said Phil. "One of the loneliest spots on the planet!"

"Thanks." I grunted.

"Let's get you unloaded. I've got to get out of here before that wind really gets up."

"You mean it's going to get worse?"

"Oh, yeah—no doubt about it. Look at those clouds."

I looked but didn't know what I was supposed to be seeing. They were certainly moving fast—like ghostly dragsters—across the peaks.

"You're going back to Hobart?"

"Right y'are, fast as a jackrabbit," said Phil.

Suddenly Hobart seemed a most seductive place in spite of its nighttime wolf packs and depressing pubs and fat-laden junk-food snack bars. I wished I was going back with him.

"Okay—let's get moving," he said.

He really did plan to get out fast. The gale smacked me like a prizefighter punch as I crawled out of the cockpit, down the wing, and onto the strip. My parka was almost ripped from my hand as I struggled to get into it and find the zipper.

Phil helped me carry my backpack to a hut at the side of the strip.

"You sure you can take off in this wind?" I asked.

"No worries, mate. But I've got to go now."

He pointed to a gale-shaped huddle of stumpy trees at the edge of the runway. "Now, listen—follow that path and you'll get to a hiker's hut just down by those trees"—the first real trees I'd seen in the last fifty miles of flying. "If Bob's around you'll see him there. If not just get the fire started and a cook-up going. M'be you can leave tomorrow if the weather's good. There may be some. . . ."

Then he turned and laughed. A figure appeared over a small scrub-covered rise above the strip, riding an odd bicycle.

"That's Barbara. Mrs. Willson." He waved.

Mrs. Willson tried to wave back, but her bike was being buffeted by the gale and she decided to hang on instead. She arrived breathless and red-faced, wrapped in an enormous yellow raincoat.

"Thought I'd miss you Phil," she gasped as she propped her

unusual bike (a British-made Moulton special with tiny wheels) against the hut. "Got some letters for you to post." Her accent wasn't Australian at all. Even in those first few words I caught the Lancashire twang of England.

"Barbara, meet Dave. He's off to do the South Coast Track."

She looked at me for the first time through guarded eyes. Her skin was bronzed and wrinkled. She appeared to be in her early fifties and as tough as the elements in which she lived.

"You're from Lancashire!" I said, hoping to establish an immediate rapport.

"Well—what of it?" she snapped.

"I'm from Yorkshire. Just over the Pennines."

She paused and her demeanor seemed to relax a little.

"Well—if you've been up in the Pennines you'll feel at home here."

I nodded and smiled. "You're right. Same colors. Same bogs—same wind!"

She smiled back—a friendlier smile this time—and then turned to Phil.

"So—give my love to Beatrice. Tell her I'll be up there next month."

"Okay, Barbara. See you in town. I'm off before that bloody wind really starts blowing."

We said our farewells to Phil and watched him scamper back to the plane as the gale tore through the scrub and bent the marsh grass in the bogs.

Barbara had mounted her Moulton and was ready to move off too.

"Listen—if you're around . . . " she seemed to hesitate, not sure if she wanted to say what she was going to say, "well, we're just a mile or so up the track there."

And then she was gone, pedaling furiously against the gale and vanishing over a low ridge. I think she'd offered me the closest thing to an invitation she could muster and I liked her for that.

Phil's plane rose ungracefully through the churning air and quickly disappeared into the skimming clouds. After a minute there was no sound except that of the gale tearing through the matted ground cover. I was alone now. I had this whole vast panoply of mountains and moors all to myself. This was the territory I had come to experience and, God willing, to conquer. It was an exciting and slightly terrifying prospect. But at least I could luxuriate for my first night in the hiker's hut. After that it would just be me and whatever was out there. The girl's words came back to me: "You feel like you're the first person ever to have walked in these places." Well—we'll see. I wasn't quite ready for that sensation yet.

I found the hut huddled low to the ground against a wood of King Billy pines. The trees grew close together and their interlocking branches presented an impenetrable barrier. No sunlight penetrated the gloomy recesses. Something resembling a path meandered off into the mossy darkness for a few yards and then gave up as if beaten back by the aggressive tangle of twigs and twisted limbs. Against the great open swaths of scenery all around, the woods offered a reluctant refuge for weary, wind-blasted hikers—but little else in the way of bucolic comforts.

I retraced my steps out of the tangle, the branches tearing at my backpack and snagging my hair. A malicious little wood—not at all welcoming. But at least in this damp hollow I was out of the gale, and for a while at least I'd accept the sinister silence here as respite.

The door to the hut squeaked open. It was a simple Quonset affair, dusty and gloomy. A large fireplace, resembling some ancient altar, separated the kitchen area from the main space, simply furnished with four double bunk beds, a long table, and a scatter of lopsided chairs and benches. The windows had not been cleaned for a long time, so what little light there was had a yellow cobwebby tinge to it.

It was cold. Really cold. Much colder than outside. The dusty plank floor, pockmarked with scourings from hikers' hobnailed boots, had streaks of white near the joints. I couldn't tell if they were ice or mildew. Probably both. The place was damp too.

A simple wooden plaque nailed to the wall declared that the hut was Deny King's gift to the wilderness wanderers he admired and loved and was built in memory of his father, Charles, who had first arrived here in 1933 to mine for tin in the peat bogs south of the airstrip. Nearby on the table was a visitors' book for hikers' remarks. It was open at a new page on which was a single in-scription by a Jay Fellows from Canada, who had spent a night here alone eight days previously and left a suitably sonorous quotation in a spidery hand:

"There are no words that can tell of the sudden spirit of the wilderness, that can reveal its mystery, its melancholy and its charm. There is delight in the silent places, unworn by man, and changed only by the slow changes of the ages through time everlasting." *Theodore Roosevelt.*

It was the "melancholy" of the wilderness that seemed to dominate my spirit at the moment as I shivered and turned the damp pages, looking for more lighthearted, more human ventings of emotion.

They came in various guises:

Thank you King Deny for the only decent place to sleep in eight days.

Never again.

We who rest here are a tiny fraternity of those who seek the wilderness to give meaning and perspective to our lives.

Myself and my frens Gunther, Andre and Hans are so ap-preciating your kindnesses Mr. Deny.

And then some wit trying to rewrite the "Evita" song:

> Don't cry for me Melaleuca
> The truth is we'll never get there
> Those fucking Ironbounds are going to get us
> We'll die up on High Camp
> So please tell our mothers.

But underlying most of the scribbled remarks, varying from boisterous to banal, you could sense a certain pride, especially in those hikers for whom this was the halfway point in their odyssey through the southwest wilderness. They had come from Scotts Peak in the north either across the Arthurs (another quote: "On the crags of Andromeda I died from utter exhaustion and someone else now occupies what was previously me.") or on the Old Port Davey Track across endless moraine-studded sedgeland plains and fast-flowing icy streams, over Mount Robinson, into the vast gloom of the Lost World Plateau, across the narrows of the magnificent fjord of Bathurst Harbor, to the meager comforts of the Melaleuca hut.

Their remarks were the most telling:

I know now that there is a God. And that he hates hikers. But I beat him!

One of the worst walks in the world. It's great to be here.

Tomorrow and tomorrow and tomorrow (and tomorrow and tomorrow and tomorrow) . . . will we ever get to the end of this bloody trail?

Some entries were a little more uplifting:

We need places like this to remind us of the difference between existing and living.

We are as small as the cages we construct for ourselves—as immense as a universe. Here I became a universe.

And finally my favorite, written by an anonymous writer whose name had been wrenched from immortality by a coffee stain on the page:

From the top of the mountains I can see clear into forever. In the creamy diffused light there is no horizon. Sky merges into mountain, the distant mountains float. . . . This is not only a place where I began my first excursion into wilderness, but it is also where I began to explore my own mind.

Time to warm this dank and gloomy hut.

Someone had left kindling and logs in a neat stack by the fireplace. At first the damp overcame my efforts to get a flame, but after a dozen matches and a room full of expletives, the twigs caught and the smoke rose and heat began to permeate the place.

I decided it would take at least half an hour to eradicate the chill and, as it was warmer outside, what better time to go exploring around my temporary home?

The gale had dropped to a gentle breeze. Shafts of gold light through the clouds swept across the mountains, transforming patches of dun-colored rock and scrub into rich palettes of bronze, ocher, and Irish-green. For a moment I had a flash of déjà vu: I'd been here before, or somewhere very like it. Then I remembered. The Outer Hebrides Islands of western Scotland. The same tree-less barrens, the same sedgeland and buttongrass plains of bog and marsh, the same bold and brittle-ridged mountains—and the same colors. The colors found in the tweeds made by the lonely crofters of Harris. The only difference was in the people. Here—with the exception of the two Willsons and occasional hikers—there were none. The land existed in its own right, untouched unmolested, unchanged for millennia. In the Hebrides, even in the wildest spots, you'd find the welcoming curlicues of blue-gray peat smoke rising up from the chimneys of crofters' homes set in rocky hollows or nestled in sheltered coves. They were hard to spot. Built of local bedrock gneiss and thatched in marsh grass they blended perfectly with the colors and textures of the surrounding land. But they were *there* —and on the days when the sea squalls hullaballooed across the moors or the westerlies smashed the surf on those scimitar sweeps of white sand they were a welcome reminder that comfort, warmth, and maybe even a spirit-raising glass of malt would greet any wayward walker of the wilds who happened to hammer on their thick oak doors.

Here there were no such compensatory comforts. The land was as it looked—lonely, aloof, indifferent. You carried your own nurturing with you—or you did without. There were no half measures.

Well—almost none.

A surprise awaited me as I set off on a path that rose from behind the hikers' hut and eased over a low ridge to another huddle of wind-shaped pines beside a slow-moving, peat-bronzed stream.

A house!

Something I hadn't expected.

Set by the side of the stream and sheltered from the elements by a thick grove of trees and bushes was another Quonset hut, originally painted in turquoise and red, and now faded over time to a pale eggshell blue and rusty sienna. A perfect hermit's hideaway. I edged closer and then noticed the name painted in small letters on the wall by the door. DENY KING. PLEASE KNOCK FIRST.

I'd found Deny's home.

The outbuildings were full of implements—axes, shovels, spades, forks, rakes—all neatly lined against wood and tin walls as if Deny might come along at any moment to select his favorite piece and set to work clearing his now-overgrown patches of garden on the slope between the house and the stream.

But of course no one would come. Deny was gone. He'd died only a short time ago, according to my pilot friend, and no one was living here.

Yet it didn't feel that way. Peering through the cobwebby windows of his home I saw a simple kitchen with a wood-burning stove littered with pans and old coffee cans and cooking utensils. On the side of the house overlooking the stream and the boat-house (Deny's boat still neatly roped to the dock) was a sunlit room with a large window facing the mountains.

Books lay scattered on a low table and on top of an old upright piano, the fireplace was full of half-burned squares of dried peat; an old couch occupied the niche by the window. I could imagine Deny lying there looking out over the vast sprawl of marsh plains and mountains, reading his books (they filled every shelf and nook and cranny in the living room), getting up every now and then to heat some coffee, and then taking a stroll along the narrow paths that divided his garden into neat oblong patches.

Whoever, whatever this man had been, I sensed him. I sensed his spirit in this little home—the kind of place that many of us fantasize about when we dream of a simple life. A life unmolested by irrelevant details and distractions, untouched by the traumas of city life, unplagued by pension-bound perspectives and the petty politics of existence. I sensed peace, simplicity, and whole-ness here. A tangible lesson in the less-is-more ethic.

Accompanied by the shrieks of shrike-thrushes feeding in his gardens, I wandered around Deny's little compound. There were more wooden sheds filled with lifejackets, oilskins, and piles of driftwood, jars of nails and screws, hammers, saws, and screw-drivers. There were compost heaps, a boat yard where he'd been repairing an old wooden dinghy, an ancient wind-up telephone hung on a wall. (Presumably for decoration. There were no telephones out here.)

Farther along a mossy path that bounced gently as I walked on it and across which the sunshine cast strips of soft, moist light, I came to a studio, open to the elements. Everything was in place for a day's painting—the brushes were neatly arranged on a small table alongside squeezed tubes of oil. An easel stood with a canvas already on it, half completed—an evening scene of golds and crimsons over blue-hazed mountains. In the corner beyond the table were a dozen other empty canvases, awaiting Deny's inspiration.

Eerie. And yet somehow strangely sublime. I had entered into his little private world and, although he was no longer around to sit and talk, artist to artist, about his life and his dreams, I felt welcome. Nothing had been touched. It was as though he'd merely left off one day in the middle of things and just never come back. His body had moved on elsewhere. But his spirit remained. Intact, inviolate, unmolested. Like the land here.

Farther down the path, past more patches of cultivated garden, was another shed, larger than the others, with windows that were less laced in webs and dust. The door was unlocked and I went in.

The sensation that hit me is hard to analyze—even, to quote Wordsworth, with the benefit of "emotion recollected in tranquility."

Only twice—maybe three times—in my life have I entered a space that has truly spoken to me. The most memorable occasion was a decade or so ago on Cliff Island in Maine's Casco Bay when I was exploring some of the less-known islands of America's Atlantic Coast for my *Secluded Islands* book. It was a misty early morning and I had arrived earlier than expected on the ferry from Portland. No one seemed to be around at the dock, so I decided to wander for a while through the forest that fringed the little coves of the western shore.

After a couple of miles I came across one of those places that hopeful hermits dream about—a tiny hand-built A-frame house sheltered in pines with windows overlooking the bay, and a natural boat ramp up a slab of exposed Maine granite bedrock. It was still misty and the waves slopped lazily up a small sand beach enclosed by huge boulders. There was no boat, so I presumed the owner was off for a spell of early morning fishing. The yard was neatly organized: three piles of cleanly split wood, each of a different size, covered with tarpaulin; stacks of lobster traps surrounded by coiled ropes, buoys, and large blue plastic pickle barrels for the catch; an outside refrigerator stocked with beer and basics; and a small outbuilding used as a toilet and storeroom. Everywhere a sense of harmony and order.

Inside had a similar well-organized feel. A single room, maybe twenty by twenty feet, rising to a pyramidal apex and equipped with all the necessities of the simple life—propane gas range, wood-burning stove, stereo, CB radio, an old sofa covered with a worn quilt, scattered rugs, a well-stacked library (with a bias toward books on ecology and small-scale farming) on shelves supported by gray cinder blocks. On a low table was a manual for constructing a solar greenhouse.

Above the compact kitchen was a raised platform reached by a rough-cut ladder which housed a foam-mattress bed and more piles of books. Sunlight tickled through segments of stained glass.

And that, basically, was it. A totally self-sufficient home— economical, cozy, and full of its owner's personality. And it spoke to me, clear and clean as larks' song: "This could be your home. What else would you ever need?"

Now, I've lived the gypsy life for years, sharing a modest motor home with my wife and two cats as we've ventured off on the backroads of America or down into the hidden corners of Britain and Southern Europe and farther beyond. I admit to a penchant for small, compact, well-organized spaces. But this little home on this quiet Maine island seemed to envelop me in its pure—and simple—totality. It wanted me to stay, to sprawl by a blazing fire in the cast-iron stove, cook up a few mussels and fish caught fresh from the bay outside the door, listen to fine music on the stereo, or read for days from books that I've long promised myself I'd read but never have.

It was with almost unbearable reluctance I closed the door of that house behind me and walked back through the misty forest to the dock on that early morning on Cliff Island. But although I left the place, it has remained with me, clear and crisp in every detail, for all the subsequent years.

300

And that's precisely what happened in Deny's little one-room shack up the path from his home. The moment I stepped in the door and looked around at his hand-made furniture (sofa, two chairs, a table by the window overlooking the mountains), the wood stove, a sleeping nook on a platform reached by a ladder made of barely trimmed branches, an old gas stove and tiny kitchen area—that same sense that somehow this was mine swept over me in a wave of certainty and serendipity. The room welcomed me as if I'd been away for a while on a hard journey and had returned, tired and torn, to recuperate and find my "centering" once again in its simple security.

I sat on a chair made of branches and planks and rested my head on the table by the window. Outside, shafts of sunlight were playing across the plain, silvering strips and patches of marsh and bog. The mountains around the plain were purple and deep blue. On the table was a small box of writing implements—old ballpoint pens, pencils with the ends slightly gnawed, an eraser broken into two ragged-edged pieces, and some sheets of yellowing lined paper.

"Write here," the room said to me. "Stay—and write here. What more do you need?"

Was Deny a writer as well as an artist? His little room reminded me of the small gardening shed used by Dylan Thomas at Laugharne in southern Wales. The same broad sweeping vistas, the same sense of being away from it all, the same sense of a place without distractions and superfluous ornamentation where one could focus—both inwardly and outwardly—and send the creative juices spilling and splashing over canvases, lined paper, or whatever medium you chose.

The silence in the room was total.

Whoever Deny was, I liked him. His spirit was alive and well in this cluster of ramshackle buildings by this stream in this magical place—one of the wildest and least-visited places on earth.

The silence continued and I sat quietly, not writing, not really thinking. Just being in the place. Letting my own silence rise up to greet the silence that surrounded me.

Until the silence ceased.

"G'day."

I jolted in my seat as if bumped in the rump by a billy goat.

The silence collapsed in shards of silver. My stillness was whisked away like gale-blown clouds.

Nothing for a few seconds, and then "Hello . . . g'day."

For a fleeting moment I thought—Deny! Maybe all this reverie and introspection into the life of Deny King had, in the intensity of the silence, metamorphosed his tangible spirit into an even more tangible incarnation.

A face peered at mine through the cobwebby window. A large man, red cheeks, big nose bulging in odd places (a drinker's nose?), richly tanned face etched deeply with lines (or scars), and firm chin set on a thick-muscled neck.

No, it wasn't Deny. From Phil's descriptions, Deny was a small, wiry kind of man who walked with a bit of a stoop.

The newcomer was altogether larger; his face folds moved like thick lava from a scowl to a pleasant, open smile.

"Thought I might find you here," he mouthed through the glass. "Okay if I come in?"

"Fine." I tried to smile back but felt embarrassed to be discovered trespassing in Deny's hideaway.

As soon as he entered the door, bending his huge head to avoid the low beam, the room shrank. He was a giant, or at least appeared so against the modest scale of the space and its meager furnishings.

"Hey—sorry to disturb you, but I thought I might find you here. Just came back in the boat from the beach. Saw your fire at the hut. You're a good fire man. S'going beaut now. Toasty as all blazes back there."

I must have still looked a little confused by his sudden appearance.

"Sorry mate—forgot me manners—Bob Geeves. Wilderness Tours. Out of Hobart. I do the honors at the camp down the beach there."

Obviously my confusion confused him.

"Er . . . the camp, y'know—on Melaleuca inlet by Bathurst. I take the camping trips. . . . "

My voice finally returned. "Oh—Bob Geeves. I've heard of you from Phil. Hi. Good to meet you." I introduced myself.

"Well—and g'day to you, Dave. Heard you might be stayin'

over awhile. Thought I'd come up and see you're all right and stuff like that. Y'okay for food?"

"Food? Oh, yes, fine. I was just going back to cook some dinner. You want to join me?"

"Sure thing. Brought a couple of fish. Caught them on me way back. You like fish, right?"

"I'd prefer anything to that dehydrated rubbish I'm carrying with me."

He exploded with a sudden gale of laughter. The small room seemed to shake. "Good on yer, mate! Yeah—that's crap in't but s'bout all you can carry on the trail. And it keeps you goin'. But I'll tell you, five days on and you'd give your left testicle for a plate of fish 'n' chips in a sweaty snack bar."

Together we strolled slowly back to the hiker's hut, past Deny's studio, past his neat rows of gardening implements, past the blue and red house, and up over the moor ridge.

The fire was indeed "beaut" and the bunk room toasty. I prepared the bread and a salad I'd carried in with me while Bob grilled the fish by the fire and started to tell me about my new-found friend-of-the-spirit, Deny King.

"He was a real outback man—tin miner, naturalist, meteor-ologist, artist, and—when you got him going—a great storyteller. God, he'd tell tales that'd scare the beejeez outa you. He was 'bout eighty when he died just a while back and—I tell you—he'd done jus' 'bout anything a man has to do down here to stay alive. The only thing he didn't do was go hunting whales like some of the crazy boyos did here 'bout a hundred years ago. Did a bit of lumbering—big trade in Huon pine from Bathurst early on. But what he and his dad, Charlie, were really after was gold. They first came on down in 1930, but nothing panned out and they went back to their farm—Sunset Ranch—not far from Hobart. Then they hit bad luck—loads of it. Bush fire wiped out the ranch in '34, Charlie's wife, Olive, died '35, so he and Deny came back here to get in on the tin-mining bonanza in 1935. Deny was twenty-four, m'be twenty-five, then. He wanted to be an engineer but gave it up to help his dad until the war. Came back again in '45 and built that house you saw—called it Melaleuca, after all those trees down by the creek."

"It must have been a tough life."

"Well, early on they had plenty of company. Twenty men or more working the peat beds for tin. But the price got bad and after a while it was just the two of them. They got mail and supplies every month or two from fishing boats that came into Bathurst. Made a bit of extra cash from the Bureau of Meteorology—he built that wooden tower with a wind gauge—didn't you see that? Y'must have come in the back way. He clocked a real roarin' forties gale there in '48—more'n a hundred and twenty miles per hour! Told me when he climbed up to take the readin' he lost all his clobber down to his vest an' boots!"

"You get winds like that?"

"Dead right we do—and rain—a hundred and ten inches average—some years double that. This is crazy territory down here. Remember that Snowdon fella from Buck Palace, photographer, married Princess Margaret—he came here doing a book on Tasmania in 1980. Got stuck down in Melaleuca with Deny for three days. Planes wouldn't fly in from Hobart. Said it was suicidal. Fella only came for a day to photograph Deny. Ended up becoming a mate for life! Hillary came down too—y'remember Sir Edmund Hillary—fella who got up Everest? Called Deny "a real pioneer." Deny liked that. Y'know, they even named a plant after him—*Euphrasia Kingii*—some new specimen he discovered on one of his botany expeditions. I tell you, Dave—he was a rare man."

"Did he ever marry?"

"Deny—sure he did. Margaret. Lovely girl. Gave her a wedding ring made out of gold he'd panned 'round here. He always said he'd find the lode—somewhere in there with the tin an' all. Never did. Just flakes and a few nuggets. Nothing much. They got two daughters—Mary and Janet. They still come down—painting like their dad. He did a lot of that when the price of tin went down."

"I saw one of his paintings. Looked pretty good."

"Oh, Deny was an okay painter, all right. Sold all his stuff. When he died he had twenty on order."

Crash!

Our chat by the fire over Bob's grilled fish was suddenly interrupted by a great bang on the hut door.

I jumped. Bob looked up and smiled.

"Cheeky bugger," he mumbled.

"Who—what?" I spluttered and fish bits flew from my mouth.

"Bloody possum," said Bob, and stood up. "Cheeky as hell. She always knows when I'm eatin' . . . bangs on that door like a bloody landlord!"

He extracted a particularly succulent piece of fish from the pan.

"You do without this?"

I was hungry but decided to be polite. "Sure."

He strolled to the door, his huge frame making the floorboards groan, and opened it slowly to reveal the cutest, cuddliest kangaroo-type creature I'd yet seen in Australia.

"There y'are, you cheeky bugger. Get that down yer."

The possum extended delicate raccoonlike fingers and took the offering gracefully. It was not much larger than a big cat, with a thick woolly gray coat, long bushy tail, pink ears and nose, and what looked like a permanent grin set in a cherubic round face. Its eyes glowed deep red in the reflected light of the hut lamp.

"She's weaning, Dave. Y'see that—a little Joey!"

Bob pointed to the possum's pouch set way down her stomach, out of which peered a miniature version of the mother, grinning too.

"That little whippersnapper'll stay there till it's five months old. Watch her when she feeds it."

The mother carefully tore off pieces of the grilled fish, chewed them up with the discerning air of a professional food taster, and then fed morsels to her baby, who winked at us every time it got a mouthful.

"Cute little buggers. Call 'em brush-tailed possums. Used to be real popular for fur. Still are, even though they're protecting 'em now."

The fish vanished fast. I hoped Bob didn't plan to feed her the last piece. I needed sustenance for my hike.

"Okay, darlin'—bloody cheeky sheila—that's it. Come back tomorrow for scraps."

The possum seemed to understand. She nodded, gave what looked like a gentle curtsy, then hopped off into the woody thicket near the outhouse toilet. Bob closed the door quietly and smiled. "Sorry 'bout your fish."

"Forget it. It was worth it. She was beautiful."

"Yeah. Real beaut." For such a tall backwoodsman, Bob's face looked almost childlike as he returned, grinning, to the fire.

"I'm glad it wasn't a Tasmanian tiger," I said.

"Oh—y'know about those? The thylacine—that's their right name. Big weird things—like a huge dog, with tiger stripes all down their backs. Been doing some reading?"

"I saw some articles about them. Didn't sound like the kind of creature I'd like to meet alone on a dark night."

"Yeah—they were pretty fierce. My dad killed one once— when I was a lad—way up in the northeast. Not too many around now. M'be none. They said one was shot at Sandy Cape in '61. 'Course, y'always get people claimin' to see 'em. M'be they're the same oddballs as claim to get kidnapped by Martians!"

His great boom of laughter rocked the hut again.

"You think they're extinct?"

He stopped laughing. The light outside was sliding into evening gloom; an eerie yellow-purple glow sheened the cobweb-encrusted windows.

"Y'know, Dave, Tasmania's a funny place. North islanders laugh at it 'cause it's so small. But when you live here it don't seem that small. There's so many places where no one's really been. Like where we are. We get the hikers and that, but they stick to the paths—if they didn't they wouldn't last ten minutes in some of these bogs. So most of this area—this South-West— well, no one's really ever seen it. Could be all kinds things out there. . . . Sometimes, well—sometimes . . . "

He was searching for the right words.

" . . . I dunno. Sometimes you see odd things. Just for a few seconds or so . . . y'know . . . things that don't make any sense."

"Like what?"

He smiled a half smile. "Well—no matter. . . . "

"C'mon, Bob. Don't do that. Tell me."

He studied my eyes to see if I was likely to laugh at him.

"Well . . . I haven't told this to many folks. . . . "

I decided to say nothing and wait until he was ready.

"Okay. No worries. If you laugh I'll belt you one, but I've

seen some weird things in my time—real odd—but the strangest time was just a few weeks back when I was down at the beach, the place where I take the campers—if you hang around another day I'll show you there."

"Great. I'd like that."

"Well, anyway, like I said, it was a few weeks back and I was down there by myself just checkin' on things. It was 'bout this time. Evening. Bit cloudy like tonight. Not much light. And I was sittin' on the beach, doin' nothin', just sitting and looking . . . Mount Rugby was up there, right across the water, all purple and red on top . . . beaut . . . like there was a light inside it. . . . So—I was sitting, doing nothing. No worries. Then there was this noise. Further up the beach a ways. Up where it narrows and the pines comes real close to the water. Now, you get kangas and your possums and all that 'round here. Quite a few, if you know where to look. But this was something I'd never seen before. I mean, Dave—it was big. Bloody big. Bigger than anything I've spotted anywhere on Tassie."

"How big? Like a cow—a gorilla?"

"Never seen a gorilla. M'be big as a big steer calf. It was hard to tell. But it had a low back end—high up front."

"Aren't the Tasmanian tigers like that? Bit like a lynx or a hyena? Low in the back?"

"Yeah, bit like that. Only this was lower. Maybe it was hurt. I dunno. It seemed to drag its back end."

"It wasn't a forester kangaroo? I read they grow pretty big in Tasmania."

"No—not a forester. I've seen plenty of them up in the midlands. No—this was something I'd never seen before."

"What was it doing?"

"Moving down the beach to the water. Slowly like. Maybe for a drink, I dunno. It was very wary. Kept moving back and forward. Maybe it was pickin' up my scent. There was a bit of breeze. Nothin' much. But enough."

"So what happened?"

"Well—it turned my way and looked down where I was. And . . . " He paused. The memory was obviously very powerful. He even looked uneasy. "Well, I'll tell you, Dave, I've never seen a head—a face—like that. Body was a bit vague in the light, but that face . . . I mean, maybe it was a freak of some kind—a badly hurt kanga, who knows, maybe even a Tassie tiger. Its jaw seemed to hang loose. Huge teeth. Massive bloody eyes. I mean . . . it was a bloody monster. Head wasn't symmetrical. Sort of lopsided. But I'll tell you. It scared the crap out of me. Really did. I've been a bushman on and off since as long as I can remember and I don't get scared easy—but this bloody thing . . . "

I waited.

"Well, it must have got wind of me. It stopped dead—right there in the sand by the rocks—then it turned and sort of pulled itself back into the trees. Stopped once and looked at me again. I mean, David, it was really the worst-lookin' thing I've ever seen. Evil. It looked pure evil. I was beginning to think where I'd run if it came at me . . . but it didn't. Seemed to want to growl or cry or something—opened its mouth real wide . . . jeez, those teeth . . . but no sound came out. . . . "

I wondered if he was putting me on, inventing tall bushman tales. The embers in the fire rose in a flurry of sparks and sprayed Bob's face with scarlet light. The lines in his forehead and cheeks had deep shadows and there was no sign of laughter in them.

"Then it just disappeared. No noise. No nothing. I mean, a thing that size makes some noise, right? Cracking twigs. Whatever. But there was no sound . . . nothing."

It was very quiet in the hut. The last of the evening light had gone from the window. A shiver scurried down my spine and across my buttocks.

"Do you think it was a Tasmanian tiger? Maybe wounded or something?"

"Honest, Dave, I've no idea what it was. If it was a tiger it was the most disfigured one that I've ever heard of. I know they're strange-looking buggers—they've got heads a bit like wolves, fifteen or so stripes across their back and a rear end, with kangaroo-type legs, only upright, and a long rigid tail, bit like a real tiger. They're real vicious too—blood feeders. Only eat fresh meat, and from what they say they weren't too fussy 'bout whose meat."

"But they're extinct now, right?"

"That's what they say, Dave. But . . . in places like this . . . well, you never know. Might be other things too. Things no one's ever seen. It's not impossible. . . . "

I pulled closer to the fire, wondering what creatures, other than that "beaut" of a possum we'd fed, I might find on this walk through one of the least-explored parts of the world. I had to ask him.

"So—anything else you should warn me about before I set off?"

Bob laughed. Some of his bushman bravado returned. He sat up straight, poked the fire, and nonchalantly offered: "Well—they told you about the leeches, right?"

"Leeches! What leeches?"

"Oh, they didn't. Well—you didn't do enough reading, Dave—wait till you get to the Ironbounds. There's rain forest over there. That's where you'll find 'em. But you got gaiters and all that stuff, right?"

"Yes, I've got gaiters. But I hate leeches! Last time I got them was in Iran a few years back, when I was working on another book. I can still feel them. Worse, I can still see them. Inflating themselves like little black balloons. Filling up with my blood."

"Well," said Bob, knowing he'd gotten my attention. "Let's see what else . . . oh—there's the devil—Tasmanian devil. You know about that little critter?"

"A bit. Not much. I thought they were mainly in zoos now."

"Lord—no. No, no! All over the damn place. Not too many down this end though. More in the west—Cradle Lake, Overland Track—'round there. But I've seen a few. Bad-tempered little blighters. Though if you get 'em young and tame 'em they can be quite normal. Friendly—but I still wouldn't trust a bugger with teeth like that. And a stinker—wow, what a stink it puts out! Takes a week to get rid of it. And as black as night. 'Bout as big as a rabbit—big bare ears, long whiskers. Y'should see it eat a fowl—or a possum. Eats every blinkin' scrap—skin, bones, fur, feathers. The lot. Growls and snarls like a demon, spits and barks—and fights like a pit bull. . . . when they get mad you'll know about it."

"Great. Nice place I've come to."

"It's okay, Dave. Doubt if you'll see one way down here. Maybe hear one once in a while. You'll be okay. You'll get mainly possums, wallabies, and those small scrub wallabies—pademelons—lizards, quoils, that kind of thing. Maybe a spotted cat—bit

A TASMANIAN DEVIL!

like a weasel or a tiger cat—they're a bit devilish in spirit. Y'might see a platypus or two in the streams. Maybe a wombat—now, there's a nice cuddly little critter. Very shy."

"And leeches."

"Oh, yeah—leeches. Definitely leeches, Dave."

Bang!

Another knock on the door. This lost world was turning out to be a far busier place than I'd envisaged. Maybe the possum was back for more fish. Well—tough. I'd finished it off long ago.

Bob rose, stretched, and smiled. "Now, here's a guy that'll tell you 'bout the nicer things down here."

He pulled open the door to reveal a small, thin man with an enormous black beard and mustache, circular John Lennon spectacles, and a mop of unruly black hair.

"Steve—c'mon in. You're just in time, boyo. I was telling Dave here about our wildlife and he thinks he'll be eaten alive soon as he sets off on the track."

"Which track?"

"South Coast Track."

"Poor bugger."

"Yeah—that's what I told him," said Bob.

"You by yourself?" asked Steve, blinking ferociously behind his thick glasses. He reminded me of a smaller version of Steven Spielberg.

"Hi, Steve," I said. "Yes, I'm by myself."

"Oh." He didn't seem to be able to focus on my face. Either that or he was nervous.

"Been tellin' Dave 'bout the leeches 'round Ironbound."

"Oh, yes," said Steve.

"Maybe a devil or two. Wadda you think?"

"Unlikely, I think."

"Yeah, so do I," said Bob.

"Spiders, though," said Steve quietly.

"Oh, God! I forgot those!" said Bob, his face cracking into a thousand laugh lines. "By God—I forgot the bloody spiders. Sit down, Steve. Tell him about the spiders."

Steve joined us by the fire, which now roared with new vigor as Bob piled on fresh logs.

312

I decided to bluff this one out. Bob was obviously enjoying himself far too much at my expense.

"So, Steve," I said. "Tell me about the spiders."

"Sure you want to know?" He smiled for the first time. His walrus mustache shook with repressed chuckles.

"Sure, I've seen quite a few supposedly deadly spiders around the world. Most of them are not half as bad as their reputations."

"That's very true." Steve smiled. "Same here."

"Good. Well, that's fine."

"Except for the wolf spider—their venom can give you a bit of an ache."

"Great—I'll remember that."

"And the black house spider, though you won't find those here."

"Fine."

"And the red-back. That was a killer once, but now there's an antivenin. No one's died since the sixties."

"Well, great. That's it?"

"Well, no. They haven't found an antivenin for the funnel-web yet."

"What's a funnel-web?"

"Nasty bugger. Lives down in a burrow which it lines with silky thread and opens it up like a funnel with trip lines that extend out from the tube. The male venom is real potent."

"How potent?"

"You die," said Steve with a serious professorial look on his face.

"Die?"

"Sure."

"Am I likely to find any down here?"

"Well—the worst ones are up around Sydney. They build their funnels near drains, in wood piles, gardens—cool, shady places."

"Sydney's a hell of a long way from here."

"Right."

"So, I'm okay?"

"Oh, I'd think so . . . just be careful."

"You mean I might find some?"

313

"Unlikely. Don't you think so, Bob?"

"Yeah, I'd think so," said Bob. "Don't remember seeing one 'round here . . ."

"Good," I said.

" . . . recently," said Bob, and burst out laughing again.

"The hell with you two!" But I couldn't help laughing. "You're not going to put me off this hike."

"Wouldn't dream of it," said Bob.

" 'Course not," agreed Steve.

"Good. So—no more spider crap. Bob says you can tell me about some of the 'nicer' things down here."

"Oh, he did."

"Like your birds," prodded Bob. "Steve's quite a famous person down here. He's helping reintroduce the orange-bellied parrot—it's almost extinct, but who knows, this could be where it makes a comeback."

"That right, Steve?" I asked.

"Well, forget the famous bit. I'm just an assistant—a volunteer. But that's what we're doing. This is their only breeding ground and we're trying to get them reestablished. It's early days yet. I'll be down here another few months helping them get adjusted."

"I've read quite a bit on the 'greening' of Tasmania since I arrived. In fact the night I came into Hobart the Green party thought they'd got the government by the short 'n' hairies. Some scandal about logging rights?"

"Oh, God," said Steve with a sigh. "That's been a problem here for decades. Not enough controls. We've lost tens of thousands of hectares to those logging operations—you'll see what they've done when you get to the end of the South Coast Track. Like night and day. Soon as you cross the World Heritage boundary there's whole stretches of foothills where the forest has been clear-felled. Nothing left."

For the first time I sensed vigor and anger in Steve's mellow manner.

"Is it changing? Is the government getting into selective felling?"

"All bloody nonsense, that 'selective felling.' All euphemisms and rhetoric—like 'managed forests,' 'replanting schemes'—honestly, we've heard all the cowclap for decades. Now we're saying—stop everything. No more felling. Tasmania's a small place and we need all the forest we can keep. There's not that much left. Less than a tenth of what we once had. Wildlife is being wiped out, the rain forest is dying, we're getting erosion, the bloody dams are filling up with runoff soil. Half of them will be useless by the end of the century. They're so dumb in Hobart! Bloody 'bludgers' " (a word I was to hear often in Tasmania, apparently referring to those nefarious members of society who live off the sweat of other people's brows).

Bob nodded and chuckled, "He's right, David. Few years back the Greens were laughed off as a bunch of pot-heads and leftover hippies. But now they've got some clout—and things are happening. . . . Tasmania could become the place to make a stand . . . set an example."

Our conversation rolled on into the night as the fire glowed and crackled. With people like Bob and Steve it seemed Tasmania might have a chance. I finally curled up on one of the bunk-bed platforms and, with the exception of a series of wall-shaking snore barrages from Bob, slept a quiet and dreamless sleep.

The smell of coffee and bacon awoke me.

"God—you sleep deep," said Bob, bringing a chipped enamel mug steaming with a thick black brew. "You'll likely need a few of these to get you going."

Getting going is not one of my God-given talents. I mumbled thanks and sipped the scalding coffee.

"Listen, Dave, I was thinking. You gonna leave today or d'you wanna spend a bit more time here?"

Thinking in the early morning is another skill I haven't yet mastered.

"Not sure yet. Why?"

"Well—I could take you out to the beach. Show you a bit of Bathurst Harbor. Then there's the Willsons. You wanna go over and visit?"

"Sounds fine." I wasn't really ready for the lonely hike. I was enjoying Bob's company and the prospect of six, maybe more days out on that trail (leeches, Tasmanian tigers, funnel-web spi-

315

ders, et al.) didn't appeal yet. And anyway it was all mist and drizzle outside. Not an auspicious time to begin a big trek.

Bob's bacon and fried-bread sandwiches were greasy and delicious. I'd catch up on my muesli, bran, and fruit later, in less challenging climes. Cholesterol and caffeine were fine for the moment.

When we emerged from the hut the mists were clearing and there was warmth in the early sun.

"She'll be a good un'," mumbled Bob as we headed past Deny's house to the boat jetty on the creek. I found it hard to share his confidence. From what I'd heard about the fickle moods and tantrums of the climate down here, such pronouncements seemed dangerous invitations to providence. But then again, he was the bushman. I was merely passing through.

"Maybe catch up a few yabbies for lunch," said Bob as he untied the small motorboat and kick-started the engine.

"Yabbies? What are they—fish?"

"No—sorry mate—keep thinkin' you know all this bush talk—they're crayfish. Freshwater crayfish. Cook 'em up in boiling water. Eat 'em with melted butter. Bloody marvelous." The crackle of the engine destroyed the early morning silence. Two herons flapped in an ungainly manner up out of the shallows on the other side of the creek and headed upstream in search of quieter hunting grounds.

The water wound lazily through dense thickets of King Billy pine and stunted myrtle, their roots exposed mangrove-fashion in tortured coils and grasping tentacles. They looked alive in an animal sense, as if embroiled in some slow and macabre dance. Slivers of mist were still tangled in their upper branches and hung across the peat-bronzed waters like wraiths. Once in a while I'd spot a lonely pandanius, that strange variant on a tropical palm found in isolated clumps all over the southwest heathlands. Its slender trunk can reach fifteen feet and is topped by a crown of arched yard-long leaves. Decades of dead leaves cover the trunk like the hairy hide of some prehistoric monolith. Strange creatures indeed, which enhance this region's lost-world flavor.

Gradually the creek widened out into Bathurst Harbor and the thick vegetation drew back revealing vistas of mountains. To the far north, the hazy quartzite arêtes and pinnacles of the Arthurs; closer in the morose-looking mound of Mount Melaleuca around which winds yet another trail, the South-West Cape path, and, across the water, the rocky summits of Mount Rugby and Mount Stokes, bathed in a watery silver light. A majestic if melancholy scene, now even more reminiscent of western Scotland, particularly the remote Torridon region, one of my favorite wild places.

Without warning, as we left the shelter of the creek, a blustery wind from the north set the boat bobbing like an empty bottle on the choppy broil of the fjord. It was a cold wind too, cutting right through my three layers of vest, shirt, and sweater.

"Put your parka on, Dave. It can get real brass monkeyish."

Bob was right. I was already shivering and as I pulled on the waterproof jacket, my fingers turned into a messy mélange of red and purple splotches. He was sitting on the floor of the boat to reduce the bone-numbing blast. I joined him and peered over the side like a child on his first boat ride—open-eyed and just a little awed by the swell which made our small craft thump and bang its way across the waves.

"There's our beach."

Bob pointed to a long strand of white sand on the edge of a thick junglelike confusion of eucalyptus, pine, and myrtle.

We shifted direction. Now we had the wind behind us and rode more easily with the waves toward the shore.

The boat ground to a gravelly halt a few feet from the beach. Bob had his long rubber boots on and pulled us effortlessly higher up the sand. The water still had that gold-ocher color to it but was as clear as a Caribbean lagoon. Tiny fish darted in the shallows. The dark forest ahead of us was silent. A broody kind of place.

"So—is this where you saw that creature—whatever it was?" It was very quiet and still now.

"Yeah," said Bob. "Right down there by those rocks."

"Doesn't look like anyone's ever been here before. Feels like we just discovered this place."

"Well—that's the way I like it. I don't bring big parties here—half a dozen or so for a week, sometimes more, sometimes less. Real back-to-basics stuff. Catch our own fish and yabbies. Everybody chips in."

317

"Sounds great."

"Well—most of 'em like it. You get a few who *think* they're going to like it but then find it's a bit too quiet. No TV. No radio. No telephones."

He led the way into the gloom following a barely defined path between the tangled branches, fallen trees, flurries of pandani and ferns, and heaping mounds of soggy moss.

"This is weird," I said. "It's almost like a rain forest."

"Right y'are. That's what it is. Scenery switches fast here. You can go from buttongrass marshes to myrtle to pines to rain forest in ten minutes. All depends on the microclimate and the soils. That's what makes this place so special. Half a dozen different environments in a short walk. Nowhere else on earth like this."

"Yeah," I said. "It feels different. Bit spooky too."

"Spooky's right. Takes a bit of getting used to."

The "camp" appeared suddenly in the half-light. It was barely distinguishable from the rest of the forest except for a broad tarpaulin stretched between four trees to shelter the camp kitchen and eating area. A riot of ragged eucalyptus, tree ferns, laurels, and dense rhododendron bushes surrounded us.

"Rain can get real bad, so I decided we gotta have one place we can all sit and keep warm and dry. I'm going to start up the fire and then see if I can get us some lunch."

"Okay. I'm going to take a look at this rain forest."

"Fine. See you back soon. Don't get lost!"

I laughed. Lost? Me!

I wasn't laughing fifteen minutes later. I couldn't have wandered more than a couple of hundred yards from the camp, but somehow I'd misgauged my orientation. The sun was no help. It was lurking behind clouds and remnants of morning mist, so there were no shadows. Just murky gloom. Damp and tangly. And dense thickets of myrtle and rotting trunks that I tried to circle around and in the convoluted process got all turned about. Totally topsy-turvyed, in fact. Usually my sense of direction is excellent. My wife, Anne, claims I've got some kind of built-in compass, possibly a leftover from my days as a city planner when working with maps was a daily necessity. But in this messy mangle of a forest I'd lost it. Clean gone. I had no idea where the hell I was and, like an idiot, had left no marked path and ignored all the basics of Scouting 101.

Bloody stupid cocky complacent sod! The self-retribution was beginning (my alter ego has always had far higher expectations than I could ever live up to).

I'd read somewhere (you see how much reading I do about my lost worlds; my alter ego is pleased about that) that the vegetation of South-West Tasmania is considered to be a remnant of Gondwanaland—that enormous supercontinent floating on a vast reservoir of magma which gradually split apart around a hundred million years ago to form the separate continents on today's globe. Specific evidence of ancient plant forms are the eucalyptus, the wattles, the myrtles, the Huon pines, and the myriad complexities of the heathland shrubs and ground-hugging bushes. Unlike the geologically recent and dramatic shifts to aridity on mainland Australia, the environment and climate of western Tasmania have remained essentially the same for tens of millions of years, thus preserving rain forest species that once prevailed throughout the southern sector of Gondwanaland and, after the continent shift, in Antarctica itself.

So here I was, discombobulated and disoriented in one of the earth's most ancient prehistoric forests whose groping, snagging, scratching confusion of strange species with mossbound trunks and straggling, slippery roots made the whole thing into an increasingly nightmarish experience. Sticky too. I was covered in sticky spider-webby goo and guck. In places I was over my boots in slime and glop. Any moment I expected to find leeches.

"Bob!"

My voice sounded thick. There was no echo in the spongy morass.

"Bob!"

Louder but no more effective.

My mind still possessed a little island of calm. It suggested the only solution—radial lines of exploration from a central and immediately recognizable landmark.

I found a fine landmark. An enormous eucalyptus whose bark hung in ocher and sand-colored tatters from a white trunk. It overshadowed everything around. A truly beautiful rain forest specimen which, in any other mood, I'd have been happy to

319

sketch and photograph. At the moment, however, sketching was the last thing on my mind.

The plan worked well. I set off on my first tangent from this splendid center point in what I thought was most likely the right direction back to the camp and then a retrace of the two hundred steps to the center point, and off again on a thirty-degree variant.

After the first four tangents I had discovered nothing except even denser thickets and muddier swampy morasses. Maybe I'd wandered farther than I thought. Maybe two hundred steps weren't enough. Maybe I'd missed the camp by a few meager yards. . . . My mind whirled with doubts, but there was nothing left to do except persevere until I'd completed a whole 360 degrees of tangents.

On the eighth tangent I was losing confidence in the whole exercise. I was a muddy, weary mess. Lunch back at camp began to seem not only a most attractive proposition but also vital to my metabolic well-being. And then, as I continued thrashing through the thickets, I became aware of what seemed like an echo in the gloom. When I moved and stumbled through the forest, something else was moving. Something not so far away. When I stopped it seemed to stop. But not every time. Sometimes the muffled crack and rustle of leaves and branches would continue a few seconds longer and then pause. When I started up again it would start up too. . . .

I was about to call out to Bob again when a thought dropped itself like a little pernicious demon into what was left of my thinking mind.

What if it wasn't Bob?

Well, who else could it be?

Not any*body*. Some *thing*.

What thing?

Like the thing that Bob saw on the beach . . .

Oh, *that* thing.

Not a pleasant thought at all. What did Bob call it? "A bloody monster . . . the worst-lookin' thing I've ever seen . . . pure evil." I stopped and tried not to make a sound. Of course, when you do that everything starts to get as noisy as hell—your breathing, your heartbeat, your pulse. . . . Normally I never notice how much noise I make puffing and panting when I walk in tough terrain.

Now I realized that I must be the noisiest breather on earth and trying to suppress the panting only made my gasps sound more wheezy and phlegmatic.

I crouched down and remained as still as I could.

At first there was silence. Then the cracking of twigs and rattling of leaves started up again. Maybe it was a wallaby—they make quite a racket with those huge hind legs and prehensile tail. Maybe . . . and maybe not. I wasn't going to take a chance.

It seemed to be moving around me, first to my right and then at my back and then on my left.

And it was definitely getting closer.

And then I saw something, about thirty yards away, something shadowy in the gloom, hunched and black. What light there was filtering through the tightly packed trees produced nothing more than a dim outline of shape. But it was certainly big. I eased behind a tree, slimy with moss and forest dew, and lifted myself up a little higher. The sounds were louder now, coming closer. The thing had long groping arms. It was carrying something under one arm. A bundle? A baby? But a baby what?

Then it growled. Only it wasn't a growl. It was a well-defined, highly recognizable syllable of sound.

"Shit!" it said.

And there was my monster, now in plain view, struggling to break a fallen branch.

"Oh, hi, Bob." My voice sounded cracked. My mouth felt as dry as a desert.

"Jeez!" Bob shot to an upright position, dropping his load of wood in surprise. "Jeez, David—don't do that. I wondered what the hell you were."

"Well—I wasn't too sure about you either." Brain pictures of mythical monsters scurried back to their lair deep in my overactive subconscious and I felt better already. "What're you doing?"

"We're low on wood. Fire's going fine, but we need more. Got some yabbies for lunch. You hungry?"

"Sure I'm hungry. Which way's camp?"

"Camp? It's right there."

He pointed in the gloom and although there was nothing I could recognize, I decided to keep up the nonchalance.

"Great. Thought I was on the right track. Easy to get lost in here, though."

"Easy for some," mumbled Bob. "You almost made me piss my pants. You must be a hell of a silent walker."

"Yeah," I said.

And the yabbies were wonderful. Quite the best lunch in weeks.

Later in the afternoon we returned across the fjord and moved slowly up the creek to the jetty. The sky was blue now in patches. Birds were twittering away in the bushes and across the heath.

"Think I'll go and see the Willsons for a while."

"Sure. No worries. See you back at the hut. You better check your gear when you get back if you're leaving early tomorrow. See if you need anything. I've got a few things lying around you can have."

"Thanks, mate. Good on yer."

"Don't you get bloody Strine on me. I'm the character. You're just passing through!" He laughed. "Well, passin' through or passin' on. Not sure which for certain!"

"Thanks, Bob."

"No—she's right," he said reassuringly. "You'll make it."

I hoped I would. Although after that overheated little terror among the trees I was beginning to wonder.

The path to the Willsons' mining operations and home took me across the landing strip and through thickets of heathland scrub. It was pleasant to be alone in such familiar surroundings. I felt as if I were tramping across the high Pennine moorlands of the Brontë country near my one-time home in Yorkshire, England. The colors, the textures, the vastness of the scene reminded me of Ted Hughes's landscape poems in which he makes all his images so tangible, so powerful, and—so similar to the underlying mood of the Brontë novels—somehow brooding and sinister. Hughes, husband of the late Sylvia Plath and Britain's poet laureate, always seemed to be as much part of those wind-scoured upland places as the weather, the bracken, and the tattered fragments of pure lark song. He absorbed the landscape in his works

and gave it back—rugged, strong, and cruel. One pungent frag-
ment of his lines returned to me:

> Where the millstone of sky
> Grinds light and shadow so purple-fine
> And has ground it so long
> Grinding the skin off the earth
> Earth bleeds her raw true darkness
> A land naked now as a wound
> That the sun swabs and dabs.

That's the Brontë country all right, up around Hughes's favorite
millstone-grit village of Heptonstall perched on the edge of black
crags, with enormous vistas of mountains and moors in all directions.

And that was here too, except all the grinding of the "skin
off the earth" had been undertaken by man and not the elements.
Small domes of overgrown detritus rose out of the heathland,
remnants of earlier tin-mining activities back in the thirties and
forties.

The boundary of the World Heritage area carefully skirts this
mini-moonscape of mounds and ponds. Purists would doubtless
prefer that this blot on the otherwise untouched landscape be
returned to its natural state, but I found it strangely comforting—
a meager sign of man's presence in a vast, hardly explored wilderness.

A small clapboard and tar-paper shack appeared around a
bend. It nestled in a secluded spot among the mounds, protected
by a huddle of wind-bent trees. Old mining machinery lay scattered about the yard; a rusting bulldozer sat lopsided in the scrub,
broken and gutted for parts. A wind chime tinkled in the chilly
breeze.

I knocked on the door. There was no reply. I pulled a string
latch and let myself in.

It was warm and cozy inside. A wood stove had a few glowing
embers in it. There were shelves of books, some old LPs, a couple
of well-used armchairs, a stereo, a shortwave radio, and a kitchen
table cluttered with empty pickling jars. Beyond the stove were
scores of liter-sized beer bottles with the labels washed off. One

stood open by the sink, half full of an amber liquid. It had that rich, malty aroma of homemade beer. I sensed a proud self-sufficiency here. Supplies would be expensive and cumbersome to bring into this remote spot, so back to the old basics—salting, pickling, home brews, and a contentment in the simple things of life.

No one was around and I felt like an intruder. As at Deny's nestlike home, this place seemed to invite me to stay, but I was uncomfortable and left after a brief warming by the wood stove.

Farther along the track, deeper into the mounds, I heard the sound of machinery. Engines were running and something was grinding and grating. The alien sounds increased. It was odd to hear such a racket in this place of sweeping silences.

The noise maker was an amazing erector-set extravaganza of ramps, rotating drums, and chutes supported by a flimsy skeleton of bleached pine beams that wobbled and shook and looked ready to fall apart at any moment. I'd seen similar abandoned contraptions during my days, many years ago, exploring the gold-rush country of northern California. But I'd never seen one actually working before. The noise was mind-numbing.

Someone was shouting and waving—a small figure in a green sweater, baggy jogging pants and a wrinkled canvas hat. I walked faster. It was Barbara Willson, pushing with a battered shovel at a pile of rocks, pebbles, and earth that slowly descended down a chute into an enormous churning cylinder punched with thousands of small holes.

"Hold on a minute—let me finish this load."

She was sweating despite the chill breeze and worked furiously with her shovel, easing the boggy mass down the chute. Chunks of bedrock, a few the size of small boulders, slipped down into the maw of the churning drum. This looked like tough work.

"Okay." She finally pushed the last part of the load down the chute, put her shovel down, and wiped her brow. Even under the shadow of her floppy canvas hat I saw a pair of dark, determined eyes. "So—you made it."

"Yes—thanks for asking me. I stopped by the house, but there was no one around."

"No—not till sundown. We're up here all day. Peter—my husband—he's out in the bog."

She pointed across the gray-brown bleakness of the plain. I saw a tiny yellow dump trunk way in the distance digging into the earth.

"That's the new bed he's working on. Took the peat off couple of days ago—down to the gravels. Then he brings the loads back here for sorting."

"And that's where the tin is?"

"Yep—down in the gravels. Gold too."

"Gold! I thought they'd given up on gold 'round here years back."

"Oh you still get some. In among the gravels. But not much. You'd never make a living."

"But you can from tin?"

"Well—almost. Price is down at the moment, so it's marginal—but there's only the two of us."

"How long have you been here?"

Her eyes twinkled. "Forever!"

"I bet it feels like that. This looks like hard work!"

"Y'get used to it. Keeps you fit."

"I think I'd prefer other ways."

She grinned. "So would I sometimes. But there's compensations."

"Like what?"

"Freedom." She said the word the way it should be said—with vigor. "And . . . well . . . all this. . . . " A sweep of her arm encompassed the whole wilderness around us.

She reminded me of others I'd met on my lost-world journeys. Individuals who had found everything they needed in a remote, seemingly inhospitable environment. They usually used the same expression—the same outstretched arms to encompass the spirit, the magic of lonely places. I always admired—maybe even envied—their apparent wholeness and certainty. Rarely have I found such a sentiment in cities, where restlessness, anxiety, insecurity, and burnout seem to be the rewards for lives lived out of synch, in pursuit of elusive carrots on overlong sticks, with happiness and contentment always a dream of tomorrow—and tomorrow.

"Y'ever seen what tin looks like?"

"No. Actually, I haven't."

"Well—take a look."

She led me down a slope of gravelly white rocks, skirting the edge of the clammering drum. The size of the gravels and rocks became smaller at each new chute in the vibrating contraption until the sandlike fragments of tin ore finally emerged and slithered in a steady stream into iron drums.

I dipped my hand into the dark brown powder. It was heavy, like lead. I had somehow imagined something white and talcumy—maybe even shiny.

"This is the oxide. It goes a lighter color when it's purified."

"Doesn't seem much compared to what you load in the top end."

"Y'right. Thousand tons of gravel maybe gets you a ton of ore. If you're lucky."

"And are you lucky?"

"We manage. We run test bores to find out where the best pockets are. We found a really rich area last week. We'll start scraping maybe in a month or two."

"And what happens when you're finished working the old beds?"

"We put the peat and the earth back. They didn't used to. That's why you get all those mounds you worked through. But we put it back. In a few years you can't tell where we've worked. Goes back to the way it was."

"Hey—what about some help up here!"

A small thin man peered down at us from the top of the shaking, banging "sorter," or whatever they call this strange contraption. Barbara smiled. "Slave driver," she whispered.

We climbed back to the top of the ramp and Barbara introduced me to Peter.

"Yeah, she mentioned some Yorkshireman might come snooping around," he said, smiling.

"Well, being from Yorkshire, I wouldn't normally go visiting Lancashire folk, but seeing as you're the only people in these parts . . ."

"Cheeky bugger. What part of Yorkshire y'from?"

I told him.

"So y'know Leeds, then?" he asked.

"Sure. I went to university there."

326

"So did I, mate. Thirty years back. Used to live near Roth-well."

"Rothwell. I lived just a few miles from there, just outside Swillington."

"Swillington! I know Swillington...."

And so it went on—a mutual naming of pubs, churches, rivers, secret places. A rejoicing in this unexpected bond, with Barbara smiling and wondering if we'd turn out to be long-lost cousins.

Finally she broke in. "Thought you wanted to get this load moving."

He looked at me and winked. "Bloody woman. Never lets me rest."

"Doesn't look like either of you rest much."

"Aye, well," said Peter. "The way prices are, you gotta keep going. It's just us two, y'know."

"Well, it looks like you're enjoying the life."

He laughed. "I guess you could say that. Don't know what else we'd do. Right, love?"

But Barbara was back at work, heaving the gravels and rocks down the first chute with her battered shovel. Way out in the middle of this vast nothingness, two people committed to a hard way of life that would make most of us weary even at the thought of it.

"Listen," said Peter as he jumped back on the dump truck. "If you want a beer and a chat later on..."

I agreed to come back to the house after sundown.

It turned out to be an evening of pure northern England hospitality—pies, pickles, home-brewed beer, and long conversations about a homeland I hadn't visited in far too long.

I rolled onto my bunk bed at the hiker's hut much later that night, set the alarm for an early start, and sank into happy oblivion, uninterrupted even by Bob's shattering cascades of snores.

A dour dawn. No sign of any sun. And one of those stiff breezes that felt as if it would cut through all my carefully layered hiking clothes. I could have stayed another day at the hut, I suppose. But I decided to start the journey.

"Well—see you back in Hobart," said Bob in a cheery morning mood. "With luck!"

The coffee had failed to clear my brain. Either that or Peter's home-brewed beer had been a lot stronger than it tasted.

Bob looked at me closely. "And it looks like you're gonna need all the luck you can get, mate."

"I'm fine. Got to bed late."

"Yeah, I know. Y'were snoring fit to wake Deny King."

"I was snoring! You've got to be joking. You're the noisiest bloody . . ."

Bob gave one of those wall-wobbling laughs.

"Now—that's better. Bit of fire in your eyes! Y'll be right, mate. Just don't rush it. Pace yourself. Oh—and you'll find a few things you might need in the left pocket of your pack."

"What kind of things?"

"Oh, nothing much. Just a few things to get you over the hard bits. . . . See you in Hobart, mate."

And that was that. A quick handshake and I was finally off on the lonely hike I'd come so far to experience.

Thankfully there were no "hard bits" for the first few miles. I felt as if I were walking on soft clouds across the bouncy buttongrass path that headed southeast from Melaleuca toward Cox Bight, my first destination on this six- or seven-day odyssey.

It was a couple of hours before the silence began to creep in and I realized that seven days of solitude suddenly seemed like a hell of a long time. On most of my long-distance hikes I've usually had company for at least part of the journey. But on this one, I had no one and no real prospect of hearing a human voice for a week or more unless I met someone coming the other way. What should I do with all that time? Dictate some short stories into my tape? Start my autobiography? Compose a few songs? Compress all my meager world-wanderer wisdoms into a few pungent anagrams? Or merely go mad, howling at this desolate unpeopled place like a hyped-up hyena?

Goethe got it right, as he usually did: "In every parting there is a latent germ of madness." Or Father Navarette: "It is no small contradiction to human nature to leave one's home." Well—home was a long way off, just about as far as it could be on any part of the globe. But I'd found a temporary home of sorts in Deny's little fiefdom, populated by Bob and Steve and the Willsons. Was I crazy to have left there? Should I have stayed and learned more about Bob's thirty years in the bush, or Steve's love for the orange-bellied parrot, or the tenacity of the Willsons' hard lives?

The balance will come, I told myself. It always does. In any situation, a benign reality usually composes itself out of the oddest of circumstances. Just let it come in its own time. Let the journey take on its own rhythm and pace and flow. And just flow with it. . . .

The path stuck to the plain, which narrowed gradually between the misty New Harbour and Bathurst Ranges. Mount Counsel with its quartzite flanks glowered down. My map showed an enticing place—Hidden Valley—high on its upper flanks and normally I'd be tempted to take such a diversion. But the land discouraged such fancies. I knew this kind of country well from my days among the Pennine bogs of Yorkshire. I knew how the seductively soft surface of the heath could give way without warning to pernicious mud holes that sucked and gurgled at unsuspecting limbs and devoured boots with malicious glee, leaving walkers in goo-laden stockings while their footwear was absorbed forever into the acidic mulch of the mire. The hardy walkers who ignore trails across such territory are known as "bog-trotters," as they leap like oversized, overweight ballet dancers from tussock to tussock. Some are lucky and escape the embarrassing boot-losing predicaments. Many do not and end up being half carried, half dragged off the stagnant plateaus by their grinning colleagues, to the warmth and nurture of valley inns.

I hadn't brought a spare pair of boots, only some soft sneakers for evenings by my campfires. If I lost my boots I wondered what I'd do—or, more precisely, what the trail would do—to my feet. Not to mention the leeches. . . .

Here it starts, I thought. The old mind-yammer. The silly fantasy-plagued "what if" scenarios that can wear a bouyant spirit down to a morose depression in a few unchecked reveries. None of those on this trip, please. All I have is me this time. No company, no helping hands, no jolly singsongs in the evening chills, no one to set perspectives straight, no one to calm fears and chase away fickle thoughts that appear—unexpected and univited—out of the miasma of the singular mind.

I tried to lift my confidence with memories of other solo journeys: that trek through Panama's Darien, those days on the deserted beaches of Barbuda; my unsuccessful climb up the Ruwenzori. They all began this way—a little wobbly at first as the spirit finds the fine line between freewheeling fantasy and the darker deeps of the mind, and then on into the days of balance and balm when the experience becomes pure, clean adventure.

Back in the United States before leaving on these lost-world journeys, I'd read Eric J. Leed's *The Mind of the Traveler* and was intrigued by some of the quotations he'd selected to explain the altruism of travel. I noted one twelfth-century excerpt in my journal from Chrétien de Troyes's poem "Ywain" in which a knight attempts to seek stimulus for his altruistic journey from a peasant who, when asked to identify himself, explains simply, "I am a man. . . . I am nothing but myself." The concept of adventure for adventuring's sake was obviously unfamiliar to such an individual:

> "I am, as you see, a knight
> Seeking what I cannot find;
> I've hunted and I've found—nothing."
>
> "And what are you trying to find?"
>
> "Adventures, to test my bravery,
> To prove my courage. And now
> I ask you and beg you, if you can,
> To counsel me, tell me—if you know one—
> Of some adventure, some marvel."
>
> "As for that," the peasant said,
> I know nothing of any 'adventures'
> No one's ever told me
> Any."

Sometimes I wonder who I admire most, the adventure-seeking knight or the "realness" of the peasant. Was the knight's admission—"I am, as you see . . . seeking what I cannot find"—

the admission of a lifelong dilemma or merely a plea for specifics? Possibly both. My "adventures" create a schizophrenic situation—the search for specifics: history, people, experiences, insights, joys, adrenaline highs but couched in a context that is less definitive—the search for something deeper and far more elusive. Myself? My spirit? My "soul"? A pushing out of boundaries in order to find a higher boundary? Or merely a perpetual discontent with the "smallness" of things—an inability to find the universe in a daisy's petal, a rejection of the predictable, a constant search for the "new" experience?

Claude Lévi-Strauss bitterly denounces the paradoxes encountered in travel for travel's sake:

> Now that the Polynesian islands have been smothered in concrete . . . when the whole of Asia is beginning to look like a dingy suburb . . . what else can the so-called escapism of travelling do than confront us with the unfortunate aspects of our history? The first thing we see as we travel round the world is our own filth, thrown in the face of mankind.

Leed himself sums up the quandary of today's adventure-traveler:

> The need for escape and self-definition through detachments from the familiar is rooted in a history that has generated an ideology requiring a wilderness, a domain of alternative realities, in which the self can assume its uniqueness and recover its freedom in the climate of the new and unexpected—just when history has all but terminated the possibility of that alternative.

Yet I know such "alternatives" still exist. Hence my search for—and exploration of—"wild places" and "lost worlds." To know that such places are present on our poor, overworked, blighted earth, I find one of the most stimulating and exciting of prospects. To be in such places, to sense their moods, to attempt to understand even a little of their complexities and beauties, is adventure enough. To share such experiences with others who may never choose or who are unable to experience these places for themselves is reward enough. To be "here" is all; to understand the inner impetus that drives me "here" is perhaps not all that important. Or, as Alan Watts once said, possibly impossible:

SOUTH-WEST TASMANIA
— all mine!

Like trying to bite your own teeth.

I am here and—for the moment, at least—that is enough.

The sun was giving me more of those bright light shafts between the ominous clouds. The heath was speckled with pools of color: I saw bosky clusters of *Melaleuca squamea*, with pretty pink thistlelike blossoms and the brilliant iciclelike shafts of the white waratah; I could smell the lemon-scented leaves of the boronia, speckled with white, four-petal flowers. The vast dunness of the plain at first seems devoid of anything except the bitter stalks of buttongrass, rattling and moving like slow tides as the wind sweeps across their dry tops. But as you look closer you see not only the tiny shrubs and bush blossoms, but the green, spotted backs of carab beetles, the beautiful deep bronze of grasshoppers, the antics of a tiny gray-furred jumping spider; you can hear the high-pitched *e-gypt-e-gypt* cry of the tiny honey eater with a strange, dark crescent of feathers across its upper breast and splashes of gold-yellow on its wings.

The plain appeared as timeless as the mountains, although the peat beds that form the nurturing ground for buttongrass are possibly less than four thousand years old. The Willsons had told me that occasionally, five or six feet down into the peat, they come across complete pine trees preserved in the acidic accumulation of decayed shrubs and grasses. Farther down they hit the hard bedrock of Precambrian metamorphic strata. They painted an enticing word-picture of vast forests along this southwestern coast in which evidence has been found of human habitation more than thirty thousand years ago. The explorer George Augustus Robinson recorded sightings of Aborigines in Louisa Bay in 1830 and noted the use of flaked stone for spear and arrow making and the skinning of animals. During the last ice age, when the sea level was almost four hundred feet lower than today's level and a broad land bridge existed across the Bass Strait linking mainland Australia with Tasmania, early inhabitants moved from the north across the bridge and lived along the more hospitable coastal margins of Tasmania below the towering glacier-filled ranges. Caves have been discovered, particularly in the magnificent gorges of the Franklin River eighty miles or so to the north of Melaleuca, decorated with "hand paintings" created by blowing a moist mix of dust, animal fat, and blood over hands pressed on the rock walls. Shards of chert, crystal quartz, and quartzite found in abundance in such places suggest that they were used both as workshops for the fashioning of tools and hunting instruments and as seasonal lodgings.

I had been told that Louisa Bay at the foot of the Ironbound Range was perhaps one of the richest sites of Aboriginal occupation in Tasmania and I hoped to arrive there tomorrow. Meanwhile, I had another two hours of bouncy hiking across the buttongrass to reach my first camp at Cox Bight.

What could have been a rather dull journey turned out to be full of unexpected delights and one not-so-pleasant moment.

I was learning to look into the plain and see its signs: the networks of runways through the marshy sedgeland that were the routes of swamp rats (otherwise known by the far more illustrious Latin name of *Rattus lutreolus velutinus*!) to their nests among the marshy buttongrass clumps; I noted the apparently innocent-looking mounds of stone and vegetation fragments that mark the home of the notorious jumper ants, whose bite can leave allergy sufferers with severe respiratory problems (Bob gave me a small plastic bag of antihistamine "just in case y'get unlucky, mate"); I saw the tiny burrows of delicious yabbies around peaty ponds but never caught a glimpse of these shy nocturnal crayfish.

And I learned to listen too. I heard the faint clicks and chirps of frogs off in the hidden pools, the frantic scurrying of the marsupial mouse deep in the knotted grasses, the odd ticking call of the flame robin, and the ringing "whit-whit-whit" of the shrike-thrush. Steve had told me to look out for the elusive ground parrot, whose orange and green plumage resembled that of his favorite, the orange-bellied parrot. "You more'n likely won't see them during the day. They like the dusk best—or the sunrise. Just before the sun comes up listen for a sound of little bells—like a wind chime. That'll be them. Lovely way to wake up."

I liked Steve. Here was a young man—a student of engineering—who'd decided to give a few months of his life to the preservation of one relatively obscure bird. He expected little, and received little, in the way of material recompense. But you could tell by the way he spoke and the way his eyes gleamed when he described his activities in this lovely place that he was finding other, far more satisfying rewards.

It was a rather wet and cold walker that dragged himself across the last half mile of open plain to the sweeping arc of Cox Bight. The light had been dwindling for an hour or so into a golden dusk that flecked the tops of the enormous fifteen-hundred-foot-high quartzite cliffs of the New Habour Range. They tumbled in brittle, sparkling majesty down to the surf.

A narrow granite promontory split the bay into two separate parts and I wondered about camping on its tip, close to the surging waves.

But then, to my right, I noticed the lagoon, a deep-purple circle of water separated from the bight by a long finger of dunes edged by what looked like a miniature rain forest. The tide was out, so I crossed the narrow inlet dividing the lagoon from the ocean and sank down into the soft white sand of a sweeping beach. In the lee of the dunes the constant battering of the winds from the west ceased. For the first time in hours I felt warm and protected. Maybe I wouldn't bother with the tent after all. My waterproof sleeping bag had seen me through many a cold night and a sleep on an open beach would be an appropriately romantic beginning for this back-to-nature odyssey.

But before the light vanished altogether I had to explore the miniature rain forest or whatever it was on the backside of the dunes.

By the time I'd clambered over the dunes and through huge bushes of native fuchsia I began to wish I'd left exploration until the following morning. I entered another one of those eerie worlds of ferns and tangled, stunted trees which reduced the dusk light to a green-gray gloom. Vines that dropped from higher branches or serpentined around moss-coated trunks snagged at my ankles. They seemed alive. My face and hands were soon coated in sticky spider webs and shards of cloying lichens. The ground was spongy with a rotted mass of dead and putrefying vegetation.

The silence was perhaps the most unsettling feature of the place. Only a few yards in, the hiss and skitter of the surf ceased and I felt cocooned in a soundless tomb. Even the wind had gone. Nothing moved in the tentacled darkness. There were no friendly bird calls, no frogs, no crickets. Nothing except the crunch of my boots on dead twigs and the slithering of wet ferns against my body.

I'm sure, had I been more of a botanist, I would have enjoyed days of delight exploring this quirky little forestscape in an otherwise treeless wilderness. But, while I find occasional fascination in recording plants and flowers and berries and buds, all I felt here was a kind of intuitive dread, tinged with that inevitable intrigue of the unknown that Wordsworth once described as the "ideal" condition of the wanderer:

> Whither shall I turn,
> By road or pathway, or through trackless wood,
> Up hill or down, or shall some floating thing,
> Upon a river point me out my course?

This wood was certainly trackless, and as I moved farther in it seemed that nothing tangible would "point me out my course." The place absorbed me into itself as if it had no intention of letting me go.

Michael Crichton once explained the driving force behind his own wanderings. "I felt a need for rejuvenation, for experiences that would take me away from things I usually did, the life I usually led. . . . I felt the urge to do something for no reason at all."

And so, for no reason at all other than maybe maudlin curiosity and a fascination with "feared things," I moved even deeper into the dark, groping tangle. I was determined not to lose my way as I had done at Bob's camp, so my route was as straight as I could make it, keeping my back to the ocean.

It was almost dark when I finally extricated myself from the dwarf forest and rejoined my lonely backpack on the beach. I was relieved to hear the surf and wind again. Familiar elements, familiar rhythms. Occasionally in my travels I feel, to paraphrase Dennison Nash, an outsider in a world of ambiguity, inconsistency, and flux. The forest had reminded me of that state—confusion tinged with frissons of fear—in an unfamiliar environment. But back on the beach, with my hands dug into the soft sand and a pack of sandwiches ready for dinner, I was home again. . . .

Sleep came easily this night.

337

But not for long.

Maybe my sleeping bag was not as waterproof as usual, or maybe the rain was harder than any rain had a right to be. Whatever the cause, I awoke just before dawn in the middle of a horrendous downpour to find myself soaked.

Rolling up the errant bag and cramming scattered belongings into my backpack, I scurried over the dunes and into the forest. Ignoring the snagging vines and moss-coated trunks, I plunged in until I found a dell edged by ferns where the rain merely dripped and splattered, rather than pounded with the ferocity of a sledgehammer.

Fortunately, my butane stove worked and I treated myself to steaming bouillon and a mushy mix of dehydrated rice and something that resembled chicken pieces in appearance but tasted of stewed cardboard. Whatever. It was food and I was hungry.

John Locke once wrote, "So far as a man has the power to think or not to think, to move or not to move . . . so far is a man free."

I decided not to think and not to move. Ergo—I was free! Only I didn't enjoy the freedom. I felt trapped as the rain continued its pounding.

Looking back, I realized I should have relished these moments of pause. After all, there were no jumping ants, no funnel-web spiders, no leeches, no mosquitoes—merely a little rain and a gray dawn. The food was filling and I had a clean, dry set of clothes to climb into. Looking back, it should have been a pleasantly benevolent interlude. . . .

Two hours later the downpour eased and I was more than ready to be off. Again, looking back, I should have stayed where I was and read a book for the day. That would have allowed time for the deluge to be absorbed into the earth, for color to return to the wilderness, and for my somewhat deflated spirits to balloon again into the bombast and braggadocio that often carries me through the "bad bits" of journeys.

But—ever restless for movement and momentum—I didn't do any of that. Instead I set off around seven-thirty into the moist morning, leaping swollen creeks, plowing along a trail that had now become a mire as I crossed the undulating moor, and climbing up into mists on Red Point Hills. Somewhere below me was

Louisa Bay, but all I could see was more mist, cold and clammy. I'd planned to take a detour down to the bay to catch a glimpse of fur seals and other summertime visitors from the Maatsuyker Islands just a few miles offshore, or leopard seals from Macquarie Island to the south, or watch the breeding rituals of the short-tailed shearwaters on adjoining Louisa Island. Most of all I wanted to see the three-thousand-year-old Aborigine middens that were said to dot the shoreline.

I was particularly curious about these few tangible remnants of Tasmania's Aboriginal culture. This little state has a notorious and embarrassing reputation as instigator of genocidal policies against the thousands of natives who had enjoyed a relatively tranquil subsistence life since around 1000 B.C. in the forests and along the coastal bays. Tranquil, that is, until the arrival of the nineteenth-century explorers and settlers who interpreted occasional protests by the Aborigines as tantamount to anticolonial rebellions. When George Arthur, governor of the fledgling colony of Van Diemen's Land, failed either to destroy or round up the natives in a campaign mounted in 1830, he sent the explorer George Augustus Robinson as a conciliator to find them and "persuade" them to relocate on the uninhabited islands of the Bass Strait. At that time Louisa Bay was a key focus of Aboriginal settlements, but within a short period of time not a single native was left on these wild shores. In fact, so effective were the government's destruction and relocation strategies that by 1876 no pure-blooded Tasmanian Aborigine existed anywhere except in the form of mummified specimens which toured the world in gaudy anthropological displays.

I remember reading a moving passage in a magazine that captured the terrible sadness of this decimated culture:

The Aborigines believed their souls to be white, the negation of their charcoaled flesh; the arrival of white men sailing down from the north must have seemed a second coming of spectres. Against this incursion, the Aborigines were helpless. Since their sagas were of dreaming not fighting, they produced no bellicose Sitting Bulls or Geronimos; they resigned themselves to their own obsolescence.

And so it was done. Rapidly, cruelly, and, for decades, without remorse. Today, however, I found a belated sadness in many Tasmanians I met and a sense of shame, occasionally tempered with claims of "benevolent relocation" or such odd rationales as "Look—disease had almost wiped them out anyhow. There were so few left. They were moved to help them help themselves." But generally it's not a subject of discussion likely to enhance beery camaraderie at the local pub. "Best leave it alone, mate," one elderly farmer advised me in a smoky bar in Hobart. "Stick to Alan Bond or dwarf tossing. Much safer."

And I left Louisa Bay alone too. I missed the detour track completely in the clouds on Red Point Hills. When I realized my error I was so bogbound and disheartened by the constant gray drizzle that I just plowed on to my muddy camping ground at the foot of the notorious Ironbound Range.

Some things are inherently amusing—like nose hairs and tables full of empty stubbies; some are not, like gray drizzly days in deepest Tasmania.

It was a day I'd prefer to forget.

And the next day too. Although for different reasons.

Dawn was promising enough: a crystal-clean light pushing the night clouds out to sea and touching the land with gold. No rain, no winds. A fine day for walking. The surly Ironbounds rose up in front of me; gilded peaks with jagged summits, flecks of ice and snow on the ridges. An ancient bulwark of Precambrian metamorphic rocks. Very impressive.

A majestic bird flew overhead as I collapsed the tent and loaded the backpack. The large white head was hawklike and its white belly sparkled as it soared the updrafts with a broad wingspan of five feet or more. I learned later I'd seen a sea eagle, a voracious eater of reptiles, other birds, and, when available, even penguins. Not a very pleasant creature—but on that sparkling morning it seemed an omen of better days ahead.

The path climbed steadily up open sedgeland onto a broad subalpine zone. Pockets of King Billy pine clustered in gullies and sheltered places, their deeply furrowed trunks and branches contorted, juniper-fashion. Small white daisies with golden centers

340

glowed in the wind-scoured scrub; compact clusters of dainty red Christmas bells rose among the grasses.

In spite of their ominous name, the Ironbounds peak at little more than three thousand feet, and while the climbing was tough going, it was made easier by the benign weather and ever-broadening vistas of mountains and bays. The wind increased as I approached the summit and I spotted places where previous walkers had camped, huddled in the low bushes. I considered calling an early halt to the day and hunkering down to enjoy the views, but my legs kept on moving and I followed the contours around the northern rim of the massif, humming happy songs and wondering how to prepare a celebratory feast of my one solitary steak (another gift from Bob) for dinner that night.

I saw new patterns of vegetation from these heights, patterns that were invisible at lower elevations—brilliant green swatches of sphagnum moss invading the small ponds and pools that lay scattered across the mosaics of darker green and bronze cushion-plant plains. The patterns were jigsawlike, thousands of micro-environments from the sedge grasses to the mosses to the lichen-blotched rocks and strata. Patches of pink mountain rocket and cheeseberry bushes adorned with bright red berries gave a rich resonance to the more muted tones of the buttongrass plateaus.

On a dull day the colors would doubtless be leeched out to an army-tent khaki, but today the sun revealed the land's true richness: a brilliant panoply of tones and textures that made me wish for canvas, palette, and brushes; a magnificent display of the subtleties, the intricate juxtapositions and meldings of plant colonies set beside the milky whorls and snakelike doodlings of sand patterns beneath the blue-green waters of the bays. And yet, despite all these delights, I could sense the restless riot of the land itself: towering broken cliffs; spars of brittle basalt; fjord-like incisions where the warmer, higher post–ice-age waters had penetrated deep into once-forested valleys; bold bluffs and phallic intrusions of dolerite into the spuming surf; the bleedings of frost-shattered ridges and razored escarpments in the form of peat-brown streams pouring from the hills; the bleached bones of ancient bedrocks protruding through the sloozy-oozy mud; the wind-torn trunks of trees, blasted of bark, blanched and twisted by a tempestuous climate that just never lets up—scratching and

341

scraping the land down to its ultimate peneplain in the hollow howling vastness that is South-West Tasmania.

I had a sudden flash of the neat little hedge-rimmed fields, ordered orchards, and Ireland-green, sheep-studded vales that awaited me way to the east around Hobart, far beyond these tumultuous ranges. I thought of the curling country roads, the pie shops smelling of fresh-baked pastry, the rowdy smoke-filled pubs, and the demure tin-roofed bungalows adorned with red and white trim and set in gardens of privet, hollyhocks, and geraniums.

I would be there soon, I promised myself—showered, de-loused, primed up on Foster's ale, choosing dinner from menus with frilly borders, sleeping on soft mattresses, dry and warm, and savoring all the wonders of a world that, up here, seemed very far away.

But enough of such hedonistic imaginings! I was less than halfway to such bucolic destinations, with a lot of tough hiking ahead and challenges to be overcome.

And the challenges came fast. Actually a mere hour or so after my contemplations on that Ironbound ridge, as I left the heights and began my descent toward the long beach of Prion Bay, everything changed. The bare, wind-tossed tops gave way to some of the thickest, most tangled and tortured rain forest it has ever been my misfortune to encounter. Out of the bright light and into a gray-green gloom of a nefarious netherworld.

Now, rain forests have their fascinations. Even that eerie dwarf forest I'd discovered at Cox Bight possessed, in daylight, a certain rampant, raging charm. But this was altogether differ-ent—a far more intense, menacing place where there seemed to be little in the way of order or subtleties. The forest just flared up and thrust me into it, following a trail that had the remarkable ability of vanishing in the difficult places, leaving me scrambling through mud and slime and decaying moss beds without any sense of direction—except down.

And down and down, deeper into the sticky gloom of ancient Gondwanaland species—more tall King Billy pines, eucalyptus, myrtles, celery-top pine, and a tangled understory of laurel, whitey wood, waratah, dwarf beech, and ferns, all competing for scarce light and root space—oh, and mosses too, in strange and exotic forms: pillars, mattresses, balls, bouquets, and furry smotherings of trunks and branches. Had the mood been more conducive I might have dallied here and undertaken a photographic essay of these myriad species, possibly even bagged a few samples for later identification. But the mood was definitely not conducive to anything except survival and eventual extrication on the beaches of Prion Bay, far, far below.

And then I noticed the leeches.

Well—not so much noticed. I merely sensed something peculiar on my left arm under layers of damp clothing. Something moving very slowly. Almost like an involuntary muscle spasm except it was happening in three distinct places simultaneously.

I looked down. I'd forgotten to fasten the Velcro cuff of my parka. Either that or it had been ripped open in my frequent fights with vines and branches. And so there it was, dangling loose, allowing whatever it was easy access to the soft flesh of my lower arm.

Actually, I knew what I would see even before I pulled back the layers. Once before, during my adventures in the marshlands of the Caspian Sea (recounted in a previous book, *The Back of Beyond*), I had experienced the stomach-wrenching sight of slimy black creatures growing bigger by the second as they sucked the blood from my legs and shins.

And, oh, yes, there they were. Three big ones this time, happily slurping away on my precious life fluid, oblivious to the discomfort they were causing in the pit of my stomach. . . .

Think back. How did my friends tell me to get rid of them in Iran? Something hot. A cigarette tip, a match—burn their tails and off they drop. But I remembered that method had not been too successful. In their haste to remove their blood-gorged, balloonlike bodies from my flesh they forgot to coagulate their incisions and left oozing wounds in their abandoned snacking spots. But what the hell? Anything was better than watching these miniature monsters have their way with me. So out with the lighter: flick . . . another flick . . . and another . . . and nothing. Not even a spark. Certainly nothing like a flame. Useless damned things, these lighters. A bit of damp and they seize up like oil-starved engines.

Okay. Next solution? Salt. That's it. A scattering of salt on

343

INTO THE RAINFOREST
South-West Tasmania

the tail and off they come. But I didn't have any salt. All the dehydrated fare I carried in little aluminum pouches was already presalted. I had a tiny bottle of soy sauce I always carried with me to perk up bland restaurant meals, but . . . aha! I did have one possible resource. Bob's bag of "emergency goodies." I'd already found his antihistamines for the bites of jumping ants. But what other delights had he shoved into the left-side pocket of my backpack?

With amazing grace and delicacy, I removed my backpack and used my right hand to burrow into the pocket. His gift was larger and more varied than I'd realized—mosquito repellent, high-energy health bars, Band-Aids, a large bandage, iodine, hydrogen peroxide, and—voilà—a small cylindrical container of common table salt. A message was scrawled on the outside. "So—they got you too! Best. Bob!" Yes, very amusing, my friend. Quite droll, really. You knew the damned creatures would find a way in somewhere. Well—you were right. And thank you for your gift of salt.

It worked. I tested the fattest one first. A few sprinkles on its lower regions and the thing tightened into a ball like a frightened snail, slowly released its suckers, and fell off with a sickening thump onto the wet moss of the path. This time it had thoughtfully sealed the tiny wound (maybe hoping for a comeback) and nothing except a little trickle of blood escaped. The other two behaved equally politely, so I resisted the temptation to stomp them into a gooey pulp and let them digest their stolen snack undisturbed by a quick belt from my boot. I cleaned the bluish wounds with peroxide, rolled down my shirtsleeve, and zipped the parka, fastening the Velcro catches as tight as a tourniquet.

But I was still curious about these evil black things. I hadn't seen any sign of them higher up. Maybe I'd been too concerned with keeping to the almost-invisible trail. Now I began to investigate the vegetation more closely and, lo!—there they were, camouflaged among the leaves and ferns in thready black shadows, nothing like the bloated horrors still digesting their meal on the mossy path.

I vowed to be more cautious, more aware. I also vowed to get out of this foul place as fast as my legs and spirit would carry me.

I arrived a few hours later at the graceful arc of Deadman's Bay enclosing yet another soft white sand beach. Most of the rain forest lay behind me but exuberant flurries of vegetation encroached on the shore and clustered thickly along either bank of Deadman's Creek. I was tempted to camp for the night but as dusk was a way off and the sky still contained slivers of blue I decided to continue on around Menzies Bluff to the four-mile linear strand of Prion Beach.

New vistas awaited me here. Behind the dwarf forest on the ancient dunes lay the large inland New River Lagoon and, towering over the landscape, the white mass of Precipitous Bluff. Tall eucalyptus forests clung to its lower slopes and rising out of this luxuriant green mass were striated dolerite crags whipped by clouds and sparkling in patches of sunshine. To camp beneath such crags would be fitting relief from a long, weary day.

But as I walked the seemingly endless strand, a dark sense of loneliness and utter isolation descended on me. The place looked so empty. So untouched. Somehow its drama and beauty exaggerated the intensity of my strange mood. Surely I shouldn't feel depressed in the midst of such magnificent scenery. I should feel elated, full of a sense of achievement. After all I was now well over halfway. Only another three days at most before the cozy comforts of Cockle Creek.

But the mood wouldn't lift. The beach seemed to go on forever. No footprints. No signs of campsites. Nothing—except me and this enormous awesome space.

Something felt to be banging against the edges of my mind. I remembered a quote from James Hillman: "The way through the world is more difficult to find than the way beyond it." I sensed I had reached an impasse of sorts. My expectations of this experience did not correspond with the actuality. And what made it so odd was that, as soon as that impasse occurred, I began hunting my head for a rationale, a definition of my "problem"— my unexpected depression. What's happening? my mind called out. This is not the way it's supposed to be. But something on the other side, a whisper, a mere breath of thought, came through: There's no "meant to be," there's only "is." And a memory. A memory of lines from Thomas Moore's splendid book *Care of the Soul* (I found the quotation later):

Modern psychology . . . is often seen as a way of being saved from the very messes that most deeply mark human life as human. We want to sidestep negative moods and emotion, bad life choices and unhealthy habits. But if our purpose is first to observe the soul as it is, then we may have to discard the salvational wish and find deeper respect for what is actually there. By trying to avoid human mistakes and failures, we move beyond the reach of the soul.

And later—at the end of Moore's magic book:

We know soul is being cared for when our pleasures [in my case the opposite, but the point's the same] feel deeper than usual, when we can let go of the need to be free of complexity and confusion, and when compassion takes the place of distrust and fear.

It is the "letting go" that is the key. The releasing of expectations and predigested experiences and the acceptance of "what is"—good, bad, elating, depressing, hurtful, ecstatic—all the myriad range of emotions and feelings and insights that have always been and always will be part of our complex human fabric.

Only then, according to Moore, does soul coalesce "into the mysterious philosopher's stone, that rich, solid core of personality the alchemists sought, or it opens into the peacock's tail—a revelation of the soul's colors and a display of its dappled brilliance." Moore ended his book with these words and his image of the peacock's tail had endured in my mind.

And it came at just the right moment. Something was happening. As I slowly began to accept the strange mood that had abruptly swept over me, it no longer seemed to be a problem but merely another nuance, another facet, of the journey's multifaceted sequence. It didn't really matter much whether I felt sadness or gladness; the mood was irrelevant to the process—the learning, the insights, the new ways of seeing that were now somehow encompassing the depression and leading me on to another level of perception.

Something definitely was happening. Something I remembered from a Tom Robbins novel (I forget which) that suggested the difference between an adventure and a suicide is that the adventurer leaves himself a margin of escape, and the narrower the margin, the greater the adventure. Well, I certainly hadn't come all this way for a lonely suicide in this desolate land; I'd come on an adventure, to narrow the margins, follow the escape routes, and see where they led.

And this one was leading to somewhere rather wonderful, a place an Aborigine had tried to explain to me a few weeks previously during my journeys in the wilds of western Australia. He talked of a web, a web of song (songlines) and legends that enveloped the world, a web in which time was irrelevant. Everything that is and ever was is part of that web—everything in constant interaction—everything in kinship within the web—all humans, all creatures, all mountains, rivers and streams, trees, even individual rocks, all animate and interrelated within an all-enveloping web.

My walk was no longer a morose, bad-mood-bound plod. In fact, I was now unaware of actually walking on this immense sandy strand. I was becoming part of it; the still silent place was buzzing with "presence"; the web was forming. The sheafs of dune grass, the fuzzy huddle of dwarf forest on the lee side of the dunes, the soft slitheriness of trillions of sand grains, the tiny marks and footprints etched in the grains, the hiss and suck of the surf, the breezes swirling among the marram grass, the slowly undulating movements of the clouds, the fractured complexities of the distant dolerite crags—even the silence itself both in the land and, growing more each minute, in my mind . . . all part of this eternal web. Another reality, where things are not fractured, fragmented, labeled, separated, but rather bound together in an inevitable totality that melts the barriers of insight, merges the boundaries between things, and lets the incredible wholeness and completeness of everything come roaring through into a previously blinkered and now suddenly unlocked perception.

All the clever doodads of the mind—rationales, expectations, critical faculties, intellectual framings, prejudices, fears, measurements, discretions, manners (you know all the rest)—seemed to drown in a deluge from some subconscious force that had laid dormant for too long and was now released with such vigor and clarity that "moods" seemed to be easily breachable barriers—

even welcome doors—into the miracle of the *now*, the infinitely intricate web of a reality without time and without boundaries.

The inner self becomes turned inside out. It no longer resides with the head but transforms into a transparent funnel linking mind and this newfound actuality. I've experienced similar fleeting sensations before, particularly in spaces whose immensity seems to threaten the stability of the rational mind. It occurred when I was crossing the Sahara with the "Blue People" of Morocco, the Tuareg tribesmen. Left for hours above the infinities of sand on a camel's back, I found my mind at first desperately rushing around within itself trying to maintain the edges, the flimsy superstructure, of sanity. It was only when I learned to let go and become part of the rhythm and flow of the journey itself, to enter into its timelessness, that the antics of my overcharged brain no longer seemed relevant to the larger patterns of perception emerging out of that apparent nothingness.

And in other places too—on the plains of Venezuela's Los Llanos, in the vastness of the Inner Mongolian grasslands, across the white infinities of India's Rann of Kutch, and even in the intense head-blasting riot of stimuli that is Nepal's Kathmandu— all places where nothing makes any sense until you stop trying to make sense and let the incredibly rich totality of each place deluge and envelop you in its own overwhelming web.

And so back to my beach, my seemingly endless strand of soft sand, where my bad mood was no longer even a memory and I gave myself up, for the first time on the journey, to the wholeness and wonder of the place itself. And my soul slowly became a peacock's tail. . . .

At the end of Prion Beach a campsite was indicated on my map. Unfortunately, it happened to be on the other side of a fast-flowing river linking the New River Lagoon to the ocean. On the map it was a mere trace of blue, hardly noticeable. In actuality it was almost a quarter of a mile wide and deep in the middle, where the water eddied and churned through the inlet. Someone had arranged a remarkably civilized way of crossing in the form of two boats, one at one side and one at the other. However, on this particular evening, both boats were on the other side. Some

thoughtless hikers had forgotten that they were supposed to return one of the boats to its starting point on my side.

Normally I might have indulged in a minor fit of curses and
expletives, thrashed the sand into muddy pulp on the riverbank,
and wished all kinds of calamities upon the lives of the boats'
previous users. But now it didn't seem to matter at all. The boat
wasn't there, so I could either swim across and then return with
the boat for my backpack or I could wait and see what else tran-
spired. I felt the water. It was bitterly cold. So—no swimming
tonight. I decided to make camp on the edge of the dunes and
let the problem resolve itself. Tomorrow.

And it did. As such things usually do, if you give them
enough time.

Shortly after dawn my tent began a Saint Vitus' dance followed
shortly by a roar of sound that broke into my sleep in such forms
as "Oi," "Ay," "Anybody home round 'ere," "Jeez, you must be
a bloody 'eavy sleeper, mate," and more of the same.

I slowly unzipped the flap and peered into a face—a human
face. My first in four days.

And a very peculiar face it was—a broad, sun-scorched, furrowed face framed by a long mop of once-ginger hair and a matted
beard of indiscriminate color. And a grin—an enormous grin that
revealed a mass of stained chipped teeth behind a mustache that
hadn't been trimmed in months.

"Well, g'day, mate. The boatman has arrived. Betcha weren't
looking forward to a cold swim, were yer?"

I blinked, wiped sticky sleep from my eyes, and heard my
cracked, unsteady voice mumble some inanities. I hadn't spoken
aloud in a long time, except for occasional curses and quiet conversations with my maker. I don't know what I said.

"Gawd, blimey, y'need some coffee, mate. Y'still got a bit of
fire out here. Y'wanna get dressed and I'll get a billy on."

"Good idea," I think I said.

"Right y'are, mate. Take yer time. S'good morning out here.
Bit on the chill side, so wrap up. See yer." The flap dropped and
then opened again. "Name's Lanny, Lanny Riley." I shook a huge

hand and introduced myself. "Right, Dave—well, take your time, mate."

And he vanished. Beard, willowy mustache, big grin, and teeth.

I heard him blowing the embers back to life and rattling pans.

How nice. Coffee being served by a stranger. A noisy stranger too, who began to sing what I later learned was one of Tasmania's unofficial anthems—a microcosm in song of Tasmanian history. The tune was rather unsteady and off-key and the words were not clear (I found them in a folksong book a few days later in Hobart), but it went something like this:

> Come all you gallant poachers that ramble void of care,
> While walking out one moonlit night with gun and dog
>   and snare,
> With hares and lofty pheasants in your pocket and your hand,
> Not thinking of your last career upon Van Diemen's Land.
>
> It's poor Tom Brown from Nottingham, Jack Williams and
>   poor Joe,
> They were three daring poachers, boys, the country well did
>   know;
> At night they were caught by the keepers hid in sand—
> For fourteen years transported, boys, upon Van Diemen's
>   Land.
>
> The very day we landed upon the fatal shore,
> The planters they stood 'round us full twenty score and more;
> They ranked us up like horses and sold us out of hand,
> They roped us to the plow, brave boys, to plow Van Diemen's
>   Land
>
> The cottage that we lived in was built of sods and clay,
> And rotten straw for bed, and we dare not say nay,
> Our cots were fenced with fire, to slumber when we can,
> To drive away wolves and tigers come by Van Diemen's Land.
>
> It's ofttimes when I slumber I have a pleasant dream;
> With my pretty girl I've been roving down by a sparkling
>   stream;

In England I've been roving with her at my command,
But I wake broken-hearted upon Van Diemen's Land.

Come all you gallant poachers, give hearing to my song:
I give you all my good advice, I'll not detain you long:
O lay aside your dogs and snares, to you I must speak plain
For if you know our miseries you'd never poach again.

Between coughs and spits and all the sounds that suggest
the sear of early morning cigarettes, his raspy voice rolled around
the campsite, setting birds singing in the dunes and in the forest
along the shores of New River Lagoon.

Out of the rear "window" of my small tent I could see the
surf gently prattling up and back on the sunlit strand. A huge
black bird, a wedge-tailed eagle, soared on the air currents off
Precipitous Bluff and peered down intently at our camp. Its enormous tail feathers and six-foot wingspan distinguished it from
the smaller white-bellied sea eagle I'd seen a couple of days back.
It looked a very serious and determined prey-seeking creature. I
learned later that its strength and broad talons enable it to attack
not only lizards and mice but even moderately sized wallabies. It
seemed to be sizing us up for a possible breakfast snack.

"Well—welcome to the world, Dave. Grab yourself some coffee, mate."

I emerged in a semi-somnolent state, but the coffee worked
its magic as Lanny began to pull out exotic delights from his
backpack. No dehydrated mulch for him. Instead he carried lean
bacon, fat Australian sausages, and thick slabs of bread.

"Fancy a bit of this bush-tucker? Nice sausage and bacon
sandwich? Was gonna make you some real 'damper' bread, but
this stuff's okay, right?"

"Sure," I gushed.

"Y'need decent breakfasts on this trip. What yer been eatin'?"

I almost apologized for my meager morning fare of muesli
and raisins.

"Well—that stuff's okay. But you need stayin' power. Bit o'
meat and fat. Nothing like it for getting goin'."

He was so right. My palate pounced on the now-unfamiliar

353

textures and flavors. The fat oozed out of the thick slices of bread onto my jeans as I gorged on these forbidden delights.

"Lanny—this tastes great!" I managed to get out between chews and swallows.

"Right y'are, mate. Grab another one. Y'can get worn down on this walk. Need yer tucker."

We chewed in silence. The coffee gurgled in the billy; the eagle still hovered above, and gentle breezes blew over the dune tops. We finished by wiping the pan clean of every morsel of food and fat with more slabs of soft bread.

"Good on you, Dave. No need to wash this lot. Cleaner than when I started."

"You carry stuff like this with you—bacon, sausages, bread. . . ."

"First couple of days. After that it gets more basic. But I like to start off right."

"You've done this walk before?"

"Done the lot, mate. Overland Track over Cradle Mountain, Walls of Jericho, Port Davey Track, the Arthurs, South West Cape. . . . Done this one, South Coast Track, three times. This's my fourth."

"By yourself? You walk by yourself?"

"Most the time. Best way. Too much baloney when you go with company. If I want company I go to the pubs. Here I just wanna . . . well . . . y'know. . . ."

I knew. Walking alone, shrouded in solitude, is an acquired habit but one that can become addictive.

"I'm glad you turned up this morning. I wasn't looking forward to swimming across for the boat."

"Don't blame y'mate. Catch yer bloody death in that stream. Dangerous too. Them currents a bit rougher than you think. . . ."

(Mind pictures of me being carried out to sea in the treacherous swirls of the stream . . . and the eagle hanging there, waiting to dive down for a tasty morsel of drowning Dave. . . . My wife would not have been pleased.)

"Y'want some chocolate?" I asked. "I've got some left."

"Naw, Dave, keep it. You've got a few tough patches up ahead before Cockle Creek. You'll need it. This'll do me fine."

And he brought out yet one more delight from his bulging backpack, a sticky square of malt loaf full of raisins and nuts.

"Try some a this, mate. Beaut way to round off yer breakfast."

And it was. I felt gorged and stuffed and utterly satisfied. Unfortunately, I didn't feel like walking. At least not just yet. So we talked instead.

Lanny's story was a familiar one in Tasmania. He was a descendant of Irish convicts sent over in the mid-1800s for petty crimes in the homeland. Unlike many Australians, who don't care to pry overmuch into their murky backgrounds (but often maintain a deep-seated resentment of the British and their cruel convict colonies), Lanny seemed proud of—or at least curious about—his origins.

He extracted a couple of books from his enormous backpack.

"You carry books too—along with the bacon?"

"Right y'are, mate. Best place to do some readin', this trail. Lots of beaches. Find a spot out of the blast and you can read as long as you want."

"What kind of books?"

"All kinds. Bird books, plant books, couple of thrillers, history books. . . . " He tapped the two he'd pulled out of his map pocket. "Now, these'll give you a bit on what Tassie's all about." He flicked through one looking for a certain page. "Listen to this, Dave."

He cleared his throat, threw his third cigarette of the morning into the embers, and began to read at an uneven pace as if reading aloud was an unfamiliar activity:

"This was written by a convict brought over back in the 1850s: 'And over the soft, swelling slope of the hill, embowered so gracefully in trees, what building stands? Is it a temple crowning the promontory as the pillared portico crowns Sunium? Or a Villa carrying you back to Baiae. Damnation! It is a convict barrack!' "

He looked at me and grinned—"Nice bit a writing, eh, Dave? Fancy stuff until he realizes he's seeing a bloody prison. He's talking about Port Arthur, near Hobart.

"And listen to this about the old-crawlers, the prisoners who were let out on probation after their sentences to go scroungin' around the countryside for jobs. This is what one of the rich land-grabbin' guys said about one of his old-crawlers: 'I've had this

355

man flogged times without number. . . . I have put a rope around his neck and on horseback, dragged him back and forth through that pond, but it was all of no use. The man would not leave my service. He'd become so used to punishment that it had become a kind of necessity to him, and likely he felt at times uneasy if he did not receive any; all that was human in his nature must have been lashed out of him, leaving nothing but the nature of a spaniel dog.' "

He paused and I thought. Tasmania is such a powerfully beautiful place, it's hard to imagine the cruelties and fascistlike regimes that were the cornerstones of its social and economic foundations. I started to put something into words.

"It's weird, Lanny. So much of Tasmania looks like England, gentle, rolling green hills. . . . "

"Y'right there, Dave—dead right—listen to this—" he flicked to another page, "this was written by that first guy I read to you, that English prisoner: 'The roads are excellent, the houses good. The coachmen and guards are in manners, dress and behavior as like untransported English guards and coachmen as it is possible to conceive. The wayside inns we passed are thoroughly British; even, I regret to say, to the very brandy they sell. The passengers all speak with an English accent; every sight and sound, reminds me that I am in a small, misshapen, transported bastard England; and the legitimate England itself is not so dear to me that I can love this convict copy.' "

There was silence for a while. I realized, as I had done so many times with my companions in the Bungle Bungle, that Lanny was another one of these split-personality Australians whose bar-and-beer bonhomie belies a far more sensitive individual, deeply caring about his history, his background—and often angered by the cruel origins of his race. Lanny in this respect was true to form. Maybe it was only in the solitude, and the sudden friendships of passing wanderers, that he felt comfortable in revealing this side of his nature. I certainly wouldn't have taken him for a man who placed much value in books, and certainly not to the point of carrying them with him in a backpack that looked already far too large for his struggles ahead over the Ironbounds.

I tried to think of something to break the silence.

"It's hard to imagine this place—this little island—having such a hard history."

Lanny laughed, revealing those huge teeth again. "Wait a minute. You wanna know how hard? Listen to this." He flurried through the pages again.

"Okay. Now, this is about a small penal colony up the west coast at Macquarie Harbour. They called it the Place of Ultra Banishment and Punishment. There was this guy Sorell, William Sorell, lieutenant governor of Van Diemen's Land in the 1820s—he said it was a place that 'held a larger portion, that perhaps ever fell to the same number in any country, of the most depraved and unprincipled people in the universe.' So he decided to build this prison on Macquarie Harbour for 'the most disorderly and irreclaimable convicts' and he told the guards . . . where is it, hold on—" more flicking of pages, "okay . . . he told them: 'You will consider that the constant, active, unremitting employment of every individual in very hard labor is the grand and main design of this settlement. They must dread the very idea of being sent here. You must find constant work and labor for them, even if it consists of opening cavities and filling them up again. Prisoners upon trial declared that they would rather suffer death than be sent back to Macquarie Harbour. It is a feeling I am most anxious to keep alive.' "

Lanny read on. Apparently Sorell's orders were followed to the extreme. Daily floggings were commonplace—a hundred lashes for the most minor offenses with a cat-o'-nine-tails consisting of nine thick leather thongs, each four feet long, knotted at six-inch intervals and tipped with coarsely wound wire that slashed skin and flesh into bloody pulp. One description of a typical flogging (recorded by a convict named Davies in 1825) left my overburdened, breakfast-filled stomach churning:

> The place of punishment was a low point almost levil with the sea, and just above high water mark was a planked Gangway 100 yards long. By the side of it in the center stands the Triangles to which a man is tied with his side towards the platform on which the Commandant and the Doctor walked so that they could see the man's face and back alternately. . . . It was their costome to walk 100 yards between each lash;

consequently those who received 100 lashes were tied up from one Hour to One Hour and a Quarter—and the moment it was over unless it were at the Meal Hours or at Nights he was immediately sent to work, his back like Bullock's Liver and most likely his shoes full of Blood, and not permitted to go to the Hospital until next morning when his back would be washed by the Doctor's mate and a little Hog's Lard spread on with a piece of Tow, and so off to work . . . and it often happened that the same man would be flogged the following day for Neglect of Work.

In addition to those terrible floggings, prisoners were often placed in forty-five-pound leg fetters that ground the flesh off ankles to the bone. They worked sixteen-hour days, never received fresh vegetable or meat, only two-year-old salted beef, and thus suffered terribly from scurvy. And for the accidental error of breaking an ax or saw (Macquarie Harbour became a lumber-felling center) they received the dreaded regimen of cat-o'-nine-tails lashings. In the case of more severe misdemeanors, executions were ordered in the form of public hangings attended by all the inmates. Not surprisingly, the executions were often a welcome release for the miserable miscreants. Lanny read from the records of one of the officers:

Their execution produced a feeling, I should say, of the most disgusting description. . . . So buoyant were the feelings of the men who were about to be executed, and so little did they seem to care about it, that they absolutely kicked their shoes off among the crowd as they were about to be executed, in order, as the term expressed by them was, that they might "die game"; it seemed . . . more like a parting of friends who were going a distant journey on land, than of individuals who were about to separate from each other for ever; the expressions used on that occasion were "Good bye, Bob" and "Good bye, Jack," and expressions of that kind, among those in the crowd, to those who were about to be executed.

We were silent again. Lanny put down the book and stirred the embers under the billy. The eagle had gone. The sun was over the dunes now, warming us. I couldn't think of anything to

say. This beautiful majestic land had now become another place—
a place of terrible terrors and cruelties, a hellhole of man's in-
humanity to man.

I'd read somewhere that as late as the turn of the century
most "Vandemonians" had experienced the convict life before
being released and probationed as "old-crawlers" and left to create
what they could of a life in the valleys and emerging towns of
the island.

Peter Conrad, a repatriot Tasmanian, expressed his feelings
in *Behind the Mountain* on the residue of this appalling era:

> The problem is our forgetfulness. Tasmania has unwritten its
> own history. Citizens who had made good vandalized the
> state archives to eliminate the record of their convict ancestry.
> A self-protective incuriosity about origins is an instinct bred
> into you . . . it was simply a matter of agreeing not to remem-
> ber things which were painful . . . a convenient amnesia over-
> takes . . . but a past which isn't acknowledged can't be
> overcome.

Conrad calls it the "Tasmanian Ailment" and it pervades his
finely crafted prose like bitter bile.

I looked at Lanny. Was he plagued by the same deep-seated
ailment? Was that why he carried such books with him to these
lonely, remote places? To digest? To face the truths of his origins?
To destroy the demons of Van Diemen's Land and return released,
refreshed, to a more familiar life?

I waited for him to speak, but as I waited I could sense him
slipping back into the hearty, outback swagger of your typical
Australian "mate." I had to catch him before the transformation
was complete.

"And you said your family was part of all this, right?"

He looked up, tottering between truth and bar-brain braggadocio.

He chose truth.

"Yeah, Dave. They were part of it. All of 'em. But they
wouldn't talk much. . . . " He paused. "I mean, this was still going
on less than a hundred years ago. My grandfather had seen it all.
But . . . well, for him, for all of them, it was over. It stopped. And
they just wanted to forget the whole bloody mess. You can't go

through life carrying that kind of crap inside your head, 'least, not in the head you use every day. Best thing—grab a few stubbies and the racing forms and a bunch of mates and get on with things. Little things. Anything."

I left it at that and very soon the Lanny of the bacon-and-sausage breakfast returned, grinning, rubbing his straggly beard and talking again like the happy hiker I'd taken him for in the early morning.

"So—let's get the boats organized and at least you'll be saved a swim, mate."

So we rowed the boat across the creek, and he returned to the other side, leaving me dry and safe on the eastern shore.

But not without one gesture. . . .

"Here, Dave, take this book. You seemed like you were interested in the stuff I was reading."

I looked at the cover. It was Robert Hughes's *The Fatal Shore*, a book I'd been meaning to find and read ever since I arrived in Australia.

"No, c'mon, Lanny, I can't take this."

"You bloody can and you bloody will. Teach you a hell of a lot 'bout this country. Lot of stuff that people'd rather forget!"

I accepted the gift and shook his hand. In his smile I saw the two Lannys again—the silent backpack wanderer in search of himself and his heritage, and the cocky roustabout that I knew he'd be if I'd met him in a Hobart pub. I liked them both.

I silently promised that if I ever wrote about the journey for this book, he'd be one of the first to receive a copy, fresh off the press, and signed with affection.

And I did—and he was.

So—off again into another sparkling day. (Two in a row in South-West Tasmania is a most unusual event.) The straggly, beach-hugging forest had returned, but I managed to skirt around the thickest sections by keeping to a narrow stretch of sand fronting the New River Lagoon inlet. Below Wierah Hill the path turned inland for a while, crossing Tylers Creek, which trickled through patches of buttongrass moor down to Osmiridium Beach. After an hour I was back on open sand again at Surprise Bay. And the bay did indeed have its surprises—vast swaths of Ordovician limestone that originated in the murky depths of the ocean over five hundred million years ago and contained a wealth of trilobite fossils. These blind, beetlelike creatures once wandered the steeply sloping sea floor at a depth of at least one thousand feet, fed on updrafts of plankton-rich currents, and died in countless billions to form dense layers of what we so casually categorize as limestone.

A sensation returned that I'd had a few years back exploring the peculiar limestone scenery of the Yorkshire Dales in England. There, in the midst of sheep-cropped plateaus and steep dry white gorges, the layers of limestone were piled, one upon the other, like books awaiting stacking. The oceans, specifically the Irish Sea and the North Sea, are now both fifty miles or more away from these bleak uplands, and yet the limestone with its myriad fossil fragments told tales of other times, eons ago, when these bleak regions were deep under oceans and teeming with primitive aquatic life.

I think it was the abrupt contrast between the silence of these open, windswept Yorkshire heights and the turbulence of their ancient creations and accumulations that impressed me. I was walking across a vast cemetery, hundreds of feet thick, composed of nothing else but once-living, eating, breeding, and, who knows, maybe even thinking creatures. I had walked these hills many times before and never been struck by this thought. I knew limestone was essentially a composite of shells and calcium and the white detritus of once-living creatures, and that seemed an adequate explanation. But when I looked "into" the rock and touched the fragments of heads, bodies, legs, tails (even the whorling excreta deposits of ancient sandworms), the stuff seemed to come alive.

My fingertips buzzed and crackled as I ran them over the rough edges of the strata exposed at Surprise Bay. Maybe I was beginning to sense what the Australian Aborigines have always known—the total wholeness of all created things, even the very rocks themselves, whose rocklike exterior contains far more fluid and dynamic creative forces and origins.

Eleanor Wilner once wrote:

We are but nature given eyes and, by a twist
of DNA, earth given to our care.

The Aborigines, with their web of songlines, sensed that the earth had to be constantly "sung" into existence and that it was each bushman's duty to learn and continually "sing" his songline in order that the earth be maintained in its completeness. Otherwise it would simply disappear.

Maybe in our steadily increasing awareness of the need to see, understand, and work with the world as an intermeshed totality (the Gaia concept of the earth) we will be able to give form and strategy to our cardinal obligation of "earth given to our care." And yet the mysteries remain, manifesting themselves in flickers of perception and awareness that are still not wholly comprehended as we touch the earth and wonder.

Henry Blount said it well in 1634:

Far above all other senses, the eye having the most immediate and quick commerce with the soul, gives it a more smart touch than the rest, leaving in the fancy something unutterable; so that an eye-witness of things conceives them with an imagination more complete, strong and and intuitive, than he can either apprehend or deliver by way of relation.

In other words—the magic remains!

And Surprise Bay possessed such magic. It touched me in the same way as those lonely hills of Yorkshire, even though its juxtaposition with the ocean made the limestone layers seem more plausible. Nonetheless, I felt that sense of "life-in-everything" again and the continuity of all things as I sat on a ledge and stroked my hands across the externalities of the strata.

Once again I was tempted to linger and reign in the flow of the journey itself.

And this time I did. I remained at Surprise Bay. After all, I had no one to meet, no deadlines, no schedules, and a day spent lingering and looking here wouldn't matter a damn in the grand scheme of things.

I was pleased by my decision. Sometimes the momentum of movement for movement's sake becomes tiresome and rather pointless. Every journey is, or can be, a means to larger ends. If it is not, then the integral point and purpose of the journey—of journeying—can be lost.

In one of my notebooks I'd jotted a couple of lines from Aitareya Brahmana:

There is no happinesss for the man who does not travel. Living in the society of men, the best man becomes a sinner. Therefore wander!

Close by was another quote—one of the briefest—said to be the last words of Buddha to his followers:

Walk on!

Both used the wandering and walking metaphors to suggest a broader meaning which, in my particular circumstance at Surprise Bay, I took to imply the inner journey, the journey of self- or soul exploration. So that day I gave myself the gift of open-ended time and walked inwardly. My blister-plagued feet tingled with gratitude at this time off from their external journey.

Eric Leed suggests that travel today, "once the agent of our liberty, has become a means for the revelation of our containment" and indeed, in much current travel literature, even the epics of V. S. Naipaul, Paul Theroux, John Krich, and Claude Lévi-Strauss seem to echo such a sentiment.

Leed continues: "The modern structure of global tourism annihilates a time-honored escape from the limits that have always defined human existence; a means of liberty from a fixed and predictable death; a method of extending the persona in time and space . . . travel is no longer heroic or individualizing."

Even Paul Fussell, that most notable exponent of the travel genre, finds the dominant emotions of what he labels "post-tourism" to be "annoyance, boredom, disillusion, even anger."

I occasionally seek solace from the hard-edged perceptions and cynicism of many contemporary travel writers in the more dulcet tones of a Jan Morris essay or the exuberance-in-solitude of Freya Stark, who wrote: "People who know nothing about these things will tell you that there is no additional pleasure in having a landscape to yourself. But this is not true. It is a pleasure exclusive, unreasoning and real."

Yes, indeed. Following my little frisson of last night I delighted even more in the solitude of my journey. I had the land all to myself but, much more than that, I was, as an Aborigine might say, "in" the land, bound to it, immersed within its own spirit and completeness. Leed also returns to this idea, perhaps his most compelling, that contemporary barriers to true "exploration-travel" and the predominance of homogenized experiences "create a necessity for the journey back, inward, to origins and what has been left behind. Thus originates a new species of the old tradition of philosophical travel, a search for origins, stimulated by a hunger for meaning and content which is itself a product of generations of wasting, simplifying, and reductive journeys. On these return journeys the old motives may operate in a new way, and a modern death may be avoided, postponed. Those do not die who connect their endings to their beginnings. Therefore wander."

And wandering (both inner and outer) is what I intend to keep on doing as long as the leeches and the lions and lonely challenges of solitude do not block or eliminate my serpentine paths.

That day at Surprise Bay brought to the journey a depth and a peace that is not always present in the itinerary of my other adventures. I felt whole again and saw the world, as my high school art teacher used to say, with "fresh eyes."

I'd been warned by Bob back at Melaleuca that the last day and a half would be the most wearying of the walk. He was right in one way. The land delighted in its own extravagance and exuberance, making me clamber up and down roller-coasting, scrub-cloaked ridges, across the sandstone-capped dolerite plateau of the South Cape Range (easily resisting the temptation to take an even harder trail to the nearby summit of Pindars Peak) and then plunging down again through more tangled, tortured rain forest to a cold little campsite on South Cape Bay at the side of the boisterous South Cape Rivulet. All in all, one of the most exhausting segments of the journey.

And yet as I sat by my evening fire on that last night of the journey, nursing my blisters and massaging my crampy thighs, I sensed my temporary tiredness easing away and being replaced by more of what I'd now labeled my "Surprise Bay mood"—a

364

glow of inner contentment, merged with a tolerance and acceptance of the walk's vicissitudes; a sacrifice of body, bones, and blisters on the altar of innocence and wide-eyed wonderment at everything around me. It no longer really mattered what the weather was like, how hard and how high the hills, how deep and cold the streams and bogs . . . or even how tasteless those terrible dehydrated food packages had become. Whatever happened was fine. The journey was teaching me many things, giving me new insights, and, in a way, a new sense of me and my relationship to everything within me and around me. I had become the journey itself and the journey had become me. And that was more than enough.

Even the wade through the blood-freezing (and overdeep) South Cape Rivulet in the early morning in no way diminished my mood. I knew this was my last day in the wilderness and although the external journey would soon be over, the inner journey that had begun would continue, and continue.

A period of soft walking along the beaches of South Cape Bay led me across an unusual outcrop of exposed Triassic coal seams, hard and black against the seething surf. Then it was time to climb the sand dunes and turn inland along the heathland bottoms of Blowhole Valley. The winds blew hard off Pindars Peak and Mount Leillateah, whipped through the scrub and over the two ponderous domes, Bare Hill and Honey Smith Hill, to the south. A last blast of farewell from the wild elements. I left the beaches that had been my resting place behind me and passed over the watershed to the sinuous curl of Cockle Creek and the deep blue of Rocky Bay.

Already the hedonistic pleasures of Hobart beckoned me. I thought of frothy beer, the camaraderie of pubs, grilled steaks and other "real" food, a soft bed, music, company—and tales to tell. I had no idea how I'd reach the city, but, as usual, something came up in the form of a farmer in a four-wheel drive truck who greeted me with an oh-so-welcome "Jeez, mate, you look like you could do with a bit of sit-down for a while. . . . "

And so I sat down on the unfamiliar softness of his truck seat and we banged and clattered off along rough roads into the greenness of small fields and farms and orchards and places with people.

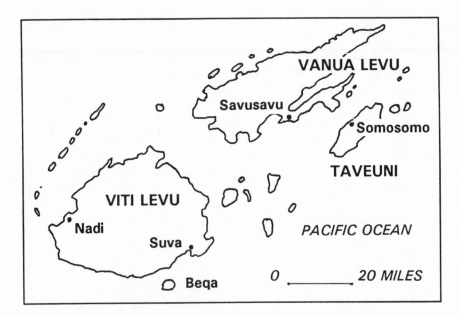

9. FIJI
The Temptations of Taveuni

My ticket read: Sydney—Los Angeles—New York (actually it was in gobbledeygook: Syd-LAX-NY/JFK).

Flight times all set. Just a matter of hauling in my dust-stained baggage (the red dust of Australia releases itself reluctantly), smiling nicely at all the nice, smiling form-fillers and ticket-stampers, drinking a final stubbie or two at the airport bar, and then off into the crisp blue infinities, couched in plushy comfort, nibbling nuts, sipping sodas or something stronger, and sleeping whenever I felt like sleeping. . . .

And then I'd be home. Bit of a long flight, but I like the limbo of flying and I had three unread books I'd been dragging around the outback with me. So there wouldn't be too much in the way of angst or aggravation. A stroll up and down the aisles once in a while to prevent bloated ankles and feet. Maybe meet a few interesting passengers, although I admit to antisociability on planes. I enjoy those listless hours of floating around my own head for a while and usually don't encourage interruptions.

After twenty-odd hours I'd be back in my big city. Back to the tangles of JFK; back to the roaring New York aggressiveness and an atmosphere energized by expletives and explosive exuberances.

And there was my flight. Up on the board already, even though I was hours ahead of schedule (another idiosyncracy; I like lots of dawdle time at airports). And on time too. Everything set. All I had to do was check my bags.

So why was I hesitating?

C'mon, I told myself. Ten weeks in the Australian outback and down in the wilds of South-West Tasmania is enough for any weary world wanderer. Get yourself home. Go back to your wife, your lake, the cats, the squirrels and the last lingerings of fall in the trees by the boat dock.

But I just stood there, surrounded by my grubby bags, watching the lights flicker on the departure board and all those exotic destinations flashing by—Honolulu, Bangkok, Port Moresby, Christchurch, Tokyo, Beijing.

Something was not right . . .

Had I forgotten something? Had I lost something? Had I gotten the days mixed up?

Checking through checklists once again. No, everything's okay. Twelve thousand miles all around this vast continent and here I am, on time, nothing lost, nothing forgotten, nothing mixed up. Everything ready for the flight. Just hand over the bags and then . . . nothing more to think about until New York. No more lists, no more near-drownings, no more riding around in crazy helicopters with no doors, no more leeches, no more tanglings with the red oozing mud of outback roads, no more blisters and a body badly in need of bathing.

The departure board continued to flash and flicker . . . Nairobi, Manila, Calcutta, Istanbul. . . .

And then it was there.

Fiji.

Something smiled inside.

Fiji.

Palm trees, sloppy warm surf, lovely open faces, quiet island beaches, cocktails overlooking purple-haze mountains, strolls by frisky waterfalls, lobster dinners by moonlight across silver-flecked bays. . . .

Fiji.

Of course! That's what was missing. A place to pause on the way home. Somewhere to reacclimatize before the rush of hugs and the surge of familiar things. . . .

Another lost-world adventure, maybe?

No, c'mon. Enough! For once you could just go somewhere as a tourist and enjoy a few days of relaxation. Forget about your books, your photography, your sketches, and all your searches for places and things unknown.

And the inner journeys?

Forget about those too. Give your head a rest. Reward yourself with a few indulgences. Let your feet and weary body float mindlessly in a swimming pool for a while, basking in wide Fijian smiles.

Eric Berne once wrote a lovely description of Fijian smiles—"these rare jewels of the world":

It starts slowly; it illuminates the whole face; it rests there long enough to be clearly recognized and recognize clearly, and it fades with secret slowness as it passes by.

Fiji.

That's what I was looking for. And that's why I was off to change my flight plans.

And that's how I came to be skimming in low a few hours later over a patch of brilliant blue South Pacific ocean, gliding over the fantasy-profiled mountaintops of Viti Levu Island and fastening my seat belt for a puffball landing at the Nadi airport . . .

Fiji felt very right.

For three days I allowed the other me to emerge. The one that likes lounging around, doing nothing, thinking nothing, wondering about nothing except the size and sweetness of dinnertime lobsters and whether tomorrow will be as warm and worry-free as today. . . .

And then the fourth day came, and things changed.

I was restless again.

Dammit. The wandering was over. The book was almost completed; what could be wrong with a few more days of seamless R and R? Even Anne had been understanding when I'd called her from the Sydney airport.

"That's a great idea," she'd said when I told her about my spontaneous stopover plans for Fiji. "Then you'll be almost normal when you get home."

(Wasn't too certain about the "almost" bit.)

So why couldn't I be "normal"? Why couldn't I just lie back for a few days and soak up the sun and the surf, the smiles of lovely girls, the company of a newfound world-wanderer friend, and all the serendipities of the soft life?

"What I'd like to find is an unusual island that's not too far away where there aren't too many people, a place that's unspoiled," I heard myself saying to a man at the tourist office in Nadi.

"We have over three hundred islands in Fiji, sir—three hundred and twenty-two, actually." The man was trying to be helpful but obviously needed more information.

"Well—I'd like some mountains, a few cheap hotels, waterfalls, lovely beaches, good weather, unusual food, interesting local people. A place small enough to explore in a few days."

"Ah, yes." He was an Indian gentleman and attempting to be traditionally Indian in his organized selection of alternatives for my consideration. "Well—there are a few rather exclusive islands—very small—with lovely resorts on them. . . . Mr. Forbes has one on—"

"No, I want something a bit more authentic. Something that reflects the old Fiji. I can do without fancy resorts."

"Oh, yes. I understand." His brow was deeply furrowed as he flipped through his pamphlets and colorful brochures with all the intense efficiency of a railroad clerk in Bombay's Victoria Station. "There are so many, you see."

His young Fijian assistant was a study in complete contrasts. He was lolling back in his office chair, stroking his thick black hair and smiling a very tolerant smile as he watched his superior anxiously trying to satisfy my ill-defined whims. It was a smile I was to see often in the next few days.

Outsiders, particularly the Indians, who are the majority of the population in Fiji and whose families have been citizens for generations, are invariably regarded with amused disdain by the natives. Strict controls are placed on their property ownership, voting privileges, and other rights. The Fijians are determined that, even though now a minority, they will keep as much control, political power, and land in their hands as they can. Naturally they will work if they have to. But after all, in this sprinkling of South Pacific island paradises, work is merely a small part of a far more enticing range of daily enjoyments—cricket, rugby, kava drinking (of which much more later), discussing matters of enormous worldly consequence with family and friends, cooking, singing, lovemaking, fishing—and, of course, more kava drinking. If the Indians wish to labor themselves into early graves and accumulate far too many material possessions, well, that is their business. But the Fijian tradition of *kerekere* discourages such myopic pursuits by the indigenous populace. Overt success is frowned upon by less fortunate family members and villagers, and material things are not meant to be possessed alone but to be shared—on demand, if necessary—with kin. All a nephew or an uncle or a son or even a cousin thrice-removed has to do is say *kerekere* ["I would like . . . "] and whatever object—video player, chicken, pig, stereo set, dress, or even a room in the house—is desired has to be given, freely and with grace, as a familial obligation. So what's the point of overdoing anything? If you become wealthy you are immediately vulnerable to the ancient traditions of *kerekere*. Best therefore to take it easy, share your good fortune if and when it came, demand it from others if and when it didn't, and generally enjoy the freer things of life in a spirit of mutual unambitiousness—respecting the "collective ego of the clan" (the *tokatoka* and the *matagala*).

"Ah!" A smile appeared on the face of my Indian adviser.

I smiled back in encouragement.

He was nodding furiously, spectacles bouncing on his narrow nose.

"Taveuni!" he said with eureka! enthusiasm.

370

"Taveuni?"

"Yes, sir. I think you will enjoy Taveuni. We call it the Garden Island. It has all that you mention—mountains, beaches, waterfalls, not many tourists, inexpensive hotels and guest houses, and . . ."

"And what?"

"Well, sir—Taveuni has lovely . . . ladies, sir."

"Oh, good."

"Oh, yes. Very beautiful ladies. Very beautiful island. I think you will be being very happy on Taveuni."

"Well—that's fine. Taveuni it shall be."

I looked over at his assistant, still smirking and polishing his thick black hair, for confirmation. He smiled a warm Fijian smile at me but didn't seem to be particularly interested in our conversation. I tried to include him in.

"Have you been to Taveuni? Is it beautiful?"

The Fijian nodded without enthusiasm. "Of course. All our islands are beautiful."

Even from the little I'd seen at my hotel hideaway I imagined he was right.

I decided to stick with my Indian adviser.

"Have you been to Taveuni?"

"Oh, no, sir," he said sadly, the furrowed brow returning. "Unfortunately, I do not travel among the islands very much. I am always very busy here."

"Ah."

"But from everything I have heard and from all the peoples I have spoken to in this office, I think you will like it very much."

"Well—thank you. You've been very helpful."

"Oh, not at all, sir. It is my job—and my pleasure. Pleased to be taking some of these brochures."

He assembled a neat little pile of colorful leaflets, placed them carefully into an envelope with the Fiji tourist office logo on it, and wrote in a stiff hand: "Taveuni Island. For Mr. David."

"I hope you will be having a most enjoyable journey, sir."

"Well, thanks to you, I think I will."

"Most kind of you, sir. Thank you."

As I left the office the young Fijian was still polishing his black hair. There was something about his attitude that annoyed me and I wasn't keen at all that smirking at his boss . . . but what the heck? This was his country. This was Fiji. And Fiji, as I was to learn, had many unusual attributes.

So out again into a sparkling blue morning and off to make plans for a trip to Taveuni.

"Excuse me."

Someone tapped my shoulder and I turned to find the Fijian following me down the street, smiling broadly now.

"I was born in Taveuni. It is a good place to go. I would like you to visit my family. I have written the address down." He handed me a torn strip of paper.

I was surprised by his sudden change of attitude.

"Well—thanks. I'll try and do that."

"They will make you very welcome."

Then he handed me a small plastic bag filled with a gray-white powder. "You should give them this *sevusevu* as a gift when you visit."

I looked at the bag and then at the young Fijian. The contents resembled something I'd once seen in a police station in Vene-zuela. Something very expensive, very illegal, and guaranteed to slam you behind bars, preparatory, in some countries, to a brief farewell to life in front of a firing squad.

"I'm not sure. . . . "

"Please—it is only a little gift. It is a tradition."

"Yes, well, but . . . what kind of tradition is it?"

"Kava. The kava ceremony. You will be their guest and they will invite you to join them in kava drinking."

"Oh, yes?"

"Yes." He laughed suddenly and his face became one of those enticing, open, welcoming faces I was to see so often in the next four days. "What d'you think I'm giving you?"

"I really don't know—I wondered if—"

His high-pitched laughter bounced down the narrow street, echoing off the little stores and cafés. "I know what you won-dered! But it isn't. This is kava. This is powdered kava. In the old days, most people took the *yaqona* (yanggona) roots and they bashed them up and chewed them too."

"They eat it?"

"No, no. they chewed it up till it's like a paste and then they added water and stirred it up and—well, in a while . . . you drink it."

"And that's kava?"

"Oh, yes. A good drink. Makes you very happy. Very nice. You will enjoy it."

"So what do you do with this powder?"

"Well, you don't need to chew this. You just add water and stir."

"I'm glad to hear it."

"Hear what?"

"About the chewing—I'm glad to know no one has to chew it first."

"Oh—I told you—that's the old way. The best way, really. The chewing has to be done by virgins of the village. But the powder is faster. So—you will go and visit them?"

"Well—I'll certainly try."

"Good. So have a nice journey."

"Yes—thank you—*vinaka*—I will."

One last, flashing smile and off he went, back to his desk and to his hair polishing.

I tucked the bag deep into my trouser pocket and hoped that this wasn't some kind of setup for vulnerable tourists.

I'd never really given much thought to Fiji before my arrival and I certainly hadn't expected to find a South Pacific nation of 322 islands and a population of close on a million. But there they were, a few thousand feet below me as I floated above a sapphire-blue sea in a tiny twenty-seat Sunflower Air plane peering down at dozens of little palm-shrouded islets and atolls, each edged by pink-white and gold-white sands. Most of them seemed uninhabited. Tiny tropical paradises, untouched, unmolested. And in the hazy distance, more and more of them, fading over a blue-on-blue horizon.

But it's all a little deceiving.

Fiji's complex and convoluted history is in marked contrast to its benign South Pacific "paradise" appearance. Tribal chiefs exercised ruthless "club law" here for centuries and, according to a missionary in 1830, "No eastern tyrants can rule with more absolute terror than the Chiefs do here, and few people are more thoroughly enslaved and trampled than are these islanders."

Looking into the shining, smiling eyes of a typical Fijian today, it's hard to imagine the great wars that were fought between and across the islands here; the hideous ritual slaughters, sacrifices, and feasting on the bodies of enemies; the guile, cunning, and open graft of intertribal conflicts; the multigenerational grudges that set clan against clan for decades; and the unfortunate fates of so many widowed women, strangled by their own sons so that they might accompany their husbands into the afterlife.

Intrusion of the West and Western values came slowly in the wake of such notable explorers as Wilson, Tasman, Cook, and the unfortunate Captain Bligh, who was pursued through much of the archipelago in 1789 by armed tribesmen in huge drua boats. Bligh and his eighteen loyal officers, who had been left only the ship's launch and meager supplies by the notorious mutineers of the *Bounty*, would have doubtless met gory deaths among the treacherous reefs had it not been for sudden storms and other fortuitous occurrences that enabled them to escape bloodthirsty Fijians and Tongans and eventually, after over forty days in the open ocean, reach the relative tranquility of the Dutch island of Timor, over four thousand miles west of Fiji. Somehow, despite all the horrors of this journey, the indefatigable Bligh made accurate charts of the "Bligh Islands," as he called them, which were used for almost a century afterward by other explorers and traders.

At first the Fijians regarded such intruders with suspicion and resentment, but as the gifts from these outsiders increased, they willingly allowed them to gather precious sandalwood and later the odd but oh-so-valuable bêche-de-mer (sea cucumber) in exchange for muskets and mercenary assistance during the almost-constant tribal conflicts.

Slow consolidations of power were made, particularly during the reign of Chief Cakabau, one of the most Machiavellian of all Fiji's rulers. Described by one observer in the mid-1800s as "arrogant, cruel, cunning, devious and bold . . . a man who thinks of nothing else but war" and by another as "every inch a monarch," Cakabau ruled as self-proclaimed king of Fiji from the tiny island outpost of Bau off the southeastern coast of the main island of Viti Levu. Early missionaries sought to convert the firebrand chief to Christianity but he was quite content with his own gods and spirits, who seemed to be forming his fortunes most advantageously, and sent them packing.

But missionaries were learning their own ways of wile and guile and used the influence of Christianized Tongan islanders, who had long traded and resided in Fiji, to "persuade" Cakabau that quick conversion could be the key to his kingly ambitions. He acquiesced but, in doing so, alienated many of the independent chiefs he sought to defeat or cajole into mutually beneficial alliances.

Then, when an unfortunate priest, the Reverend Baker, was unceremoniously clubbed to death, decapitated, and eaten by a tribe in the remote highlands of Viti Levu, Cakabau was obliged by the increasingly dominant British traders to lead a reprisal attack. The Kai Colo—the hill people—denounced Christianity as "Cakabau's religion" and decimated his forces.

Cakabau's power began to decline as news of his defeat spread and by 1874 he, along with other chiefs, finally ceded the islands to Queen Victoria, at which time vast colonial-development plantation schemes were initiated, requiring the importation of indentured laborers—mainly Hindu and Muslim Indians. Thousands of these virtual slave immigrants lived in appalling conditions at "coolie-line" barracks until Gandhi's vehement protests led to an abandonment of the system in 1920.

Fijians proved to be loyal supporters of Britain and the United States in the two world wars and the Malaysian conflict, and this led, after years of political machinations, to the granting of independence in 1970. The young Prince Charles officiated at the elaborate ceremonies and has remained a favorite "royal" among islanders ever since.

"He is like our sugar," one Fijian told me in Nandi, "sweet and very civilized."

And sugar has certainly been the "civilizing" element of the islands, along with such other lucrative economic staples as copra, cocoa, ginger, and, more recently, tourism. Somehow the organizational skills of Indians, Europeans, Chinese, the *Kai-loma* (part-Europeans), and the Tongans have helped balance the subsistence agrarian traditions of old Fijian society and the debilitating *kerekere* ethics of shared wealth to form a richly varied cultural mix (hardly homogeneous, as the Fijians cling proudly to their special "rights") that is certainly fascinating, friendly—and fun. And graceful too. I had sensed that already in my brief stay. Generosity, quiet pride and dignity, a love of ceremony, politeness, and enjoyment of good and plentiful food and drink all combine to create a graciousness of living even in the simple villages of thatch and mud *bure* huts strung around their central green, or *rara*. At appointed times during the day the village *lali* drums can be heard echoing in the hills and you know that life goes on, slow-paced and warm-spirited, permeating every nuance of this intriguing society, still happy with its old ways in the midst of inevitable and ever-increasing change.

I hoped to learn and see much more in my brief stay here.

"Please fasten your seat belts. We shall be landing in a few minutes . . . you can see Taveuni to our right."

And there she was. Third largest of the Fijian archipelago, about twenty-eight miles long and six miles wide, and with a population of around nine thousand. Bolder and far more dramatically profiled than most of the other islands. A buckled spine of volcanic cones cloaked in thick green forest running her whole length, tiny bays with white sand, flashes of waterfalls tumbling from the ridges, scatterings of cottages with palm frond roofs, large coconut palm plantations, sinewy paths disappearing into dense forest, and tatters of clouds trailing off four-thousand-foot Uluinggalau, Taveuni's highest peak. All in all a rather mysterious-looking place (no sign of exotic tourist resorts here), a place to explore rather than tour.

We landed with a sudden thump on a grassy strip at the northern tip of the island and taxied to a standstill by a couple of huts that made do as the terminal, set in a profusion of flowering bushes—great showers of red hibiscus and explosions of bougainvillea and frangipani.

Most of my fellow passengers were Fijians visiting family and friends for the weekend. The remaining half dozen or so were avid Australian scuba divers, whose conversation on the flight over had been full of convoluted aquatic technicalities and references to such exotic-sounding diving locales on Taveuni as the Great White Wall, the Ledge, Pandora's Box, Rainbow Reef, Blue-Ribbon Eel Reef, and the Pinnacle. Apparently I'd arrived in one of the South Pacific's finest scuba-diving islands and wondered if I'd have the time, or the inclination after that near-death fracas up in the Ningaloo, to do a little subaquatic exploration myself.

Taveuni also apparently had a more recent claim to fame. A cinema poster on the wall of one of the airport huts proclaimed proudly, TAVEUNI—HOME OF THE BLUE LAGOON.

"What's that?" I asked Maika, the young, bright-eyed driver of a ramshackle "cab," who had appointed himself as my instant guide as soon as my bags were unceremoniously dumped from the plane onto the grass.

"Oh, we are very famous here," he gushed. "All the movie people came to film *Return to the Blue Lagoon.* Very big drinkers—all of them. Some crazy times . . . they filmed not far from here, near Bouma on the other side of the island, very beautiful waterfalls and beaches."

I vaguely remember reviews of that unfortunate movie. New York critics blasted just about everything except the scenery. I think it ran in Manhattan for three days and then vanished.

"Have you seen the movie?"

"Oh, yes. It was at the cinema in Wariki two weeks ago."

"Any good?"

"No—it was a very bad film."

"Really?"

"Oh, yes—very bad . . . except for the waterfalls and the mountains."

Well—chalk one up for the New York critics.

"So—where are you going?" Maika asked.

"I've no idea—let's just drive for a while and when I see a place I'd like to stay, I'll tell you. Okay?"

"Okay."

And so off we went, at first on a narrow tarmac road following the wriggles of the western bay-dotted coastline, which soon became an even narrower dust and gravel road, generously punctuated with potholes.

"Many holes and bumps, we have much rain on this island. Thirty feet a year."

"Thirty what?"

"Thirty feet, three hundred and sixty inches. Sometimes more."

"Is this the wet season now?"

He turned and smiled another one of those gleaming Fijian smiles. "It's always the wet season on Taveuni!"

Great. No one had thought to mention that. But at least this day was blue and cloudless. The water in the bays sparkled, the palms by the roadside wafted in warm breezes. There were fishermen offshore in tiny dugout canoes carved from single tree trunks. Night-black mynah birds squawked in the bushes. Children played in the shallows and waved when they saw my pink, sun-scorched face. I waved back and heard their screams of "*vinaka, vinaka*" ("thank you, thank you") echo through the trees.

I breathed in the rich air that rushed through the open window and smelled the moist perfumes of blossoms wrapped in that deeper, more mysterious aroma of jungle—a peaty, rotting, musky mix of tumultuous growth and death made more pungent by abundant rain and thick mossbound decay . . . the aroma of irrepressible life.

We passed through a small village where the men, wrapped in traditional skirtlike sulus, walked in a kind of cheerful stupor and called out welcomes of "*Bula! Bula!*" waving their arms like drunken traffic cops.

"They seem happy enough."

"Oh, yes—they are—today is a kava day. A national holiday."

"Really—which one?"

"Prince Charles's birthday."

"Prince Charles of Britain?"

"Of course."

"You celebrate his birthday!?"

"On Taveuni we celebrate all kinds of things. We like celebrations—parties. One a week, usually. Sometimes more. Prince Charles is very special man to us. We have named a beach for him. He wrote us a lovely letter to say thank you."

How strange. I'm sure most Britishers have no idea of the

Prince's birth date. Certainly there's no national celebration. But here, in this little outpost of ex-colonialism, one discovers a whole day of fun and frivolity for the monarch-to-be. (Even Queen Elizabeth II looks young and happy on the bank notes of Fiji—very different from her stern, aged portraits on British pound notes.)

"Any other celebrations in the next week or so?" I asked.

"Not official ones, I don't think."

"No fire walking and that kind of thing?"

"No—that's only in the island of Beqa, off Viti Levu."

"What about *nagols*—jumping off hundred-foot-high trees with vines tied around your ankles?"

"Oh, no—we never had the *nagols* here, sir. Never on any island in Fiji. That's to the west in the Vanuatu Islands, near the Solomons. Are you going there?"

"No—not this time."

"They say it is very frightening. Many people badly hurt."

"Yes—so I've heard."

"I can take you to our Lake Tagimaucia—very strange place high up by Des Voeux Peak—in an old volcano, in a crater."

"What's up there?"

"Very rare flowers—the *tagimaucia*—big red blooms with white hearts. Only grow here. Nowhere else in the world. We have a very sad tale about these flowers—everyone in Fiji knows it. It happened when Taveuni was very young—when the first people came. There was a little girl called Maucia who lived in a small *bure*—a cottage—by the ocean. Very pretty. But she had a stepmother who was very cruel to her, so one day Maucia ran away—ran far away—deep into the forest, into the mountains. But she became lost and the vines wrapped themselves all around her. She tried to get away, but the vines were very strong—like those strangler figs—" he pointed to a group of forest trees at the roadside smothered in snakelike vines, "you see them everywhere on Taveuni—and as she struggled more and more the vines got tighter and tighter. And she cried—she wept—and the tears became red blood and they rolled down her cheeks and down her arms and her legs and fell onto the ground and when they went into the earth of the forest they turned into tiny red flowers—the flowers we call *tagimaucia*. It means 'Cry Maucia.' "

I waited for more, but Maika had apparently finished his tale.

TAVEUNI
BEACH SCENE
— Fiji

"So what happened to the little girl?"

He seemed surprised by the question. "She died," he said.

"You mean there's no happy ending?"

"Well—there are the flowers. The *tagimaucia*. She became the flowers."

"I was hoping for a Cinderella sort of ending."

"Cinder-who?"

"Never mind, Maika."

I found my small hotel in the village of Waiyevo, about halfway down the western coast. Perched right on the beach, the Garden Island Resort was well within my modest budget and refreshingly devoid of scuba-diving enthusiasts at the time of my visit even though Rainbow Reef was only half a mile or so offshore.

"D'you think you'll be doing any diving?" asked Lela Prym, owner of the hotel, as we sat by the pool sipping cocktails brimming with freshly squeezed mango juice.

"I'm not sure. I don't know what I'm going to do—except explore and enjoy myself."

"You sound Fijian already." Lela had a real Julia Roberts grin that filled her face.

"And with a smile like that, you look Fijian."

"Well, I'm not," said Lela. "I'm American. I used to live in Washington, D.C."

"You've obviously recovered from that."

"Taveuni does that to you."

"Let's hope it does it to me."

"Oh, it will," she said, still grinning her *Pretty Woman* grin.

The days slipped by so gently. From time to time there were showers punctuated by brilliant shafts of sunlight that made the leaves and blossoms shine as if hand polished. One early morning there was a rainstorm so powerful it pounded the weaker palm fronds off the trees and flattened them into the running rivulets of gold and ocher mud. By lunchtime the rain was gone and the whole island basked under brilliant skies, smelling so richly of

382

washed earth and moss and refreshed jungle that you could almost drink the air in great liquid gulps.

I did silly, pointless things, for no reason.

On a nearby beach, shaded by thick vine-bound jungle, I built a sand castle out of the damp white sand. Quite an impressive affair, really, with turrets and battlements and an enormous arched entrance across a moat which filled as the tide edged in and began to crumble my creation. I remembered that as a child on the beaches of Yorkshire I would cry as my castles collapsed. And even though this time I was laughing at the idiocy of this middle-aged world wanderer building sand castles after decades of abstinence, something deep down, very faint, was crying a little as it fell.

On another beach I discovered a sign proclaiming that I now stood astride the international dateline—the 180 degree median— so I bounced backward and forward from Tuesday into Wednesday and Wednesday into Tuesday and smiled at what a funny thing time is.

In fact, time became irrelevant. I discarded my watch and marked the days' progress by the movement of the sun over the high volcanic ridges. If it became too hot I wandered off into the forest dappled with musty light and followed narrow trails up the lower slopes of the mountains. Parrots, fantailed cuckoos, and pigeons floated in and out of the trees. If it rained that silky warm island rain, I'd lie back on the ground and let it soak me with its freshness, sip its sweet taste, and listen to the land crabs clicking their claws in their earthbound burrows.

At other times I'd set off for long walks on the narrow highway that serpentined around the coves and bays and when I was tired I'd hitch a lift back with whatever was going in the right direction. Once I rode with fishermen in the rear of an ancient truck, all sitting on the bare metal floor admiring their catch of large colorful fish and identifying them for me—a butterfly fish, a damsel fish, a goatfish, a blue-striped snapper, a rabbit fish, and a rainbow-hued parrot fish. All good eating, they assured me. Particularly when washed down with fresh kava from a communal *tanoa* bowl scooped up in cups made from halved green coconut shells that are marinated for a week or two in swamp water to give them their customary color and "reek."

One of the older fishermen told me of the "good old days" when villagers would join together for regular fish dives, or *yavayava*.

"Much kava—much, much kava! In big *tanoa* bowls, sometimes four feet across, made of the *vesi* wood—very sacred tree. We prayed to our ancestors—the Vu—everything had to be done right. Very important ceremony. We prayed for our vine ropes—the *walai*, for the nets, and we prayed to the statue of Gonedau who watched over the dive. He was in a special boat—the bigger boats, the *ladi*, were for the fishermen out by the reef. And then as we pulled in the big nets and rowed in to the beach, we would pray that the nets would not break and that we would have a good catch for everyone in the village. Oh, it was so much noise and singing . . . lots of fish . . . lots of kava!"

The other men were nodding and smiling. There hadn't been a real fish dive in a long time and they remembered the old days with relish. I was sorry to leave them.

"*Vinaka,*" I said, thanking them for the lift. "*Vinaka,*" came the collective reply out of wide-grinning faces.

Another time I rode with a thin and rather nervous Indian, owner of an "everything shop," in Somosomo, the main village on the west coast and home of Fiji's high chief, Ganilau. The Indian invited me in and showed me his wares piled high in a dark warehouselike store that seemed to go on forever in a damp, jungly gloom. Lots of cheap Naugahyde furniture, mounds of bananas, ripe tropical fruit and coconuts, bottles of Fijian rum, columns of cigarette cartons, enormous aluminum cooking pots, fishing nets, cheap stereo boomboxes and even cheaper pirated cassette tapes, big black and crudely welded cooking stoves, a table of secondhand books and magazines, racks of shapeless jackets, dresses, and trousers (also maybe secondhand, it was hard to tell), some glittery T-shirts adorned with Ninja Turtles and other Western-inspired instant images, a pile of just-caught fish in a huge enamel basin by the door, and—in prominent display—a miniature forest of bundled yanggona roots for kava making.

"Well—you seem to have thought of everything," I congratulated the storekeeper, who followed me, rubbing his long, thin fingers, as I admired his remarkable range of offerings.

"Yes. Everything, I think. We are also having TVs next week. We should be receiving our first programs soon."

"There's no TV in Fiji?"

"Well, not until recently. The government allowed TVs for some very important rugby matches—World Cup matches—and now the people say they want some more."

"It was banned before?"

"Well, the government said TV was not good for family life and interfered with the children's education, you see. So . . . "

"How courageous of the government!"

He looked at me curiously.

"Just joking," I said.

"Oh, yes, joking. Of course."

He tried a bit of a laugh, but it didn't come naturally.

A dear friend of mine in Suva who works with the blind in Fiji and other South Pacific islands would have described this as a distinct case of "optorectitus"—"an ailment where the optical nerve gets crossed with the rectal nerve and you end up with a shitty outlook on life." The storekeeper did not seem familiar with the Fijian enthusiasm for laughter.

In fact, most Indians in Fiji have still not learned the easy-going, easy-smiling ways of the native Fijians. They seem to be far too busy running most of the businesses, worrying about their children's education, and wondering how to grab a little more political power over a native population reluctant to relinquish any controls to "outsiders"—even outsiders who have lived here for almost a hundred years.

Ormond Eyre, owner of the tiny Maravu Plantation Resort near the airport, sympathized with the predicament of such outsiders. Descendant of an old part-European family of plantation owners on Taveuni, he still sensed some reluctance on the part of natives to see him as one of them.

"It's subtle—never overt. And it's something I've got used to. I've been off-island for many years—I was a steward with Quantas for a while. Did all kinds of things. Traveled everywhere. But I always wanted to come home and run my own hotel. Something this small—we've only got eight cottages—*bures*—done in the traditional style with palm-frond roofs—but it's nicer that way. I don't need—I don't really want—any more. I get to meet everybody and learn about their lives. You've got to know when to say 'enough' in this life. If you don't you'll spend most of your time doing things you don't really want to do for reasons you can't remember—or understand."

I enjoyed one of my best dinners in Fiji here in Ormond's open-air, thatch-walled and -roofed dining room—pungent garlic prawns *en croute* followed by roast chicken with tarragon, stir-fried bok choy and celery, and fried plantains in a Thai-flavored peanut sauce. Flaming banana crêpes, liqueurs, and Fijian folk songs sung by a local group playing guitars, ukuleles, and tambourines, brought the meal to a delicious close as the moon eased up over the volcanoes and bathed the rolling lawns in silver light. . . .

But I hadn't come for too much of this, I reminded myself the next day. Time to get out and find that family I'd been invited to visit by the young man in Nandi. See what really goes on behind the pastel-painted walls of the *bure* homes in the roadside villages. Time to experience Taveuni in the raw, so to speak.

The following day I passed a village market, a casual sprawl of rickety tables and blankets spread on the ground. In addition to the rainbow-hued mounds of just-caught fish, I saw baskets brimming with shiny pawpaws, mangoes, melons, pineapples, clusters of burgundy-red grapes, and great orange moons of halved pumpkins scooped out and ready to eat. On separate tables were the muscular, bulbous staples of yams, breadfruit, taro, cassava, rich purple dalo, and small wizened potatolike morsels whose name seemed to vary, depending on whom I asked. And of course the inevitable forests of bundled yanggona wrapped in torn sheets of the Fiji *Times* and awaiting the ritual pounding for innumerable kava celebrations.

Under a shady awning of sackcloth, an old and very fat woman clad in an enormous togalike dress was cooking morsels of fish in a cast-iron caldron bubbling with palm oil. I remembered all the warnings about this particular oil but bought a handful of pieces anyway, brown and crisp on the outside and soft as whipped cream within. It needed no seasoning, although, encouraged by the cook, I tried a sprinkling of hot pepper sauce and immediately wished I hadn't. I stood with lips burning, eyes streaming, accompanied by the grins and soft laughter of on-lookers.

"It's too hot for you!" the large cook said, trying to suppress her amusement.

I tried to say something funny, but it came out more like an inebriated squawk.

That was too much for her. She collapsed in a great explosion of giggles and fell heavily onto her stool covered with a square of ancient tapa cloth that looked as though it had been polished by her generous buttocks for years. The ancient patternings of bronze, white, and black dyes had been reduced to subtle shadowy hues, and the once-rough texture of the inner mulberry bark from which the "cloth" is beaten, looked smooth as shot silk.

Unfortunately, she fell a little too heavily. The stool gave a sad groan, buckled, and with sudden and very final snaps, two of the bamboo legs gave way and sent the giggling cook sprawling across her pandanus-leaf ground mat, whose broad dimensions defined the size of her impromptu kitchen.

There was a sudden silence—and then a hullabaloo of hilarity. My temporary discomfort with the pepper sauce was abruptly forgotten. Everybody turned to watch the poor cook struggle to pull herself upright. She rolled and struggled but couldn't seem to raise her generous bulk from the prime position. The laughter increased. Then she reached out for the table on which the huge caldron of oil was bubbling away. God, I thought, she's going to bring the whole damned thing down on herself. The table was starting to tip as she used it to drag herself up; no one seemed to see what was about to happen—they were far too busy guffawing at her ungainly struggles. I jumped forward and grabbed the table before it finally toppled.

Churned by the rocking table, the oil spat and leapt. A few drops splashed my arm. I could smell singed hair and seared flesh. But at least she now had the leverage she needed and slowly raised herself up, still laughing. The squashed stool lay spread-eagled on the ground under the tapa cloth. She didn't seem to mind. Instead she took one look at my smoking arm, scooped up a fistful of something greasy and gray from an ancient coffee tin, grabbed my wrist, and proceeded to plaster the rancid-smelling whatever-it-was over the reddening oil-burn marks.

It all happened so quickly I never really felt the pain or the burning. I was amazed by the speed of this apparently ungainly woman.

"*Vinaka*—thank you very much," I said.

"No," she said, still grinning but trying to be serious. "No—*vinaka* to you—you would now be covering all of me with this grease if the pot had fallen—*vinaka*."

There was a ripple of echoed "*vinakas*" in the crowd. Someone patted my back; an old man stepped up, looked me in the eyes, and rubbed my unburned elbow as if it were a kind of good-fortune talisman.

"*Bula, bula*. You were very fast, sir. That was a very good thing for you to do."

More mumbled agreement from the market crowd. I had suddenly been transformed from a foreign fool with a pepper-scorched palate into some kind of hero-of-the-day. All within a few seconds.

"Are you all right?" I asked the cook.

"Oh, yes—thanks to you."

"What about your stool?"

"Ah—it was a bad stool. For a year it's been creaking and wobbling. Now I can get a new one!"

The smiles and laughter began again.

One of the fishermen who had been standing off to the side behind his pile of parrot fish approached with an enormous specimen in his arms.

"This is for you," he said shyly.

"What—oh, no. No, I don't need any fish. *Vinaka*. That's very kind of you, but honestly—I have nowhere to cook it—thank you for a very kind thought."

He stood holding his fish and looking a little sad. It turned out that he was the husband of the cook and felt obliged to say thank you in the traditionally generous Fijian way of giving something of value.

The cook looked at him sternly as if to say, "That is not enough." Then she bent down and picked up the beautiful old tapa that lay buckled over the crumpled stool.

"No fish. This is for you."

She began to roll the tapa slowly.

"This would have been all burned too—just like me!" she said, grinning. "So now it's yours."

It was a superb piece of bark-cloth. Altogether different from the stuff I saw in Nandi's tourist stores. Its stains and discolorations from years of use, and smoothed patches where the cook's behind had rested for countless hours, made it even more authentic and precious. I was very tempted.

"No—honestly. I can't accept this. It is very beautiful—but it belongs to you."

Now she was the one to look sad.

"Listen," I said, desperately trying to think of a way to avoid offending anyone. "Y'know what I'd really like . . . some more of your lovely fried fish. It's the best I've tasted in Fiji. I'd like some of that—only without your special sauce!"

The crowd broke into raucous laughter and started applauding. This was all getting a little embarrassing.

"Is that okay with you?" I asked, hoping I'd said the right thing.

She looked at me, and then "into" me—deeply. (Fijians have a special way of focusing their eyes into your eyes that makes you feel as though they're peering into your soul.) There was what seemed like a long, long silence. And then she laughed.

"I will make you some special fish. You will not need your dinner tonight."

And she did. The cook and her husband filleted the large fish he'd carried over, cut the large steaks into small cubes, which she rolled in her flour mix ("My secret," she whispered), and then deep-fried them in the still-bubbling caldron.

I left with enough golden brown fish pieces to feed the whole market and they were, as I knew they would be, utterly delicious.

And—she was right—I didn't need dinner that night.

Snorkeling—I had to go snorkeling. Overcoming residual fears from the Ningaloo experience in Australia, I decided that as Taveuni had been proclaimed one of the top five diving areas in the world, there was no way I could avoid the experience.

I'd been advised to avoid the treacherous currents of Rainbow Reef and the "bottomless" chasms of the Great White Wall. So I hired a boatman to take me out to the benignly named Blue-Ribbon Eel Reef and swam along its shallow slopes, circling around a couple of fiercely striped (and very poisonous) lionfish, grinning at the fat-tomato clownfish that played among the swaying anemone, and chasing a pufferfish that grew ever larger as it propelled itself through the coral reefs with a tiny, almost invisible tail fin.

There were scores of gray and dark red bêche-de-mer among the explosions of coral. We know them by far less graceful names, of which sea slug or sea cucumber are the most familiar. Lovers of Chinese food will have seen them listed on menus in the more authentic restaurants and the Chinese themselves revere them as restoratives of sexual prowess. I can't vouch for this particular quality and neither can I really recommend them as a memorable dish. Bland, colorless, gelatinous, and resembling floppy slices of dill pickle, they are quickly overwhelmed by other flavors at a Chinese banquet. Even when eaten along with minimal accompaniments I still fail to understand their appeal. And yet vast fortunes were made by the traders who visited here in the early 1800s to supervise their collection and curing. The "black-bêche" were considered the most valuable and formed the basis for a lucrative trade with the Orient.

These mature creatures, around ten inches long, three inches thick, covered with warty bumps, and coated in a thick sticky goo, were harvested by Fijian fishermen from the reefs. Carried to shore in great straw baskets, they were split, boiled for a few minutes, and then smoked, sometimes for days, over green twigs and branches in a smokehouse, or *vata*. The results were shriveled leatherlike strips which were piled into sacks or baskets, each weighing around 140 pounds (a *picul*), considered to be a reasonable load to be carried on a man's back. And off the trading ships sailed to Manila and other Oriental ports to sell these odd wizened creatures for ten to twenty times the cost of their processing.

There was only one problem with this seemingly lucrative trade. The Fijian chiefs began to hear of these enormous profits and became discontent with the paltry payments of the traders, usually in the form of iron implements, rusty muskets, and, as the whaling industry increased, the polished teeth of sperm whales (*tabua*). They were particularly incensed by the stinginess of the New England traders, who were notorious for hard bargaining and duplicitous deal making.

On one particular occasion in 1834 the chief of Ono Island reasoned that the sailing skills of his subjects were more than a match for those of the wily New Englanders and that there was no reason for him not to confiscate a trading ship and arrange his own export ventures with the Orientals.

So one warm September afternoon he sent his warriors to the smokehouse on the island, with orders to destroy it and club to death the whole Yankee crew. Ten men were killed within minutes and it was only the shot from a single cannon on the trading ship, the *Charles Doggett*, that prevented the chief from realizing his schemes of easy riches and glory.

A similar attack occurred around the same time on the English brig *Sir David Ogilvie*. The Fijian chief, who was actually a guest on board, suddenly clubbed to death the unfortunate Captain Hutchins with whom he had been chatting on the quarterdeck. This was the sign for attack. Warrior canoes immediately sailed out from shore to complete the rout, only to be driven back by frantic musket fire from a terrified crew. The chief was shot as he sat in the captain's cabin wearing Mr. Hutchins's gold-braided hat.

It took regular visits by British and American men-of-war ships to subdue these occasional uprisings. Eventually better terms were offered to the angry chiefs and the trade continued, albeit on less friendly terms.

And there they were—the cause of all these problems—scores of fat, floppy sea cucumbers between the coral sprays, benignly oblivious to the battles that had once raged around these reefs, all for the sake of improving the sexual potency of already overpotent, overpopulated Asian nations.

In contrast to the gray anonymity of these sluglike creatures, the coral itself exploded in bouquets of rainbow colors and effervescent shapes: hard knotty clusters of polyps, delicate fanlike sprays of soft coral, bulbous mounds of brain coral, strange gardens of cabbage coral, the aggressive spikes of aptly named staghorn, fluffy sponges, and a dozen other less familiar species displayed in a welter of golds, jades, crimsons, blues, purples, and pinks.

391

Snorkeling is a very seductive pastime. No matter how many times or how many oceans I swim in, each experience reveals new wonders of form, color, and texture, new delights at the incredible variety—and intensity—of aquatic life. Even more so with scuba diving, although this time I erred on the side of caution and stuck with my snorkel mask and tube. I was disappointed with myself but gave in to the urge of self-preservation, even though the deep purple-blue depths of the cliffs and canyons below the surface reefs beckoned me with fleeting images of enormous groupers and lithe-bodied whitetip sharks.

I drifted through the satiny, sun-dappled shallows, among the butterfly fish and golden shoals of anthias, watching the dark-green tentacles of the sea worm emerge from their white warty tubes and sway ballerinalike in slow graceful dances. I could sense the warmth of the sun on my back and the soft lapping of the water on my outstretched arms. That old familiar feeling of weightlessness eased in—a lovely limbo of effortless movement through a landscape of infinite beauties where fish come up to kiss you and golden wings of lace coral wave at you like old friends and you wonder why you can't just float on like this forever, buoyed by a benevolent ocean, lost in mushy-minded reveries, where all the plans and perils and petty concerns of life on land dissolve away and you allow your fantasies free rein to play, hour after hour, day after day. . . .

I hadn't seen the shark.

It must have been trailing me, keeping its distance, mimicking my lazy meanderings. I was moving over a field of cabbage coral, great blue-green sprays of leaflike clusters, when I noticed that my own dappled shadow appeared to be followed by a second shadow, almost of the same length. I thought it must be some trick of the light—some form of double reflection—and then slowly realized that the movement of the shadow behind was not identical to mine. Similar, but not quite the same.

With a quick flap of my flippers I turned . . . and there it was. A whitetip, almost five feet in length, but similar in almost every detail to far larger—and deadlier—specimens. There was the dull-gray smoothness of its streamlined head, the ridge of its nose, the dark pectoral fins like honed knifeblades, the scimitar-shaped mouth slightly open and generously endowed with layer upon layer of razored teeth . . . and its eyes. God—how I hate the eyes of a shark, any shark, even those of the little puny dogfishlike sharklets. The eyes are always the same. Wide open, metallic, cold, angry, cruel—utterly merciless. Nothing like the cute little button eyes of the tomato clown fish or the bright gold jewel eyes of the anthias or the conical domes of the puffer.

Previously I had been warm, buoying about in the sunny shallows. Now I suddenly felt cold—death cold—as I looked right into the eyes of a killer. Only whitetips weren't killers . . . or so I'd been told. But maybe this one hadn't heard about its benevolent reputation. Or maybe this was the day when it was contemplating a new direction in life, a little human flesh maybe, to enliven an all too regular diet of puny defenseless fish. A nice fat mouthful of thigh, possibly, or a juicy arm.

If only the thing would blink once in a while . . . a smile would be too much to ask, and anyway, that crescent slit of a mouth seemed to possess a perpetual smile of gustatory anticipation . . . but a little blink of those deathly, malevolent eyes would be very nice, a little reassuring gesture, an indication that this was something more than just an endlessly avaricious eating machine.

But it didn't.

So—what to do?

No way was I going to turn my back on it or try to swim around the creature. Maybe a hand gesture? I slowly allowed my arms to drift together until my hands were touching. Then I clapped them together, hoping a sudden movement would persuade it to wander on in search of less aggressive prey. But it did nothing except wriggle its dorsal fin and keep staring right at me.

There were branches of staghorn coral a few feet below me. Maybe I could use one of those as a spear and give him a quick jab on the nose. After all, the tips were supposed to contain some unpleasant poison . . . but that might make him mad at me and then . . . well, I'd be a quick lunch and that would be that.

In the end it was a standoff. I kept staring and it kept staring back and then I think it just became bored. With a quick flick of its tail fin it vanished. Off over the edge of the shallow reef and down into the purple depths of a canyon to my left.

I decided not to wait around to see if it had second thoughts and swam back to the boat as quickly as I could, expecting at any second to feel those incisor teeth and that ghastly maw of a mouth closing on one of my flapping legs.

"Oh, no, the whitetips are fine, man," the boatman assured me. "Never had no problems."

"Well, that's what I assumed," I bluffed. "Never really thought it would do anything." Fear was easing away; my confidence was returning.

"No, not 'round here," he replied with a big reassuring grin.

"Right."

" 'Course, if you'd been up in the Solomons . . . "

"Off Papua New Guinea?"

"Yeah tha's right, man."

"Why would that be different?"

"Man, tha's very different up there. They eatin' people all the time. Blacktips, whitetips, they all doin' it. They really like people meat 'round those islands. They got used to it a'suppose. Before all them missionaries, the people'd leave out the bodies of them that died on the reefs for the sharks. Faster'n cremation, man. Few seconds and they'd be gone. So y'see, they got this taste for people meat. No one likes the water up there."

"But that's never happened around Fiji?"

"No, man—oh, no—we got different ways of doin' things here."

"Like burying the dead—not feeding them to the sharks?"

"No, man—no! Like eatin' 'em instead!" His laughter made our small boat rock as if hit by a hurricane, and all the way into shore he kept repeating his punch line.

"Like eatin' 'em instead!"

I was soon to learn much more about the ancient tribal customs of this seemingly benevolent little island.

I made another island friend—a young black-haired man named Mitieli. He just happened to be around when I emerged from the hotel one morning and we started talking. I liked his eyes and his conversations and he seemed to enjoy the role as newfound friend—and tutor.

We were strolling on a narrow stretch of beach just beyond

the school at Somosomo when he pointed to a pile of driftwood lying in the roots of wind-bent palms at the high edge of the sand.

"Pieces of the Ra Marama," he said in a soft voice. "Could be...."

"What's a Ra Marama?" The locals kept doing this to me, dropping references to Taveuni history as if anyone who had taken the trouble to come to the island would at least know something about its intriguing (and gruesome) background and traditions.

"Ah—you don't know about the Ra Marama?"

I'd read enough about the early adventures of Hannah and John Hunt, farmer-missionaries from Lincolnshire, England, to realize that whatever story Mitieli was about to tell me would be both colorful and violent.

The Hunts apparently arrived here in the 1840s to preach their Methodist doctrines to an extraordinarily savage population. The king of the reef, Tui Thakau, had loaned them a tribal *bure* but made it clear that their presence was merely tolerated, not welcome.

"Cruelty is law in this place," John Hunt wrote in one of his journals. Hardly had they landed when they were confronted with "giants with spears in their hands and great heads of hair, two or three feet in diameter, their bodies naked except for a loincloth of masi and behind them were the tall thatched steeples of their heathen temples and the jagged peaks and rainclouds of Taveuni." He noted in understated English prose, "The first sight of a Feejee man is rather appalling."

The initiation of this young, God-fearing couple into the vicious rites of the "Feejee" men occurred suddenly, within a week of their arrival. One of the king's sons was drowned one morning in a boating accident and immediately the king ordered the execution of sixteen attractive widows so that his son might be attended by enticing female companions in the spirit world. According to tribal custom their deaths were to be by strangling.

The poor Hunts protested and begged the king to reconsider, but the gentler ways of Christians had not yet begun to permeate tribal mores. The king dismissed their pleas with a wave of the two royal spears and ordered the Hunts to witness the horrifying spectacle. John recorded the gory details:

We were obliged to be in the midst of it and truly their cries and wailings were awful. . . . They took a long piece of Native cloth and tied two knots about the middle and putting one knot on the throat and the other on the back of the neck some pulled at one end and some at another until they were strangled. Soon after they were murdered they were brought to be buried about twenty yards from our house. They were folded up in mats and were carefully covered over with stones; the cloth which formed the rope for strangling them was hung over them.

The poor Hunts were in for more gruesome rites the following day—the celebration of circumcision for the young men of the tribe.

When the ceremony was performed with knives made from split bamboo, the cloth on which some of the blood had been sprinkled was brought into the king's yard and put on a stick, and the persons who had been circumcised danced round it. Their dancing consisted in walking and jumping and singing and shouting and yelling, etc., a most heathenish affair to be sure and continued several nights. . . . In connection with this ceremony many females and some men had one of their joints of their fingers cut off.

One can only admire the Hunts for their perseverance in the face of so much cruelty. They witnessed more ritual slaughters, the great festivities and feasts (the *mekes*), the pounding of the great *lali* drums made of tree trunks as the bodies of enemies were cooked and devoured with glee. They were also aware of the ancient tradition of implanting the bodies of captives upright and alive as foundation supports for the main posts of *bures* and tribal buildings to ensure *mana* (spiritual harmony) for each construction. Nevertheless, they continued to preach, teach, and collect a few converts while sacrifices and rituals continued unabated. They tried at one point to hide from the horrors of the tribe's cannibalistic rites when captured enemies were slaughtered, roasted, and eaten with great relish by the tribe. John, ever loyal to his journals, described one such event when the Hunts had closed all the doors of their *bure*, which was located only a few yards from the king's own house, to block out the appalling activities in the royal compound:

> The king came in during the time the bodies were cooking and enquired why we had closed all the doors of the house. We told him the true reason which was because we hated the smell of the bodies which were cooking at which he was not pleased. As soon as Mrs. H. saw the king she began to cry. We spoke strongly to the king on the conduct he was pursuing, etc., at which he became angry and among other things said if we did not cease to reprove him he would kill us. I think he was particularly displeased because Mrs. Hunt wept.

Missionaries like the Hunts were often ill-informed prior to their arrival about the meticulous ritual-bound lives of the Fiji Islanders. What to them were despicably gruesome excesses, to the islanders—particularly the fierce Taveunians—were essential elements of a delicately balanced relationship between the gods and the tribe. Any omission, any abbreviation of ancient ceremonies, even a careless error in the long recitations of chants and war epics and accolades to the bravery of fallen enemies, could disturb this balance and make the chief and all his followers liable to divine punishment and retribution. Critical battles, it was thought, could be lost because of a single forgotten line in a thousand line monologue; villages, even whole kingdoms could be destroyed by such thoughtlessness. The gods were intolerant of the foibles of man. They expected perfection from their chiefs, warriors, and worshipers. The far more benign teachings of the missionaries with their "loving, forgiving God" seemed curiously unmasculine to many Fijian chiefs. They preferred the rigid rituals which they claimed would guarantee success and joy in life, in battle, and in the hereafter.

So—having learned at length some of the details of nineteenth-century tribal life on Taveuni, I prepared myself for Mitieli's doubtless stomach-churning story of the Ra Marama.

"This was a splendid boat," he began, "a great double canoe over a hundred feet long and twenty feet wide which took the boat makers over seven years to carve. They built a large platform and a place for the King—Ratu Thakobau—to sit when it was on the ocean. It was really a beautiful boat and all the rituals were done according to tradition. There were some human sacrifices and men were clubbed and killed with big wooden sticks when the boat was launched."

"Why were they clubbed?" I asked.

"I don't know. It was tradition. A kind of blessing on the boat, I suppose. Anyway, after the boat was on the ocean something went wrong. They were lowering the big sail and it snapped, killing one of the men on the boat and hurting some others. The king became very worried and said this was a sign of anger from the gods because not enough men had been sacrificed. So they found twenty more men and sacrificed them quickly."

"And then everything was okay?"

"I don't know. The boat seemed to have a kind of curse on it. It wasn't used very much. People were afraid of it. And when Thakobau died it was returned to Somosomo—here—where it was built, and the people decided that as a sign of respect for the king, it would never sail again. So they put it high up on the beach and left it to rot."

"And you think these are pieces from the Ra Marama?"

Mitieli smiled. "I don't know. I was just joking, really, so that I could tell you this story!"

"Ah, yes. Joking."

"Well, I tell good stories. Don't you think?"

"Indeed you do, Mitieli."

"So where's my *tabua*?"

Oh, God, here we go again. Mitieli's segues into island traditions and legends were never subtle.

"Okay. What's a *tabua*? Tell me all about *tabuas*."

"Well," he said with a grin. "I'm glad you asked . . . and it's not *tabua*. You say it *tam-boo-a*."

This was turning into a real Abbott and Costello routine.

"*Tabuas* are very valuable in Fiji. They are the teeth of sperm whales and are given as tokens of thanks and respect. Sometimes as polite bribes—y'know, if you want someone to do something for you. You give him a large *tabua* and if he accepts it, then he usually will do what you ask."

"So you think I should bribe you with one of these *tabuas*?"

"Well—is there anything you need me to do?"

"No—not really. Just keep telling me your stories."

"Okay, then. So—this would be a thank-you *tabua* for all my wonderful stories. A nice big tooth—about eight inches wide would be fine—just like we used to get from the whaling boats that came to the islands over a hundred and fifty years ago. You'll have to scrape and clean it, sand it with coral sand, then rub it with coconut oil and polish it till it shines with the leaves of the *masi ni tabua* tree."

"Okay—sounds easy enough."

"I haven't finished yet. Then, when it's all nice and shiny and polished, you'll have to smoke it over a fire or stain it with tumeric until it turns a lovely deep orange. Then you plait some *magimagi* rope using pandanus leaves and tie this around both ends of my lovely tooth so that I can carry it around."

"And that's it?"

"No—that isn't it. Then you have to wrap it up in a piece of tapa cloth and put in a special *kato* basket with a polished *tinai ni tabua* stone—one about the same size—so that they lie together."

"Why a stone?"

"I don't know. When there were not so many whale teeth they used to use polished stones or even *tabuas* made from trochus shells. But I don't know why they put both of them into the *kato* basket."

"And that's it?"

"No. Then you have to present it to me as a gift. You have to kneel down on a special straw mat—a *masi*—and tell me that this gift is *sa ka tudei*—a thing that will not change—something that will last forever. And then I accept your gift, give a nice speech, and tell you more stories."

"How about a bottle of rum instead?"

"Okay. Now?"

"No, not now, later. After more of your stories."

"A big bottle, right? Not one of those little things for your back pocket?"

"Okay—a big bottle."

"Good—well that's all settled. Now, how about a climb up to Lake Tagimaucia?"

"To see the flowers?"

"To see . . . everything!"

"Okay."
"Okay."
"When?"
"Tomorrow."
"Right."

Wrong. Definitely a wrong decision. On the map it looked like an easy enough hike. Take the track behind the Mormon church (the islanders are very tolerant of divergent Christian sects) in Somosomo and then a brisk walk up the mountain to the lake and back down for a lunch of Indian samoasas or Fijian poached fish in coconut sauce. A pleasant morning walk. Nothing more.

But maps are often nothing more than deceitful, mean little shards of useless printed paper. At least this one certainly was. For a start it had rained overnight and, although the day was bright and blue, the almost invisible path remained a quagmire of mud holes and hidden ankle-snapping rocks. And then the map indicated a walk of no more than a mile or so into the center of the island. It felt more like a hundred. And it didn't show that we had to climb three thousand feet from the beach.

Mitieli didn't complain, however, so I kept my peace and followed him as the route became steeper and steeper, winding between enormous forest trees festooned with vines that snagged my arms, backpack, and legs. In places the path seemed to take on the characteristics of a stream bed, with cascades of water bouncing off the roots and rocks with silvery abandon.

"It gets a little tough now," said Mitieli cheerfully, hardly panting.

I was wheezing like a retired warhorse. The air was thick and hot. There were no breezes in the dense layers of rain forest and little light permeated the dark canopy. My lungs screamed uselessly for cool dry air.

"Bit steep now," called out Mitieli, way ahead of me in the sticky gloom. I didn't bother to respond. I needed all my energy just to breathe.

On and on we climbed for what seemed hours through the forest . . . until we came to the mist.

The terrain had leveled out a little, but now it became difficult

400

to see anything. We entered a warm, white miasma in which the trees were blurred and boot-snagging roots hard to spot.

"Well," said Mitieli, "we're here. Normally you get a good view of the lake. You can usually see *tagimaucia* flowers."

He explained that we had reached a ridge overlooking the lake, couched in its ancient volcanic crater, about three thousand feet above the doubtless sun-baked beaches far below.

"So now I should be photographing the lake and taking a few close-ups of the flowers."

"Yes." Mitieli smiled his disarming Fijian smile.

"Only I can't see a bloody thing." I was grumpy. Surely we hadn't climbed all this way just to stand in a clammy mist.

"Well—maybe we should have some lunch."

We had lunch. I've forgotten what we ate. I was too impatient for the mist to clear.

If anything, it got thicker. An hour passed and I could hardly see Mitieli even though he was sitting, actually dozing, only a few feet away.

"Okay!" I half shouted, and was delighted to see him jarred out of his doubtlessly blissful catnap. My grumpiness had not been alleviated by lunch. "We might as well go down."

"Maybe in another hour."

"Mitieli—it's getting worse, not better. I can hardly see you."

"On Taveuni the weather changes very fast." He was doing his Fiji smile thing again.

"Forget it. I'm going down."

"Okay."

We started to slip and skid back down the long quagmire path.

"Maybe we come tomorrow. It's a lovely lake."

I didn't bother to answer.

A couple of days later I hitchhiked to the Wairiki Mission with another bunch of fishermen (no one seems to take fishing too seriously here—it seems more like a relaxing pastime between long bouts of kava drinking and impromptu *meke* sessions of clapping songs and storytelling). Most of the churches on the island are modest structures, gaily painted with the same mauve, green, blue, and apricot-yellow abandon as the homes, but at Wairiki I found an imposing stone edifice of Catholic prominence set way back from the road on a bluff overlooking a rugby field (another national pastime, this one taken more seriously). Behind the tall towers the forest climbed, thick and viny, up the misty slopes of Des Voeux Peak.

The mists had never left the ridges since my climb with Mitieli, so I'd spent many hours on the beach since then learning more about Fiji's long and gory history. Now it was the turn of the fishermen to add their tales. Sometimes I wondered if Taveunians would be happy to return to their warlike ways. Their ancient battle exploits seem to be one of the most popular topics of conversation.

"This is where we beat them Tongans," one of the men told me. Apparently in the mid-1800s the fierce Tongan warriors in their enormous *drua* boats had pretty well reduced the Fijian islands to vassal states. Only little Taveuni remained as a stronghold of proud but ill-equipped natives determined to preserve their independence.

"The missionaries told us what to do. They were real clever and when the Tongans got to the beaches just down there we got 'em so bad there weren't a man left—we got all of 'em. Clubbed 'em, speared 'em, chopped 'em up, and cooked 'em." His eyes shone as he told of the exploits of the brave Taveuni warriors, vastly outnumbered but trained by the missionaries in devious guerrilla tactics.

"Wouldn't be a Fiji if we hadn't chopped 'em up like we did." He was licking his lips in a most peculiar way. "They must have tasted real good."

This battle was a breakthrough for proponents of the Christian God. After years of benign—and amused—tolerance the missionaries now became revered members of Fijian society. Chiefs were converted by the dozen and their subjects were required to adopt the strange and stringent Christian codes of modest dress and a discontinuance of their penchant for boiled and barbecued human flesh.

"We built them this mission," the fisherman pointed proudly to the enormous church. "We're clever people here on Taveuni!"

And fun people too. The fishermen were heading for the

402

southern tip of the island to visit friends in Navakawau (End of the Road) village and invited me to continue on with them.

Jolting and crashing down a potholed road in the rear of an ancient Toyota truck would not have been my first choice of transportation, but the company of this jolly band was something I couldn't resist. So, forgetting cramped legs and a numb and bruised backside, I joined in their singing, drank their beer, and handed around cigars as we rattled and thrashed along the unpaved track, passing lovely coves with untouched beaches, avoiding broken tree limbs (there had been a fierce storm the previous night), and watching strands of sunlight snaking through the tall forest trees at the roadside, dancing and flashing in our dust cloud.

We drove on the edge of rugged cliffs and past an enormous blowhole where the surf rushed through caves and exploded out of the earth in a huge geyser. Then we crossed plateaus of exposed lava flows in which there are deep tunnels where the Taveunians once buried their fiercest warriors.

"When they died it was a secret. They didn't want their enemies to know. So they put them in these lava tunnels," one of the fishermen told me.

"Are they still there?" I asked.

"No—they took most of the bones out about thirty years ago. Only they missed a few places."

The other fishermen smiled and nodded.

"Taveuni seems to have a lot of secret places."

"Well," said the oldest fisherman, a thin, wiry man with an enormous mop of frizzly gray hair, "We been here a long time. . . ."

After a couple of hours of constant bone-jarring driving we finally arrived in Navakawau to find a colorful collection of brightly painted cottages and a few more traditional *bures* scattered around the village *rara*. I expected the men to go off fishing with their friends, but it turned out they had other far more important things in mind.

And so it was that I finally came to participate in my first real kava-drinking ceremony, something I'd been hoping for since my arrival.

Many of the details were lost on me, particularly after the

fifth cup of mint-smelling "muddy water" scooped from a three-foot-wide six-legged kava bowl. But I remember bits . . . vaguely.

And one thing in particular. Hardly had we arrived in the village and said our hellos to the people gathered around us when a large, potbellied gentleman with a huge halo of black hair stepped forward and hugged me.

I was touched but unused to such profuse greetings.

"We have been expecting you," he said, smiling widely.

"Me?"

"My son in Nandi said you would be coming to see us."

The penny—as they say—dropped. This was the father of the young man at the tourist office. The family I'd promised to visit.

"Oh, I'm so glad to meet you," I gasped. "I had no idea."

"Taveuni is a very small place," he said, and hugged me again. "We knew you would come."

I was embarrassed. I'd brought no *sevusevu*—no gift. My pathetic little bag of yanggona was back in the hotel . . . this whole trip had been unexpected and spontaneous. I tried to apologize.

"You need no *sevusevu* with us. You are here and we are pleased you come."

I felt very happy.

The "ceremony" (actually it was more like a boisterous bacchanal) took place around one of the thatch-roofed *bures*. Like most island houses it was sparsely furnished—a couple of chairs, a low table, a small wood-fired cooking stove, and broad expanses of pandanus mats for sleeping. A few household utensils, a frying pan, a large caldron, an ancient and cracked kava bowl hung on the wooden walls near the stove. A rather gray and mottled print of King Thakobau dangled next to a more colorful photograph of Queen Elizabeth II looking (as she always does in Fiji) young and happy.

Although the *bure* was simple, there were strict etiquettes about its use. Usually the rear of the space was private and, unless specifically invited, strangers did not stray beyond an invisible line roughly demarked by the ridge pole of the home. All the real activity takes place up front by the open windows and doors. This is where one enjoys the occasional *meke* feast, and where visitors sit, if it's raining outside, to imbibe endless coconut-shell cups of kava.

It wasn't raining, so we sat outside on mats rolled across the red earth.

The kava had already been mixed at the back of the *bure* (I hoped it was powdered yanggona, not the saliva-drenched and pounded root variety) and was carried in the great *tanoa* bowl to the center of our circle of reclining bodies.

Conversation ceased. Maybe in my honor the man of the family recited a short verse which translates something like this:

> Wake up!
> We have slept well and now
> The sun is high above us
> So—go pull the *yaqona* from the earth,
> prepare the root and sing!
> Our praise rises to the sky
> —may it reach the whole earth.

Everything was very quiet. I could hear the gentle surf prattling on the beach below the village. The palm fronds and leaves of scattered forest trees gave a pleasant rattling sound, like distant hand clapping.

Then there was a sudden clap of hands right in front of me. My host smiled at me and said loudly, *"E dua na bilo?"*

Fortunately, one of my fisherman colleagues was sitting to my right. "He says he would like you to try a cup—a *bilo*—of kava. You say yes."

"Yes. I would love to. Thank you."

The man smiled again, filled the *bilo* with the muddy earth-colored mixture, rose up, and carried the cup around the circle to where I sat.

I was about to rise when the fisherman (Eroni was his name) whispered, "Don't get up. Before he gives you the cup say *Bula!* and clap, then take it and drink it—in one drink. Don't sip!"

I did as I was instructed.

"Bula!" I shouted, then clapped, then accepted the bowl in both hands and downed the contents in a couple of gulps without worrying about the taste.

Everyone seemed delighted, clapped three times and shouted "*Macca!*" signifying that the cup was emptied.

The host returned with the empty *bilo*, seemingly pleased by my performance, and the identical ritual was repeated with each member of the circled group.

The taste? Well, it was an odd mix of minty-flavored cold tea—and diluted mud. Nothing overwhelming or mind-blowing. A tingle on the lips—on the tongue. A slight relaxing of muscles. And a smile that gets wider with each cup.

And there were many cups. I lost count after five but noticed that we all seemed to be drawing closer to the bowl as if some magnetic force were merging our bodies.

There were so many smiles. Smiles that grew wider and wider as the ceremony progressed. Smiles full of gold teeth, missing teeth, no teeth—but smiles that seemed to ease through my eyes and touch something way, way inside.

Odd things were happening to me here in Taveuni. I don't think I've ever smiled so much in my life. I felt buoyed by a spirit of utter happiness. Time eased by so gently. I felt welcome everywhere I went, especially in this little village at "the end of the road." I was learning so much. . . .

I learned to look deeper by looking into those open eyes that look so deeply into mine. I learned to listen to the quiet voices of villagers and hear shards of old wisdom as the *ta lanoa* (the conversation) drifted on. I learned more of Taveuni's long, long history in which today's events and crises are mere sprinklings of raindrops on a vast ocean of time. I sensed a knowledge—no, not knowledge, deep empathy—with nature, so rich and entrancing—so alive—it makes the laborious researches of our scientists and students of nature seem like babies playing in a sandbox.

Someone told me the story of the yanggona plant as we sat in the evening glow of an amber sun. Something about the Fijian god Degei ("he who is from heaven to the soil and through the earth") who gave the gift of yanggona and other more powerful hallucinogenics as "angel's cap" and "Yaqoyaqona" to the earthbound to lift their minds and calm their spirits.

I sensed both. Soon I was reclining on the pandanus mats with the others, watching the evening rays of sun move slowly across the compound, gilding the earth, and stroking our faces with sheens of trembling light. I wasn't drunk; I wasn't on a narcotic high. But I was somewhere different. Somewhere I'd never been before. Exploring unfamiliar sensations in a benevolent miasma of ease and familial well-being.

Food came later. A modest *lovo* in the form of large platters of mashed taro, fat slices of yams, chunks of fried fish, and other dishes I couldn't readily identify. But it didn't really matter. The food was warm, soft, and juicy and, as I remember, delicious. Someone played a guitar. We sang (I hummed, mostly). It was not the big Fijian *meke* but something smaller. Family-styled. There was a *lali* drum in the distance, a strange, sad, echoing sound above the skitter of surf and the rasp of slowly moving sand. Songs and conversation eased on. I joined in when I could understand the gist; otherwise I just sort of half lay there, letting my eyes do their own traveling from the kava bowl, to the candelit *bures*, to the guitarist, and to the purple strands of cirrus clouds above us in the last of the dusk light. Young girls flitted like little moths in the shadows; the older women sat on the edge of the circle, smiling.

I vaguely remember some discussion about staying the night, but the fishermen decided to drive back to Somosomo. Maybe I should go with them . . . maybe I should stay. . . .

Apparently I went back with them because I woke in my hotel room very late the following morning and never remembered anything of the journey back along that chronically potholed road. Amazing what good company, good food—and yanggona—does to neutralize the adversities of travel.

The days following my return from the kava bout passed slowly, punctuated by sudden downpours and aftermaths of sticky sluggish air smelling of jungle and rich, wet earth. One morning I drove north past the landing strip to Bouma Falls. Hidden deep in the rain forest, the place was all mine. I sketched the sixty-foot-high cascade and then stripped, dived into the pool at its base, and floated on my back, listening to the roar of the falls and watching two orange-breasted doves do what doves love to do, which seems to consist of making soft reassuring coos and gently nudging one another in an almost constant reaffirmation of their mutual fidelity. A bit sloppy but seductively entrancing. Especially when you're all alone in a warm, forestbound pool, thinking of home and someone there waiting for you, wondering when your own little reaffirmations would begin again.

I continued on past Bouma into one of the most beautiful corners of this lovely island. No wonder the crew of *Return to the Blue Lagoon* chose the traditional village of Lavena, with its thatched *bures*, its blinding white sands and translucent aquamarine bay, as the setting for its ultraromantic, if notoriously short-lived epic of young love in a South Pacific paradise.

My list of places I'd like to retire to (Retire from what? dear friends ask) keeps growing longer as I continue my travels around the world, but Lavena is somewhere up there close to the top. It's hard to imagine a more idyllic place: dense forest encroaching on small perfect beaches, the Tobu Vei Tui Falls hidden in the foothills of the island's mountain spine, another cascade that tumbles off a high clifftop near the village directly into the ocean (World War II ships used to pause at the base of the falls here to refill their freshwater tanks), and a sense of ease and grace of living that makes one seriously question the modern materialistic mores back home.

All I'd need here would be a cozy palm-frond *bure*, a wraparound sulu for daily dress, a fishing net into which dinner would nonchalantly swim each evening, a basket to collect the fruits that grow abundantly in the wild, a bunch of local friends (kava connoisseurs, of course), a couple of pet doves to make bill 'n' coo sounds all day long, a shortwave radio so that I could smile (Fijian style, of course) at the frenzied foibles of the world beyond the beach, a lot of sketch pads and writing paper, the occasional barbecued wild pig shared with village friends . . . and Anne.

So why the hesitation? Why not just move here and stop the fantasizing?

"You could live like a king!" whispered the little seductive enticer inside my head.

I remember something I'd read in the *Cyclopedia of Fiji* about the life of island kings, and it didn't sound so bad at all:

The duties of a king allowed him abundant leisure, except when he was much engaged in feasting or fighting. Like potentates of ancient times, he knew how to reconcile manual labour with an elevated position and the affairs of state. With a simplicity quite patriarchal he wielded by turn the sceptre, the spear and the spade and, if unusually industrious, amused himself inside by plaiting sinet. Should he be one of the rare exceptions who saw old age, he existed, during his last days, near a comfortable fire, lying or sitting in drowsy silence.

Invariably his Majesty had two or three attendants about his person, who fed him and performed more than servile offices on his behalf. An attendant priest or two, and a number of wives, completed the accompaniments of Fijian royalty.

I suppose the "number of wives" bit might create a few domestic disharmonies with Anne, but other than that she's a pretty easygoing person, well experienced in the traveling life, undemanding when it comes to material possessions, and a great lover of fresh-caught fish, fruit, and all the simple frivolities of endless time in the surf and the sun.

How should I explain to her my emerging idea of a new life here at Lavena?

"Listen, darling, rent the house—pay the bills, pack a few books and things, give everything else away, load up the cats"— oh, yes, Freddie and Friskie would love it here—"and I'll meet you in Taveuni and bring you down to this palm-frond *bure* I've just built on the beach and we'll have a kava celebration and then we'll go fishing and make a *meke* and then . . . "

I think she'd like the idea.

So—make the call.

When?

Now.

Now?

Why not?

Well—I just might. . . .

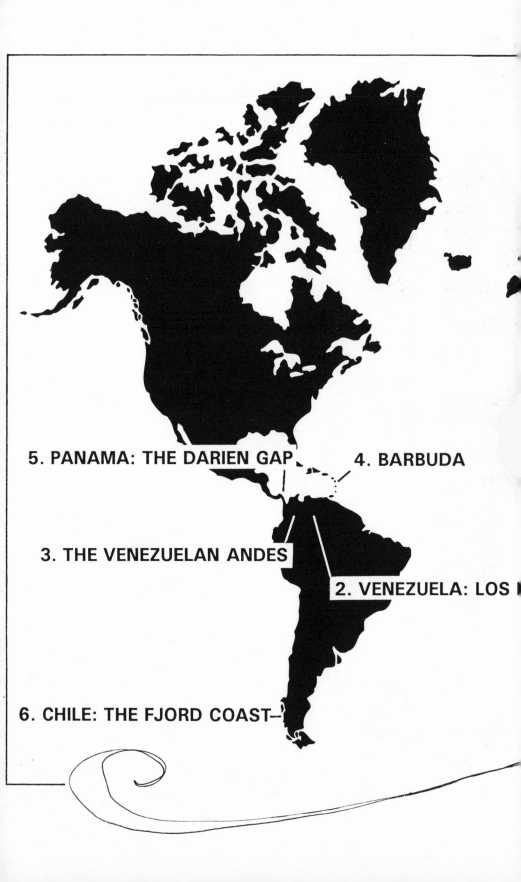

5. PANAMA: THE DARIEN GAP

4. BARBUDA

3. THE VENEZUELAN ANDES

2. VENEZUELA: LOS

6. CHILE: THE FJORD COAST